The Political Discourse of Carl Schmitt

The Political Discourse of Carl Schmitt

A Mystic of Order

Montserrat Herrero

ROWMAN & LITTLEFIELD
INTERNATIONAL

London • New York

Published by Rowman & Littlefield International, Ltd.
Unit A, Whitacre Mews, 26-34 Stannary Street, London SE11 4AB
www.rowmaninternational.com

Rowman & Littlefield International, Ltd. is an affiliate of Rowman & Littlefield
4501 Forbes Boulevard, Suite 200, Lanham, Maryland 20706, USA
With additional offices in Boulder, New York, Toronto (Canada), and London (UK)
www.rowman.com

British Library Cataloguing in Publication Information Available
A catalogue record for this book is available from the British Library

ISBN: HB 978-1-78348-454-6
ISBN: PB 978-1-78348-455-3

Library of Congress Cataloging-in-Publication Data

Library of Congress Cataloging-in-Publication Data Available

ISBN 978-1-78348-454-6 (cloth : alk. paper) -- ISBN 978-1-78348-455-3 (pbk. : alk. paper) -- ISBN
978-1-78348-456-0 (electronic)

♾™ The paper used in this publication meets the minimum requirements of American
National Standard for Information Sciences Permanence of Paper for Printed Library
Materials, ANSI/NISO Z39.48-1992.

Printed in the United States of America

Contents

Preliminary Note

This book is based on the study I did of Carl Schmitt in the 1990s. That work resulted in my first book on Carl Schmitt published in Spain and entitled *El nomos y lo político: La filosofía política de Carl Schmitt*. The book I now present also takes advantage of some parts of that first book, but it is not a mere translation of it. Many parts of the book, for example the last chapter, are completely new. The other parts have been rewritten and reordered. In addition, a new bibliography has been included. Nevertheless, the main thesis remains. After years of continuing work on Schmittian topics, I am convinced of the centrality of the main thesis of the book for a correct understanding of Schmitt's works. In quoting Schmitt's books, I have mainly used published English translations of Carl Schmitt's works. Christa Byker translated Carl Schmitt's texts that are not yet published in English, as well as the main text of this book.

Acknowledgments

Since the first version of this book was released in Spain, awareness of my gratitude to all those who have made it possible has only grown. First of all, I am grateful to Rafael Alvira for having persisted in channeling my efforts toward an author as suggestive, sharp, and deep as Schmitt, whose every word is notable. I am also in debt to Álvaro d'Ors, whose correspondence with Schmitt I edited between 2000 and 2004. I cannot forget the afternoons, always from seven until nine, in August of 2000, that we spent in his Pontevedra office conversing on political theory, recent Spanish history, music, literature, art, and theology. I always left his house with my attention on something new.

I also had occasional help from José María Beneyto, Dalmacio Negro Pavón, and Alfredo Cruz-Prados in Spain and from German specialists of Carl Schmitt's thought, among them Günther Maschke, Reinhart Koselleck, and Ernst-Wolfgang Böckenförde. Each of them openly trusted me with their points of view.

I fondly remember Koselleck's effort in getting me to visit the archive and his initial surprise at my stubbornness and refusal to carry out archivistic work: "Your thesis is not far off, but you should consult the files," he would say. In the end, I took his advice and, with his recommendation, he opened up the doors to Schmitt's legacy for me. I cannot forget our visit to Bielefeld, with his explanation of each monument and the museum; nor can I forget his surprise at my name: a place name that ends in t—a scandal for a woman's name!

I would also like to thank Joseph Kaiser, who gave me access to Carl Schmitt's archive in Düsseldorf, as well as Werner Weber, who helped me there. They permitted me access to many references that enriched my work.

I also appreciate Jaume Aurell and Andrea Mura's inspiration in leading me to consider a possible English-language revision of my first book, which has now been so profoundly revised that it can be said that it is another book entirely. My thanks also goes to all those who have taken my first book into consideration, critically or otherwise; your comments and reviews have offered me real food for thought.

I also want to thank those who helped me in correcting this book at its different stages, particularly Christa Byker for her translation work. Finally, I want to thank Anna Reeve from Rowman & Littlefield for her confidence in this project. One of any author's dreams is to have great publishers.

Introduction

"Whoever wishes to discuss the political, cannot keep quiet about Carl Schmitt."[1] This sentence appeared in one of the most widely read German newspapers in the early 1990s. When dealing with political theory today, reference to Schmitt is also required. Once you have read him, it is difficult to continue thinking about the political without referring to his concepts and definitions.

His work, silenced during the last years of his life, is becoming increasingly important due, in large part, to the variety of traditions in which his work has been received. Schmitt's ideas have interested "the right" as much as "the left," democrats and reactionaries, as well as revolutionaries. Schmitt's influence is well known, for example, on German neoconservatism, as Armin Mohler showed, and on the Frankfurt School, as Ellen Kennedy revealed.

Schmitt's aura is broad and his influence has long crossed over German borders, as documented, only two years after his death, in Günter Maschke's book, *Der Tod des Carl Schmitt*.[2] Since then, the ranks of Schmitt scholars have only increased.

Studies of Schmitt's work proliferated outside his home country, especially in Italy, as Ilse Staff's publication, *Staatsdenken im Italien des 20. Jahrhunderts: Ein Beitrag zur Carl Schmitt-Rezeption* shows.[3] This was also the case in France thanks to the efforts of Alain de Benoist and, before that, to Julien Freund, among others, and in the United States thanks to Georg Schwab, Ellen Kennedy, Joseph W. Bendersky, Gary L. Ulmen, and others. In Spain, the number of scholars is smaller, but notably includes Álvaro d'Ors, one of the most knowledgeable interpreters of Schmitt's work.[4] Recent studies in Germany mainly focus on the study of unpublished manuscripts found in the *Nordrhein-Westfälischen Hauptstaatsarchivs Düsseldorf,*

1

which Ingeborg Villinger and Dirk van Laak have primarily worked on. Many of the correspondences that Schmitt maintained with other twentieth-century intellectuals have been published in recent years, for example, those with Ernst Jünger, Hans Blumenberg, Armin Mohler, Álvaro d'Ors, Hugo Ball, Werner Becker, Luís Cabral de Moncada, Jacob Taubes, and Rudolf Smend. Paul Noack undertook an important, pending task in writing the biography of Carl Schmitt. The book has already been widely reviewed.

In addition, new editions of Schmitt's diaries have been published, including *Carl Schmitt Tagebücher vom Oktober 1912 bis Februar 1915*, edited by Ernst Hüsmert; *Carl Schmitt. Die Militärzeit 1915 bis 1919*, edited by Ernst Hüsmert and Gerd Giesler; *Carl Schmitt: Tagebücher 1930 bis 1934*, edited by Wolfgang Schuller and Gerd Giesler; and *Glossarium. Aufzeichnungen der Jahre 1947–1951*, edited by Eberhard Freiherr von Medem. Also Günter Maschke's collections of Schmitt's articles *Frieden oder Pazifismus? Arbeiten zum Völkerrecht und zur internationalen Politik 1924–1978* and *Staat, Großraum, Nomos: Arbeiten aus den Jahren 1916–1969* are much appreciated for the original material they offer. Helmut Quaritsch's book *Antworten in Nürnberg* was also much anticipated.

The aim of this book is not, however, "manuscript discovery," even if it also includes references to Schmitt's archive; rather, it aims to fill a gap left by research on this author, research whose *status questionis* was clearly defined for the last time, while Schmitt was still alive, at a 1986 conference organized at the *Hochschule für Verwaltungswissenschaften Speyer*, which involved many of the most significant contemporary representatives of Schmitt's commentarists, including Piet Tommissen, Ernst-Wolfgang Böckenförde, Armin Mohler, Günter Maschke, Ellen Kennedy, Joseph Kaiser, Gary L. Ulmen, Helmut Quaritsch, Pasquale Pasquino, Julien Freund, Georg Schwab, Gianfranco Miglio, and Michele Nicoletti, among others. Thereafter, many workshops and conferences dedicated to the Plettenberg jurist sprung up across the world.

In first surveying the existing literature on Schmitt's work, it is evident that practically all of the questions that the Plettenberg jurist noted in his writings have been studied in depth. Special monographs that deal with specific aspects of his writings—the concept of the political is perhaps the most common, as well as his legal theory—have been widely published. There have even been some attempts to issue an overall interpretation of Schmitt's thought, examining the work as a whole. In this sense, one of the most successful attempts can be found in Peter Schneider's book *Ausnahmezustand und Norm*.[5] In addition, Carlo Galli's *Genealogia della politica: Carl Schmitt e la crisi del pensiero político moderno* and Reinhard Mehring's *Carl Schmitt: Aufstieg und Fall* fit into this category of research. The focus of these studies is not philosophical, although a few others do have a philosophical focus, including Matthias Kaufmann's *Recht ohne Regeln? Die phi-*

losophische Prinzipien in Carl Schmitts Staats- und Rechtslehre, which seeks to deepen typically Schmittian concepts and the role they acquire in the author's work taken as a whole.

What does the present book add to this body of research? The study here carried out is also like the books by Schneider, Galli, Mehring, or Kaufmann quoted above in that it is a reassessment of Carl Schmitt's work. It intends not only to analyze the fundamental concepts that make up Schmitt's discourse, but also to show the basic thread that runs through it and give specific meaning to these concepts. Order is Carl Schmitt's first and the last word. This is the main thesis of the book. In the course of Schmitt's writings, we can see how an idea that was developed in the 1920s and 1930s became the central idea in the 1950s organizing his political and juridical discourse. This initial intuition is the constitutive role of the *nomos of the earth* in history and politics. We can find this idea in the first of Schmitt's writings, including the 1916 text, *Theodor Däublers "Nordlicht": Drei Studien über die Elemente, den Geist und die Aktualität des Werkes*, and the short 1925 article, "Illyrien: Notizen von einer dalmatinischen Reise," and particularly in his 1934 book, *Über die drei Arten des rechtswissenschaftlichen Denkens*. His increasing interest in this idea and further formulation of it can be seen in the titles of his publications in the fifties: *Der Nomos der Erde*, 1950; *Raum und Rom: Zur Phonetik des Wortes Raum* and *Recht und Raum*, 1951; *Die Einheit der Welt*, 1952; *Nehmen, Teilen, Weiden*, 1955; *Der neue Nomos der Erde*, 1958; *Gespräch über den neuen Raum*, 1958; *Nomos, Nahme, Name*, 1959.

This thesis is a "continuist" one. It allows for continuity in Schmitt's discourse. Continuity can be argued, for if we distinguish between the different rhetorical moments in every Schmittian text, we can distinguish between the purely theoretical ones in which he shows his own position and the contextual-critical ones in which he describes or criticizes the Modern State or the Constitution of the *bürgerliche Rechtsstaat*, the Weimar Republic or the *Drittes Reich*. On the contrary, many of Schmitt's interpreters distinguish different periods and argue that there is a shift in his production. Consequently, they usually label his thinking as opportunist.

When presenting this work it is necessary to highlight what has been done "starting from Schmitt." Some of Schmitt's theses have been interpreted in light of others without departing from their own assumptions by taking into account different criteria for analyzing texts, including chronological, rhetorical, and logical criteria. The first criterion is used because each of his publications springs from reflection on a specific historical-political situation from which his writings cannot be completely disentangled. The second criterion pertains to the literary style that characterizes Schmitt, with which he subtly employs rhetoric that creates apparent paradoxes between his different works. It is important to distinguish between different types of work, recognizing when he presents the situation of his particular historical period, when he is critical, when he employs political propaganda, when he reveals his own position, and when he uses irony. Above all, I have read Schmitt's works in an effort to discover the discursive structure of his writings and I have done so by starting from the end of his body of work.

The present book's chapter structure corresponds to the latter criterion. I begin by examining the *nomos* of the earth, which is one of Schmitt's fundamental philosophical concepts, corresponding mainly to his later theoretical contributions. A society's economic, judicial, and political situation logically depends on the *nomos*. In light of the *nomos*, Schmitt's work takes on an internal unity, whose fullness will be revealed in the last chapter of this book when dealing with political theology, which corresponds to one of Schmitt's first works.

This systematic aspiration—that is, to put Schmitt's position together in a single discourse, still seems crucial; Schmitt was a true master of language and, in connecting each of his formulations, they fully shine. These formulations include friend-enemy, political theology, political romanticism, catholic political form, concrete order, *Großraum*, sovereignty, *nomos* of the earth, and *ex captivitate salus*. Into what strange world does Schmitt bring us through all of these somewhat cryptic expressions? Certainly, he does not bring us into the strangeness of Wonderland, but rather into the persistently diaphanous world of reality. In a language that many have described as almost mythical, Schmitt paradoxically does not enter into an abstract and nebulous world, but rather he takes us out of legal-political fictions to expose their contrast with reality.

Schmitt's passion is the name of the game and constitutes his access to reality, the "serious" case, *Ernstfall*, as he said. But this involves a lot of back and forth: One can only reach the game by approaching it from that which is most serious. He who knows where to find what truly matters can take everything else pretty lightly. Peace is reached from conflict, friendship from enmity, God from politics, the universe from earthly limits. Contrary to common opinion, I cannot help but think that Schmitt's real proposal is closer to a true peace settlement than the sacred contemporary ideals that everyone seems to hold rather insincerely: Our age excludes war and enmity as a real possibility, yet accepts a new mixture of violence and politics that is unmatched in history.

To understand an author, one must try to get inside both his personal and intellectual worlds. Beginning with condemnation does not work well for this kind of study. Here, the relevance of Schmitt's historical circumstances in shaping his thinking must also be noted. Schmitt found himself in the tradition in which he was inserted, in his education, and in the historical period that he lived in, which happened to coincide with a period that was perfect for examining the specifically political. The historical vantage point from which he wrote was unique and included the collapse of the Second Reich—

that is, the absolute end of a world centered on the imperial idea—the First World War, the emergence of the Weimar Republic and its agony in the hands of the Third Reich, the Second World War, and finally the new international order that was configured from its fall with the humiliation of Germany and what Schmitt considered the triumph of American liberal imperialism. Within this historical trajectory, Schmitt's most accurate insight comes to be the weakness of the liberal democratic state abandoned to the fictions and contradictions of a constitutional utopia that leads to the deterioration of the principle of authority and the effectiveness of the state. "The question of legality,"[6] so goes the title of one of his most famous articles, is perhaps the central problem within Schmitt's political analysis.

> I am the last conscious representative of the *jus publicum europaeum*, its last theorizer and researcher in an existential sense, and I endure its end as Benito Cereno endured his journey aboard the pirate ship. It is the time and place for silence.[7]

Schmitt recognized the beginning and the end of the state era. He found himself, in a sense, before it because, by tradition, he was not a modern thinker, but rather a premodern one. In a certain sense, he also came after it since he could see its breaking points from within modernity.

He accepted his position as a theorist of *jus publicum europaeum* because of his intellectual tradition and, above all, because of historical necessity: The Modern State was an adequate response to the needs of the era. However, he recognized its beginning and its end, which were closely connected. The beginning is found in the separation of legal science from theology, and the end comes in the form of the death of the state due to the poisonous action of technique and, as a consequence, the disappearance of the political. He foretold political modernity all while knowing that, given his classical tradition, it was doomed to fail from the beginning.

As Schmitt said of Bodin and Hobbes, whom he referred to as his "cellmates": "They were set between the old and the brand new and, therefore, were attacked and maligned by both sides. According to theologians, they were atheists and, according to radical rationalists, they were merely hypocrites and opportunists."[8] In turn, today, the same can be said of Schmitt.

Schmitt was an enemy of absolute war, an enemy of the criminalization of enmity, an enemy of falsehood, an enemy of the part of liberalism that exerts superficial mildness, and an enemy of frivolous intelligentsia. Indeed, he was a soldier for peace and clear thinking, despite all of the paradoxes. This again seems to me to be the true face of that Christian Epimetheus.[9]

Chapter One

Biographical Sketch

Who was Carl Schmitt?[1] In the only book in which he talks about his life, *Ex Captivitate Salus*, Schmitt tells of how, on one occasion, this same question—"Who are you?"—put him in an "existential trance."[2] Despite the difficulty in doing so, he was able to give a definition of himself as a "Christian Epimetheus."[3] He even wished to make this definition his epitaph; however, the inscription on his tomb reads (in Greek): "He met the *nomos*."[4]

It is very difficult to define a personality as rich and multifaceted as that of Carl Schmitt; however, an outline of his life is certainly a necessary part of understanding his intellectual path. With Schmitt's biographical timeline in focus, one can better understand the development of his thought. This is especially true for someone whose life was continually marked by historical circumstance, politics, and legal science.

One cannot speak of complete discontinuity in Schmitt's biography, but his life and work are certainly capable of some periodization, as he himself claimed.[5] In 1958 he characterized his timeline as follows:

1. Childhood: 1888–1900. In the Catholic Sauerland
2. Adolescence: 1900–1907. Clericalism with a liberal education
3. Young adulthood: 1907–1918. De-Hegelianized Prussianism impregnated by Wilhelmism and neo-Kantianism
4. Adulthood: 1919–1932. De-Prussianized German patriotism in the Weimar liberal democracy, with strong nationalistic reactions (anti-Versailles)

(Influences):

on 1: An old priest, a good person with memories of the *Kulturkampf*
on 2: Convent director and patriotic manufacturers

on 3: Civil servants and officials (fundamentally decent people)
on 4: Authentic pluralism and a lot of freedom

The content of this book does not follow or extend this timeline so as not to distort the discursive unity of Schmitt's theoretical contribution, which is the principal aim of the book. Thus, before delving in to the systematic development of Schmitt's thought, this chapter will present a biographical sketch in which Schmitt's work will be presented in faithful chronological order with three criteria in mind, namely, historical circumstance, Schmitt's scholarly production, and his personal situation.

FICTION AND REALITY: 1888–1920

Schmitt was born on July 11, 1888, the same year that William I died, in the Westphalian Sauerland city of Plettenberg to a rural Catholic family. With Frederick III, German liberals had buried their hopes and the new conservatism of William II was imposed, which, twenty-five years later, would result in the First World War. He was born in a time of change and in a region that rejected Catholicism during the diaspora of Catholics from Protestant regions.[6] In this environment, Schmitt formed his first feelings of animosity, which remained throughout his life. Schmitt's position was not merely negative criticism to Protestant *Kulturkampf*, but rather was expressed in a kind of eulogy to the Catholic Church that explicitly appeared in his early writings *Die Sichtbarkeit der Kirche* (1917) and *Romischer Katholizismus und politische Form* (1923).

He was first educated, between 1900 and 1907, at a Catholic school, the *Rivius Gymnasium* in Attendorn, where he also lived in a Catholic convent that served as his lodging. By this time, he began to show signs of his literary skill and he read everything he could get his hands on. In March of 1907, he passed his high school exams and decided to study philology, for which he moved to Lorraine, where he had relatives who could house him. Once there, his uncle diverted Schmitt from philology and advised him to study law, which brought him to Berlin in 1907, where he found himself standing in from of the *Juristische Fakultät* sign.

The first months in Berlin proved decisive in his education. He went from a provincial area to the big city, which at first dazzled him, but could not hide the masks and lies. Schmitt described his impressions thusly:

> I entered the University reverently: I thought it would be a temple of high spirituality. But the cult that I saw there was absolutely confusing and I was not inspired to join in on it. Their priests were somehow contradictory and particularly busy with themselves. They represented both an armored self and a frenzied self. Within the internal contradiction of their armored frenzy, the ground they walked on became a stage for displaying themselves. The whole

era was histrionic and, consequently, the temple felt like a theater. . . . I was a dark young man of modest origins. I was neither understood within the dominant social stratum, nor within any opposing current that might arise. I would not formalize a relationship to any party, or any circle, nor did anyone come looking for me. I was, neither for myself nor for others, not interesting enough. Poverty and modesty were my two guardian angels that kept me in the dark, meaning that I remained in the dark and, from there, contemplated a glowing space. . . . In any case, to remain in darkness is an advantage. *L'obscurité protège mieux.*[7]

There, he met Josef Kohler, an eminent jurist, and the great Greek scholar Ulrich von Wilamowitz-Moellendorf, son-in-law to the famous scholar Theodore Mommsen, both of whom completely dazzled him at first. They, and many others, joined in on the stage described above.

At that time, Schmitt drank deeply from the artistic and intellectual currents then in vogue and that interacted in the big city, forming a truly psychedelic scene: Darwinism, romanticism, Nietzscheism, pantheism, expressionism, and cubism. He faced them with a critical attitude in an attempt to separate truth from fiction. Schmitt found new enemies in these currents, which lasted until the end of his days and which were characterized, a few years later, in *Schattenrisse* (1913), namely, Romantic subjectivism, Darwinism, pantheism, optimistic progressivism, and nihilism. In those early years, and as shown in the previously cited work, Schmitt clearly demonstrated a trend toward literary fiction and play through language and images. *Die Buribunken* (1918), another of his first writings, resulted from this same inquietude.

In any case, Schmitt spent relatively little time in Berlin. He studied two semesters there, one in Munich, and the last three in Strasbourg, where, in 1910, he presented his dissertation, entitled *Über Schuld und Schuldarten: Eine terminologische Untersuchung*, under the direction of Professor van Calker. Neo-Kantianism was in the air in the legal field and Schmitt composed his early writings faithful to its assumptions, but gradually began distancing himself from them. In his Strasbourg years, he frequented a circle of expressionist writers where, in 1912, he met Theodor Däubler. Their friendship and conversation inspired the work *Theodor Däublers "Nordlicht": Drei Studien über die Elemente, den Geist und die Aktualität des Werkes* (1916). Through this poet's writings, Schmitt discovered the world of language, which had fascinated him ever since his father had taught him stenography. Words have a real reference that completely permeates them to the point of becoming a reality themselves. Language, words might say more than what they refer to. Through them, one can create a new world of meanings. Discourse is the place in which reality is born. Until the end of his days, Schmitt was interested in these topics.[8]

After submitting his dissertation, Schmitt worked as an intern until 1915 in the service of the Prussian justice Hugo am Zehnhoff, a lawyer in Dusseldorf, a representative of the "Centrum" party and later the Prussian minister of justice from 1920 to 1927. During those five years, Schmitt published a series of works influenced by the intellectual ground he walked on and in which his position as a jurist was not yet clear: "Der Wahnmonolog und eine Philosophie des Als-ob" (1912), *Gesetz und Urteil: Eine Untersuchung zum Problem der Rechtspraxis* (1912), "Schopenhauers Rechtsphilosophie außerhalb seines philosophischen Systems" (1913), and "Juristische Fiktionen" (1913). In 1914, he published his habilitation thesis, *Der Wert des Staates und die Bedeutung des Einzelnen*, in which he distanced himself from the normativism, Kantianism, and rationalism that reigned around him. He did not make a *plädoyer* for the absolute State, but rather for the absoluteness of law in a strong state. In my opinion, Schmitt does not disclose his real view in this publication.

In January 1915, he passed the *Assessorexamen* in Berlin. A few months later, he served as an Adjunct Professor (*Privatdozent*) at the University of Strasbourg until it closed. In February 1915, he married Pawla Dorotic, a marriage that failed since, soon after marrying, he found out that she had hidden her true identity. By 1918 they already lived separately, although they were still legally married. In the end, she left him, taking part of their furniture and library. In 1924, the marriage was declared void under civil law, although, despite his relentless efforts, he never obtained an annulment from the Catholic Church.

From 1915 to 1919, he served in the military, enlisting as a volunteer in the infantry in Munich. He was first a corporal until September 1917, then top noncommissioned officer, and thereafter highest official. During those years, he met luminaries from Bavarian intellectual and artistic circles. In 1917, for example, he met Konrad Weiss, who was a decisive influence in his life and with whom he maintained a lifelong friendship. He also initiated a friendship with Georg and Lilly von Schitzler, founders of the *Europäische Revue*. His relationship with writer Franz Blei is also worth mentioning; in 1920, Blei wrote a series of satires and parodies entitled *Das Bestiarium der modernen Literatur*. Schmitt's fondness for literature, fiction, and satire was still intact.

From 1919 to 1921, he was lecturer (*Dozent*) at the Munich *Handelshochschule*, during which time he attended Max Weber's seminars. Schmitt's years in Munich were influential in the development of his thought and during that time he underwent a change that transformed his taste for fiction, which until then he favored, into a preference for reality; the game turned into seriousness, literary digression into political reflection. The contrast between these worlds is especially apparent in *Politische Romantik*, published in 1919, which was his last work as a young adult. Some commentators believe that, in this work, Schmitt not only fought the subjectivism of his time, but he also immunized himself against the romanticism that gripped his generation, paralyzing his contemporaries when making decisions, incapacitating them from taking a political stance, and abandoning them to a bourgeois life dedicated solely to aesthetic enjoyment.[9]

Schmitt's thinking was inexorably marked by his contact with the war and by having endured in 1919, just as he left military service, the Government of the Soviet Republic in Munich, which constituted a real state of exception. It can be said that, in Munich, Schmitt's fear of chaos went from being a feeling to being a theory. At this point, the political spirit had taken root in Schmitt, which became obvious in his subsequent publications.

THE DISCOVERING OF THE POLITICAL SPIRIT: 1920–1932

Schmitt changed pace and changed his tune. Guided by his discovery of *decision*, opposed to the "eternal dialogue" of aesthetics' logic, he wrote what would become a central part of his thought: *Die Diktatur* (1921), *Politische Theologie* (1922), *Die geistesgeschichtliche Lage des heutigen Parlamentarismus* (1923), *Der Begriff des Politischen* (1927), *Verfassungslehre* (1928), *Der Hüter der Verfassung* (1931), and *Legalität und Legitimität* (1932). At this point, before his National Socialist period, he generally described himself as a decisionist. Certainly his 1912 work, *Gesetz und Urteil*, had primed his thinking about the centrality of the decision.

These represented difficult times for Schmitt, corresponding to the period in which his marriage had just ended and to the experience of the First World War and the consequent peace with dire consequences for Germany. He was also faced with positioning himself professionally; in 1921 he was appointed Professor of Public Law at the University of Greifswald, where he only remained one year. In 1922, and until 1928, he moved to Bonn, where he joined the University as a regular professor in the School of Law, succeeding Rudolf Smend. They were quiet years in which Schmitt participated fully in university life, including giving classes, discussions, supervision of doctoral theses—in four years, approximately twenty-one—co-director of the Political Science Seminar, and so on. He liked to talk with and advise students and even paid for a few students' doctoral studies. He invited students to his house and sustained a friendship with many of them. Later, while in Berlin, he became famous for his house's motto: "Welcome, good and bad alike." Hugo Ball, founder of Dadaism and Hermann Hesse's first biographer, was among those who frequented his house; there, they struck up a close friendship.

In 1925, he fell in love with the woman he would marry one year later—a Serbian woman named Duschka Todorovic, who was his student in Bonn.

According to both his "friends and enemies," his second wife was an exceptional woman. Since he was unable to marry her in the Church, as he would have wished, he remained outside of the Church until her death in 1950, a fact that caused Schmitt true anguish.[10] He returned to the Church after her death. The couple had one daughter, Anima Louise,[11] who was born in 1931.

Despite the stability that he enjoyed in Bonn, his spirit of adventure—of "intellectual adventure," as he described it at the Nuremberg trials—guided him toward the center of interest, toward where ideas were moving and where new streams of thought were forming: "Berlin was his destiny," as his wife once said.[12]

In August 1927, he began making plans to move to Berlin and in April 1928, during the golden era of the Weimar Republic, he began to give classes at a business college (*Handelshochschule*). Shortly afterward, in 1929, the gross domestic product fell in Germany from 89 to 58 billion marks and unemployment numbers increased by one and a half million to more than three million in one year. The situation became increasingly critical and instability was in the air again. At this time, he forged new friendships. In 1929, for example, he met Johannes Popitz, specialist in tax and financial law, Honorary Professor at the *Handelshochschule*, and, at the same time, secretary of state in the Ministry of Finance. He taught Schmitt the uniqueness of the State, administration, and the Prussian style, without which, according to Schmitt, his education would have been incomplete.[13] Their friendship lasted until Popitz's execution, as a member of the German Resistance, in February 1945.

Schmitt's friendship with Ernst Jünger also sprang up during these years, a testament to which is found in the letters between them, clearly demonstrating that they shared readings, thoughts, and ideas.[14] At the time, Jünger was the star of the "conservative revolution" in Germany; he was a symbol of the 1914 generation, the generation of the "front." His use of language was a weapon to fight "civil" Weimar society; he was a mixture of "heroic realism" and radical right dashed with socialism. Bendersky notes that their friendship was based on the admiration each had for the other's intellectual power.[15] The dialogue between them went through difficult times, not only for historical reasons, as might be the case regarding the different positions that each took on National Socialism, but also because they had different spirits. Schmitt disliked that Jünger indiscriminately included the content of their conversations and letters in his diary. Schmitt also kept a diary, but most of it is still untouched because it is written in shorthand that is impossible to decipher. Schmitt was incapable of talking about himself, let alone publishing something so personal. He only did so once, in *Ex Captivitate Salus*, and only by taking sufficient distance from himself.

Schmitt also established contact with Walter Benjamin during this time. Benjamin wrote him a letter motivated by the publication of *Der Ursprung des deutschen Trauerspiels* to thank him for his publications, which greatly influenced his recent writing. Benjamin was fascinated by Schmitt's thought because of its aspiration for integrity and interdisciplinarity. Their positions were far apart, but both had declared war on compromise, parliamentarianism, and political liberalism; both understood that the highest manifestation of the spirit takes place in exception, and both were inclined to think in absolute terms and by starting from theology. [16]

As he did in Bonn, and especially in Munich, Schmitt surrounded himself with writers, artists, and publicists in Berlin. This group included liberals, nationalists, young conservatives, and even revolutionaries. He became interested in both contemporary and classic painting, including painters such as Gilles, Nay, Heldt, Velázquez, and Bosco.

Returning to political events, in 1930 the Weimar Republic began to fall into crisis. Estévez Araujo describes this period in his analysis of the decline of the Weimar Constitution as follows:

> From 1930 until Hitler's rise to power, governments did not depend on Parliament's trust, but rather exclusively on the president's. To carry out this constitutional change, President Hindenburg used his power to dissolve parliament. This practice began with Brüning in July 1930 when Parliament refused to approve the measures proposed by the Chancellor and the President dissolved Parliament, while maintaining the Chancellor in his position. [17]

Moreover, in that same year, the interpretation of Article 48's second paragraph of the Weimar Republic reached its final point. The article read:

> If public security and order are seriously disturbed or endangered within the German Reich, the President of the Reich may take measures necessary for their restoration; intervening if need be with the assistance of the armed forces. For this purpose he may suspend for a while, in whole or in part, the fundamental rights provided in Articles 114, 115, 117, 118, 123, 124 and 153. [personal freedom, inviolability of the home, confidential correspondence, freedom of the press, freedom of assembly, freedom of association, and private property].

Facing the approaching cataclysm, Schmitt attempted to save the constituted state even though he was not a friend of the system. With this intention, and not to prime Hitler's dictatorship as has been assumed so many times, he wrote *Der Hüter der Verfassung*—Who can defend the Constitution in a case of extreme peril?—and he offered an interpretation of the aforementioned article. According to this interpretation, the president cannot abolish the Constitution and undermine the "organizational minimum" that is a prerequisite for its very existence. Article 48.2 does not give the president legislative or judicial power: He may violate law, but not create it. Here, Schmitt sought to give the rule of law's legislative and judiciary apparatus an organ whose specific function is to decide, within certain limits, when and to what extent it is in the state's interest to violate the law.

POLITICAL ACTION: 1932–1937

With the Weimar crisis, Schmitt also initiated his involvement in political life. [18] The contact he maintained, beginning in early 1932, with von Papen and Schleicher was decisive. Through them, Schmitt was given the duty of defending the Reich in the process of 29 October 1932 against Prussia because of the "*Preußenschlag*" on July 20. The process dealt with what was referenced in Article 48. The resolution of this process was crucial to the future of the Weimar Constitution. The progressive influence of two other circumstances was also crucial to the agony of the Republic: the fear of the possibility of civil war and doubt about how the Republic would react to the clear majority that the Nazi party was gaining. Schmitt's contribution to the interpretation of Article 48 undoubtedly influenced the transformation of the German parliamentary system into a presidential system. However, he also feared this new majority, as shown in the following statement from July 19:

> Whoever provides the majority to the Nazis on July 31, though not himself a national socialist and only sees the lesser evil in this party, foolishly acts and gives this ideological, political, mature movement the chance to change the Constitution, to establish a national church, to dissolve trade unions, etc. He delivers Germany to that group. Thus, it was good—always taking the circumstances into account—to promote the movement to resist Hitler; after July 31 it could be extremely dangerous, because 51 percent of the NSDAP represents a political will of incalculable consequences. [19]

Schmitt wanted to save the Weimar Republic from both a weak parliamentarianism and a strong dictatorship. The change in government seemed imminent; Germany's fascination with this new movement was an incontrovertible fact. Carl Schmitt clearly saw the danger, perhaps better than anyone, and could not, however, do anything other than submit to it. The year 1932 presented improved "hopes" for Schmitt. He explains his situation in an interview with the Spanish newspaper *La Noche*, on Saturday, April 7, 1962, in Santiago. To the question: "Rumors have emerged that your thinking at that time had shifted, is that not true?" He answers:

> No, I was a staunch defender of the German Republic, but the Weimar Constitution was susceptible to many interpretations. During this regime I was an advisor to General Schleicher, who represented the only chance to prevent Hitler's rise to power. Bourgeois democrats, given the fact that General Schleicher was military, started talking of "militarism" and facilitated Hitler's

triumph. President Hindenburg has the great responsibility of not only having given Hitler power but . . . the Constitution. [20]

Indeed, Hitler finally came to power on January 30, 1933. I copy two of Schmitt's journal entries from those days: [21]

> January 27, 1933
> The Hindenburg myth has come to an end. The old man was ultimately merely a MacMahon. Horrible situation. Schleicher has retired; Papen or Hitler will rise. The old man has gone mad. I came home on a horrible, cold night around eleven.

> January 30, 1933
> Then I went to Kutscherer cafe where everything was very stirred up by the appointment of Hitler as Chancellor.

Starting then, much of his activity, according to his own words, was designed to establish adequate dialogue with the regime, despite the fact that it burned everything possible. At the beginning of the new regime, Schmitt performed several legislative tasks. In March, he started working at the behest of his friend Popitz on the *Reichsstatthaltergesetz* of April 7, 1933; later, he worked on the *Preussische Gemeindeverfassungsgesetz* of December 15, 1933; months later he participated in discussions about the *Strafverfahrenordnung*. In April of that year, the new regime appointed him Professor of Legal Science at the University of Cologne. There, he worked with Hans Kelsen, with whom he did not like to discuss much, and he met Erik Peterson. Both were like a counterpoint to his thesis. He was never friends with Kelsen, although he was friends with Peterson, to the extent that some say that Peterson, a Protestant theologian, converted to Catholicism in part because of Schmitt's influence. [22] Schmitt also forged another relevant friendship at that time with the canonist Hans Barion. In the same month, Schmitt entered the Party: "I enrolled in the local chapter in Cologne at the end of April 1933; there was a long line. I let them sign me up, like many others." [23] Here begins Schmitt's short political career.

On Jellinek's recommendation, Schmitt was offered the Anschütz chair in Heidelberg, but in July he was appointed advisor to the Prussian State, an appointment that Göring planned. He believed in Schmitt's worth and protected him until the end of the regime. Hitler, meanwhile, never met Schmitt, as Schmitt described in the interview referred to above: To the question "What is your personal opinion of Hitler," he replied:

> I never got to talk to him. His hatred of jurists was even stronger than his hatred for Jews; I learned this from Hans Frank [who had been the Bavarian justice minister and later was governor of Poland]. Hans Frank frequently dealt with Hitler and knew his attitude on jurists. Once Frank told me that talking

with the Chancellor would mean disgrace for me. For my part, as I say, I could
only observe him: He was a *halbgebildet*[24] man and his sparse culture led him
to hate educated men.

In August, he was offered a new appointment at the University of Munich,
but he refused. Finally, in October 1933, he arrived to the University of
Berlin, where he was Professor of Legal Science until December 1945, when
he was fired.

After that, his duties came in quick succession, but did not last long. As of
November of 1933, he was director of the so-called *Fachgruppe Hochschul-
lehrer im Bund Nat. Soz. Deutscher Juristen.* On June 1, 1934, he was given
the responsibility of editing *Deutscher Juristen-Zeitung*, in which only a few
months later the article "Der Führer Schütz das Recht"[25] was published,
which was as controversial as, according to Schmitt, it was misinterpreted.

Despite his efforts to win the confidence of the regime, nearly the entire
Nazi hierarchy suspected him because of his Catholicism, his friendship with
Jewish personalities, and his scholarly strength. In the summer of 1936, the
State Security Service opened a dossier on Schmitt and began an investiga-
tion into his life and activities. As a result of this decision, on October 3 and
4, 1936, several attacks against Schmitt appeared in the newspaper of the SS,
Das Schwarze Korps. Although Göring was able to stop the attacks,
Schmitt's career in the Nazi regime had ended. In December 1936 Frank
wrote:

> I have dismissed, despite everything, the State Advisor Carl Schmitt of all his
> duties. . . . Professor Carl Schmitt will not be employed in any official posi-
> tion, the League of Lawyers, or the Academy.[26]

During the three years of political commitment to the regime, Schmitt
published several articles. Perhaps the most representative of them, as can
already be seen in the title, is *Die deutsche Rechtswissenschaft im Kampf
gegen den jüdischen Geist.*[27] The content does not directly attack the Jewish
race, but rather demystifies Jewish jurisprudence and intended, supposedly, a
display of German jurisprudence overconfidence. This article was written
when the SS had Schmitt under investigation. He undoubtedly tried to concede everything possible to the Party. However, at this time, Schmitt also
wrote things that can be more consistently related to his thinking and that are
not so directly related to the Nazi reality. This applies, for example, to the
1934 book, *Über die drei Arten des rechtswissenschaftlichen Denkens*,[28] in
which he outlined his position on what the law is, which remained consistent
from thereon out. That is, even then, as always, he was focused on jurisprudence.

TIMES OF FEAR: 1937–1945

Beginning in 1936, Schmitt went through some hard times. He continued giving classes at the university and began to write since he had no other tasks. He mainly developed his theory of space, which took shape until resulting in the 1950 publication *Der Nomos der Erde*. His theory of space was scientific, but it could serve the Nazis by justifying their power and ploys, which allowed Schmitt to continue publishing his writings. These were years in which "you had to pretend to be . . ." Schmitt commented on this in the *La Noche* interview:

> It was the most dangerous moment of my life. Being attacked by a totalitarian state in the party newspaper is extremely dangerous. When I talk about this, people say I just want to excuse myself. What I can do?

At this time, Schmitt published many of his core writings. Among the most significant are: *Der Leviathan in der Staatslehre des Thomas Hobbes. Sinn und eines Fehlschlag politischen Symbols* (1938); *Völkerrechtliche Großraumordnung mit Interventionsverbot für Raumfremde Mächte* (1939); *Land und Meer. Eine weltgeschichtliche Betrachtung* (1942).

The pressure he felt, however, did not prevent Schmitt from having a social life. His house was still a meeting point, even in the war years. His guestbook attests to visits from Ivo Andric, Ernst Jünger, Werner Gilles, Ernst Wilhelm Nay, Emil Nolde, Werner Heldt, Prinz Rohan, Lilly von Schnitzler, Heinrich Oberheid, Bishop Schulz, Hans Freyer, Werner Weber, Werner Sombart, Johannes Popitz, Erich Marcks, and many students and doctoral candidates, among others recorded between 1938 and 1940.

Starting in 1941, he went on several trips. He visited Paris, where he lectured at the Ritz. A year later he also traveled to Bordeaux, Lille, and Brussels. In Budapest, where his friend Hans Freyer was exiled, he spoke in May 1941 and November 1943. In February 1943 in Bucharest, he gave the same conference that he had given in these other cities: *Die Lage der europäischen Rechtswissenschaft*, which he also presented in Spain—Barcelona, Madrid, and Granada—in April–May 1944 and in Lisbon in May and June 1944.[29]

THE SECURITY OF THE SILENCE: 1945–1985

Immediately following the war, Schmitt was sent to a concentration camp in Berlin (*Lichterfelde Süd*), under the "automatic arrests" that the victors staged, where he stayed a few months during 1945 and 1946. During that time, he wrote *Ex Captivitate Salus*, a summary of what he saw as the meaning of his existence. On August 22, 1946, he was able to return to his home in Berlin until March 19, 1947, when he was again imprisoned at

Nuremberg as a witness. On April 3, 21, and 29, 1947, he was questioned by
Robert Kempner[30] in Berlin and declared innocent. In reality, he was not
charged with anything by the victors, but rather was taken as a witness; they
were interested in Schmitt's impression of what happened in Germany during
those years. At trial, he was questioned on three points in relation to his
activity[31]; namely, to what extent did you theoretically justify Hitler's expan-
sionist policy (*Großraumpolitik*)? Were you decisively involved in preparing
the offensive war and the criminal acts associated with it? What position did
the ministers and the head of the Reich Chancellery take? Schmitt filled a
few notebooks to answer these questions.[32] A substantial portion of the latter
question's answer is published in the article *Das Problem der Legalität.*[33]

Just after the war, the Rector and the University Senate decided to fire all
the teachers who had been involved with National Socialism. Schmitt was
therefore dismissed from the university, where he was never to work again.
In a February 1946 report to Erich Przywara, Schmitt reflected on his situation; here are some significant lines:

> This testimony refers to knowledge and insights that can only originate from
> the most intimate of events in Germany and can only be made from a German
> Catholic experience, that is, by a German who has had his legitimate participa-
> tion, total *participation*, in German history of the last century without identify-
> ing with it.[34]

His only option was to return to Plettenberg, his homeland, and he did so in
1947 to live with his family, and stayed there until his death. His retreat
saved him from the "denazification" (*Entnazifizierung*) that took place in
Germany for many years and he was granted a pension. His house in Plettenberg, which he called "San Casciano," evoking Machiavelli, came to be a
place of rest and security, "the safety of silence," as he called it.

In December 1950, his wife died and shortly thereafter his daughter,
Anima, left home to study. Before then, and especially thereafter, "San Casciano" became a must-visit place for old friends and a number of intellectuals, politicians, journalists, and theologians, who came to talk with him.
Among his most common known visitors were Ernst Jünger, Ernst-Wolfgang
Böckenförde, Reinhart Koselleck, Hans Barion, Joseph Kaiser, Piet Tommissen, Paul Adams, Gerhard Nebel, Hanno Kesting, Peter Schneider, Günther
Krauss, Heinrich Oberheid, and Armin Mohler. Outside Germany, Schmitt
had a remarkable influence in Spain, not only because of the quantity of his
disciples, but also because of the ideological disparity of the people he influenced, including Tierno Galván, Fraga Iribarne, Father Valverde, Sánchez
Agesta, and Legaz y Lacambra (who directed José Caamaño's doctoral thesis
on Schmitt). Starting in 1944, he struck up a friendship with Álvaro d'Ors,
who dedicated his 1954 book, "De la Guerra y de la Paz" (*On War and*

Peace), to Schmitt. He admired Spain, especially its character, its art and its history.

Schmitt's intellectual output not only did not stop, but was strengthened. He wrote despite the difficulty of not being able to work in a library and, not having much of a library himself, he largely cited texts from memory. Although finished in 1945, in 1950, *Der Nomos der Erde* was published, followed by years of related publications. In 1970, *Politische Theologie II* was published, representing another central work in his thought. Meanwhile, he wrote many articles and never retired from public dialogue. In fact, officially he was retired—since he never retracted his past—which was reason enough to keep him out of the public forum. But, in reality, he continued to participate. He continued to influence the currents of thought and political life through his friends. Throughout his life and in these years as well, he maintained constant correspondence, as can be seen in the index of the published catalog.[35] He almost never failed in answering a letter.

The death of his daughter, Anima, married to Professor Alfonso Otero, in June 1983, came as a huge blow[36] that nearly finished him. In December 1984, he was diagnosed with a serious illness—cerebral sclerosis—that deprived him of his use of reason in the last months of his life. He died on April 7, 1985 at the Plettenberg hospital.

After some years of being banned internationally, Schmitt's figure has rapidly risen in recent years, especially in Italy and in Germany itself, but also in the United States. It seems clear that his thinking has a force—some would say a "fascination"—that will keep him at the center of the controversies that arise in political thought for generations to come.

Chapter Two

Space and *Nomos*

nomos— land appropriation
is critical to the
political

Schmitt's name is inevitably intertwined with characteristic phrases that correspond to his theoretical contributions, the most famous of which include, "friend-enemy distinction," "exception," "concrete-order thinking," "large space," as well as "political theology" and the last one, chronologically speaking, "the *nomos* of the earth." This cluster of curious phrases made the Plettenberg jurist's discourse appear somewhat extravagant; however, a lucid and coherent discourse can be found by deciphering the questions contained in these expressions.[1] This book aims to engage in this deciphering task and the key to it is found precisely in the latter theoretical discovery: the *nomos* of the earth, that is, the appropriation of space by its inhabitants, the settlement of peoples on earth.

Theory always arises in Schmitt in response to legal practice, and his theoretical innovation is always oriented toward the search for an authentic foundation of Legal Science. This foundation is not based in natural law or in a rational construction, but in history—that is, in temporarily constituted nature. In this sense, Schmitt recognized himself as an heir to Savigny and Bachofen.[2]

Keeping in mind the principal object of his research concerning *nomos*, I intend to go deep into the meaning that this concept acquires throughout his discourse.[3] So, while Schmitt, in *The Nomos of the Earth*, designates "land-appropriation as a constitutive process of international law,"[4] by looking to smaller publications on the subject, which Schmitt developed over time, we can go further and say that *nomos* is the constitutive action of any political community.

Considering the import of *The Nomos of the Earth in the International Law of Jus Publicum Europaeum* (1950), along with many more of his books—including *Über die drei Arten des rechtswissenschaftlichen Denkens*

(1934) and *Völkerrechtliche Großraumordnung mit Interventionsverbot für Raumfremde Mächte* (1939), and with other smaller writings that are no less significant such as *Der Reichsbegriff im Völkerrecht* (1939), *Großraumordnung gegen Universalismus* (1939), *Der neue Raumbegriff* (1940), *Reich und Raum* (1940), *Raum und Großraum in Völkerrecht* (1941), *Land and Sea* (1942), *Die Raumrevolution: Vom Geist des Abendlandes* (1942), *Über die phonetische Bedeutung des Wortes Raum* (1950), published also as *Raum und Rom* one year after (1951, which he considers as the corollarie number 6 of *The Nomos of the Earth*), *Recht und Raum* (1951), *Nehmen, Teilen, Weiden* (1953, which he considers as the corollarie number 7 of the Nomos of the Earth),[5] *Der Neue Nomos der Erde* (1955), *Die Geschichtliche Struktur des heutigen Weltgegensätzes von Ost und West* (1955), *Gespräch über den neuen Raum* (1958), *Nomos-Nahme-Name* (1959), *Glossarium, Aufzeichnungen der Jahre 1947–1951* (1991), and *El orden del mundo después de la Segunda Guerra Mundial* (1962)[6]—the concept of *nomos* is fully sketched with the meaning that Schmitt intended for it. These writings were published over a thirty-year time span, showing that Schmitt's research on *nomos*—although more explicitly thematic in the last part of his work—was a constant and not limited to a particular historical moment. The first time he used the word *nomos* was in a 1934 text on Legal Science: *Über die drei Arten des rechtswissenschaftlichen Denkens*,[7] which, although not specifically written about space or *nomos*, is related to it. In Schmitt's discourse, the concepts of order, space, and *nomos* correspond to each other. What is meant by the first two words is definitively clarified in the concept of *nomos*.

NOMOS OF THE EARTH

The fact that Schmitt devoted so much of his writing to the subject is worthy of consideration and not irrelevant when attempting an interpretation of his work. Research on *nomos*, therefore, is not inapt and neither is it just a mythical game.[8] It is the thread that runs throughout his political discourse. Everything has to be situated in the order of earthly space.

Original man's appropriation of land opens up the possibilities of history.[9] This is the moment in which man first employs his relationship with earthly space, which conditions all future relationships between men.[10] This same historical event continues to take place in various forms to this day: Land appropriations can happen again in historical reality either by settlements caused by conquest and migration or because of a political decision in the defense of a country against an enemy.[11] This original fact is necessarily repeated again and again, to the point that it can be considered as a historical constant, and it has its foundation in the human spirit's very constitution: Man cannot live without appropriating. This is the condition of human sociality—that is, an original act that conditions and accounts for man's way of formally manifesting human sociality, which corresponds to law, economics, and politics. [12] The *nomos* of the earth reveals every social act as, in the first place, an act of appropriation. That is, to speak of any kind of relationship in society and, therefore, of economics, law, and politics, it is necessary to refer to this original fact of an existential nature that arises with man's appearance in the world. Property, economics, international and civil law, and the conception of the political can only be understood starting from man's appropriation of the earth. In Schmitt's discourse, even political theology belongs to the *nomos* of the earth.

EARTH, SPACE, ORDER

In order to fully understand what *nomos,* in all its breadth, means, we must first define man's relationship with the earth. Any consideration made of man, of everything that has to do with him and his journey in time, must refer to one element: the earth. It is therefore possible to meaningfully characterize man as a terrestrial being:

> Man is a terrestrial, a groundling. He lives, moves and walks on the firmly-grounded Earth. It is his standpoint and his base. He derives his points of view from it, which is also to say that his impressions are determined by it and his world outlook is conditioned by it. [13]

In fact, man calls the place where he dwells "earth," although it has large areas of water. Earth is so significant for man because it is the first thing he comes in contact with and because it is necessary for his survival. Given that man confronts land's dimensions when he cultivates and grows, the primary mode of this man-earth relationship is found in agrarian activity. [14] Cultivation, upon making contact with land's dimensions, is the first form of culture. This first type of relationship with the earth gives way to other relational modes in society, which, although they may seem different or superior, always maintain a certain relationship with that first settlement and common use of the land. Later forms of this relationship are, for example, types of property, family, race, caste, neighborhood types, and modes of power and dominion. [15] Man's relationship with the sea is different. The sea is not safe ground for him and resists ownership claims. Certainly, man eventually became capable of inhabiting the sea, although only for short periods of time and, in so doing, mimics what it's like to dwell on land in the form of a boat.

Man's—a people's—form of historical existence largely depends on their relationship with space, which is seen clearly in, for example, the different ways that landlocked and coastal countries have evolved. These inhabitants' imagination, language, and very ways of thinking develop differently, depending on their geographic position. Schmitt, however, adds a nuance, namely that *conditioned* does not mean *determined*: Man confronts the earth, is conditioned by it, but he does not allow himself to be absorbed by its edges. Man can use the land and, in that relationship, conquer his own existence and consciousness. This is what land appropriation implies, since man's reference to space is not confined to a physical relationship with it, but rather a spiritual relationship that gives way to various forms of awareness and social relationships. Thus, in *Land and Sea*, Schmitt notes that if man had a determinate geographical context, he could not be differentiated from animals.[16] This reference to animals is not trivial. They also live in relation to space; however, they cannot use it in the same way as man, which first requires putting a reality as such into objective terms. An animal can use things in space and move in it, but it cannot know it as such; therefore, an animal cannot possess it in the same way and, thus, cannot express its measurement in the same way. Ultimately, man can appropriate the land thanks to his spiritual element, where land is a necessary condition of spiritual development.[17]

In his early works, Schmitt used the word "space" instead of *nomos* to describe man's relationship with the elements—earth, air, and sea. *Raum* (space) is the existential condition of man. In any reality, there is a disposition of parts with the consequent distances between them, which form space. *Nomos* adds a nuance to mere space, namely, man's entrance into space and with respect to it, along with two specifically human capacities: appropriation and measurement. *Raum* can exist without man, but *nomos* cannot. Since man's first activity on earth was appropriation, space in general must have been one of man's first concepts: "Space is one of any language's first words. It is an original word of the original language."[18] From a genealogical point of view, in the formation of concepts, land comes before space. With the first land-appropriation (*Landnahme*), man forges the concept of space, precisely because the first measurement of land emerges. The idea of space in Schmitt's thought contains implications for a concept of land and land-appropriation that he did not formally frame until 1950, but they were implicit during 1939–1941, when writing about *Raum* and *Großraum*, and even in 1934, when, for the first time, he explicitly mentioned the word *nomos* and first outlined its meaning. Schmitt analyzes the meaning of space from multiple, complementary perspectives and the concept acquires so much relevance in his thought that we could say that all the expressions he uses are in a way "spacialized."[19] We begin with the phonetic approach that Schmitt offered, taken from the Jacob and Wilhelm Grimm German dictionary: The vowels *A* and *U* refer to A and Ω, the beginning and end of time and, therefore, a temporal reference. The consonants *R* and *M* demarcate a place without any material limit.[20] *R* constitutes an active start and *M* the foreseeable end. With these phonetic reference points, Schmitt offers the following definition:

> Space is not a closed circle, it is not an enclosure; rather, it is the world and that world is not an empty space nor is it in an empty space. Our space is a world full of tensions between different elements.[21]

In opposition to the word *Raum* (space), the word *Meer* (sea) is used, whose repetition of vowels indicates an empty space. Schmitt makes a phonetic description in order to show that all *real* space is qualitative, has a shape, and is not a void. It has a certain form because it is inhabited. Therefore, as opposed to *Raum*, *Meer* is a space that is undifferentiated in itself; it is without form and homogeneous. *Meer* can be considered space only in reference to land, because land sets its limits. Thus, insofar as the sea has a shore, it is considered a space, but if we do not look beyond maritime space, it is impossible to establish anything because no fixed point can be set and it lacks diversity.[22] Consequently, it is impossible to establish an order; maritime space cannot be organized, nor lived in—it is merely a transitory place. *Raum* and *Meer* or, better yet, *Erde* (earth) and *Meer* are names that correspond to two kinds of space.

Having thus defined space, Schmitt does not detain himself in pure materiality, but rather analogically transports its meaning to other areas. Space is analogous. First, for Schmitt, the word *space* has some metaphysical-anthropological connotations. One can speak of a *Raum-Sein*[23] (space-being) analogy. At this point the long-standing space-time dialectic appears. Time takes on a sense of finitude versus space, which acquires hints of eternity.[24] Both time and space have to do with life, but in two different senses.[25] Natural chronological time represents the dynamism of a living being, while material space represents the dialogic nature of that same being. Time has an end in the same way that temporal life does, but life itself does not.[26] When referring to temporal life in the *Glossarium*, Schmitt puts it thusly: "Life itself is a joke of time and time has an end."[27] But life gains and retrieves the time that passes in the form of spirit, form, being. Both form and being are space. The being that lives and consumes time, gains interior space, spirit. This thought recurs in Schmitt's work: "Ich verliere meine Zeit und gewinne meinen Raum."[28] "I lose my time and earn my space." Where there is no space, there is no being. There is nothing. In that sense, the spatial conception of the self faces nihilism.[29] Schmitt refers to Nietzsche saying, "This phrase is also eternal (even surprising in the context of Nietzsche language): With man's chin up, space is originated against the great nothing. Where there is space, there is being."[30] And he further states that the essence of being is to be spatial, saying, "The essence of being is spatial being, position, space and power; it is not a temporal succession; it is presence, i.e., space. . . . God is dead means space is dead, corporeality is dead."[31]

How should we understand this relationship between space and being? To the extent that "the point" does not really exist and is a pure abstraction, every being is spatial, including the spirit. It is understood that he is talking of space in an analogous sense and, in this way, it can be defined as anything that involves a unifying force of distant positions; in a way, it is unity in diversity. Given this characterization of space, time appears as nonbeing. Time is the abandonment of unity: disintegration and, therefore, secondary to space. How is it possible to combine this concept with the historical awareness that Schmitt undoubtedly had in mind?[32] Time is also in space and only occurs in space.[33] To evoke history's spatial-temporal assimilation, he plays with the relationship between the words *Raum* and *Rom* (space-Rome): "I'm sure *Raum* and *Rom* are the same word."[34] He also notes that "Space is the same word as Rome. Hence the hatred of the word space; that hatred is only a variant of anti-Roman temper."[35] Álvaro d'Ors explains how Schmitt saw the word *Raum* as an echo of Catholic Rome.[36] No doubt the parallelism between the two words is forced; however, their relationship gives us the key to understanding that when Schmitt refers to space. Rome is not just physical space, but rather is also a spiritual space that extends over the entire world. It could mean the Roman Empire and its significance for world history, but it could also mean the Catholic Church. The Church of Rome is visible; it is a space at once spiritual and terrestrial, but it is present anywhere believers meet in the name of Christ.[37] This is only possible if Rome means more than a physical space. Indeed, Rome is a symbol of civilization, that is, of the space that constitutes a sublime form of humanization. *Raum* and *Rom* express the fact that significant space for man is humanized space, that is, *nomos*. Rome is thus seen as a symbol of all *nomos*. Still, there is a second significant feature derived from conserving Rome not just as a symbol, but also as the center of civilization. Real space is always qualitative. A homogeneous space only exists in abstract mathematical science. A qualitatively configured space has a form that configures it as a non-void. It must also have a supporting point from which its peculiar configuration arises because, if not, it would be a divine monad. The civilized world has its center in a concrete place from which the last light of human civilization radiates. It also constitutes the origin of the greatest civilization in the history of the world, a civilization from which we originate.[38] All human space is civilized. Therefore, the center of all civilization is Rome, meaning that what it symbolizes is the center of all humanization of space—that is, of all *nomos*.

We still have to consider a new extension of the concept of space, one that has more political connotations, namely the *Raum-Realität-Ort-Ordnung* (space-reality-position-orientation) relationship. The importance of space in political theory ensures realism over utopia. Reality for political theory is:

Der Mensch in Raum, not just *Der Mensch und die Menschen*.[39] Man in space is the setting for any realism in legal, political, or economic theory. Both, the autonomization of the object versus the personal sphere and of the territorial sphere versus the communal sphere, are false. A community of people is not possible without regard to objects and space. When this is lost from sight or is not taken into account, space becomes a weapon. As Schmitt says,

> It is no longer given by nature or by God, but by chance, chosen arbitrarily and freely, made, built by people for people, built on flat surface such that it no longer involves any particular place.[40]

Space is then dissociated from particular place, a position (*Ort*), and becomes an unorganized, homogeneous space, an abstract mathematical idea that man can handle at will, thus creating the possibility of utopia: "It is, in other words, overall planning, which also includes natural realities of the human *physis* and *psique* in its de-localization."[41] Ultimately, the disordering of space is a danger to the conceptions of law and policy, since, in such a space, the notion of concrete order is lost and opens up to arbitrariness and opportunism.[42] If space is qualitative and not merely quantitative—that is, homogeneous or void, then it is an order made up of formal unity in diversity with a sustaining center or internal reference. An ordered space is, by definition, located (*Ort*) and differentiated space. By contrast, in a space in which all points are the same—as far as space as such—one cannot be differentiated from another and any one point in this space cannot be fully located because location requires a reference difference. In quantitative, mathematical space, points are indistinguishable—there is no particular center—and, therefore, nothing can be fixed in a location.

In *Illyrien*, Schmitt gave an example of the notion of concrete order in relation to a differentiated space in itself. This article dealt with what is called Illyria, a space that later became Serbia and then was divided between Italy (Trieste and Istria); Albania; and the Serbian, Croat, and Slovak kingdoms, which were later included in Yugoslavia. Schmitt claims that the latter name is not a name, but rather a political label. In this long historical period, Illyria was a *political object*. Its soil has been the scene of many political happenings, through which Rome, Byzantium, the Normans, the Turks, the French, and the Austrians have all passed, making for a significant mix of these races.[43] Despite so much historical change, the land remains the same,[44] although it gained a characteristic feature, that of housing a polyglot people. The development of this polyglot capacity is not due to the need to accommodate many peoples, but rather is due to a psychological attitude that amounts to having affection for the foreign without sacrificing everything proper to a people. This does not pertain to an international movement of peoples, but rather, in the words of Schmitt, to

> a particular disposition of the spirit, a waiver of utilitarian and practical com-
> promises, an ability to let other languages coexist as companions and talk with
> them as people, without instrumentalizing them. [45]

This particular character of the Balkan peoples is not shaped by their bloodline, but rather is found in their land. [46] Particularity arises from the original *nomos* and, therefore, any attempt to homogenize space fails sooner or later since it is nothing more than an imposed political label. Illyria consti-tutes a concrete example of the *nomos* of the earth. Once the event with which all human history begins has been partially described, we will careful-ly consider the original meaning of the word *nomos*.

THE POLITICAL RELEVANCE OF THE *NOMOS OF THE EARTH*

The Semantics of *Nomos*

The first thesis that Schmitt offered concerning the meaning of the word *nomos* indicates that it has more to do with the land than with the law. To prove this thesis, Schmitt again outlined considerations of a philological nature. Words that end in *nomos* generally refer to an object, words that end in *-kratie* or *-archie* refer to a subject, as for example, *Monarchie, Demokra-tie*, and *Oikonomie*. The former refers to a single subject, the second to a group of subjects, while the latter refers to *oikos*, or house, an object. [47] This is also true for the majority of the words that end in *nomie*, such as *Astro-nomie, Geonomie, Gastronomie*, with one exception: *Patronomie*. Still, the reference that *nomos* makes to an object can be generally accepted. Second, *nomos* alludes to the root *Nem*, inasmuch as *nomos* comes before the verb *nemein*. Schmitt notes that Laroche, in his study *Histoire de la racine –nem*, observes that words with this root always indicate organization, order, and economy. It could mean *Weide*, pasture, as well as *Stückland*, piece of land, and *Wohnsitz*, settlement. Later, in the Roman world, *nomos* would be trans-lated for *lex* in the work of Cicero. [48]

The noun *nomos* comes from the verb *nemein*. [49] These kinds of nouns are *nomine actionis* and indicate a fact that acquires its content through the verb itself, thus *legein-logos*; *sprechen-Sprache*. *Nomos* refers to *nemein* action, in German *nehmen*. Therefore, the first meaning of *nomos* is *Nahme*, or "something appropriated." Schmitt described the result of this action by say-ing that the former is not the division of the land, but rather the land as a possession in which division later takes place. In the beginning, there was no fundamental norm (*Grund Norm*), but rather an original possession (*Grund*

Nahme). This is the fundamental condition to give, divide, or distribute any-thing. Without land appropriation, one cannot carry out any action on it—and to take land, it must be given.[50]

As mentioned, the concept of *nomos* implies a nuance absent from the concept of space, namely the appearance of man in space. Without man, *Raum* can exist, but not *nomos*. *Nomos* has its origin in the first measure of the land and this appears with man. To speak of *nomos* means thinking of land as a whole and man as an inhabitant in it. Schmitt explained it this way:

> I speak of a new *nomos* of the earth. That mean that I consider the earth, the planet in which we live, as a whole, as a globe, and seek to understand its global division and order.[51]

The earth as an "appropriated" whole is *Nahme*. However, no historical *nemein* is original, but rather is always carried out on an earlier *Nahme* and, ultimately, on the first *nomos* that came from an original act of God unknown to man, inhabitant of the earth.[52] Thus, there is a profound relationship be-tween *nomos* and *logos* as given actions that precede human action. There is an "original" political theology. Just as *logos* is an intellectual space, the *nomos* is a practical one. Therefore, *nomos* makes division possible and *nomos* itself is already a certain original appropriation in the same way that a particular *logos* is always participating in a common *logos*. Now, for division to be made possible, the earth has to appear as a whole and, inasmuch, manifests itself as an objective order. Since the earth has a given internal objective measure, any appropriation or division of it cannot be totally arbi-trary. This is reflected in Schmitt's thought in the following assertion: "All human *nomoi* are 'nourished' by a single divine nomos."[53] Human *nemein* is not possible without a nonhuman original *Nahme*, as already noted. No one can give anything without first taking it.[54] At this point, Schmitt, as stated, referred back to the origin of the world. In the beginning there is only that which is given[55]—that is, the earth with its internal measurement—within which one's action can take place in the pursuit of creating a habitat and constituting a relationship with the land. Thus, the novelty in studying man's common life—constituted by economics, law, and politics—is renewed by the unity of a *nomos*, whatever it may be, in each historical period.[56] From this original fact, the history of later land grabs is explained. This relation-ship is described as follows:

> Thus, in some form, the constitutive process of a land-appropriation is found at the beginning of the history of every settled people, every commonwealth, every empire. This is true as well for the beginning of every historical epoch. Not only logically, but also historically, land-appropriation precedes the order that follows from it. It constitutes the original spatial order, the source of all further concrete order and all further law.[57]

Nomos was the word that originally designated this fact. Later, it was used to designate a positive law or legal system, but originally it "is and remains the real core of a wholly concrete, historical and political event: a land-appropriation."[58]

In Greek culture, the term was used to designate the first measurement on which all subsequent measurements, partitions, and basic distribution were based. Over time, this meaning has disappeared, becoming one of simple rule, without reference to anything but positive formulation, unrelated to space. What was once original has become a means. Beginning with the Sophist era, the relationship between *nomos* and the appropriation of the earth was lost from sight. For Plato, *nomos* took on the sense of rule and utopian plan, in the same way as modern laws. Aristotle distinguished a *politeia*'s individual *nomoi* or specific order from the whole. However, his description seems to have some reference to the original distribution of the land. With time, the term underwent changes in its use and lost its meaning. The most significant subsequent use comes from the Sophist current and assumes a distinction between *nomos* and *physis*. In this opposition, the concept of *nomos* comes to mean a convention or imposition and is separated from any connotation to being. According to Schmitt, however, the term does not indicate a mere disposition in which "is" and "ought" can be separated. This confusion has influenced the German word *Gesetz* and weighs on the language of modern science, which has been called nomothetic science. For example, according to the latter's conception of things, natural law does not indicate substance, only calculable function.

Appropriation, distribution, production

As earlier stated, Schmitt sought a basis for law and found it in history, specifically in the concept of *nomos* insofar as it contains "primal processes of human history, three acts of the primal drama."[59] There are appropriation, distribution and production.

Appropriation consists in a settlement, that is, in establishing the life of a human group in a space. This group of people, a society, with their habitation, configures space. Any time there is an appropriation of land two measures merge: the measure of the land and man's measure with which he relates to the land.[60] In this fusion, the condition that makes settlement possible is born. Thus, as Erich Pryzwara, referring to Schmitt, indicated, under the defining idea of an absolute order, the real person remains in a "*Nomos der Erde*," which is based on a "*Kyrios der Erde*," on a lord of the earth.[61] God originally placed people to have dominion over the earth, and within it they have been situated. Thus, man's task on earth is plagued by a tension between the tendency to make order in a given space and the need for a genuine occupation of places in the world, ranging from the appropriation of land, to the conquest of the sea and air, until the total conquest of the world's space. In the beginning there must have been a cosmic order, but ever since men have been living on the earth and appropriating it, a non-absolute unique political order emerged. The political order is always constituted through a pluriverse—that is, the establishment of measurements that are neither cosmic nor absolute.[62] This constitutes the reason for Schmitt's constant reference to a particular order that cannot disregard the appropriation of land. Every people acquire a certain position—*Ortung*—with respect to other spatial boundaries that are not their own. And in this particular position, demarcated by territorial boundaries, an order is created—*Ordnung*. To become aware of a position involves realizing that one's own settlement leaves other spaces out of it that can become, or already are, distinct settlements. That is, it involves a conception of global space that is not abstract, but rather "located." Thus, it is an inward and outward ordering of space. Because of the dialectic that is established between the exterior and the interior in every settlement, *nomos* can be considered the origin of coexistence among peoples and, therefore, of juridical and political relations. When a society is located in a space and makes contact with the earth, they begin to demarcate the earth and immediately they develop a culture.[63] In *Glossarium* we find a description of the *nomos* as "Order and position: house and property: city and country, land and sea; my body, my dress, my house (my country), my land."[64] Any subsequent law refers to the observation of a primitive order, of a reality. The *nomos* of the earth contains an order with two directions: one that is outward and found in the relationship between diverse spatial orders; the other is inward and found in the organization of law, economics, and other social relationships.[65]

However, the term *nomos* does not designate any stability; Schmitt did not intend to use it to establish a static object, nor a particular type of action. It designates a "verbal disposition," a general course of action with respect to space that is comprised of three actions: appropriation, division, and production. The act of land appropriation and its results are always united, although not identical. In that sense, hereinafter, we will discuss various "moments" in the content thereof so as not to speak of succession. Schmitt vividly termed these "moments" *dreiaktigen Urdramas*,[66] or acts of an original drama. *Nomos*, just as *logos*, possess a dynamism that does not arrive at an end and is never exhausted. *Nomos* involves all the potential locked up in the first act of land appropriation that is expressed as the possibilities of life in occupied space. Different categories of man's common life correspond to a primary act—that is, *nomos*—all of which remain *nomos*: *nehmen, teilen, weiden*.[67]

The first moment of *nomos* is *nemein*, in German *nehmen*, in English, to have, possess, or appropriate. This category expresses the essence of what Schmitt calls "existential fact." It is a historical event. It is not an arbitrary factual happening, but rather something that occurs and, even though it cannot be fully explained, it is not arbitrary. The essential characteristic of this existential fact is that "it is given."[68] In the specific case of *nomos*, that which "is given" corresponds to the conquest of human existence in relation with the "elements" that man finds in his habitat.[69] Schmitt's "existential logic" starts on this point. With the first possession came the first division and the resulting distribution, which is the source of all distributive justice and, therefore, of the first constitution (*Urverfassung*), of the first norm (*Ur-norm*),[70] and of law. Schmitt cited Kant at this point to support his own argument: The first thing that was acquired can be nothing other than land, Kant claims.[71] Land, the foundation of all productivity and the assumption of all law, must have been appropriated at some point. He would also agree with Hegel's writings on property.[72] Persons have the right to insert their will in everything, which, for the will, is what immediately distinguishes it from a free spirit. It is merely the exterior and lacks personality, right, and freedom. When a person involves his will, he claims the thing for himself. This refers to man's right to possess things. Contract comes later, as a mediation when a piece of property is not just held in relation to one's will with something, but at the same time by another will and, therefore, a common will is generated. From a philosophical perspective, we can say that man is the only being that, in the strict sense, inhabits, is conscious of his *externality* and of the *distance* between himself and what he is not, so that he can act and enrich himself in relationship to both material and spiritual externalities. By speaking of possession, we are dealing with the first mode of having, which arises from man's relationship with the land and stimulates other modes of having. Schmitt refers to the latter with a few examples, one from institutions and the other from mysticism. The first example[73] refers to marriage and family. There is a possessive relationship that is superior to the taking of the land herein discussed. A husband takes a wife, the first possessive relationship, and the wife recognizes her husband as her own and takes his name, the second possessive relationship. The second example refers to mysticism, specifically to Simone Weil's book, *Attente de Dieu*, which tells of how, while Simone Weil was writing a poem in the form of a prayer, Christ "took" her: *Il m'a pris. Er hat mich genommen.* In both cases, we see how taking possession makes reference to a name. Traditionally, the woman is taken and, in the process, changes her last name in the same way that persons consecrated to God acquire a new name. A name always accompanies any authentic appropriation of land, so much so that a settlement is only consolidated once the person who has appropriated it can give it a name.[74] As seen in the previous examples, this also happens in any appropriation that is higher than land appropriation, such as in the case of knowledge or a personal relationship. A thing is not known until it is properly given a name.

Once men have settled the earth, speech takes on another meaning: *teilen*.[75] This is the second major category of human common life and takes on the meaning of *divisio primaeva* as a first precedence and action of subsequent partitions and distributions. It is an *Ur-Teil* and its *Ergebnis*.[76] Therefore, *nomos* is, secondly, law in the sense of the part that each one has, the *suum cuique* or property. When explaining this, Schmitt did so in a graphic way, stating,

> Abstractly speaking, nomos is law and property, i.e., the part or share of goods. Concretely speaking, *nomos* is, for example, the chicken in every pot that every peasant living under a good king has on Sunday, the parcel of land every farmer cultivates as his property, and the car every American worker has parked in his garage.[77]

In referring to law, Schmitt does not speak of statutes, but rather of property, which constitutes the condition for any subsequent law,[78] although he does not identify law and property titles. At this point, it is worth touching on the question of whether property was originally private or public. According to Schmitt, these distinctions come up later and assume the act of settling land in common. Land occupation always creates, in the internal sense, a kind of ultimate property of the community as a whole, despite posterior distribution. Free private property is recognized in the case of individual persons.[79] The appropriation of land, the delimitation of a space, makes an order possible within its limits. Therefore, a settlement is also the origin of all order and property rights. It is impossible to separate the concepts *Ortung-Ordnung-Recht* (localization-order-law): "Every order constitutes a specific, located law. Law is only law in an exact place, on this side of the line!"[80] *Nomos*, as a condition of any subsequent law, is, I would say, "a force of law."[81] Every constitution refers to this kind of source.[82] What often happens is that positive law obscures the latter condition. Schmitt used the rediscovery of the word *nomos* in the field of law to argue against legal positivism. The concept of *nomos* preserves the unity of "is" and "ought" because it takes into account the spatial structure of a concrete ordering. The translation of the word *nomos* to *lex* (statute) belongs to a decadent age that is incapable of establishing legal science's evolutionary connection to its origin and beginning; it also does not distinguish fundamental law, as order and concrete settlements, from diverse dispositions, regulations, measures, and provisions that the development of relationships within a community brings with it. Precisely because law relates to a space that is qualitatively configured as a given, once constituted, it continues to refer back to that space. In this sense, concrete law and concrete situations are absolutely dependent.

Any settlement establishes an inward and outward law. One is inward because the first division of land coincides with the establishment of the first order of all the conditions for possession and property. The other is outward because any group that settles on land will potentially interact with other groups occupying other land that are, therefore, outside of the borders. These relations become political when tension between friends and enemies arises.

The third meaning of *nomos*, once land has been divided, is *Weiden*,[83] which corresponds to the productive work that takes place within the property. Furthermore, *Weiden* is the source of all commutative justice. *Nomos*, in this sense, is a kind of pasturing (*weiden*), economizing (*Wirtschaften*), taking advantage (*nutzen*), producing (*produzieren*). Schmitt thought of the verb *nutzen* as particularly relevant when characterizing this activity since it contains a reference to production and consumption, doing away with the false antagonism between the two.[84] Through the meaning of *Oikonomia*, Schmitt revealed the foundational relationship between *nomos* and *weiden*, that is, between living in a place and economizing. The term *Oikonomos* appeared in the sixth century before Christ and, in its original sense, was used to describe the economy of the house (*Haushaltung*) with connotations of foresight, saving, and planning. When humans were nomadic, *nomos* was *weiden* par excellence in the sense of pasturing. This was the primary activity to the extent that the pastor, *nomeus*, was the typical symbol of sovereignty and dominion. Since that time, *nomos* in the sense of *weiden*, has undergone many changes throughout history. The most significant came with the transition from nomadic tents to fixed houses, to *Oikos*. This change represents a different appropriation of land, going from provisional land ownership and distribution proper to nomadic peoples to permanent ownership proper to agricultural peoples. The permanence that a house represents established the unity of *nomos* and a stable concept of ownership that enables production and, with it, economizing.[85] From that establishment until today, a kind of development emerged that seeks increases in production, which is also referred to as progress. This impetus is seen starting with simple nomadic settlements and moved through feudal agrarian culture, continued with the appropriation of the sea during the sixteenth century to the nineteenth century, as well as the technical-industrial appropriation and the subsequent division of the world into developed and underdeveloped regions, until reaching the current appropriation of air and space, making them economically profitable as well. Many times this progress, which always pursues production, forgets its relationship with the originating *nomos* and the action of *nemein*, leading to the disruption of social life where all categories are related.[86] This has been especially true since the Industrial Revolution.

Schmitt's reflection on the economy led him to criticize the fundamental categories of liberalism. Despite what it may seem, this critique is not a denigration of economic activity; rather, it seeks to restore economic activities' proper place within the social framework. Schmitt intends to locate the economy in its appropriate place within the categories of human common life.[87]

In the nineteenth century, the economy was associated with words that, for Schmitt, have a negative meaning, such as: rationalism, bourgeoisie, technical nature, liberalism, pluralism, and privacy. With these words, the economy became the focus around which all other areas of life and interests of any other kind revolve. This has been detrimental to the value of other spheres of common life, especially politics, and the consequences of this economic conception can be summarized in the term "neutrality."[88] Schmitt developed an example of the spirit that gives breath to liberalism at length in his study of Romanticism.[89] Nineteenth-century romanticism represents a link between the moral life of the eighteenth century and the "economic life's style" of the nineteenth century. For romanticism, morality overlaps with aesthetics, and the laws of economics must govern aesthetic enjoyment, which is pure consumption—that is, romanticism's survival is sustained by robust economic activity. Therefore, economic activity becomes, with aesthetic nuances, central to romanticism.

By the way, historically, economicism is accompanied by the development of technique, both of which, in their development and rising absolutism, have increasingly neutralized other areas of human life, such as metaphysics, theology, and morality. Spiritual life's center has been shifted to the economic and technical sphere. The economy is central to this process because, in its essence, it is a means. Both economics and technique are characterized by being "at the service of." They can be at the service of any ideal, religion, or political intention; they cannot, however, by themselves, force the spirit to adopt a neutral stance. Thus, an economic motive always hides some kind of political motive or, at least, power, since someone profits. This indicates, once again, that all social categories always appear in the life of every society, even if their expression is reduced in trying to "neutralize" them.

Schmitt's critique of liberalism can be summarized in the following points[90]: criticism of bourgeois *Rechtsstaat*; criticism of the undemocratic nature of the parliamentary system of said rule of law; and critical opinion of liberal instrumentalization of all aspects of existence. It should be noted that, while criticism of parliamentarianism does appear explicitly in his writings, the rest of the above critique is not stated as such, although it is deducible in many of his texts. These criticisms are based on three motives. The first is a theological motive based on his professed Catholicism, as we can read in his *Roman Catholicism and Political Form*, perhaps influenced by counterrevolutionary thinkers, particularly Bonald, de Maistre, and Donoso Cortés, and perhaps by Pope Pius XI's anti-liberal argumentation and on the French and German *Renouveau Catholique* discourse.[91] His Catholicism is laced with a strong critique of modernity, represented by the liberal currents of the nineteenth century and characterized by secularization, individualism, and the denial of both original sin and the idea that the devil exists. These ideas led, consequently, to the assertion of the natural goodness of people, whose ends are freedom and happiness, which they can achieve based on their autonomous reason. Supported by these principles, an economized and modernized world emerges with a socializing mechanism in the form of moral humanitarianism that Schmitt despised.[92] As will be seen throughout this book, the category that places Schmitt outside of liberal and modern thought amounts to *order*, which is also part of Catholic tradition. By accepting order as the fundamental element that sustains the rest of his legal and political thought, Schmitt opts for an existential position.

The second motive is aimed at domestic politics and focuses its critique on parliamentarianism as a political manifestation of liberalism. According to Schmitt, it is racked by contradiction and obscures the essence of politics.[93] He analyzes each of its principles, including: public debate, publicity, separation and balance of powers, and the concept of legislation. Parliamentarianism is the inevitable result of putting democracy into practice, which contains many contradictions and is weakened by its defense as the lesser of two evils. Its worst consequence is in destroying politics, because it turns representation (*Repräsentation*) into a set of private actions (*Vertretung*).

The third motive for his antiliberalism deals with foreign politics and can be summarized in the criticism of methods proper to international law that sustain modern universalism, which are genuinely liberal. This deals with imperialism in the form of humanitarian ideology that is familiar with legality, but not with *nomos*. With it, a pacifist vocabulary has developed that expresses the banishment of power with the use of mere economic means. Watchwords in this discourse include, for example: sanction, policing, peacekeeping, and security measures aimed at peace. Forms of control and intervention emerge that obscure the war-peace relationship. It ultimately aims to banish war and, with the elimination of war from the political framework, it also seeks to eliminate the category of enemy from humanity. An enemy becomes someone that is outside of humanity itself.

As this reflection on economics shows, once *nomos*'s formal categories—*nehmen, teilen, weiden*—are recognized, a problem arises in assigning their proper order and assuring its consistency.[94] Until the Industrial Revolution, there was an unchanging order in the existential categories related to *nomos* consisting of land appropriation, law, economics, and politics; after it, this sequence no longer seemed so clear, both for liberalism, as well as for socialism. Both agree that the elements in this sequence can be mixed up: Production becomes independent of distribution and the *nomos*.[95] Liberalism is a theory of freedom and, among other things and first, of freedom of economic production, of the free market and of consumer choice. These freedoms are invariable principles, where other factors of social life are dependent variables of these principles. The categories pertaining to production and economization—*weiden*—become paramount in social life. Socialism responds to this ideology with an appeal to equitable redistribution, which is its theoretical basis. In this case, it seems that the social category *teilen* dominates the organization of society. However, historically, socialist theory has generally developed by focusing on production. Thus, for example, for Fourier, any problem in the order of property and distribution seeks resolution in production. Proudhon, for his part, argued that any good expropriation should be done through a series of divisions and fair redistribution to favor the real producers and consumers. Marx accepted and developed the assertion of an indefinite increase in production that is typical of progressive liberalism; the question of distribution and division came later in his work. His reflection centers on the expropriation of the expropriators; the expropriation of long-standing proprietors opens up new possibilities for appropriation. In its last phase, *nehmen* becomes paramount.

Today, the question of the *nomos of the earth* amounts to questioning the current status of worldwide unity: Is the earth really conceived as possessed in its totality such that, objectively, no new appropriation is possible? That is, no new land appropriations are possible? Has appropriation really ceased such that it is no longer possible to divide and distribute? Or perhaps only production is left? In that case, we must ask after the principal proprietor of the enormous division and distribution of the planet or after what drives and orders the unity of global production.[96]

Nomos as Original Power

A concrete act of land appropriation refers to a settlement that happens outside of the limits of a particular power[97] and is, therefore, directly related to the political sphere. A power is defined by the proper relationship of the human will with space, starting with, as we have seen, owning land. For the will, a limit represents the scope of its power. Schmitt noted that, "Space is the image of our power and time the image of our impotence. . . . Space is power."[98] However, in a space, as Schmitt considered it—that is, a space qualitatively configured with an internal measurement—power is different from force. That is, power cannot be exercised any which way, but rather must respect space's internal measure. Space is differentiated, but a single space allows for various configurations, which vary according to the history of peoples on the land. The transformation of a spatial configuration involves a change in the configuration of power. Therefore, the attempt to establish equilibrium between spaces—corresponding to Schmitt's theory of the *Großräume*, which we will see later—is itself an attempt to limit power.

Schmitt described how in the legal-political sphere and over the course of history—that is, over successive land appropriations—there are authentic and inauthentic appropriations of land. The former have a principle of spatial order, the latter are taken as an act of "raw power" and do not have a principle of order, but rather the order they want to establish has to be constantly imposed by force. The first type of *nomos* wears with time; the second, on the other hand, lasts a certain amount of time, until a new spatial order replaces it.[99] The two are distinguished from each other only in retrospect, or, at least, Schmitt did not outline any other way of distinguishing between them other than historical continuity. Objects and situations "resist" the control of the will; this resistance guides force, making it a "located" force—that is, a power. Schmitt puts it this way, "Space is a power in presence, not strength. Time is neither the one nor the other. Forces are powers that have not yet been located; powers are located forces."[100] The only thing that the will can do against time, as we have seen, is overcome it in the form of space. For Schmitt, it makes no sense to speak of a space without considering the connection between the spatial order and the political sphere. He, therefore, argues, for us, there are no political ideas outside of a space or, vice versa, spaces or spatial principles without political ideas.[101]

The entirety of Schmitt's political theory aims toward finding the true source of power.[102] Space is not power's source, but rather its condition.[103] First, power has to do with secrecy; it is the "secret and terrible finality."[104] Second, it is a center, a position. Third, facing toward secrecy, there is an opposing direction toward dissemination. There, power appears as *Archie* and *Kratie*. *Archie* means coming from the origin; *Kratie* is power through arrogance and occupation. The former refers to the metaphysical association of the subject; the latter, to its implementation. In any case, for power to arise, a settlement, a taking of the land, is necessary.[105] There is no earthly power that does not first claim some possession, because the first form of power is power over the earth.

Certainly, what is considered space, as well as forms of power, varies in each historical period. For example, one can speak of a market space or industrial space. In fact, industrial progress is accompanied by a vital space that is mainly characterized as economic. Thus, in this sense, Schmitt recognized an *Industrien-Nahme* (industry-appropriation) and a *Luft-Nahme* (air-appropriation).[106] In the last stage of his life, Schmitt referred to the conquest of space not so much through military or aviation means, as he does in *The Nomos of the Earth*, but rather to the conquest of space through technology using sound waves (*Tonwellen*). Since technology made it possible to communicate through waves, the concept of space changed. The distances between one point and another on earth have changed essentially. In many cases, you might even say that there is no distance, making the protection against a possible enemy increasingly difficult. In the *Glossarium*, Schmitt often refers to this idea; some of his most significant statements are included below:

I win my space. Is this not a bit boastful? Strange sound waves pass by with a silent whistle, but they really do cross through my space. The fact that I do not hear them does not improve my spatial situation. It is as if there were invisible spheres surrounding me that shoot at me and fail to reach me. Can I then say: What I do not know does not bother me? Unfortunately, I do know. [107]

The unlimited diffusion of the waves is not power, but rather influence. [108]

But all these determinations of space ultimately refer to territoriality. With a new concept of space come changed modes of manifesting power. One of them is what Schmitt called influence. Where there is no limit, one cannot know the scope of his own power. By persisting in influence, in undifferentiated space, power may inadvertently and indiscriminately grow. This applies, for example, to propaganda in the media, which amounts to power with no exact limit. When publicity is absent from power and from the powerful, it falls into economism, which is accompanied by disregard for *nomos*. An appropriation always implies a power whose publicity is associated with the name of the person who brought it about. [109] With this name, abstraction and secrecy turn to concrete reality and publicity.

The idea that a settlement determines a power, in ultimate territorial terms, implies that it determines a limit to space—that is, borders—while also establishing power as such. These borders determine who is and who is not a foreigner and, in the extreme case, an enemy, as well as the kind of warfare practiced. [110] When a space is taken and limited, the ability to determine an enemy emerges; in this moment, it becomes political. [111]

A NARRATIVE OF LAND'S APPROPRIATION

In *The Nomos of the Earth*, Schmitt devoted ample space to historical description in order to show the intrinsic relationship between the land appropriation and legal and political orders. He pauses at each significant milestone in the history of land appropriation and points out how each one has resulted in a legal order, in a political configuration, and, therefore, in a criterion for enmity and in a way of making war. [112] It could be said, in this regard, that modern man's way of life has come down to us from the history of the successive land appropriations. World history is the history of successive land and sea appropriations, the struggle between land and sea powers, which can be expressed mythically as the struggle between the *Leviathan*, the powerful fish, and *Behemoth*, the powerful terrestrial monster. [113]

The unfolding of history has been accompanied by spatial revolutions. While it is true that space determines the life of man, science and technological transformations play a major role in the discovery of new spaces. The configurations of space that have taken place in history are always formalized—made positive—in international law. For a long time, man had a mythical image of space. There have always been territorial divisions on earth, but they were, at first, made unconsciously. Until man could measure the contour of the land as a whole, he did not possess a *nomos* and was not aware of taking a piece of land or of having thereby created an order. Therefore, space was first understood in a pre-global way.[114] The first peoples to inhabit the earth did not grasp anything other than a common space in which each settlement constituted one commonwealth against another, where both had absolute claim. The concept of coexistence between empires—that is, between large independent territories within a common space—lacked any ordering force, since the concept of a common measure of space that would cover the whole earth did not exist. Consequently, until such a measure was developed, wars were carried out as wars of destruction:

> Every powerful people considered themselves to be the center of the earth and their dominion to be the domicile of freedom, beyond which war, barbarism, and chaos ruled. Practically this meant that in the outer world and with good conscience one could conquer and plunder to a certain boundary. Then they built a fence, a line, a Chinese wall, or consider the pillars of Hercules or the sea to be the end of the world.[115]

The organization of the *Respublica Christiana*, the Empire of Christian Europe during the Middle Ages, serves as an exception to this spatial conception. Schmitt considered it to be a special case of ordering within a pre-global conception of space. Although it was also a pre-global ordering, it had the judicial title to create an international law of a global nature. With it, in the sixteenth century, human rights between European states were developed, which emerged from the dissolution of medieval spatial ordering based on empire.[116] Medieval ordering was born from takeovers of the earth during the migration of peoples. Their coexistence fueled new political units and a kind of European international law. The unity of this international law in medieval Europe was called *Respublica Christiana*. The peculiar thing here was that there was already an ordering to the extent that a territorial, qualitative distinction was made between the Christian territories and those of the pagans. There was no equality between them in that one was considered conquered territory and the other open to the Christian mission. Thus, for example, Islamic lands were considered enemy territory and could be conquered and annexed through the Crusades. Two forms of government carried out the ordering of the *Respublica Christiana* unit: the empire and the priesthood, which were visibly represented by the emperor and the pope, respectively. In this spatial unit, characteristic of the Christian Middle Ages, distinguishing territory was determined by a historical force: The continuity of great historic imperial power depended on *Katechon*.[117] Empire, in this context, implies the historical force, a restraint, capable of stopping the appearance of the Antichrist and the consequent end of the present era. Only the Roman Empire and its Christian extension could explain the survival of that era and its conservation against the overwhelming power of evil. This mission to detain the Antichrist legitimized the land appropriation that the empire undertook. Although the empire was not the same as the Church, their missions were definitely linked. According to Schmitt, the political constructions that ensured the continuation of the Christian Empire are nothing more than apostasy and the degeneration of religiosity into scientific myth. As noted earlier, an ordering of space like this one corresponds to a certain political unity, but not assimilation, between the empire and the priesthood. In this unity, the emperor did not take on an absolute position of power that absorbed all other positions, but rather was a function of the *Katechon*. That is, it corresponded to the elevation of the crown, not just as a monarch, but also as a task that comes from heaven, from a realm outside of the kingdom. In this context, the relationship between the Church and the empire, as can be well imagined, were determined quite differently from subsequent church-state relationships. The conceptions of empire that do not correspond to the *Respublica Christiana* disregard the idea of *Katechon* and immediately foster Caesarism.[118]

In the Christian republic, conducting war was confined to what is known as "just war," and a *iusta causa* was needed to declare war. The criterion for justice came from the aforementioned distinction between Christians and pagans. Over time, this position presented many problems and the first arguments against *iusta causa* came from humanists, who claimed that any party that declares war believes their cause to be just. Such discussions, and the hostility of the time, led to a new concept of war that began with the State era. Along with the distortion of the idea of just cause, an awareness of the differentiation between territories and the concept of *Katechon* were lost. This process ended in what we know as the Modern State:

> [O]nce (beginning in the 13th century) political units were formed that not only factually, but increasingly also legally withdrew from the *imperium* and sought to restrict the *auctoritas* of the *sacerdotium* to purely spiritual matters, the medieval Christian order began to dissolve.[119]

The new order of space formed by the dissolution of the medieval empire was very different from the first order of space. The pre-global vision of space gave way to a global understanding, which was made possible thanks to the discovery of new land—that is, land appropriation.[120] Strictly speaking, the first spatial revolution occurred in the sixteenth and seventeenth centuries with the discovery of new land and the circumnavigation of the world. This did not simply mean an expanding horizon, but rather the awareness of a global image of our planet. During this period, it became scientific fact that the earth is round, and the idea the earth revolves around the sun in

an infinite void took hold. This idea made finding land on the other side of the
sea a discovery and every discovery involves a spatial revolution, a transformation of every spatial concept and every aspect of human existence. [121]

A new distinction of the land emerged alongside these discoveries: firm
soil and free sea. Land that was accessed through the freedom of the open sea
was considered a territory open to discovery and occupation. This New
World was not considered an enemy, but rather a space for unrestricted land
acquisition. [122] Under these conditions, inter-State human rights centered on
Europe emerged. Emerging foreign relations revolved around land and sea
appropriations in this new world. [123] The partition and division of land became a common issue for European peoples and powers. Thus, international
law has its origins in the distribution of new lands. [124] While carrying out
large territorial gains, maritime conquests were also undertaken. [125] Land
belonged to a number of sovereign states, while the sea was still open to all at
that point. People did not begin to perceive the difference between the order
of the earth and the sea, as well as between land warfare and naval warfare,
until England took possession of the seas. In the sixteenth century, ground
war was understood as war between States. Fighting forces faced each other
and no one was treated as an enemy and no one was disturbed until entering
the war. Maritime warfare has other rules, principally the destruction of the
enemy's commerce and economy. An enemy was defined as any subject
from a country whose commerce was currently or potentially seen as a competitor. Pirates, corsairs, and adventurers attracted by trade found the sea to
be their element. [126]

For the first time in the history of mankind, global lines were drawn in
order to set a spatial arrangement of the entire earth. The beginning of map-
ping enabled greater geographical knowledge and shaped the need to establish a known distribution of space on paper. These initial distributions were
not absolutely neutral, but rather included political assumptions. [127] Pope
Alexander VI's May 4, 1494, edict, *Inter cetera divinae*, initiated the tracing
of the first global lines, followed by the Treaty of Tordesillas (1494) and the
Treaty of Zaragoza (1529). Years later, the Spanish-French treaty of Cateau-
Cambresis (1559) noted the birth of a different global line: the amity line.
Between the amity line, the "Latin line" had a distributive sense, whereas the
English "amity line" was of a more competitive character. Later, with the
Monroe Doctrine (1823), the idea of the "Western hemisphere" as something
separate emerged. The former divisions referred to land occupations by European powers; however, the latter positioned itself against the claims of
European occupation, which, according to Schmitt, was an attempt at self-
isolation. This division remains to this day. [128] The peculiarity of this new
nomos of the earth, therefore, emerged from two developments: First, it is an
order of space centered on Europe and, second, it includes the land as well as
the sea. [129]

In addition to the discovery of new lands, the Protestant Reformation also confirmed the order of space and brought with it religious civil wars. [130] The political interest of the time focused on neutralizing the enmity that prevailed in these wars, [131] which was made possible by creating a new order of space, based on a balance between European continental areas, which in turn maintained relations with the English maritime empire. Schmitt describes this new order as follows:

> First, it created clear internal jurisdictions by placing feudal, territorial, estate, and church rights under the centralized legislation, administration and judiciary of a territorial ruler. Second, it ended the European civil war of churches and religious parties, and thereby neutralized creedal conflicts within the state through a centralized political unity. . . . Third, on the basis of the internal political unity the state achieved *vis-à-vis* other political unities, it constituted within and of itself a closed area with fixed borders, allowing a specific type of foreign relations with other similarly organized territorial orders. [132]

This spatial ordering did not just involve a new distinction between land and sea war, as has been noted, but also a new concept of land warfare. War on European soil became a military relationship between two States. It became a war "in form" for the mere fact that it became a war between clearly defined European states in terms of space, in a dispute between spatial entities as *personae publicae*, which, in an extreme case, could be considered *iusti hostes*. [133] This did not occur on non-European soil since it was considered free. There, any land appropriation was considered an occupation and carried with it, when a conflict between possible occupants arose, an interstate war the majority of the time. In these wars, as noted, the problem was no longer about *iusta causa*, but rather about the relationship between sovereigns with equal claim. In this new *ordo*, it was highly important to be recognized as a great power, first because, with it, recognition of *ius belli* and *iustus hostis* became more important and also because the great powers were considered bearers and guarantors of the spatial ordered that they controlled. In this framework, the concept of enemy was also limited. When carrying out a "war in form," the army occupies a territory and must maintain its public order as well as protect the local population. Given this, the population must render obedience and a spatial relationship between the occupiers and occupied is established. The enemy is not an absolute enemy. In short, one can say that the *nomos* of the earth centered on Europe and formed within the two historical milestones mentioned, is structured on two balancing points, namely, the balance between land and sea and the balance between the states of continental Europe.

The last land appropriation made in accordance with the idea of a European-centered international law was sealed in the Congo Conference of 1885. Later, between 1890 and 1918, the *Jus publicum europaeum* order began losing its force until it ceased to exist.[134] It tried to implement a new order that, despite the United States of America's isolation sealed by the 1823 Monroe Doctrine, attempted to bring America and Europe to work together toward a "European civilization."[135] However, the Paris Peace Treaty (1918–1919) revealed the fact that Europe was counting its days as the center of power. It no longer played that role in an attempt to create a common European civilization. The treaty implied a new division of space that lasted until after World War II, when Europe ceased to be the center from which decisions were made.[136]

With Europe no longer at the center of power, land distinctions were undone and *Jus publicum europaeum* gave way to a universal law. An empty normativism, which hid the lack of a new order to replace the previous one, followed the dissolution of the old order. At this point, the problem of the ordering of space was lost from sight, which meant losing sight of "the notion that European soil or soil equivalent to it had a different status in international law from that of uncivilized or non-European peoples."[137] A conception of a non-spatial global universalism and, with it, the possibility of universal political unity emerged. The dilemma between pluriversal and universal politics has always existed, where the question of whether or not the planet can survive with a single center of power is a constant in the history of political thought. In this dilemma, the Geneva Conference definitely opted for universalism. Schmitt roundly claimed that universalism remained the dogma and confession in Geneva.[138] As a result, a global free-trade and world market emerged opposite the state, such that foreign relations among states no longer refer to space or land, but rather fundamentally refer to what is now free land, the economy.[139] This new order also implies a new concept of war. A given territory, in being considered abstract, is taken into account—as already stated—for economic purposes alone. Disputes of this kind are therefore of an apolitical nature. The enemy is no longer political, but rather moral. Within this lack of differentiation, war is regarded as an international crime, an offense, and, as such, is absolutely disqualified and, at the same time, left without any limitations: War, in the case that it breaks out, could be a total war. This being so, time has proved that it is impossible to eliminate war from our planet, and not limiting war results in new forms of civil war and wars of destruction. In the event that war breaks out, it has no limit.[140] Schmitt thus returned to showing how changing spatial concepts amounts to a change in the concept of war. In this case, spatial change implies a war of destruction. The rise of the airplane is the result of attempting a habitation of space.[141] The conquest of space augments the balance between land and sea with a third element, the air. With the airplane, radio waves, satellites, and other communication components appear as a third dimension. A war of destruction takes place in the air.[142] Land warfare is characterized by the recognition of *iustus hostis*, of the just enemy. This kind of warfare was not of a criminal nature since there was no discrimination between one just and another unjust party. Meanwhile, maritime war was a war of booty, a trade war and, given that trade was a private matter according to nineteenth-century thought, private. There, hostile acts were committed against private persons. Aerial warfare, however, is characterized by destruction and has nothing to do with looting, which is impossible using air tactics alone. Aerial warfare is also unlike land warfare in that the occupation of a territory is accompanied by an interest in preserving the security and order of the occupied territory. In contrast, with aerial warfare, the territory is destroyed.[143] As means of destruction intensify and the theater of war becomes indeterminable, the labeling of an enemy becomes criminal.[144] With the emergence of aviation, a new neutralization was achieved. On the one hand, airspace makes land non-differentiable; on the other hand, by homogenizing land, a common economic space was created. This order, however neutral it may appear, is a function of some interest. All that matters now is maintaining peace, a peace that, by situating itself above all political boundaries, allows for the maximum development of the private sphere and allows for the independent operation of the economy. In this situation, the political, in the case of war, becomes a façade of defensive territorial borders since the economic sphere is what really penetrates said borders.

THE GEO-INTERPRETATION OF HISTORY

The fundamental fact of man's life—a temporal and historical being—corresponds to his inhabitation of the earth. Space and time are so intertwined in his existence that it is possible to interpret world history through the lens of space. And that is what Schmitt did in his brief essay entitled *Land and Sea*, which he first presented to his daughter, Anima, as a story. Populations have differentiated and related according to the natural opposition between land and sea. Schmitt did not speak of enmity, but rather of a "clean break"[145] between the two spaces, a contrast: Universal history is a war between sea powers and terrestrial ones.[146] This description contains biblical tradition. In the very beginning, God created the heavens and the earth; he separated water and dry land and allocated the earth, not the sea, to man as his dwelling place. In this account, the sea only appears to mark land's boundary and it even seems that it could be dangerous.[147] In the New Testament, the sea also seems to exude a sense of danger. There, the new earth is described as sinless and without evil; St. John sees a new heaven and a new earth, but not a new sea.[148]

Ernst Jünger and Arnold Toynbee offer historical interpretations that take the genius of opposites; both writers have interpreted universal history through the lens of the tension between the East and West. They have tried to make a cultural, historical, and moral inventory of these conflicting cultures and draw some conclusions.[149] Through this analysis, they describe a series of antitheses and contrasts showing the polar tension between the two blocs, making it possible for them to present a "regional iconography,"[150] in the sense Jean Gottmann[151] employed, corresponding to a grouping of the entire globe into geographical areas, each characterized by a specific form of human existence that manifests itself in the practices of public and private life, in signs, in abbreviations, in historical memories, myths, legends, symbols, taboos, and so on. Through the assignment of regional iconography, it has been concluded that, according to the juxtaposition mentioned earlier, the East is hostile to material expression, while the West has fostered it. However, according to Schmitt, although useful, analysis of East-West tension is not enough. Another interpretive lens is required because, in the East and West dilemma, the world's problems are not exhausted.[152] Moreover, the distinction between East and West is relative and always changing depending on one's starting point.[153] This perspective contributes to the Schmittian conception of history not so much by identifying some characteristic or another of the polar tension, but rather by affirming that there is no concrete historical location without some kind of "visibility."[154] That is, wherever there is a settlement, there will also necessarily be icons and iconography. The history of *nomos* is correlative to the history of culture in general. Instead of this polar tension, Schmitt suggested the aforementioned tension between land and sea, which is accompanied by a reference to a *nomos* of the earth as a fundamental interpretive point of view. The relationship between these two elements has long been taken into account and, even in the nineteenth century for example, English-Russian relations were represented as a fight between a whale and a bear.[155] Two legendary names for this tension appear in the book of Job (chapters 40 and 41), namely: *Leviathan*, a powerful whale, and *Behemoth*, an earthly monster. Kabbalists represented the image of a land power being besieged by a maritime power as a fight between these two animals and, while this Jewish representation of world history is mythical, it is based in reality.[156] Throughout history, maritime powers have been at the forefront of development, for example, Venice, another mythical name, emerged as a naval power in the Christian world[157] and, later, England likewise emerged with decisive maritime supremacy.[158] England detained the movement toward the sea with which the first part of the spatial planetary revolution concluded. At that point, England was undergoing a transformation from the *Leviathan*, a large fish, into a big machine, and its relations with the rest of the world changed.[159] This is how the Industrial Revolution came about. The Industrial Revolution first took place in a space shaped by a maritime existence because of the relationship that exists between the sea and this revolution's technique. Life at sea requires a much greater development of technology.

The aforementioned examples demonstrate how far it is possible to understand historical events from the point of view of the land-sea opposition. Now we must ask after its meaning. First, it must be noted, this does not center on a struggle between two natural elements:[160] However crucial physical reference is, if we consider land and sea as simply natural areas that are incapable of either hostility or friendship, it is impossible to simply say without further explanation that the inhabitants of the sea are friends or enemies of land inhabitants: "There is no room for an enmity that is generally determined by the contrast between land and sea."[161]

Enmity itself cannot develop between the land and sea because they are just natural elements. The relative "enmity" found between these elements is neither a facet of their nature nor of the nature of the animals that inhabit them since they inhabit different worlds and do not cross paths. Land and sea become enemies insofar as men use them as a means for friendship or enmity, a state that is based on spiritual elements, not natural ones. These elements have come about as the development of inhabitation in a space, but they do not come with the need of it. The lines of friendship and enmity are never purely physical.

It is certainly possible to speak of hostility between animals living in the same space; however, hostility, which sometimes exists between animals, is very different from that which exists between men.[162] Thus, for example, dogs and cats have an invariable hostility. Their antagonism is the necessary result of instinct, while men are able to reject an enemy and, in an extreme case, his designation as man.[163] Human hostility has its climax in civil or religious wars. In a moment of extreme hostility, the enemy is declared a criminal and is considered "outside the law" and, given that the law appears to be the model of humanity, inhumane. However, extreme hostilities do not always have to arise, which can be seen in the case of the historical tension between the land and sea. While this tension has certainly produced naval battles, it has also made the Industrial Revolution and the development of trade possible.

There are two possible interpretations of historical tension: one polar, the other dialectic. Polar tension is found in Schiller, Goethe, and Jünger, and it involves the simultaneity of the contrasts that constitute it. This refers to a repetitious simultaneity and a constantly equal structure in a kind of eternal return. These polar oppositions are, therefore, eternally valid. Now, if this were really so, it would be nothing more than a fragment of nature, and the kind of hostility between land and sea in the above sense would be unsustainable: The elements in the sense of the very nature are separated and joined again, mixed and separated. They move and transform into its circular motion in a circle of metamorphosis. The circular motion always proposes new forms and manifestations to a polar tension in the background always the same. The current opposition between East and West would therefore be a manifestation of elite eternal circulation, problems, and iconography. Against this polar interpretation, Schmitt proposed a dialectic conception that involves a consideration of history as a succession of land appropriations, given man's and peoples' capacity for this action. This dialectic cannot be understood as a universal logic of concepts or as a system of laws in a historical process. A universal theory of history is not possible because there is no functional process that corresponds to it. Historical thought can only contemplate unique situations and, therefore, only unique truths. The word *dialectic* here implies a question-answer structure of all situations and histor-ical events. [164] A historical situation can only be understood as a "call from time"—*Anruf der Zeit*[165]—and as man's response to that call: Every human word is an answer, every answer gets a sense of the question to which it responds and is meaningless to anyone who does not know the question. The meaning of the question lies, in turn, in the concrete situation in which it arises. Robert G. Collingwood has presented the idea of the Question-Answer logic in an effort to overcome naturalist positivism; however, he was too focused on the concept of nineteenth-century science to overcome the psychological-individualistic interpretation of the question-answer scheme, which does not involve a man or set of men raising a question, but rather the same story consisting in the same specific questions and answers. [166] Arnold Toynbee also wrote to this effect, referring to the Challenge-Response struc-ture of culture's history. [167] He discusses over twenty civilizations, which he characterizes by describing the call that gave them life and their response to it. However, according to Schmitt, Toynbee lost sight of the central unity of all history by focusing on the formulation of general laws and thus fell into the trap that all historical reflection faces. [168] To find true historical reflection, one must free oneself from the nineteenth-century line of thought that at-tempts generalizations removed from reality, examples of which can be found in the thought of Auguste Comte, Karl Marx, or Oswald Spengler. Given this conception, Schmitt proposes the following: When men perceive the question and call of history and try to respond to their behavior and deeds, they venture to the great test of historical capacity and are marked by a tribunal. In a word, they pass the state of nature to the state of historicity. [169] Here, Schmitt is not talking about dialectic in the Hegelian sense, but rather about the complementary nature of the question-answer structure in every historical event, which, in each event, manages to maintain the sense that history has a kind of uniqueness to it. [170] For example, this historical logic is manifest in the house and the boat as different answers to distinct historical calls: "The ship is the core of maritime existence of men as the home is the core of his earthly existence. Boathouses are not antithetical in the sense of a polar tension but different answers a different call of history."[171]

Still, it is necessary to make yet another distinction. The question is a call, but call here does not mean impetus, which is more like an artificial need produced by technological progress. Impetus comes before the call of history and is artificial. In the same way that impetus is not a question, technique cannot supply a true answer, which often implies more of a gridlock than openness to new spaces. [172] Only genuine choices—that is, responses—make history; anything else amounts to arbitrary games that, while taking place therein, do not form part of its historicity. When a decision cannot be understood as the reflexive response of man, it is clearly not a call able to solicit subsequent answers because it has not become part of history and it has not incited authentic dialogue. At best, it is an impulse.

Thus, it may seem that the historical future, the new *nomos* of the earth, will develop in a new space, namely in cosmic space. Technology has opened up this possibility, this new area of life; however, according to Schmitt, it cannot be labeled a call of history. [173]

Chapter Three

The Legal Science

Schmitt's legal thinking is difficult to reconstruct given the sheer amount and variety of texts in which it is detailed. In addition, Schmitt also thought with the thread of historical events in mind. All of this points to the fact that his theory is not compact or closed, but rather is a set of ideas in need of ordering, contributing to the impression that his writings often seem unrelated and laced with confusion, making it further understandable that he has been dismissed as an occasionalist[1] and that his thought has been labeled as *"bewegliches Denken."*[2]

While reflection motivated by specific experience is certainly a feature of all Schmittian thought, it is still possible to distinguish his programmatic writings from those of a more transitory nature that make immediate reference to the historical events of the moment. Keeping this in mind, one cannot just maintain that his thought changed circumstantially,[3] although one can certainly speak of an evolution that sometimes developed with apparent contradiction.[4]

To clarify this matter and in search of further analytic possibilities, some attempts have been made to structure Schmitt's thought on law into three stages, namely, normativism, decisionism, and concrete order. Other attempts also structure Schmitt's thought into two stages, namely, concrete order and decisionism. However, it is also possible to reach a comprehensive interpretation of Schmitt's work by clarifying each of his discursive positions—that is, by taking into account the rhetorical intentions of each of his books and by searching for unity in complementarity. It is possible to find a unified Schmittian discourse by identifying the thread that guides the unfolding of his thought, thus allowing for the formulation of congruent development and, along the way, solving contradictions and paradoxes. In what follows, the latter option will be explored.

To this end, two preliminary distinctions are required. The first is almost trivial and involves the need to distinguish the writings in which Schmitt proposes legal theory in general—that is, theoretical works that respond to questions on law, its foundation, its constitution—from others that refer either to the Weimar constitution, to *Drittes Reich*, to postwar situations, or to the description of the Modern State—that is, to concrete historical circumstances. With this first distinction in mind, for example, the state as the *status* of political unity that can take many possible forms should be distinguished from the State as a particular historical form of political unity,[5] whether that pertains to the Modern State and its derivations or to the National Socialist State[6] or to any other state model. The second distinction is crucial for both reestablishing unity among the series of changes that appear in Schmitt's theoretical legal literature, as well as for understanding that his emphasis on decision does not directly correspond to pure decisionism. The distinction between the legal idea (*Rechtsidee*), legal order (the place of statute, *positives Gesetz*), and judicial reality (the place where law is to be applied, *Rechtsverwirklichung* or *Rechtsanwendung*)[7] carries the idea of transformation and appeals to mediation that supposes the intervention of some authority (*auctoritatis interpositio*).[8] Schmitt regularly emphasized in his writings a conviction that there is a gap between that which is declared as law and its implementation.[9] The law does not become immediately effective and requires personal intercession by someone who enforces it. Decisions are, therefore, just as necessary to legal order as norms. Failure to observe this distinction makes the evaluation of Schmitt as a decisionist understandable. In addition, it is important to mention that the intellectual atmosphere in which Schmitt lived and studied was dominated by dualism resulting from the coexistence of neo-Kantianism in which Schmitt was educated as a jurist with the positivism that proclaimed the triumph of empirical objectivity.[10] This situation presented legal science with the challenge of finding a bridge that unites both realities, ideal and factual—and Schmitt accepted that challenge.

Having made these comments, I will continue by describing what law means in Schmitt's writings. In line with the aforementioned distinction, I will start by analyzing what law means as legal idea (chapter 3) and then analyze what a legal order means as law revealed in a constitution and in statute law (chapter 4). I will not focus, however, on how law unfolds in judicial practice, although I will make a side reference to this area.[11] Following the central thesis of this book, I will show that it is only possible to account for legal ideas in connection with the *nomos*.

As discussed in the previous chapter, the *nomos* is an original act, the condition that enables a human society to live together on a piece of land such that all possible novelty therein refers back to the action that made it possible.[12] Thus all research on the origin of law should be undertaken from the point of view of the original land appropriation. Law is already prefigured in that order, which is what Schmitt meant when he stated that land appropriation is a primitive act that establishes law. This observation is the starting point of an arc that culminates in the conception of law as a specific order. The unity of order and position (*Ordnung* and *Ortung*) is the key feature of law that is defined from within a *nomos* of the earth. In the same way that a specific space is constituted by the elements and distances that shape it, vital space is constituted by the life of a people on land, which requires a spatial localization and an order.[13] For example, an institution like the family encompasses the house and the "*Hof,*" the estate, and the work that sustains the family.[14]

Schmitt refers back to mythical language that characterizes the earth as "the mother of law"[15] to explain the connection between law and the land and this for three reasons: First, the land contains an internal, given measure that is independent of external or posterior action. An example of this internal measure is found in the harvest that it gives as the "answer" to or measure of cultivation. Second, the earth allows for position to be determined because it is a solid surface; indeed, the space-position relationship on earth is not found in the sea or air. Third, human society is established within these limits of the earth and its first significant and visible symbol is the house. Given these three attributes, we can establish a three-way relationship between the land and law: In this way, the earth is bound to law in three ways. She contains law within herself, as a reward of labor; she manifests law upon herself, as fixed boundaries; and she sustains law above herself, as a public sign of order.[16]

Law includes the first moment when the life of a human group appears on land. It is intrinsically related to space precisely because the first thing that man does is inhabit the earth. Law is the declaration of an order, of the order of a concrete inhabitation. The *nomos* is the origin of order, while the law is the very order for each particular historical moment and for each particular land appropriation. The occupation of the land logically and historically precedes this ordering. As Schmitt claims: "[A]ll property and every legal order has land as its precondition, and is derived from the original acquisition of the earth's soil."[17] It always starts with land measurement and distribution, as noted in the first chapter. *Teilen* has the sense of *division primaeva—Ur-teil—*the origin of subsequent partitions and distributions. Although a written constitution seems somewhat removed from a spatial order that is the result of a land appropriation, it essentially remains a *nomos*: "To talk of a constitution of a country or a continent is to talk of its fundamental order, of its *nomos.*"[18] This is so much so that a change of constitution corresponds to a change in *nomos* and vice versa. It is not a positive law in the sense of a posterior state codification or of a constitutional legal system, but rather the consequence of land appropriation. From what has been said so far, it follows that land appropriation has, in its legal aspect, a categorical character. It institutes law in two ways:

inward and outward of the bounded territory. Inwardly, it creates an order of property relationships. Outwardly, a group that takes a piece of land is situated in opposition to other settled groups that are constituted as a power over their own land. With these reflections on the relationship between *nomos* and law, Schmitt definitely situated the latter in a concrete reality. The law is a concrete order, an ordering of people in work and inhabitation contexts. [19]

What has just been described as Schmitt's fundamental position regarding the source of law was only reached after extensive research on the true nature of the legal order connected at the beginning with the problem of the difference between law and power.

LAW AND POWER

One of Carl Schmitt's first works, his 1914 Habilitation entitled *Der Wert des Staates und die Bedeutung des Einzelnen* [The Value of the State and the Importance of the Individual], [20] is controversial because, in taking the point of view of legal normativity, it appears to advocate a position that contradicts his *nomos* writings. [21] However, by making some distinctions, it is possible to leave behind the contradictions associated with reading Schmitt, making it seem more like reading Kelsen. It is important to keep in mind that, by 1912, Schmitt had already written *Gesetz und Urteil*, which he conceived as a polemic against contemporary positivism, in which he called for greater decision-making space in a judge's ruling capacity, beyond the praxis of the subsumption of a particular case under the norm. In addition, it is also important to bear in mind that a *Habilitation* does not normally entail proposing an original theory, but rather entails a detailed analysis of a topic, and I think Schmitt's *Wert des Staates* conforms to this model. Schmitt found himself in the context of a Modern State from which he sought to distance himself—that is, the liberal *Rechtsstaat*. Once situated in this context, however, he wrote as if he were ironically offering his own position. [22] This does not differ much from how he wrote the *Schattenrisse*, which was published only a year before; Schmitt's *Habilitation* is a kind of fiction in which he uses an extreme description of reality in a critical mode and thus employs irony. Despite this fictionalization, Schmitt used his *Habilitation* to launch some of the theses that would follow him throughout his intellectual career.

The key for understanding this work correctly is found in properly placing it within the general framework of theoretical writings on legal theory. It should first be noted that Schmitt's *Habilitation* marks the moment of conversion from the legal idea—ontologically abstract law (*Rechtsidee*)—to statute—ontologically effective law (*Positives Recht*)—that is, positive general legal norm (*Rechtsordnung-Rechtsnorm*). [23] Secondly, it is necessary to historically contextualize this piece within the *Rechtsstaat*. [24] As noted above, in this piece, Schmitt does not at all propose a general way of conceiving legal order; rather, he analyzes the reality of the state as *Rechtsstaat* with its own instruments and conceptual mode.[25] Thirdly, with this piece, Schmitt refuted the then contemporary theories that dominated the field of legal thought, namely, State pluralism and legalism, that is, the conversion of *Rechtstaat* into a legislative State (*Gesetzstaat*).[26] In this sense, this piece contains a defense of law against legalism, hence the insistence, which is somewhat unusual in Schmitt, on characterizing the law as the norm of norms, as a true sovereign that founds power and comes before it. This definition of law is intended to highlight the unity of the *Rechtsstaat* against the omnipotence of the legislative State.

The Value of the State and the Importance of the Individual is a purely theoretical piece. Its thesis appears in the prologue and is constantly repeated: The *Rechtsstaat* ultimately finds its meaning in the task of instituting law in the world.[27] The *Rechtsstaat* simply aims at the realization of the law, which precedes the State and all power in a sense,[28] even if there is no statute law outside the State. The individual finds his meaning and place only within the logic of this fact that characterizes the existence of modern man. To describe it, Schmitt proposes a sequence containing Law-State-Individual (*Recht-Staat-Individuum*), in which the terms are referentially defined as follows:

> The law—as pure norm that is not legitimized by facts—logically represents the first part of the series. . . . The State enforces the union of the world of thought with the world of events and empirical reality and represents the only subject of juridical *ethos*. . . . The individual as an isolated empirical essence disappears to be understood by the law and the State in their efforts to implement law and even to take its meaning and value in performing that task within that closed world according to its own norms.[29]

These definitions assume that the law is an independent variable and that the State and the individual are dependent variables, although, in Schmitt's work, the State is protagonist precisely because of its function of instituting the law.[30] Viewed from the point of view of the State, law is an abstraction that cannot be deduced from the facts because there is an insurmountable gap between abstract and concrete worlds that can only be bridged by decision.[31]

A certain disharmony can be found between this piece and later ones, suggesting that Schmitt's thought evolved regarding the concept of law until reaching his fundamental position in *On the Three Types of Juristic Thought*. However, this piece still contains certain theses that Schmitt maintained in his later writing:

(a) This book dealt with ontologically abstract law: the legal idea. He defined law from the framework of the *Rechtsstaat*, as an abstract thought that cannot be deduced from the facts and that is solely constituted by purely rational norms lacking in any will or end.[32] There is no room in it for anything that is outside of the law, and its essence is found in norm and justice, thus it is independent of any reality. The world of law is the only thing that exists for law, such that law is a stranger to its own accomplishment,[33] which depends on the will of the State. This definition of the legal idea as logically abstract is not opposed to the concept of law found in the concrete order of a *nomos*[34] because they reflect on law at two different moments in its existence. In Schmitt's *Habilitation*, it is located on the plane where the idea of law converts into statute law—that is, it analyzes the way in which a norm is enforced. It does not question how a norm rationally emerges as a legal idea and instead seeks to uncover what a valid norm means on the state level. Thus, Schmitt was able to say: "What actually happens in the world is unimportant for the content, form or justice of a judicial norm."[35] Schmitt took this thesis into consideration until the end of his legal writings,[36] and it is directly related to his aversion to naturalism that appears in the *Schattenrisse*.[37]

(b) In *Der Wert des Staates* he critiques what he calls the "theory of power" (*Machttheorie*) at certain points, which will be discussed later. Thus, for example, he critiques the following statement: "Any appeal to a law contains a reference to power."[38] However, this statement could be seamlessly integrated[39] into his *Constitutional Theory*, in which he states: "Prior to the establishment of any norm, there is a fundamental *political decision by the bearer of the constitution-making power*. In a democracy, more specifically, this is a decision by the people; in a genuine monarchy, it is a decision by the monarch."[40]

As stated, the distinction between the law and the implementation of the law is a constant in all of Schmitt's work. A norm cannot be implemented by itself and needs a will that upholds it[41] precisely because, as already mentioned, there is an insurmountable gap between the abstract and the concrete, which cannot be avoided by a gradual step where a semi-abstract or semi-concrete situation arises. The law in the *Rechtsstaat*'s context is a sphere of abstract thought. It cannot be deduced from facts, nor can it be inherent to facts. Facts or events can only be an object of the will of law's implementation. Deduction in no way exists. The problem that arises, then, is how to link the two areas. Only the will of the State can accomplish this task by an act of sovereign decision in which the State itself becomes dependent upon the law it intendeds to implement.[42] This idea became a constant thesis in Schmitt's later works.[43] One can formulate as many universal goals and rights as desired; however, since a norm is not implemented by itself, "that is a fantastic manner of speaking."[44] Only upon entering someone's tangible will can an ontologically abstract law cease to be an idea of law and become positive, thus dependent upon a concrete situation and upon the will that implements it. This idea winds through Schmitt's entire conception of law and appears throughout his work from the beginning.[45]

(c) Of all Schmitt's work, this book is perhaps the one that most deals with the distinction between ethics and law.[46] Schmitt offered an illuminating example: The phrase "love thy neighbor" is not a positive law, nor can it become one. If there were honest and brave men to implement it in legislation during a certain time, it would be a milestone in State legislation and would enter into a different sphere and the impression of seeing it in that sphere of life would also be very different.[47]

This topic can be assumed in his other works, precisely because they lack any reference to ethics.[48] This distinction is related to another distinction between outer and inner freedom and the inability to include the visible and the invisible, the temporal and the eternal, in the same concept. Ethics belongs to the interior, invisible, and eternal sphere; law belongs to the outer, visible, and temporal sphere. To illustrate this distinction Schmitt offers the following example: A saint can exist in the desert, but there he cannot be just.[49] There is, therefore, a distinction, not a separation, between an interior and exterior order.[50] He adds that:

> Any philosophy that wants to redirect the law and ethics to the same principle should not overlook the fact that, if that were so then the State and God would relate in the same way as law and ethics; both would have the same necessity and, in the same sense, would think like divinities.[51]

We can say, therefore, that Schmitt was not closed to the existence and importance of an inner world, but he did suggest that if that world wants to continue to exist, it should be differentiated with respect to the area in which men's conduct can be determined from outside, from its "visibility." Hence, Schmitt maintained a clear conviction, from the beginning of his career, with regard to separation between political and religious ethics, not in the concrete sphere, as we will see in dealing with political theology, but rather in the sphere that encompasses decision or judgment on these areas.

(d) The distinction between "is" and "ought," and, in some cases, the split between these two areas, as well as how they are articulated, is related to the aforementioned topics.[52] In Schmitt's *Habilitation* when describing the *modus operandi* of the *Rechtsstaat*, we find a favorable inclination toward the "ought" and a disregard for the "is." Law belongs to the "ought" and it is not only not deduced from the facts or individuals, but it really has nothing to do with them. It is absolutely independent. In contrast to the law, the will belongs to the "is." But, insofar as it belongs to the "is," it does not belong to law. If the law were a will that could implement itself, it would no longer be norm. In later writings, Schmitt attempted to establish the origin of the "ought" in the "is," while retaining a clear difference between the two. And he showed how an "ought" that is separated from an "is," separated from *nomos* and abstract, is dead weight in legal thought.[53] In his later perspective, the will itself mediates between the "is" and "ought." The will is "an amount of 'is' as the origin of 'ought.'"[54] What he meant to say here is, in my view, that neither fact nor possibility establish the "ought." "Ought" is found in the rational will, which also makes the fusion between the "is" and "ought" possible. This fusion is essential for the political decision making that makes law positive, as well as for concrete order, which is the premise of all law. The will as the source of "ought" is present in every man's life in society. The "is" cannot be anything other than the concrete *nomos* of the earth in which every "will" is located.

With all this in mind, it is safe to say that, from the beginning, Schmitt's real enemy in the field of legal science was legal positivism, in particular, the work of Hans Kelsen, who intends to avoid the will in the theoretical construction of the *Rechtsstaat* at any cost.[55] Schmitt was academically trained in an environment, as he himself characterized, that was like an "empire of positivism." He experienced the Weimar Constitution firsthand, a constitutional model of a parliamentary State that defended the rule of law against the rule of persons.[56] Schmitt describes this State as follows:

> [T]he bourgeois *Rechtsstaat* takes its point of departure from the idea of being able to comprehend and to limit the entire exercise of all State power without exception in written laws. In this way, political action of any given subject, whether it is the absolute monarch or the people come to political self-consciousness, even sovereignty itself is no longer possible. Instead, a diverse range of fictions must be set up, such as that there is no longer any sovereignty at all, or, what is the same thing, that the "constitution," more precisely, constitutional norms, are sovereign, etc.[57]

This kind of State seeks to end power by dividing power into three fundamental modes of execution, including legislative, executive, and judicial. Since these three modes are unable to separately govern the State, it should be limited to a joint government based on the establishment of mutual checks and balances.[58] Along with power, it sought to end any expression of personal will, establishing the statute's will everywhere, which is nothing more than a nice name used to hide a number of "apocryphal acts of sovereignty."[59]

For legal positivism, law is just statute. There are also interpretive means for the implementation of the content of statute. That which, by these means, is deduced from law, is law. Everything else is juridically irrelevant. Opposite to this, *concrete order* recognizes the source of law and the legal idea in a concrete *nomos* from which it receives its content. This approach calls into question something that has already been rejected by normativism, namely, that an order is marked and formed in real life, which legal science only updates normatively.[60] The fundamental distinction that separates Schmitt from legal positivism is found between pure "formalist-functional legality" and "substantive law and historical legitimation" (*rein formalistisch-funktionaler Legalität* and *substanzhafte Rechtsgeschichtliche Legitimität*).[61] Schmitt proposed a "substantial" legal idea rooted in *nomos* in place of empty legality, which he defined as follows:

> In a modern system, that is to say, an industrialized, thoroughly organized system, endowed with a division of labor and highly specialized, legality means a specific working and functioning method of the public body. The manner in which affairs are decided, the routine and the habits of departments, the somewhat calculable functioning, the concern to retain this kind of life and the need of a "cover" against an account demanding authority: all that belongs to the complex of legality from a bureaucratic-functionalist point of view.[62]

With legal positivism, law becomes statute in a series of "positions on positions" or "acts of will" within the continued deployment of statute; this is, in Schmitt's words, the recognition and approval of the "normative force of the factual."[63] The transformation of juristic thought into legal thought is undertaken in three steps: first, the implementation of law rests on the "will of the legislature"; second, to avoid any subjectivism, this will is passed on to statute itself and it is referred to as "the statute's will"; the third step involves the elimination of the term *will*, which is a nuisance to all legalism, and it is referred to as "statute itself" and, with it, legal legitimation is obtained. The objective of this transformation is to rid the law of any meta-juridical argument.[64]

Schmitt constantly criticizes legalism in his work.[65] Thus, in his 1978 article, *Die legale Weltrevolution; Politischer Mehrwert als Prämie auf juristische Legalität und Superlegalität*,[66] in which he describes Hitler's rise to power as a result of a legal revolution, Hitler shows legalism's last step: Legality has not only become legitimate, but also has become a revolutionary instrument. In a modern industrial society, only legal revolutions have a chance: "Even the thinking of professional revolutionaries progresses, as evidenced today in 'legal' revolution."[67]

(e) The first chapter of *Der Wert des Staates* is entitled "Law and Power." Later in 1917, Schmitt published this chapter as an article in the magazine *Summa*.[68] The dialectic between the spheres of power and the law is one of the main threads that run through Schmitt's legal theory. It is a question that is always open and that he tries to solve by way of thinking about concrete order. As we have seen, power and law are two completely different areas, two qualitatively distinct realms of being, such that, between them, no causal relationship can arise.[69] The problem is found in uniting these two areas, finding the point from which—conserving the primacy of law over power—concrete existence can influence juridical norms.[70] The dialectical relationship between law and power is mirrored in other dichotomies found in

Schmitt's work, such as: is/ought, *potestas/auctoritas*, *ratio/voluntas*, objectivity/subjectivity, impersonal norm/personal will, and state/law.[71] He again treats this problem in his commentary to Meinecke's book, *Idee der Staatsräson*. Meinecke characterized this dualism through a moral lens, identifying its movement in a series of contrasts,[72] as, for example: kratos/ethos; politics/moral; interest/ethical norm; nature/spirit; destiny/reason; evil/good; devil/God. However, as Schmitt observed, Meinecke's work contains the primacy of a moral pole.[73] Meinecke leaves dualism suspended and unsolved. There is no definitive answer, but rather a pendulum movement between the two poles of this dualism that depends on specific historical circumstances:

> The problem is not at all found in the normative content of a moral or judicial mandate, but rather in the question: Who decides? . . . The great works of the seventeenth century emphasized this "quis judicabit," especially in Hobbes and Pufendorf. Naturally, everyone wants law, morality, ethics, and peace; nobody wants to commit injustice, but the only interesting question is always who *in concreto* decides what is fair, what is peace, what is a threat or a danger to peace, how is it to be avoided, when is a situation normal and considered peaceful, etc. This "quis judicabit" shows that dualism is reintroduced within law and the general moral mandate, which takes the capacity that these concepts have in appearing as simple contrasts of power and in moving in a pendulum trajectory toward it.[74]

Schmitt's solution to the dialectic between power and law is found in his concrete order theory.

CONCRETE ORDER THINKING

Schmitt's book *On the Three Types of Juristic Thought* is the most striking example of the position he took against Kelsen's pure theory of law, which is apparent right away with the vocabulary he employed. Along with following from his earlier explorations of space, the book also demonstrates Schmitt's position on the conceptualization of the law. Schmitt rejected Kelsen's theory in the same terms that Kelsen used in his pure theory of law.[75] Kelsen and Schmitt's books were both published in 1934 and they had met the year before as professors at Cologne. Kelsen welcomed Schmitt from the beginning and even supported his appointment, believing that they would be able to maintain fruitful discussions,[76] although Schmitt did not return Kelsen's enthusiasm. Schmitt's book, however, is far from being just a critique of Kelsen's theory, taking the opportunity to outline, albeit roughly, his own legal thought, which, until then, he had not done. As is well known, Kelsen aimed to develop a theory of law that is "pure"—that is, purged of all ideology and any natural-scientific elements. Legal science, Kelsen thought, should appropriately respond to the criteria set for other sciences, especially in terms of accuracy and objectivity. Above all, Kelsen believed that law must be clearly separated from politics. Schmitt presented his position in opposition to these theses, which sometimes seem to be an exact reply to Kelsen's formulations. For Schmitt, the legal idea is primarily determined by a concrete order. Law is not primarily determined by rules or decisions, but rather by a previous order. The law is a *nomos*—or we might say that the law "assumes" a *nomos* if it were possible to pinpoint a moment in man's life on earth that still did not have a *suum*. All law can be no more than a "located" law.

In "concrete order thinking's" logic, order does not first mean legislation—that is, a set of rules or the sum of a set of rules, as Kelsen claimed; rather, order denotes the visibility of a *nomos*. Concrete order is what comes to be regarded in the juristic field as a "normal" situation. The concept of normality, from which the idea of a norm comes, is not created in an abstract or hypothetical realm, but rather is born of concrete life's juridical substance. In a subsequent stage, it becomes expressed in general rules, but only as an explanation of said substance, as a demonstration of its particularity and internal order. In this context, a norm is no longer an otherworldly ideal. It becomes the manifestation of an order, a means for the realization of the law, which depends on a concrete order and loses its validity when it no longer corresponds to it.

On the Three Types of Juristic Thought is a treatise on *nomos*.[77] In it, Schmitt takes his first steps toward the relationship between law and *nomos*, which he only years later came to definitively shape. In any case, Schmitt certainly considers order in his early writings, where, as considered earlier, he was truly fascinated with the order of language and naming. This does not mean that Schmitt wrote *The Nomos of the Earth* to try to justify what he had sketched many years earlier as juristic thought,[78] but rather, in the course of his writings, what was an intuition in 1934 became the center of his interests. The theory of *nomos* of the 1950s represents a true discovery in Schmitt's work that illuminated his 1934 intuition and his previous writings without invalidating them. In his 1934 essay, he set out the possibilities open to a jurist when forming a legal idea. In his opinion, every jurist consciously or unconsciously holds a concept of law, which becomes the supposition from which he practices his science.[79] This concept takes three main forms, where (1) a jurist mainly ascribes to the realm of decision, (2) he mainly ascribes to the realm of rules and regulations, or (3) he conceives of it as a concrete order. A fourth possibility is found in a mix of two of them, which can be clearly seen in the legal positivism of the nineteenth century. The positivist system is both normative and decisionist because, within it, everything is subject to decisions made by the legislature that represents state power and, at the same time, there is a clear attempt to validate any decision as norm. This results in something rather contradictory: the state legislature, while making a decision on statute, subjects itself to that statute and its interpretation.[80] The result of this combination is not, however, a synthesis between norm and decision, but ultimately, a position of almost absolute power to the extent that it puts power and authority in the same hands. The state apparatus conceals a political decision under the soft cloak of statute.[81]

Obviously any way of looking at law involves rules, orders, and decisions; however, one of these elements always becomes the most important and the other two end up referring to it.[82] Different types of juristic thought emerge depending on which of these elements is chosen as most important. For example, juristic thought founded on decision is called decisionism or, as Schmitt once called it,[83] a theory of power (*Machtstheorie*). Juristic thought founded on rules is referred to as a normativism or what, in contrast to the term *Machtstheorie*, can be called a theory of law, *Rechtstheorie*. But establishing the differences between decision and norm, decision and order, and order and norm does not clarify anything and instead requires the establishment of relationships as well, which is what Schmitt tried to do.

Sustaining a certain kind of juristic thought is not at all arbitrary or neutral with regard to societal and political structure. On the one hand, the presence of a certain type of juristic thought depends on the situation—that is, on the specific time and place, in which it develops. Thus, different modes of juristic thought are found in a variety of human peoples and races,[84] which is why, for example, one cannot make blanket statements about English, French, American, or German law.[85] On the other hand, the fact that a certain type of juristic thought or another materializes depends on historical circumstances.[86] The reference system of legal order is, ultimately, a people's specific mode of existence. Schmitt gave the following example:

> There are peoples that, without territory, without a state, and without a church, exist only in "law." To them normativist thought is the only reasonable legal thought, and every other type of thought appears inconceivable, mystical, fantastic and ridiculous. The Germanic thinking of the Middle Ages, in contrast, was through-and-through concrete-order thinking; however the reception of Roman law in Germany since the fifteenth century has displace this kind of thought among German jurists and advanced an abstract normativism.[87]

Schmitt ascribed his concept of law to the kind of juristic thought that corresponds to concrete order (*Konkretes Ordnungsdenken*). Here, the legal idea is primarily determined by a concrete order, which is later made explicit in a legal order (*Rechtsordnung*). With the distinction between order (*Ordnung*) and legal order (*Rechtsordnung*), law brushes off the impression that it is nothing more than empty normativity.[88] Juristic thought on concrete order is also a juridical mind-set, a philosophical position on law.[89] For this mind-set, law is not primarily determined by rules or decisions, but rather by a previous concrete order. It presupposes an order or, what is the same, law presupposes a *nomos*. Thus, all law can be no more than a "located law" or a "situational law."[90]

As already mentioned, order does not first mean legislation—that is, a set of rules or the sum of a set of rules. Rather, rule is a part of order, a means for realizing it, but it does not create order.[91] Order is *nomos* made visible, and *nomos* is the development of communities of men in space thanks to the natural relationships between them, to labor and tradition, and to man's natural way of being, as well as that of a particular people. Substantial juridical order is, therefore, an anthropological expression. It is a concrete time and place because human life happens in space and time. It is labor and relationship because man is a social being. Order connotes, in short, a mixture of moral and rational principles that are shaped by customs, feelings, environmental constraints, and by the fact that human beings can only live in relationship with other human beings.

Statute law is, then, the "positive" expression of a set of principles, practices, and attitudes that have crystallized over time in the relational life of a people that occupy a given space. Law reveals an internal order through an external structure[92] and, thus, Schmitt describes it as the public sign of order. Rules and regularities do not create the order, but rather serve it,[93] which is why a legal order necessarily presumes a normal situation and excludes an exceptional one. Exception and conflict no longer belong to the legal field, but rather, as we shall see, to politics.[94] An order's visibility is achieved through specific forms. The most appropriate way to reflect this order is found in institutions because any order that belongs to the sphere of life cannot be shaped through systematic-technical means, but only through institutions.[95] Institution means nothing other than the duration and strength of an order or a social disposition's living presence.[96] In this sense, although no doubt there is a close relationship between *nomos* and statute, it is inappropriate to translate the term *nomos* for statute, rule, or regulation, as it has traditionally been translated, but rather—in one of its meanings—for law, which is as much norm as decision, but above all, order. Any subject of law always refers back to a specific institutional order. Schmitt gives the example of a king, a monarch, a guardian, a ruler, or a judge and points out that "one can speak of a true *nomos* as true king only if *nomos* means precisely the concept of *Recht* encompassing concrete order and *Gemeinschaft*."[97] The family institution offers also an excellent example of this topic:

> One can portray general and abstract norms as the "constitution" of the international legal community to the same limited degree that one can find the "constitution" of a family in general norms such as that "you should honor your father and mother" or "love your neighbor."[98]

The ontological supposition that reality itself is ordered is juxtaposed to theories that conceive of social reality primarily as conflict, an example of which is found in Hobbes's state of nature and consequently in the idea that every civil society must be artificially constructed. [99] On the contrary, Schmitt's thought is underlined by the belief that human society itself unfolds relationships that, in its persistence throughout history, appear differently in different times and places.

Schmitt uses this type of juristic thought in defining the concepts he employs, which he also does with the constitution, the State, and *Großraum*. For example, he speaks of the constitution in the following terms:

> Because every being is a concrete and determined existence, some kind of constitution is part of every concrete political existence. But not every entity that exists politically decides in a conscious action the form of this political existence and reaches, through its own conscious determination, the decision regarding its concrete type. [100]

The Modern State is also closely related to *nomos*. [101] It corresponds to a political form that appeared with the configuration a European order in which the land, unlike the sea or free terrain, was divided into enclosed spaces under sovereign power. This spatial configuration is essential to the State. Hegel, in his *Philosophy of Right*, also understood this. [102] The Modern State became a new organizing concept of space and it, subsequently, transformed law. The concept of "large space" (*Großraum*) also belongs to a concrete time and space, corresponding to the post–World War I era. The configuration of space in this historic moment did not give rise to the Modern State; rather, it structured globalized space with technology, industry, economy, and bureaucracy.

For Schmitt, law is thrice concrete. It is concrete in the logical sense—that is, the legal idea (*vorpositives Recht*) is concrete in the sense that legal substance is found in *nomos*. But to be even more effectively concrete, a legal idea must also be made statute (*positives Recht*), that is, it must be made positive and effectively concrete by a will that actually puts it into statute. And, thirdly, it is practically concrete to the extent that this statute applies to each particular case in judicial practice (*Rechtsanwendung*). When instituting law, it is necessary to go from that which is logically concrete to that which is practically concrete. In "concretizing" there is a certain "gap" that can only be mediated by decision. [103] Schmitt devoted many pages to clarifying this "gap" and the need for mediation inherent in all law, that is, the need for a "will." [104]

Normativism emerges against this conception of order and law. For normativism, order only consists of the correspondence between a concrete situation and general rules, with which it is also measured. [105] Any legal norm can regulate many cases and, independent or isolated, individual cases, it is absolutely objective. It is an "ought" that intends to line up with justice and that is found far from the "is" of things. Given that statute is considered perfect, normativism looks to norm to govern. All other elements of political life—the people, the king, the judge, the state—are based on objective norm. In this regard, normativist thought can be characterized as "non-personalist," if such a category makes sense, unlike the personalism of decisionist thought or the "supra-personalism" (*überpersönliche*) of concrete-order thinking. Normativist thought imposes an absolutely abstract order—that is, it is closed to the social reality that is life and, therefore, to concreteness and openness.

This approach has, according to Schmitt, two fundamental flaws: Firstly, it does not realize that, for governance by norm to be possible, the existence of a normal situation is necessary.[106] Therefore, it depends on a particular order—that is, on the situation that is considered normal. When this normality disappears, norm also disappears because it loses any juridical meaning. Secondly, it does not take account of the object that such normativism faces, namely, the life of a community in relation to things, which is changeable and does not fully comply with norm. Human life in society is nothing like rail car traffic, where interactions can be calculated with a simple mathematical function. Some spheres of human life, those in which functional interactions are meaningful, can certainly be compared to rail car traffic, corresponding to an instinctive level on which actions are repeated almost invariably. Nevertheless the majority of human spheres could not tolerate mechanical or functional planning, which would destroy the essence of its very order. These areas of life cannot be fashioned in a technical-circulatory mode, but rather must be shaped institutionally. Schmitt reproached normativists for the detachment from reality that their thought implies; on occasion, he would say, in the end, "what does a rationalist know about life?"[107] All such normativity loses sight of the fact that the "is" is the wellspring of all law.

The decisionist conception, which also opposes concrete order, is different from normativism. For decisionism, order is the result of a decision; therefore, all law is founded on a final decision's authority or sovereignty. This concept is originally found in Bodin and Hobbes and belongs to a statist era that only recognized decision in its exclusive form (*Entweder-Oder*).[108] Bodin's thought, however, was still dependent on theological conceptions of order, which is why his thought cannot be said to be typically decisionist. Hobbes's thought, on the other hand, is a classic representation of decisionism. For him, all statute, norm, and law are the result of sovereign decisions and the sovereign is nothing more than he who decides and commands: "*Auctoritas non veritas facit legem*," authority, not truth, makes statute. *Auctoritas* does not mean here an order or a pre-political authority, or even, as Bodino thought, something different from *potestas*; rather, full authority means sovereignty, that is, the power to establish peace, security, and order. According to Schmitt, decisionism starts from certain unacceptable suppositions—that is, absolute decision, as decisionists describe it, originates in a rational void and has a disordered relationship to concrete situations. Decision institutes both norm and order.[109] Before it, only the chaotic Hobbesian state of nature exists, a state of unhappiness, disorder, insecurity, and a struggle of all against all. Absolute decision is the absolute beginning.

Along with Hobbes, counterrevolutionary philosophers also emphasized decision. Their philosophy was, on the one hand, a response to the historical moment of crisis that they faced, which required a decision. On the other hand, it was also the result of a metaphysical assumption referring to the fallen nature of man. These philosophers therefore held, although not as stridently as Hobbes did, that there is an originating disorder.[110] An extreme example of this thought is found in Donoso Cortés, who purported that there is an inherent disorder in human nature that requires a decision to restore order. Decision is always initiated, as in the case of the two previous examples, by a demand for order from an inherent disorder. Within the framework of thought on concrete order, decision is dependent on concrete order, which originates in both the need to restore order and in the need to find a new order.[111] Decision must always be dependent on an order so that it is not separated from the framework of law, which is not deduced from force alone.[112] From the point of view of concrete order, both norm and decision, while always necessary for the formation of law, are understood differently from normativist or decisionist thought. As mentioned, in this context, norm is understood as a means for carrying out the law[113] and statute publicizes an order and is a manifestation of it.[114] Every institution, and even every norm, is characterized by this relationship to a state of things as an inherent premise of its existence and validity.

PHENOMENOLOGY OF DECISION

At this point, we must distinguish between disorder as it relates to social harmony and a metaphysical, radical disorder. The possibility of an absolute disorder requires an absolute decision for its resolution, which defines Hobbesian-like decisionism. The conception of a relative disorder, as in the case of Schmitt's *Ausnahmezustand*, requires sovereign decisions framed in a particular order.[115] Here, sovereign decision only becomes absolutely necessary when a disorder prevents the normal functioning of a society.

This point of view is certainly related to the classical tradition. In general conceptions of order in antiquity, an order is always represented as a supposition of decision. Pure decision emptied of content—that is, the "gap" that all decision implies, is always limited and understood by an order, such that it is possible to claim that decision is the result of a presupposed order. [116] Schmitt gives the example of Tertullian, a jurist and theologian, who argued that we are bound to something, not because it is good, but rather because God commands it. Although this statement sounds like juridical decisionism, it is not. The Christian idea of God carries with it a concept of a given order. Tertullian argued in a metaphysical context that lacked a representation of a worldly disorder, a chaos that could only be turned around by an absolute decision. [117]

Within a concrete order, decision has a "decisive" role because, thanks to it, in the first place, political decision sustains the legal framework and affords security and concreteness to the sphere of law, such that the law becomes formulated in statutes. Secondly, thanks to judicial decision, the realization of the law is ensured. [118] Now, not even a political decision—the sovereign decision, which is the quintessential form of decision and decides on an exception—[119] can dispense of concrete order. At the same time, concrete order cannot be formed without the collaboration of people's moral decisions (the level prior to political and judicial decision that connects the private and public spheres).

In the first place, the sovereign does not decide by reference to a legal order, one expressed in general legal norms; rather, he decides by reference to the concrete order of the situation in which he lives. An exception is not necessarily chaos and the exceptional state differs from anarchy. Exception is an event in which any legal order subsists. But even in this case there is some kind of order. Secondly, the sovereign can no longer be understood, as he has been understood in much of political thought to date, as a supreme, originating and judicially independent power. [120] As Schmitt would claim, there is no unyielding power that rules with the security of natural law; a sovereign must be defined in connection with power in the legal sphere. And that connection comes from dependence on concrete order. [121]

In this approach, compared to decisionist thought, order is not only a consequence, but also the foundation, of political decision. [122] This "not only" refers to the fact that, of course, decision puts an order in place since a decision about a situation necessarily changes that situation, but it should be added, following Schmitt, that decision cannot modify reality to the extent that order becomes a "pure creation" of decision. Instead, decision formalizes and identifies opportunities for order in a concrete situation. A concrete order, therefore, is partly founded on and partly the result of political decisions.

There are three types of decision that correspond to the three figures of any legal order, which is an order where statutes are established beforehand. In this legal order, the normative element of the law and the actually existing element of concrete ordering must be alive. [123] The subjects of the former element are referred to as *legislative power*, in the case of law-making power that establishes statutes and the *judge* who looks for law-setting in concrete situations; the subject of the concrete ordering is referred to as *sovereign*. The latter becomes a dictator insofar as he decides without paying attention to norm, precisely because the particular order in which that norm was valid has fallen. However, as has been said, in a way, he still depends on an order. [124] The following texts reiterate this idea:

> The content of the actions of a dictator consists in this: achieving a certain goal, "accomplishing": the enemies should be defeated, the political opponent nullified or destroyed. This always depends on "specific circumstances." [125]

> In practice the commissary dictatorship suspends the constitution in order to protect it—the very same one—in its concrete form. . . . [Sovereign] dictatorship does not suspend an existing constitution through a law based on the constitution—a constitutional law; rather it seeks to create conditions in which a constitution—a constitution that it regards as the true one—is made possible. Therefore dictatorship does not appeal to an existing constitution, but to one that is still to come. [126]

Decision is always an action that is undertaken in the pursuit of an end, that which must be done. [127] In either case, the end is uncertain. And this is so because decisions within an order refer to unique situations that are not fully specified and because the proposal is a complete novelty.

The difference between these three types of decision—sovereign, legislative, and judicial—is found in two aspects. First, its relationship with a pre-established law: A decision's configuration within a political order (a judge's decision) is found in statute or in a common law, while, in a situation that involves an exception to a legal order, a decision's configuration is found in the new order that it wants to establish or in the order that it endeavors to reestablish, but not in statute (a legislative or exceptional decision of the sovereign). The second aspect refers to time: A decision that conforms to statute comes with sufficient, preestablished time to act such that it can count on detailed and elaborate deliberation, but this does not occur when a decision is made in a situation of disorder, where the legal order must be restored as quickly as possible. Schmitt underscores this point as follows:

> Hence, in an extreme case, he has the capacity not to obey general norms. But if the concrete means of achieving a concrete goal can, under normal circumstances, be predicted with regularity—for instance when the police is entitled to maintain public security—in cases of emergency we can only say this much: the dictator is entitled to do everything that is appropriate in the actual circumstances. [128]

Schmitt continuously detailed the difference between these areas of decision in his works through the following distinctions: (a) constitution-making power and constitutional amendment[129]; (b) constitution and constitutional law[130]; (c) sovereign dictatorship and commissarial dictatorship[131]; (d) constitution-making power and constituted authority[132]; and (e) constitution and constitutional law.[133] Whoever gives the constitution is a single will that, with his decision, raises an entire people to a political order. However, a constitutional statute is less decisive. Constitutional statutes may change in part—and here Schmitt is unwavering—without the constitution itself changing, meaning that to legislate is not the same as establishing a framework for all legislation, that is, as establishing a "normal situation."

Both modes of decision are united by a "striking of the will" that can be understood as uncertainty regarding the outcome of a decision and regarding the decision itself or as the nondeductibility, in the case of norm, of the other end that is sought[134] and that depends solely on the subject and his decision. Now, that does not mean that voluntary mediation equals subjectivism, just as an act of prudence is not subjective. On this point, by maintaining that a voluntary act has an objective measure, Schmitt parts ways with decisionism.[135] Schmitt characterizes this qualitative jump as a "vacuum of reason," by which he does not refer to a "nihilist" or subjectivist conception of human action. With no guarantee on the outcome of a particular action, one must take a gap because there are many possibilities for action and, yet, it is necessary to choose one. This choice is no longer deductible from situational knowledge. A decision involves a "jump" not only because human beings lack the necessary knowledge such that action is always appropriate to the situation that requires it, but also for two additional reasons. The first is that there are situations in social reality that, because of their abnormality, need an immediate decision that must somehow be made, even though one lacks full certainty regarding the decision's appropriateness. The second is a decision's inevitable dependence on the person who makes that decision. Precisely because there are many possibilities for action, he who chooses one option and not the other becomes an immediate reference to the subject that decides, to his interpretation and, therefore, to his conscience. Here we find the novelty of Schmitt's political theory in the context of the prevailing theory at the time. In Schmitt's theory, responsibility for a decision is not diluted. A governor, and anyone who works in any capacity in a case of exception, including a judge, does not act according to statute, but rather according to prudence, that is, conscience. Prudence is "situational conscience."[136] In Schmitt, we also find that: "Everything that a man does or thinks—with or without power—passes through the hallway of human conscience and other individual human powers."[137] There is yet another place where Schmitt refers to the "ability to take a decision," and critiques the political passivity of the Romantics:

Thus the subjectified occasionalism of the romantic also accompanies what encounters it, and it should not be difficult to differentiate its organic passivity from the restraints of an active statesman that result from political experience and objectives. The criterion is whether the ability to make a decision between right and wrong is present. This ability is the principle of every political energy: the revolutionary, which appeals to natural right or human rights, as well as the conservative, which appeals to historical right.[138]

The "gap" implied in decision is measured by a sovereign or judge's conscience or, what is the same, prudence. The content of a decision is not therefore fully determinable *a priori* because it depends on the situation of things and on who interprets them.

After this analysis the question remains, why has Schmitt's theory been crossed off as decisionist?[139] Schmitt has been described as a decisionist[140] precisely because of the importance he gives to decision's qualitative gap and to its "empty content" without explaining it enough—which the previous pages have attempted to do—and without stopping to consider the type of decision he refers to in each moment and his critical approach to the decisionism elaborated by Hobbes, de Maistre, and Donoso Cortés.

Schmitt fundamentally earned this portrayal by way of the texts that refer to the second type of decision, the one that does not proceed according to statute. In stressing a difference and highlighting it against the internal point of view of the *Rechtsstaat*, he makes a distinction between decision's form and content[141] and characterizes decision, above all, as form, as an act of sheer will that appears similar to the Nietzschean will to power. In this way, Schmitt may seem to lean toward decisionism when considering texts referring to the "positive" moment of every constitution in isolation; there, he precisely intends to show that there is personal will in every conscious constitutional decision. The following texts further clarify his position:

> That is the instance of competence that renders a decision makes the decision relative, and in certain circumstances absolute and independent of the correctness of its content. This terminates any further discussion about whether there may still be some doubt. The decision becomes instantly independent of argumentative substantiation and receives an autonomous value.[142]

> The constitution is valid by virtue of the existing political will of that which establishes it. Every type of legal norm, even constitutional law, presupposes that such "will" already exists.[143]

But, for example, in a broader sense, this text from *Constitutional Theory* highlights the following:

> In contrast to mere norms, the word "will" denotes an actually existing power as the origin of a command. The will is existentially present; its power or

authority lies in its being. A norm can be valid because it is *correct*. The logical conclusion reached systematically, is natural law, not the positive constitution. The alternative is that a norm is valid because it is positively established, in other words, by virtue of an existing will. [144]

When evaluating a decision, it is important to determine whether it is made in a normal or abnormal situation—that is, whether or not it involves a decision according to statute. As noted in the preceding pages, the problem can only be correctly considered from this point of view: the question of the normality or abnormality of a particular situation. [145] It remains certain that Schmitt progressively refined the decisionist mood of his early writings. [146] His take on concrete order, outlined in *On the Three Types of Juristic Thought*, represents a maturing of the ideas in his first books, which seemed to put decision front and center. It is as if this 1934 book confronts the decisionist criticism he received that was provoked by the books *Gesetz und Urteil* (1912), *Politische Romantik* (1919), *Die Diktatur: Von den Anfängen des modernen Souveranitätsgedankens bis zum proletarischen Klassenkampf* (1921), *Politische Theologie. Vier Kapitel zur Lehre von der Souveranität* (1922), *Der Begriff des Politischen* (1927), and *Verfassungslehre* (1928). *On the Three Types of Juristic Thought* frames, closes, and gives meaning to his theory of decision developed in the previous years. [147]

JUSTICE

One question remains to be examined when dealing with Carl Schmitt's position on law, and it pertains to justice's place in the concrete-order thinking. I propose the following answer: Doing justice means that order should always be restored; justice is found in restoring order to everything. Schmitt did not frame justice in this theoretical context, but rather in a practical one. One can only speak of justice in the process of its realization because one does not really know what justice is until it is realized. The correct formulation of the question at this point is not, therefore, what is justice, but rather what is a just decision. What else could justice consist of? Schmitt only discussed this issue, therefore, from the point of view of judicial practice. [148] Here, the crucial question is: when is a judicial decision correct? [149] or even better, when, today, in juridical practice is a judicial decision considered correct? [150] In any case, it is not a question of what is just. When responding to this question, the fundamental problem in judicial practice—concerning the gap between statute (*Gesetz*) and judgment (*Urteil*)—comes to light again. Legality cannot be identified with justice; [151] a correct decision is not only or primarily measured by statute. Rather the decision aims to law's determinacy. This is a positivist assumption according to which a sentence is just when it is legal, that is, when it corresponds to positive law, when a judge submits a case to statute. However, as Schmitt would say, here lies the heart of the problem, because there is a qualitative gap between statute and judgment that precludes the deductibility between both. [152] This gap exists because, although judicial decision is a judgment on the basis of a statute, it is not clear how this process takes place given that it is not a mechanical process. The question of legal interpretation always exists, and it is not at all trivial since it has to do with real power. [153] Schmitt dismissed legal science's claim that a method for the objective interpretation of statute can be developed such that this interpretation contains the very statute's will or the legislator's will. If this were possible, a judge would decide exactly as set out in statute. [154] This approach assumes that statute's will is somehow inscribed in it, the very force that carries it out. This claim is, according to Schmitt, a fallacy that has led to many contradictions and inconsistencies, precisely because it operates based on a fiction [155]: Statute contains nothing more than "manifest content" [156] and in no way includes a will. Justice, therefore, is not deducible from the interpretation of statute. This solution only succeeds in replacing the question with another, recurring one, namely, which interpretation is correct? [157] The criterion of correctness for a judicial decision cannot be found in a "sense of justice," [158] in individual conviction, or in a mix of both when they come to an agreement. The justice of a decision cannot be left in the hands of autonomous criteria, but rather must be heteronomous. [159] Schmitt's position comes to be (1) the activity of a judge is not just a simple subsumption of a number of cases to statute, [160] and (2) the criterion for a correct decision does not rest in the subjectivity of the judge. [161] *Praxis* itself decides whether or not a decision is correct, which corresponds to the following formulation: A judicial decision is correct if another judge would have decided the same way. [162] This criterion is guided by the will of the judge to determine the law. That which is just is defined in judgment itself; there is no abstract standard of justice and, although it could be formulated, it would have no meaning for *praxis*. [163]

Chapter Four

The Legal Order

For the idea of law to be made effective it must enter the sphere of positive law, where law means statute law. Starting with the birth of the revolutionary Modern State, law becomes positive when it is expressed in a written constitution. Schmitt designated a constitution, as conceived within the framework that has been alluded to, as a positive constitution, but even in this context of "positivity," Schmitt never lost his fundamental inclination toward order seen in the previous chapters. Although modern constitutionalism has lost sight of it, every constitution is fundamentally a matter of *nomos*. Every society, every people, is already constituted in some way before its members consciously decide to formulate a positive constitution. It could be said that the original constitution, the *Urverfassung,* is found in *nomos*.

ORIGINAL CONSTITUTION

Using Schmitt's terminology, to say that a society is formed before its members politically decide on a positive constitution is akin to claiming that it contains a vital order (*Lebensordnung*) with certain forms. This has already been sufficiently discussed in previous pages; however, in what follows, some of Schmitt's comments on this point in dialogue with counterrevolutionary sociologists will be addressed.

The idea that society is in itself constituted is a classic one. A society is all the more constituted the higher its forms are, that is, the more channels for mediation that exist in it, such that a positive constitution is merely an explanation of these forms. Thus, if a society retains many customs and institutions—that is, if it contains deeply rooted modes of relating—then a positive constitution will be concrete because of the correspondence between it and the aforementioned forms. If, on the contrary, a society lacks form and barely sustains behavioral modes, then the corresponding positive constitution will be abstract and will necessarily employ coercive means in search of compliance. This is the case of contractualist theories.

The counterrevolutionary political theory is a good example of this idea. The Restoration, in the thought of counterrevolutionary sociologists, involved the reinstatement of the natural social order. Bonald, whom Schmitt recognized as the founder and father of modern sociology,[1] wrote about the constitution according to the aforementioned ideas. A society's constitution is the realization or active presence of moral truth, which is properly expressed in order, thus a constitution is the intrinsic order of society.[2] The constitutive principle of society is power[3]; however, the legitimacy of power is a function of the realization of a natural constitution. Thus, the ancien régime was considered a state of legitimacy because it was the historic realization of a constituted society, the result of history: "The constitution of a people is their history put into action."[4] "The constitution of a people is their mode of existence."[5] A constitution is rooted in the social order, which is its principle of legitimacy. Social order is not meant here as a balance of powers, but rather of institutions. Ultimately, the question of legitimacy becomes a question of legitimate social order and this is, as Bonald claimed, moral civilization, which is nothing more than Christianity applied to society. This ideal of civilization is on the always-desired and never-attained horizon because there is always a rupture in passing from the natural constitution to the positive one, from the natural constitution of society to the constitution of political society. Bonald's ideas are in line with Schmitt's constitutionalism. For counterrevolutionaries, as Schmitt would claim, human society has a historical determination, it has become a nation.[6] Not blood, but rather *nomos* makes a human group into a people, a nation.[7] As a solution to the dualistic distinction between community and society and, in opposition to universal human community, Schmitt proposed the concept of nation, which belongs to *nomos*.[8] Without the concept of nation, the unlimited human community is a revolutionary god that transcends all social and political boundaries, proclaiming the brotherhood of mankind. History shows us how this abstract community has been historically constituted in concrete places. Thus, that a people are a sociological and historical reality with statutes and a particular language that expresses its national and spiritual individuality is deduced from the fact that it is limited. Thus, Schmitt also speaks of an existing society and he does so with a nuance that he inherited partly from the German historical school and partly from counterrevolutionary philosophy.

The concrete order is already given; it is a *nomos*. A positive constitution is nothing more than an account of that order. This relationship is shown in the fact that a constitution is recognized as proper to a given community insofar as memory of the land appropriation that founded it is still alive. As soon as this memory ceases, that community is no longer valid as a positive order.[9] He speaks of a people, *Volk*, expressing a notion similar to the counterrevolutionary idea of historically determined human society. Historically determined human community in different peoples acquires a plurality of ways of being and becomes differentiated and concrete. Each town, therefore, has its own way of being and, by becoming aware of that way of being, is politically determined and gives itself a positive constitution. Thus, the State presupposes the nation in the same way that the law presupposes a particular order:

> The act of establishing a constitution as such involves not separate set of norms. Instead, it determines the entirety of the political unity in regard to its peculiar form of existence through a single instance of decision.[10]

> Every existing political unity has its value and its "right to existence" not in the rightness or usefulness of norms, but rather in its existence.[11]

> State is a certain status of a people, specifically, the status of political unity. State form is this unity's particular type of formation. The people are the subject of every conceptual definition of the State. State is a condition, the particular circumstance of a people.[12]

Schmitt does not speak of universal human society as a political subject, but rather of the concrete existence of a people organized as a nation. This existence takes on a political character when it becomes aware of its own way of being in comparison to others. The concept of society is not political, while the concept of a people is. A human group, historically determined, with a peculiar way of being is necessarily organized politically and acquires form through a constitution. Every community has the potential to be political—that is, has the ability to acquire a political *status*, which is a superior way of being. A society free of the political is a utopia. That a society is already instituted means, for Schmitt, that every society is potentially political, even more, that political reality exists in the concrete.

POSITIVE CONSTITUTION

In *Constitutional Theory*, Schmitt describes how, throughout history, different concepts of a constitution have developed. He categorized them in the following groups: Constitution in an absolute sense as unified whole,[13] constitution in a relative sense as a multitude of individual laws,[14] the positive concept of the constitution as the complete decision over the type and form of the political unity,[15] and the ideal constitution in an exemplary sense, thus named because of a certain content, which has corresponded to the constitution of bourgeois *Rechtsstaat* for some time.[16] Schmitt dedicated most of his discussion on the constitution to description and analysis of the latter kind. There, Schmitt sketches, not always explicitly, his views on the positive dimension of the constitution of a people.

In the first pages of *Constitutional Theory*, Schmitt identifies the ideal constitution with the constitution proper to the *Rechtsstaat* based on liberal principles. He ironically characterizes it as "ideal" because it is usually regarded as true or genuine compared to the other kinds, which, for not having these implied principles, are not even considered constitutions. This description of a constitution is undoubtedly ideological since every society has to organize itself and, yet, there is not just one way of doing so, exemplified by the fact that there have been a variety of constitutions throughout history. Thus, there is no such concept as an "ideal" constitution. Every constitution is such insofar as it constitutes a people. In short, an ideal constitution would fit what is understood as constitutional truth in every concrete place and historical moment,[17] yet, a constitution also belongs to a particular *nomos*, which, in considering it ideal, intends to make this *nomos* normative for every place on earth. The constitution of bourgeois *Rechtsstaat*, its *nomos*, arose from a concrete situation corresponding to the struggle of the liberal bourgeoisie against absolute monarchy in which liberal-bourgeois principles emerged victorious. From this moment on, the definition of a constitution was restricted to that which touts the principle of individual freedom and that which permits bourgeois political influence.

The distinction between constitutional and nonconstitutional states[18] can only be made with the concept of an ideal constitution in mind, that is, ideologically. This concept also implies another distinction between "constitutional constitutions" and "unconstitutional constitutions." This distinction would seem contradictory if it were not because it is easy to recognize that this adjective—nonconstitutional or constitutional—implies a political agenda—that is, for something to be regarded as a constitution or not depends on political conviction. Thus, for bourgeois liberalism, a constitution only exists if it respects private property and individual freedom. Any order that does not respect these principles is considered despotic, a dictatorship, slavery and tyranny, which, when these categories are compared to the ideal constitution, are considered all the same. However, for a Marxist, such a constitution would deserve the title of a "reactionary pseudo-constitution." For the secular state, a constitution that does not include a separation between church and state among its principles is considered unconstitutional, while a confessional state would claim the opposite. There are many examples of this and they all demonstrate that the legitimacy of an ideal constitution is not found in the constitution itself, but rather is located outside of it.[19]

Hence, since the birth of the Modern State until now, the term *constitution* has been understood as that which fits the following description: It must be written, have a system of guarantees for bourgeois freedom, and be a guarantor of the separation of powers. From here, two "organizational criteria"[20] can be deduced: First, the sphere of individual freedom should never be disturbed, unless by the force of a statute, by which statute becomes the guarantor of freedom; and second, all manifestations of state power should be measurable—that is, the control of power. With these features, the constitution becomes a system of legal norms, closed and sovereign, steadfast and politically unapproachable. The problem is that these legal elements, when realized in a particular state, need political elements in order to be made effective. This type of constitution is usually realized in parliamentary democracies, whose principles[21]—representation, publicity, and debate, combined with freedom and the separation of powers—illuminate the bourgeois *Rechtsstaat*.

After offering a sophisticated analysis of the modern constitution, Schmitt simplified his opinion on the matter until offering a single idea as truly essential to its definition, namely, all positive, and therefore modern, constitutions amount, ultimately, to a decision. At this point, it is important to remember that the very concept of constitution as a written constitution belongs to the historical and political context of the Modern State.[22] In this sense, written modern constitution is, therefore, a historical concept. To say that a constitution is essentially a decision is not immediately a decisionist position, but rather highlights the fact that the Modern State requires a decisionist concept of constitution. Without this in mind, what has been discussed about the law so far and *Constitutional Theory* could appear contradictory.

To understand the consistency of Schmitt's discourse a further step is still needed, namely, to clearly determine the moment in which the birth of the constitution takes place within the development of law. If we consider that a political situation passes through three stages—conflict, exception, political order—the constitution can be seen as a decision that opens up a path from exception to political order. The Modern State's constitution is the concrete mode of political unity's form. It is the form of the decision with which the sovereign founds political unity. The concept of positive constitution is defined by two notes and by an argument for legitimacy: "Every constitution should inherently be a political decision that unquestionably establishes the constitutional basis of state unity."[23] The meaning of all rational constitution is to provide a system of organization that allows for the formation of a political will and the institution of a government capable of governing.[24] Hence it can be said that the constitution is: "the conscious determination of the particular complete form, for which the political unity decides."[25] And also "a conscious decision, which the political unity reaches *for itself* and provides *itself* through the bearer of the constitution-making power."[26]

While constitutions may contain diverse sources of law, every constitution shares the need for a power that validates it and that, at a particular time, decides to bring it into concrete existence by being the constitution of a people. The constitution arises in a positive sense, therefore, through an act of *constitution-making power*, which does not contain abstract or general legal content, but rather the existential form of a political unity.[27] A constitution is a conscious determination of a certain political unit's concrete form. The question surrounding the constitution is, therefore, a question of constitution-making power, the political will with force or authority to make a concrete decision on all manner and form of political existence. A constitution is worth as much as the existential political will of whoever offers it. Constitutional normalization presupposes an existing will, and the question of constitution-making power is a question of who bears that power.[28] Schmitt addresses this question in a bipolar mode. When determining who has constitution-making power, it is necessary to refer to two political-formal principles, namely, the principle of identity and the principle of representation.[29] Every constitution is made up of a legal element and a political element. Norm belongs to the former—that is, constitution-making power—and formal-political principles belongs to the latter.

The legal element of a constitution is norm, which is not, as has been said, a rational construct, but rather always refers, first, to a concrete situation and, secondly, to a will. In *Constitutional Theory*, when discussing the moment in which law is made positive, Schmitt links norm, above all, to will. Any legal normalization, as well as constitutional normalization that involves the content of a constitution, presupposes a will.[30] From the "ought" itself of a norm it does not follow that this norm has to exist, that is, to be in force.[31] If this were the case, if a norm in its normativity could establish itself, it could also protect itself and would not need anyone or anything to do so. Appealing to a constitutional court, for example, would never be necessary. Theoretically, a norm can be valid in three possible ways: It can be valid on its own, valid because it is just, or valid because it is positively ordered. Practically, first it is impossible for a norm to be valid on its own since it is not possible for an "ought" to come before an "is" and because statute itself does not specify who should institute or interpret it. Second, the idea that a norm is valid because it is just assumes that justice as a value can be applied by itself. The problems that arise in this case of concrete validity—not absolute validity, since a norm is valid absolutely speaking if it is just—can be summarized in two points, namely, the just and justice are not obvious and, therefore, the recognition of justice that a norm needs in order to be valid is not assured in all societies and in all historical periods. Furthermore, justice is a later feature of a norm since a norm is just because a just man has given it, not because any quality of abstract justice actually exists. A just statute does not precede a just will such that a will must put an absolutely just norm into practice in each concrete case in which it is meant to be valid. Thus, a norm is valid according to the third possibility of validity, which will be considered in what follows, namely, a norm is valid, it becomes valid, because it is positively ordered and justice depends on the justice of the will that orders it.[32] A norm is always positive because every "ought" is born of a will: Justice is always born in a judge.

One hypothesis that seeks to eliminate the need for the will to determine a norm is that of "democratic mystique," as Schmitt would call it, which defends modern mass democracy or modern democracy based on a general Rousseaunian will. According to this mystique, justice and decision always necessarily go together because the majority has the ability to determine, as a general will, what is just, reasonable, and true. Again, the only thing that can be said in this case is that a norm is only valid because it is positively ordered and, in this light, norm is seen from concrete political and social reality. Decision is concrete because it is instated for a concrete situation that is considered a normal situation.[33] The question of the constitution does not lead to the consideration of the best constitution, but rather to its origin, a concrete will, and to its condition of possibility, a normal situation. Thus, the legitimacy of the constitution is not established from justice, but rather is established in relation to its genealogy.

A constitution is legitimate when the power and authority of the constitution-making power, on whose decision it rests, is acknowledged. The political decision reached regarding the type and form of State existence, which constitutes the substance of the constitution, is valid because the political unity whose constitution is at issue exists and because the subject of the constitution-making power can determine the type and form of this existence. The decision requires no justification via an ethical or legal norm. Instead, it makes sense in terms of political existence.[34]

The political aspect of every constitution corresponds to the constitution's guarantee that a government is capable of governing. In every constitution, the identity principle and the representation principle are united to the legal element out of necessity since the legal element does not denote a kind of government and a State requires a government. The constitution of bourgeois *Rechtsstaat* intends to be a purely legal constitution. Consequently, the State proposes itself in the constitution because it implies a set of limits and controls on political power, but says nothing about how power should be exercised. Fundamental rights and the division of powers do not at all denote a single type of government. However, in reality, governing is paramount so somehow the two above-mentioned principles must also appear, albeit under the guise of legality. However, two principles belong to the unavoidable "political element" of every constitution.

IDENTITY AND REPRESENTATION

Identity and representation are the basis for that which is politically constituted. They are principles of all constituted political form because it cannot
occur without the presence of both. And precisely because they belong to the
political element of constitution, they are existential categories. Schmitt defines them as: "opposing formative political principles. Every political unity
receives its concrete form from the realization of these principles."[35] Opposing here does not mean exclusion, but rather, in Schmitt's words they are
opposing, but complementary, "orientation points."[36] In their implementation, this complementarity can occur in different ways and to different de-
grees. If we take a people and a state as subjects through which these principles are realized within the modern political conception—that is, one in
which the subject of identity is a people and the subject of representation a
State—we can account for this complementarity through the following two
assertions: A state is not possible without a people, and a people are not
possible without a state.

No state is possible without a people. This assertion seems clear if we
consider, starting with the very concept of *nomos*, that a people exist before a
state. Thus, the existence of a people is the condition of possibility for the
existence of a state. Nevertheless, this is true only if one considers the state
as a representation in a sense that will later be discussed. If the state has
nothing to do with authentic representation, it also has nothing to do with a
people, or simply, there is no relationship because the two elements do not
exist. This is seen, for example, in Rousseau's thesis. There is no separate
state and a people, but rather a people as a state, such that he could claim that
the state is the people and there is no more sovereign. This proposition
violates one of the formal principles and it pays the price by staying locked in
abstraction.[37]

A people are also not possible without a state. This second assertion is
reciprocal of the above. As stated, a people are a condition of the state, but it
should be added that the latter is the basis for the political existence of a
people. Thanks to the state, a people gain a higher mode of existence—
political existence—that makes a group of men into a people as a political
unit.

The concept of representation is central to Schmitt's theory. It rarely
appears defined, although he often referred to it,[38] especially in *Roman Catholicism and Political Form*, in *The Crisis of Parliamentary Democracy*,
and in *Constitutional Theory*. For Schmitt, representation is mainly personification and visibility of a political unit. Representation is fundamentally characterized by presence, personality, and publicity.[39] These same descriptions
provide political life with its specific nature.[40] The characteristic activity of
any representation is mediation, which Schmitt explained through the repre-

sentation of the Catholic Church.[41] The Church represents Christ himself and takes his place in the historical present through the sacraments. This assumes a real representation to the extent that access to Christ, once he left this realm, is only possible through the Church. Similarly, he who represents the political unit is not a representative; rather, by being capable of deciding on the political unit's way of being, he is the political unit himself through his own will and not through the general will of the people.[42]

Through the three descriptions mentioned above—publicity, personality, and mediation—a clear idea of what it means to represent emerges, as well how an irreplaceable concept for responding to a qualitative reality that—although found in other areas of reality[43]—is fundamental to understanding the political realm. Regarding the first aspect, publicity, Schmitt claimed the following: "Representation can occur only in the *public* sphere."[44] Representation that unfolds in secret or that is a private matter is impossible; representation must be public, thus it is only possible in the context of a people. At this point it is necessary to distinguish between two senses of the term *representation* that, in German, are differentiated with two words: *Repräsentation* and *Vertretung*. The former corresponds to political representation and is different from the latter, which corresponds to commercial representation (*Selbstvertretung*) or committed representation (*Auftrag*). The latter belongs by its nature and origin to civil law and private contracts. Political representation, however, is not a contract because it is not an agreement between individual interests; rather, it is the public exercise of power. It is of the people and for the people, without being the people. It is not a relationship of one individual with another, or of the people with an individual. This is because the representative, as such, loses his individuality in favor of dissemination, and because individuals are not represented, but rather an entire people as a collective is represented. Only a publicly formed people can be represented, not a people that is the internally differentiated sum of voters.

Parliamentarianism purports to take a people into account in their physical or natural totality (as opposed to their existential totality) and only the sum of citizens quantified in votes can serve this purpose. This sum results in a majority that is nothing more than a product resulting from a kind of "voting commerce." But, as Schmitt noted, a set of private interests, rather than an entire people, is therein reflected. There, genuine political representation is not possible. However, the term is not given up to the extent that the terms "parliamentarianism" and "representative system" are used interchangeably.[45] In the latter phrase, representative means fair representation of the people in parliament. The question of who is then represented remains: "In this regard, all concepts and ideas are excluded that are essentially part of the spheres of the private, of private law, and of the merely economic. This includes concepts such as execution, trusteeship, and advocacy or private interests, etc."[46]

In parliamentarian democracies there is no difference between the representative and the represented because the meaning of "public" has been lost. The actions of those that make up the representative system are also private and they also act in light of interests. In the framework of parliamentary activity, an empty formality unfolds and truly important decisions are made behind the public's back. Thus, parliament may perform useful functions, but it no longer represents the political unity of a people.[47]

Representation is neither a normative phenomenon nor a procedure, but rather something with an existential nature.[48] It is public and comes with a people, both sharing in the same existential reality. After publicity, presence and visibility emerge as related attributes. A feature of being public is being seen. Publicity has nothing to do with secrecy, nor with "apocryphal acts of sovereignty." In contrast to the direction of secrecy that all power contains, power also has a counter direction toward publicity.[49] The second attribute that Schmitt mentioned related to representation is personality. A person is also the "who" that represents.[50] The representative must be a "who" because he must be able to act. There can be no true representation when the representative is a collective entity. It is a physical impossibility, because for this person to be able to represent, he would need a physical person with the ability to act.[51] In addition, by being a person, personal dignity comes into play. A people, by being represented, retains its own dignity and, with time, confers high worth to the representative figure because whoever represents a high worth cannot be deprived of it. In representation, both the representative and the represented acquire a superior dignity[52] that represents a qualitative leap, which mainly corresponds to perfection. In his subsequent political theology, this corresponds to the concept of transcendence versus immanence.[53] The third aspect corresponds to the capacity for mediation. The representative is such by virtue of his activity. A "who" becomes a representative through the elevation of a people to a political unit through a decision by which a people, absent in an active way, becomes politically present. Representation is legitimate if it is capable, if it has the power to enforce the decision of the people—that is, to establish it. Therefore, legitimacy comes by way of this function. According to Schmitt: "To represent means to make an invisible being visible and present through a publicly present one."[54] And again: "Only he who *rules* takes part in representation."[55] This capacity for mediation is characterized by the presence-absence dialectic. It is not that the people are absent or that they lack worth, but rather, because of their very way of being, although always potentially present, they must become politically present, that is, actually present.[56] A people cannot enter political life without a certain elevation of their being, without a certain unity:

> The dialectic of the concept is that the invisible is presupposed as absent and nevertheless is simultaneously made present. That is not possible with just any

type of being. Indeed, it presupposes a special type being. Something dead, something inferior or valueless, something lowly cannot be represented. It lacks the enhanced type of being that is capable of an *existence*, of rising into the public being.[57]

This dialectic consists in converting an invisible supposition into a politically visible and present element.[58] In the act of representing, the representative stands in the place of the people and, in that moment, the people become institutionally represented.[59] Whoever represents mediates between an absent people and a politically present people. The representative implements this conversion in his own person. A people cannot become a political presence in any other way. This absent-present mediation is done through a third party, in this case through political decision. Thus, a representative only truly represents if he can decide, if he can make a decision on the political existence of a people. At that time, a people become a political unit. Representation makes it possible for people to be a political unit and corresponds to constitution-making power. This is when a people glide into a political situation, a state, as Schmitt called it, which can take on different forms depending on the political unit's formation. With political representation, form emerges.[60]

The concept of form is key in Schmitt's theory. Form is visibility, presence, publicity, and permanence. The idea of form is among the hidden concepts in Schmitt's work, given that it only appears explicitly in a few places. In particular, the Church appears as a large three-part form: juridical form, aesthetic form, and a form of power. And this is so precisely because of the purity of its above-mentioned representation.[61] Sovereignty emerges as a problem of political form and decision, especially where Schmitt quotes Wolzendorf to confirm his definition of the state as the force of an order, a *form* for the life of a people. From there, Schmitt undertakes the analysis of juridical form. The latter arises because the idea of law cannot *transform itself*. To become an effective reality, the idea of law has to be formed—a transformation, and therefore an *auctoritatis interpositio,* is required.[62] Mediation emerges again. Schmitt's work is suffused with a formalization that cannot be easily captured through the previously cited cases. It can be said, in short, that form mainly corresponds to three things: On the one hand, it corresponds to a principle of unity, inasmuch as it establishes a relationship where there is separation. On the other hand, it is a principle of renewing being, inasmuch as it can be said that the more formalized a reality is, the more it "exists." From another point of view, it is a principle of intelligibility because it illuminates the understanding of reality.[63] Reference must be made to aesthetics, which does not correspond to the world of form in vain. It is possible that Schmitt's political semantics originate there. Art grasps reality through forms and not through concepts. Art manifests that there are aspects of reality that cannot be realized with concepts; something similar also occurs with certain aspects of political reality and, hence, the need for form.

With the issue of representation addressed, we are left to analyze the formal political principle of identity. What did Schmitt mean with the term *identity*? This question can be answered in just one word: the people.[64] The presence of the people is always necessary as a political sign such that representation can take place, making authentic government possible. This point deals with a problem that any political philosophy must solve: the problem of how to secure the people's will, how to "form it" in some way so that it can be represented. Today we would speak of the problem of how to build consensus. In Schmitt's wording, the problem revolves around how to secure a "substantial homogeneity" of the people (*substanzielles Gleichartig-keit*)[65] or how to perceive their way of being (*Artgleichheit*).[66] Every people has a peculiar way of being that is unique to them and that corresponds to the concrete form of its unity in many,[67] a substantial homogeneity with which every representative must be familiar.

It is thus first of all necessary to analyze the concept of a people. It becomes immediately clear that it is such a broad concept that it can only be limited and defined negatively. A people are primarily that which is not authority or state magistracy and is made up of those who, in principle, are not organized, those who do not exercise organic functions of authority, and those who do not govern. If at some point they take on some governing activity, it is merely by proxy—that is, as a function of an authority. Moreover, as Schmitt would say, when one or more parts of a people are organized, they stop being a people. In this sense it is a "negative" concept and is defined by that which it is not. And yet, Schmitt claimed that a people are before and above (based on importance) any positive constitution.[68] The fact that a people can only be defined negatively is not trivial and has nothing to do with the limits of language, but rather is key to the essence of its being.

> It would not only generally involve something sociologically essential, if one defined the people negatively in such a manner (for example the audience in a theater as the part of those present who do not perform), but this distinctive negativity also does not permit itself to be mistaken for the scholarly treatment of political theories. In a special meaning of the word, the people are everyone who is *not* honored and distinguished, everyone *not* privileged, everyone prominent not because of property, social position, or education.[69]

Thus, using the same example that Schmitt provided, during the French Revolution, the bourgeoisie was a people in contrast to the aristocracy, but as soon as the bourgeoisie became the state class, the proletariat emerged as a people and, therefore, became the bearer of a negative definition. The content of what a people might mean continuously changes, however; even if it is defined "negatively," a people is a condition of the public and therein lies its importance. If we look for a form of positivity in it, an actor, it appears as pure negativity. If we consider it as public, it is the public realm: "Only the present, truly assembled people are the people and produces the public."[70] Representation elevates political existence to a higher existence than that of pure negativity.[71]

Given this "negative" condition, how is it possible to form the will of a people? How is it possible to consolidate a certain unity to define its identity? How is consensus reached? Schmitt would say that power produces consensus and consensus produces power.[72] Beneath this distinction, we find a deep-rooted relationship between political power and a people's consent or approval (*Bereitwilligkeit*) that exists in every political form.[73] Schmitt argued that, in this relationship, the most important thing is to realize that consensus is formed through power,[74] which has its own methods, including education and school,[75] the press, radio, and television.[76]

According to Schmitt, in what relates to the formation of the people's will, the biggest error in political history[77] has been to understand universal suffrage in its two variants—both pure democracy and parliamentarianism—as the only expression of the will of the people.[78] According to democratic doctrine, the general will is obtained through a voting system that is individual and secret; according to parliamentarism, popular opinion is proportionally represented. Schmitt thought that both cases contain the same deficiency, namely, the will of the people is formed through nonpublic means[79] and, in addition, it becomes abstract because it involves transferring a general will, not a will for each case.[80] A secret and individual choice transforms a democratic citizen into a private, liberal man.[81] The link between the people and the outcome of the vote is broken at the decisive moment. The people do not vote and choose as a people, but rather as the sum of private individuals,[82] and this privacy results in the greatest paradox, namely:

> Individual voting leads disinterested or politically irresponsible parties to decide on political matters. It can even be said that, with the current method of voting, the more a group tries to ignore decision and political responsibility, the more political influence it has.[83]

An additional problem develops in pure democracy because its concept of a general will is based on a principle that cannot actually be verified, namely, the existence of a unitary, comprehensive, homogeneous, indivisible people.[84] Given this, it is assumed that all members of a people essentially want the same thing. If, in the voting process, a winning majority and a defeated minority emerge, then the majority is thought to possess the truth[85] and the minority is forced to undergo the "religious act" of identifying its will with the majority. This attitude of giving away a will can only be the result of a democratic education in which the people must be instructed.[86] It is only possible to establish a democracy among a people that thinks democratically.[87]

Parliamentarianism confronts a different problem. Here, an identification of wills is not required; rather, proportional representation is organized. The difficulty then becomes that a split will cannot govern. We must keep in mind that this division stems from the practical impossibility of democracy:

> The people in its entirety must decide, as was originally the case when all members of the community could assemble themselves under the village tree. But for practical reasons it is impossible today for everyone to come together at the same time in one place; it is also impossible to ask everyone about every detail.[88]

Now, this is not a sufficient reason to justify parliamentarianism, because if it is necessary for technical reasons that a group of people decides for the people, it is not clear why one person could not do so. Liberal ideology, as Schmitt described it, also has its own faith with dogmas to account for its way of operating: the free competition of opinions as a means to reach truth and, therefore, the belief in a preestablished harmony—that is, in the idea that truth can be found this way.[89]

Both democracy and parliamentarianism have an overreaching identity principle that is made absolute. It attempts an immediacy of the government of the people that is impossible, because one cannot govern without somehow getting organized and, when there is government and therefore organization, there is also representation and, consequently, mediation.[90] Schmitt, however, did not stop at criticism, but rather reflected on the proper way to form the will of the people. A people belongs to the public sphere, outside of which it is invisible. A people is public and produces the public realm with its presence.[91] The crucial question, then, is how a united people can adopt a concrete decision all together in its way of existing politically. Schmitt offered three objections to the possibility that the people decide in that way. First, if a people acted as a constitution-making power they would decide on things that they cannot decide on since they would have to decide on organizational matters and political form without being organized[92]; second, it would lose its status as a people because its essence is not representation[93]; third, a plurality of subjects of a constitution-making power would annul the political unit. However, a people in its "not formed state" has certain capacities that come from being a people, which is only expressed when the people are gathered.[94] Thus, there is only one way for the people to participate in representation: acclamation or protest.[95] The will of the people that corresponds to its essence is manifested by the following:

> It is part of the directness of this people's will that it can be expressed independently of every prescribed procedure and every prescribed process.[96]

The natural form of the direct expression of a people's will is the assembled multitude's declaration of their consent or their disapproval, the *acclamation*.[97]

The will of the people can be expressed just as well and perhaps better through acclamation, through something taken for granted, an obvious and unchallenged presence, than through the statistical apparatus that has been constructed with such meticulousness in the last fifty years. The stronger the power of democratic feeling, the more certain is the awareness that democracy is something other than a registration system for secret ballots. Compared to democracy that is direct, not only in the technical sense but also in a vital sense, parliament appears an artificial machinery produced by liberal reasoning, while dictatorial and Caesaristic methods not only can produce the acclamation of the people but can also be direct expressions of democratic substance and power.[98]

Acclamation, an "amen" of the people, is the most appropriate, even the most democratic, manifestation of the will of the people to show their agreement, and silence to show their disagreement.[99] Acclamation makes the "immediacy of mediation" possible. The moment of acclamation is sacramental in the political sphere. Not surprisingly, Schmitt was obsessed with Max Weber's concept of charismatic legitimacy.[100] The legitimate representative is the one who realizes his mediation function with the most "purity" because he realizes it in virtue of his own personality. Just as the notion of charisma introduced grace and the supernatural into the religious sphere, with this notion of "purity," Schmitt introduced magic, enchantment, the imperceptible, the purely qualitative and nonquantifiable.

The possible action of the people is always the same: agree with or reject something that is proposed.[101] Discussion is never involved. It is not possible to gather the people "under a linden tree" to discuss and it is not clear that it would even be useful. Acclamation is, for Schmitt, the expression of the true will of the people that, at that moment, is a real entity. The actual manifestation of a will is the expression of something sacred:

The people can only say yes or no to a single question posed to the vote, exactly formulated. If this is not the case, then every result coming from millions of individual votes could be interpreted in a very multifarious way.[102]

Liberal parliamentarianism unintentionally holds a similar idea. The concrete expression of the will that serves for universality is, in parliamentarianism, the vote. Thus, liberal parliamentarianism asserts that the vote and ballot boxes are sacred because an interior will is deposited in a ballot box, which will bring about the political constitution of the people. In addition, ultimately parliamentary forms consist of nothing more than approving or rejecting something that is proposed.[103] In this case, such approval and rejection suffer from the very public nature of the political. Just as there is no state without a people, there are no people without acclamation,[104] which does not mean it has to be a continuous phenomenon:

> In times of peaceful order, these types of expression are rare and unnecessary. That no special will is perceivably expressed simply signifies the enduring consent to the existing constitution. In critical times, the no that directs itself against an existing constitution can be clear and decisive only as negation, while the positive will is not as secure.[105]

As stated, the will of the people always becomes part of the constitution-making power, but not as the subject of a specific decision; rather, it comes about as a willingness to assent to or the rejection of a proposal or decision. However, it is important that this will be public. Only in this case are the people prior and superior to any organization and, therefore, can become part of the constitution of a state. A people are an existential reality; the public sphere is not. Both a group of people and representatives acquire a qualification as public when they relate with the people as a whole, that is, when dealing with the public sphere and not private interests or those of particular sectors. A people immediately manifest itself and the content of said manifestation is consensus. Mediation does not come from the people, but rather from representation and goes from top to bottom.[106] The representative makes explicit that which the people approved in acclamation.[107]

EXCEPTION

Within the framework of the legal order, where everything is norm and regulation, historical reality can unexpectedly barge in showing that, alongside absolute predictability, there are legal gaps. Statute cannot regulate everything. As Schmitt notes in *Constitutional Theory*:

> Such "gaps" are always possible, and an essential part of a constitutional conflict is that one can successfully present claims based on unforeseen circumstances. The uselessness of all normative types of discourse on the "sovereignty of the constitution" reveals itself here especially clearly.[108]

Exception exists. This reality gives way to the consideration of a new area of nature that is different from that of law, namely, the political sphere. In the legal tradition, the exceptional case appears as a limiting case for the law and only since the beginning of the twentieth century have there been attempts to erase the exceptional case from legal framework to avoid the constitutional vacuum that it suggests. A state of exception, beyond the case of exception, refers to a state in which not just a statute is suspended, but rather an entire legal order. In Roman law this was called *iustum* and the declaration of an *iustum* implied the suspension of ordinary law.[109] In this state, consuls could take necessary measures to resolve the exceptional situation in which the republic found itself. It was not an unconstitutional situation in itself.[110] In these cases, in situations that threatened the political community, civil government ceded power to the army. Hence Cicero's assertion: "*Silent leges inter arma*," as expressed in the words of d'Ors:

> Laws become silent where the state is powerless against the threat to the individual; laws are silent before a threat against the state: Legitimate defense in both cases: public here and private there. In both cases, the state is in crisis and its laws are inhibited before a natural law founded on self-preservation. Laws are silent because the validity of a capable state organization is absent.[111]

Schmitt referred to this same concept when speaking of the exception.[112] Schmitt devoted little space to defining it,[113] but dedicated considerable space to showing it, that is, to pointing out—starting with the classical state to nineteenth-century police and military, up to the state of financial and economic exception—how the exception is always present in history, how it is a historical constant that acquires different juridical and political forms.[114]

The first question to be answered is, whether the isolated exceptional case is conceived as an event that belongs to the judicial framework alone, or whether it can be extended to a broader context that goes beyond the framework of the law and then goes on to constitute a state of exception. The exceptional case is, in a specific sense, a limiting concept of the juridical— that is, conceptually, it is found within the juridical framework insofar as it defines the juridical by denial of what the exception signifies.

Within the framework of the legal order, the case of exception is defined negatively as that which is not codified in the existing legal order and "cannot be circumscribed factually and made to conform to a preformed law."[115] But it can also be expressed positively, namely the case of exception corresponds to that which, in some way, forces a definition of the legal order. It belongs to the political order in a positive sense and is characterized by its lack of normalization and by interrupting norm. It is a case to which existing positive norms cannot be applied. The case of exception does not belong to a special kind of law,[116] as perhaps could be interpreted, but rather, it does not come under norm at all. Nor is it the causal denial of a norm, but rather the interruption of norm in certain circumstances. Precisely because it is not a denial of norm, a case of exception can, if the situation requires it, reinstate norm. To account for the exceptional situation, an analogy with the case of exception is useful. What happens in the state of exception is so little predictable and so anomalous that legal order loses its long-standing character and becomes a measure that must be imposed again if it is to be maintained or changed. Statute belongs to the realm of normality, while measure belongs to the realm of exception. Not just any disorder, by virtue of being so, is a situation of exception, which supposes a disorder that requires an unfettered faculty for its restoration—that is, a disorder capable of interrupting the constitutive legal order.[117] The state of exception is the absence of a legal order (*Rechtsordnung*), a suspension of positive law, but it is not the exclusion of all order (*Ordnung*). Law is suspended, but the state remains. The exception causes a situation that is not anarchy or chaos, but rather a state in which juridical norms are not effective, in which a juridical vacuum exists. In this state of things the state suspends law.

The next question that arises in the context of legal order in reference to exception pertains to the question of jurisdiction—that is, the question of who has the powers that are not constitutionally regulated, who is responsible when the legal order no longer solves the problem of competency. At this point, the figure of the sovereign appears. The sovereign is he who decides on exception and who, with his decision, restores normality.[118] To end this situation, another one must be created in which norms are valid—that is, are made effective. A normal situation has to be created in which the legal order makes sense again. Normality and legal order are correlated in the constitution of a people. When a gap appears between the two—that is, when the legal order ceases to be real, a state of exception arises. Thus, an exceptional situation does not always occur because of a political conflict; it can be caused by a change in the configuration of the social order, because the concept of normality has changed. This gap is mediated or resolved by a sovereign decision. The exceptional situation is exceptional because of its contrast with normality. It is defined by the normality of which it is an exception and it is only an exception because it does not last, eventually giving way to a normal situation. If an exception becomes normal it no longer makes sense as such. Similarly, norm only arises by reference to a case of exception. This is so much so that a statute arises only in reference to the perception of some abnormal conduct and, until then, the issue of normality is not raised regarding that particular conduct.

Schmitt's effort in this regard centers on keeping both correlative concepts alive, normality and exception, since, by maintaining both concepts, neither of them loses their meaning. *Rechtsstaat* has tended to pursue its regulation with the specific intention of eliminating exception. Its attempt is reduced to precisely enumerating the cases in which the law might suspend itself.[119] Schmitt ironically details how this is not possible, asking where law finds the strength to determine a case of exception. It is not possible because the exceptional case always lacks definition and cannot be included under a general case. It can only be confirmed and, once it appears, it can only be negatively defined. It is not possible to clearly delineate when an exceptional case exists, nor is it possible to pinpoint what should be done when it occurs.[120]

Three characteristics of the exceptional situation follow from this negative definition: First, it is a state of extreme necessity (*Notfall*); second, it threatens political unity and, therefore, it is a serious case (*Ernstfall*); and third, it is unique. The fact that Schmitt considered the situation of exception as *Notfall* highlights the importance that legal order has in his political and juridical theory. Every society needs institutions and normalizations that give the relations that take place within it stability and longevity. If the legal order is compromised, society itself is endangered because chaos and, in extreme cases, war follows. Thus, Schmitt also called the exceptional situation *Ernstfall*, which corresponds to the "serious case," a decisive case in which the life of a people is endangered. In traditional political practice, the ordinary civil government ceded power to the army during situations that threatened the political community. Where statutes have lost their power, power must be exercised by force. But war is, as we shall see, the extreme case *par excellence*, the case of maximum danger. In that case, the state continues to exist as long as it has power, that is, the ability to decide in the case of exception, thus demonstrating its competence. While disorder only affects the legal order, the state continues to exist, but when disorder destroys the political unit, the state ceases to exist. This is not foreseeable, that is, the exception can only be explained by itself, and, in this sense, it is unique. It is the emergence of something in an ordered space that incites total change of that order. Thus, Schmitt made an analogy between exception and the concept of a miracle, arguing that what happens in the course of natural laws when a miracle takes place also occurs in the legal order with exception: "The exception in jurisprudence is analogous to the miracle in theology."[121]

Given this kind of event, legalistic rationalism is useless. It is proof that its rationality is only one part of a more comprehensive rationality that corresponds to a non-legal, supra-legal order, which it cannot account for. Schmitt expresses this in *Theodor Däublers "Nordlicht"* saying: "Men also have full use of reason with their sensible organizations until a case that only depends on itself arises."[122] Such a case cannot be organized, cannot be predicted, and is not accessible to human reason or human power. However, as previously indicated and as Schmitt himself suggested, we must step outside the legal order to understand what exception means.[123] In this case, legal thought is blind and must be left in the hands of philosophy.[124] Just as a certain kind of metaphysics underlies the rationalist theory of *Rechtsstaat*, inherited from naturalist scientific thinking that intended to banish exception from the human spirit, another kind of metaphysics also underlies exception. It is a conception of open reality—that is, it does not have its rationale in itself because it is not even given as a whole. The world and its history do not have an immanent rationale. Even in Hegelian metaphysics, history is open. There is a tension between the "being" and the meaning of events that does not allow for a full understanding of contingent reality in absolute terms. This requires a conception of reality that contains exception, improvisation—that is, that can give unity to historical events and that can account for the unique and the universal without having to establish a closed system. Enlightenment conceptions of the philosophy of history have failed on this point. By being rationalists they have tried to account for contingent reality with a closed, absolute approach, for which they directed their research to the discovery of general laws, completely forgetting the exceptional. Philosophy and, ultimately, theology, are responsible for accounting for the exception. Just one paragraph appears in Schmitt's work commenting on this issue and, though brief, it clearly defines his position:

> Precisely a philosophy of concrete life must not withdraw from the exception and the extreme case, but must be interested in it to the highest degree. The exception can be more important to it than the rule, not because of a romantic irony for the paradox, but because the seriousness of an insight goes deeper than the clear generalizations inferred from what ordinarily repeats itself. The exception is more interesting than the rule. The rule proves nothing; the exception proves everything: It confirms not only the rule but also its existence, which derives only from the exception. In the exception the power of real life breaks through the crust of a mechanism that has become torpid by repetition. [125]

And he confirms this text with the words of a "Protestant theologian," as he called Kierkegaard, drawn from a few paragraphs of the book *Repetition*. [126] These texts contain pointed and concealed implications that appear throughout Schmitt's work and can be summarized in the following points: (a) Exception and repetition are two irreducible, as well as interdependent, elements of historical events—that is, reality in time. Nothing would be known of exception if it were not for repetition, and there would be no rules to constitute repetition if it were not for exception. In chaos or a state of uncertainty there are neither rules nor exceptions. They cannot be ignored when configuring the law or politics because both are constant, real elements of historical events and to exclude them would distort reality. (b) If we make a distinction between nature and spirit to seek a better understanding of the reality of things, then it can be said that the natural realm is the realm of repetition, while in the spiritual realm, properly speaking, repetition does not exist. In the plant and animal kingdoms, life is cyclical, it is pure repetition, and novelty is foreign to each cycle. According to pagan philosophical conceptions, the spirit is merely a vital principle and human life also has a cyclical explanation. However, for a "philosophy of concrete life," exception opens a path between repetitions and gives meaning to novelty. What is meant by saying that a philosophy of concrete life cannot ignore exception? We could respond with Kierkegaard in affirming that, for men, it cannot, because in reality no two situations are alike. A human being's next second will never be the same as the previous one because, even when circumstances are the same, the reality of human beings has changed, including their experience and learning. Situations that repeat themselves in history are not exactly the same either. Human life has primarily to do with exception. And if this is so, history also has primarily to do with exception. Human lives and historical lives are growth, not progress according to a calculable law. Any norm established for human life or history can only represent a probable tendency toward change: Probable because new situations that require new attitudes and new decisions always arise. Still, uniqueness here is not arbitrary; the concept of exception is not at odds with order.[127] In the concept of order, exception is included insofar as order is open and dynamic. And in the case of legal order, the fact that there are exceptions is not a legal "disorder," but rather a limit thereof. As opposed to a concept of a non-geometric, dynamic, and open order, the general laws of natural science have attempted to standardize and neutralize human life's space and time. The case of exception comes to point out that homogenization is impossible. The order of life is not completely controllable and cannot be fully regulated. It is an order that can be expressed in statutes, but only statutes that are made in reference to exceptions. (c) To say that exception is characteristic of the human spirit, as opposed to the natural realm (in the sense used above), is analogous to saying that the spiritual realm is the place of freedom. The sphere of freedom is not mechanical, it cannot be determined, but rather leaves room for action and decision. (d) The concept of exception involves non-cyclical history. Repetition has pagan connotations, as discussed in the previous chapter, while exception has Christian ones, as Kierkegaard himself indicated.[128] If the philosophy of history must take the notion of exception into account, it necessarily becomes a theology of history. Precisely because history's rationality is circumstantial, changing, and unforeseen, philosophy, which deals primarily with the universal, cannot offer it, but theology can. On this point, the Christian concept of providence is key. Providentialism leaves room for contingency without losing its foundation. Philosophy, however, always tries to free itself of contingency and tends to generalize, to make absolute and universal. The rationality of history cannot be found within itself. In this context, the exception is not arbitrary in the same way that providence is not irrational, but rather supra-rational. (e) If historical reality is as described, knowledge of it cannot advance by just appealing to the general, but rather by paying attention to the particular in borderline cases. Therefore, Schmitt's thought tends to be a thought of "the unique." (f) Exception has to come before norm, precisely because it is grounded in itself. Exception reveals the origin and sets the tone for the original and for that which lacks a rationale.

Chapter Five

The Concept of the Political

A real political situation is posed when there is a conflict within the framework of law. And for a legal order, conflict is the exception, whether it is an exception to a single statute or an exception to an entire legal order. In the first case, political decision intervenes to give a definitive solution to a particular conflict or to reform a statute; in the second case, it intervenes to create a new order, because no society can live in a state of disarray. Therefore, the sphere of law depends on the political sphere for its definitive realization. At the limit of the juridical sphere there is an area of free action, the exceptional situation, which enables those who have power to apply all effective measures necessary to end a certain situation or create a new one. It corresponds to the realm of the political.

Schmitt approached the political sphere from the legal one. There is a close relationship between international law and the strictly political sphere,[1] as both focus on the relationships between different, organized human communities. However, politics solves the problem facing international law, namely, the difficulty in instituting world peace. This problem can be primarily broken down into two issues: First, there is no uniformity in the various legal orders corresponding to different political units, and, secondly, there is no such thing as an impartial judge who can mediate in the event that a conflict breaks out between them. Conflict erupts precisely because international law is incapable of resolving these issues.

There are, therefore, three key elements for understanding politics: conflict, exception, and sovereign decision, which are all reflected in Schmitt's writings in a masterful formulation that contains the political moment par excellence. This does not appear in the book *The Concept of the Political*, as might be expected, but rather, in *Political Theology*, and is stated as follows: "Sovereign is he who decides on the exception."[2] In the last period of his life,

Schmitt repeated another phrase: "Sovereign is he who controls the waves in space."[3] The latter is a particular case of the previous statement, which takes place in the modern State of the nineteenth and twentieth centuries. The change in terms is due to a change in the configuration of *nomos* and to a corresponding change in the concept of exception. In an undifferentiated space, without resistance, the exception becomes normal because there is no *nomos* and political power can be exercised continuously and without limits.

THE POLITICAL

In Schmitt's discursive logic, there is a close relationship between exception and political situation. Exception occurs when a disagreement occurs in a normal relationship, where the friend-enemy dialectic unfolds. Conversely, the friend-enemy dialectic produces the exception. If exception and conflict understand each other, it is reasonable for Schmitt to define the political situation as the determination of a friend-enemy relationship. The concept of the political that, five years later, Schmitt described in *The Concept of the Political* is prefigured in *Political Theology*. In *The Concept of the Political*, he characterized the political situation as one that reveals a conflict in the form of a relationship between friends and enemies—that is, a situation that calls political unity into question. For the law, that conflict is exceptional insofar as its validity is at stake and it calls for a political, not juridical, decision.

   The Concept of the Political is perhaps Schmitt's most controversial book for many different reasons. It is an essay with a long history.[4] Looking at the matter in the most superficial light, it is no doubt difficult to permit a conceptualization of politics centered on conflict to enter a "civilized" world.[5] Both a too general and a too analytical study of this concept of politics can be misleading. The former stops at general descriptions without clarifying them according to the indications that Schmitt himself gave elsewhere. The second intends to dive in to an analysis that it ends up being a theory of the theory that not even Schmitt could recognize.[6] However, this text does not intend to offer a theoretical analysis, but rather a practical one that conceptualizes political reality in a simple manner and in a way that is useful for juristic practice. Now, although this intention is practical, it is addressed theoretically insofar as it is formal, despite Schmitt's resistance to making a general theory.

   Schmitt's writing is always inspired by concrete history. In *The Concept of the Political*, Schmitt was intensely surrounded by a historical-political concrete fact in the form of post–World War I and the novelty of the regime set in place by the Weimar constitution. However, his conceptualization of politics is not limited to a historical moment and, therefore, is not a concept of the political for particular circumstances, but rather is formal and, hence, intends to be valid for any historical moment and for any circumstances. Through his study, Schmitt tried to find a criterion for recognizing a political situation in concrete reality. He posed the problem of recognizing "the political"[7] as it actually occurs in reality, leaving aside other issues related to the "ought" ("normative" questions) that generally appear in any political theory, such as the question of the ends that political activity should pursue, how to carry them out, and so on. In short, rather than developing a general political theory, Schmitt wanted to know what "the political" is or, more specifically, where and when a specifically political situation occurs.

The Concept of the Political was first drafted in 1927, but Schmitt repeated its main theses until the end of his days, as can be seen in the preface to the latest edition.[8] All of his writing answers the following question from different angles and considering many aspects:

> Let us assume that in the realm of morality the final distinctions are between good and evil, in aesthetics beautiful and ugly, in economics profitable and unprofitable. The question then is whether there is also a special distinction which can serve as a simple criterion of the political and of what it consists. The nature of such a political distinction is surely different from that of those others. It is independent of them and as such can speak clearly for itself.[9]

Such a criterion does exist and it amounts to the distinction between friend and enemy. Conceptually grasping the phenomenon of "the political" is not easy and theorists from every age have recognized this. It is therefore important to confirm whether or not Schmitt's text on the political explains a concept of the political that is universally valid.

A concept is explained by discerning the characteristics that properly belong to it, which are what distinguishes the essence of that particular concept. Through them, an essential definition of an object can be reached, in this case, of a political situation. From these general assumptions, it can be said that Schmitt tried to define a political situation through one of these characteristics that he judged as particularly appropriate, which he called the political criterion.[10] It does not explain the genus but the "specific difference," "the great sign of differentiation." The friend-enemy distinction is an essential feature because it cannot be reduced to any other distinction, nor can it be explained by any more fundamental distinction. This definitional mode corresponds to the proper character of political reality, which is a dynamic and changing reality. A static reality cannot be cognitively approached in the same way as a dynamic, and therefore historical, reality. The substance of the political changes according to historical circumstances in such a way that generalizations cannot be made. There is no guarantee that the object of politics or its activity will remain the same in the future.[11] It is difficult to substantially define the political such that it is universally valid and, consequently, completely detached from historical circumstances.

Schmitt's fundamental insight is found in the discovery of an unchanging relationship that he relies on for definition.[12] He realized that any societal activity represents a dynamic way of relating. Within this relational context, the political is a specific relationship that occurs in society and that is irreducible to other relationships, namely, friendship-enmity—that is, an extremely intense union or separation between human groups.[13] The definition of the political in one criterion tries to circumvent the difficulties involved in any attempt to define the political, which are as follows:[14] First, the object of the political changes with historical circumstances. Second, there are parasitic political classes that can obscure the essence of political phenomena. This happens especially when private interests are mixed in with political decisions, where the political is hidden in a set of traps, tactics, skills, intrigues, and manipulations.[15] Third, an inheritance of negative definitions weighs down its characterization. The political has often been defined as that which is not economics, that which is not moral, that which is not law. These contrasts allow us to indicate some of the political sphere's characteristics, but not its specific meaning. Fourth, another difficulty is found in the concealment of the political in the state's juridical and practical-technical definitions, and, fifth, in the marriage between the political and the State that has existed since Bodin's time, as theory and practice have recognized, these terms have come to be virtually interchangeable concepts.[16] In the seventeenth century, with the birth of the Modern State, the following equation was formed: State is equal to politics facing society. In this formula, the State is independent of society and, if the State recognizes society, it is as a rival to exert its power over society. In this dialectic, against everything concerning the State-political, a few elements stand out, including religion, culture, law, economics, and science, as politically neutral. Today the State still implies the "status" of an organized people in a defined territory—that is, State is understood as the modern *Rechtsstaat*. However, this political configuration is coming to an end; the State model is in decline. In breaking down, this configuration gives way to an intermediate situation between form and formlessness, between war and peace, that requires a new response.[17] Precisely because it no longer makes sense to continue to plan the future with reference to the State, a definition of the political that continues to include, or that presupposes in its terms the State concept, is no longer accurate.

In any case, we cannot forget that Schmitt lived and wrote at a time when the idea of the State was alive and was still the quintessential political form, as it still is in the West. This inevitably affects the way political reality is viewed. Schmitt's concept of the political tries to go beyond it.[18] The State is nothing but a political form born in a particular historical moment as an expression of political unity that will end with changing historical circumstances.

With Schmitt's access to the political justified, it is necessary to describe it. As noted, Schmitt proposed a political criterion; he did not intend to organize a system. In his opinion, the systems age has passed and we cannot return to old ways of explaining reality. Nor does the opposite position, an approach to political reality through aphorisms, seem compelling. The hopelessness of both paths led Schmitt to a third one, namely establishing a maximally explanatory criterion of the political that can be verified for each specific political situation and explain it. This political criterion is made explicit by a number of corollaries and is always open such that the criterion of the political is enriched over time through them. In terms of this approach, Schmitt was interested in its validity and that it be explanatory. That is, he hoped the approach would be useful for understanding the political in every political situation. If what is proper to the political is common to all of these situations, then the criterion is valid. In addition, if this approach is presented as the only possible explanation for understanding what is common to all these situations and for which they can qualify as political, then it is necessary. Schmitt himself used in some of his works this criterion as an explanatory key for political situations, for example, in *The Nomos of the Earth*. Therefore, the political criterion is valid if it is proven that in any political situation there is a group of friends and enemies. Thus Schmitt gave two examples that validate this approach, the first of which is proof that in every political situation said grouping exists and that all political concepts have a controversial sense.[19] By this he meant that these concepts are necessarily linked to a concrete situation whose radical characterization is a grouping into friends and enemies. If such a distinction did not exist in reality, the concepts related to it would be abstractions (*"gespenstischen Abstraktionen"*). Examples of controversial concepts include the following terms: state, republic, society, class, sovereignty, *Rechtsstaat*, absolutism, dictatorship, plan, neutral or total state, discussion, and so on. Proof that all of these concepts are political is found in the fact that, when speaking of them, everyone tends to ask, "What is understood for . . . ?" or "What is meant by . . . ?" It is necessary to specifically know—that is, in this concrete situation— which reality is referred to, what it sustains, what it denies, why they fight.[20] What is meant by these terms is unknown until they are related to or compared with a particular political situation.[21] In addition, this grouping is significant in what refers to the terms *political* and *apolitical*. Enemies are often characterized with the adjective *political* thereby indicating their lack of objectivity and moral, scientific, aesthetic, or economic purity, and so on, for their commitment to values and interests. In contrast, at other times, *apolitical* has been considered a pejorative, typical of those who intend to stay outside of society. The meaning of the adjective varies with the situation. Schmitt found another example of a controversial term in the definition of *republic*. For Machiavelli, republics are states that are not monarchies, while, for Richard Thoma, they are states that are not based on privileges. In both cases the term *republic* opposes another, but differs from each other.[22] Lastly, Schmitt discussed a final example in relation to the political nature of the controversial use of the word *tribute*. The socialists of the Second International used this word to refer to the rent that a tenant must pay the owner of the house where he lives, making it a weapon in the class struggle. However, they did not want the payments that France imposed on Germany to be called tributes and preferred the term *reparations*; although the latter term can be seen as more pejorative than the former, *reparations* was preferred to *tribute* because *tribute* was controversial at the time. Its use could equate Germans and proletarians, a comparison they wholly rejected.

Another sign that this grouping is always present in politically relevant situations is that, even when the idea of enemy is lost or, at least, eliminated from vocabulary, new meanings appear. This, for example, happens in a pluralistic party system, which aims to eliminate the concept of enemy from the political framework. However, given that every party takes a political position, it is unclear that this system can uphold the neutrality of enmity. The struggle of interests between the parties reveals the friend-enemy distinction, though very poorly, as "the scramble for office and the politics of patronage."[23] In these cases, internal politics expands and civil war becomes a potential risk.

The political can only be understood with specifically political categories. The fundamental political category is the friend-enemy discrimination. Just as there are fundamental distinctions in other areas of human activity from which we can deduce criterion for guiding action, there is also a distinction that characterizes human action itself.[24] Thus, just as morality has to do with good and evil, or aesthetics involves the beautiful and the ugly, or economics involves utility and harm, the political involves friendship and enmity. The friend-enemy relationship is a criterion that is independent of others and it characterizes action by pointing to a quality that is different from what the other distinctions allude to.[25] Schmitt did not denominate a substance, but rather he put an adjective to a substance,[26] thus why Schmitt did not use the term "politics," *Politik*, but rather the adjective noun "the political," *das Politische*. He did not speak of politics, but rather of the political.

> Thereby the inherently objective nature and autonomy of the political becomes evident by virtue of its being able to treat, distinguish, and comprehend the friend-enemy antithesis independently of other antitheses.[27]

It is a specific criterion—that is, a specific characteristic defines it—as Strauss saw in the annotations he made on Schmitt's work.[28] This point has

been one of the most controversial among Schmitt scholars, generally leading to one of several possible conclusions, including that this characterization
of the political lacks content and only points toward nihilism,[29] that it is to be
taken in a metaphorical sense, that the ultimate way out for this characterization is total politicization or totalitarianism,[30] or that it leads to a militaristic
conception of politics. However, from my point of view, all of these possible
conclusions distort the true meaning of what, for Schmitt, the political
means.[31]

To access the meaning of the friend-enemy distinction, it should be noted
that the above criterion is not autonomous in the sense that friendship or
enmity are possible without "substance"—that is, without reason. It does not
involve a "purely" existential enmity void of essence, but rather is an enmity
whose substance is not always the same, that varies with circumstance. It
should not be inferred from this, however, that for each concrete case there is
no content for enmity.[32] Schmitt did, in fact, consider this point in the speech
"The Age of Neutralizations and Depoliticizations."[33] A political situation
gathers strength from the various areas in which human life unfolds. Every
age finds the core of its human existence in a different "spiritual" sphere
from which other realities are interpreted. At one time, it was theology, after
metaphysics, morality, and so on; in the twentieth century, this "center of
gravity" corresponds to the economy. It is just in these "centers of interest"
that the conflict that determines the political situation arises.

> Every religious, moral, economic, ethical, or other antithesis transforms into a
> political one if it is sufficiently strong to group human beings effectively
> according to friend an enemy.[34]

A political situation is characterized by a concrete standoff—that is, by a
substance—which may be religious, national (ethical or cultural), economic,
etc.[35] A motive is necessary for the situation to occur, but what is properly
political about the situation, that is, that for which it may be considered
political, is found in the confrontation, the specific grouping of men into
friends and enemies.[36] The situation becomes political precisely because of
this relationship's configuration such that once a part of life has been politicized, all that matters is defining a way of being with reference to the friend-
enemy discrimination and, in so doing, losing sight of what caused the conflict.

It is important to keep in mind, when facing a political situation, that not
all areas of life are equal; some are more profound than others, depending on
whether they more or less refer directly to the core of human existence.
Grouping into friends and enemies is unusually intense in the profounder
areas. This is the case, for example, with religious conflicts, which are more
dangerous than in any other area. When religion is principal, by its very

essence, it is radically so if it enters the political sphere.[37] If conflict were always raised in this area, religion would become politics, which according to Schmitt, would be a monstrous monopoly.[38] When Schmitt spoke, in "The Age of Neutralizations and Depoliticizations," of the neutralization and de-politicization of life, he implicitly referred to this point. If all these areas were equal, the neutralization process would cease to be meaningful. The theology-metaphysics-moral-economy sequence as a progressive series of neutralization implies that theology is more radical, more fundamental than metaphysics and so on. Describing something as more radical denotes that a position taken on any issue in that area is not indifferent, but rather extremely meaningful to human existence and intensely affects other areas of life; therein, there is no middle ground when determining any question between yes and no. Political conflict is, therefore, harsher in this area than in others. For our eminently economic age, a very superficial era, political conflict tends to be purely economic and, if economic disputes can be fought in a purely mathematical way, then society itself becomes depoliticized.

One possible interpretation of this thesis is to consider it as a defense of the "total politicization" of society.[39] If everything is potentially political, then the social is commensurate with the political. However, this involves very strained reasoning that must be put into context. The politicization of any area of human life is possible because a conflict involving a grouping into friends and enemies *can occur* in any of them. "Can occur" is empha-sized because conflict does not necessarily happen, nor does it simultaneous-ly happen in all areas of life.

THE FRIEND-ENEMY CRITERION

But what exactly does the friend-enemy distinction mean? Here, we turn to some characterizations made explicit in Schmitt's writings:

(a) First, the friend-enemy distinction is a specifically political distinction to which every political action and motive must be traced back.[40]

(b) As a fundamental political category, it designates a properly political way of being within the social fabric. It is the characterization of a kind of relationship in society.

(c) It is autonomous not because it intends to be independent of other areas of human life, but because it designates a constitutive way of being that is irreducible to others.[41]

(d) It characterizes the intensity of a union or separation.[42] It involves a formal distinction, namely, it denotes a structure that includes (falls under its form) a network of possible symmetrical antitheses without properly naming them.[43]

(e) It does not designate a necessary situation, but rather a possible one. That is, it does not imply that a people has to be a friend or enemy of another forever and it does not exclude the possibility of a certain neutral or smart political decision avoiding conflict in a given moment.[44] It implies that any human group has to inform about the possibility of such a distinction.[45] Since the friend-enemy grouping is a feature of non-normality, total politicization is impossible. The case of conflict is presented as an exception and requires a decision to end it.

(f) The terms *friend* and *enemy* are not symbols or allegories, but rather have a particular reference in reality; they are measured by the intensity of the union or separation between people—that is, the intensity of an existential relationship.[46]

(g) The definition of the political excludes the term *humanity*, precisely because this term implicitly denies the differences between people. *Humanity* does not contain a reference to the friend-enemy distinction: "[T]he concept of humanity excludes the concept of enemy; because the enemy does not cease to be human being—and hence there is no specific differentiation in that concept."[47] However, even in a concept that aims to be neutral, it is possible to group friends and enemies; it is even possible to declare war on behalf of humanity. In this case, the enemy is considered inhumane, that is, he is not just considered a political enemy, but also a moral one. If the concept of crime against humanity is introduced, then, for the sake of consistency, it must be universalized. A crime against humanity and one that is not are distinguished in quantitative terms. If not, with what criterion can they be distinguished? In criminalizing war, the concept of crime against humanity was introduced, but that concept makes criminal law impossible because all crimes are against humanity or none are. According to Schmitt, all concepts that eliminate differences are ultimately political weapons for those who know how to use them, for those who know who the enemy is. This occurs, for example, in the use of popular concepts such as humanity, peace, justice, civilization, and progress.[48] As we shall see, in renouncing the concept of humanity as a political concept, Schmitt rejected the concept of absolute enemy.

(h) Here we find the most intense distinction because it is the most existential. Here the Cartesian assertion is specified: "'I think, therefore I am' and it takes on an existential aspect until it is finally clarified in a declaration mediated by the situation: I think, therefore I have enemies; I have enemies, therefore I am."[49] At this point, it is necessary to clarify what existential meant for Schmitt. A friend, he once said, is "the same way of being."[50] An enemy is someone with another way of being, the existential other.[51] Thus, existential primarily means way of being and, in an extreme case, preservation of biological being. Schmitt said no more on the subject.[52] However, "way of being" presupposes a plurality of ways of being, that is, there are

many ways of developing human social life. The possibility of difference
concerns a society's way of being in history and, in this sense, the political
criterion is conditioned by history. The clash between two different human
groups is not common to all human groups, but rather involves what is
specific and different between them, what they have created in their own
history. Now, a group becomes aware that it is different from another only
when measured with it—that is, in conflict.[53] Therefore, the possibility of
distinction herein discussed is the possibility of an existential, not essential,
difference. The other—that is, the enemy—is existentially, not essentially,
other. If he were essentially an other, conflict would not arise. Existential
enmity is not enmity without content. Without it, there would be no existential difference since there would be no means of differentiation.[54] Schmitt
gave a key to interpreting "way of being" and existential difference in the
following paragraph of *The Concept of the Political*:

> We recognize the pluralism of spiritual life and know that the central domain
> of spiritual existence cannot be a neutral domain and that it is wrong to solve a
> political problem with the antithesis of organic and mechanistic, life and
> death. . . . For life struggles not with death, spirit not with spiritlessness; spirit
> struggles with spirit, life with life, and out of the power of an integral under-
> standing of this arises the order of human things. *Ab integro nascitur ordo.*[55]

In addition, it is the most existential struggle because, in taking place, it
totally jeopardizes existence. As stated, any sphere of human life can become
political and, at the same time, it should be noted that a political decision
affects the entire sphere of social life, to the point that for the most extreme
case, war, a political decision determines that men give their lives in defense
of others.[56]

(i) The political criterion is found inductively, based on historical observation and by arguing from it. However, to assert its legitimacy, empirical
testing is not enough; rather, it requires some justification on another level,
whether metaphysical or theological. We find three modes for this justification in Schmitt's texts that are theological: (1) the dogma of original sin, (2)
eschatology, the dogma of the end of history and the coming of the Antichrist, and (3) Christology. The second mode is perhaps most directly used in
Schmitt's political theory. The Antichrist is the absolute enemy; his strength
is always present in history and it can only be stopped with the friend-enemy
distinction.[57] Later, when discussing political theology, I will refer to this
issue again.

(j) The friend-enemy distinction is oriented to the extreme case or situation. Enmity is not always explicit and is only made clear in exceptional
cases. The friend-enemy distinction is a distinction in the extreme inasmuch
as it is oriented toward the extreme case, war. For Schmitt, the political
sphere is only viable from the point of view of the exception. A few hidden

anthropological presuppositions can undoubtedly be seen behind this idea, including:

(1) An assumption that man's fallen nature is the foundation of his problematic character.[58] Man's nature is fallen, but not definitively corrupt,[59] thus it is entirely accurate to qualify Schmitt's anthropology as pessimistic:

> The problematic or unproblematic conception of man is decisive for the presupposition of every further political consideration, the answer to the question whether man is a dangerous being or not, a risky or harmless creature.[60]

Historically, two fundamental philosophical and political positions have existed that presuppose man's natural goodness,[61] including, on the one hand, anarchism, which has shown itself to be practically impossible and, on the other hand, liberalism that, in practice, is inconsistent with its principles since it is largely devoted to establishing limits and controls on certain freedoms that are thought of as dangerous. Most political thinkers, however, assume that man is a problematic being—that is, that he does not always act well and that he can become dangerous. This does not involve seeing things more or less optimistically, but rather knowing where we are situated with respect to human nature.[62] Depending on one's point of view, it can be said that man shows himself to be teachable before a teacher; before a jurist he shows himself to be good until the contrary can be proven because a normal situation (which is the only place a jurist's word has any meaning) supposes that man can easily become good; before a theologian man appears in need of redemption; before a moralist, he appears as a free being; before a political thinker, he appears to be capable of enmity. In any case, man's original problematic character becomes visible: "In a good world among good people, only peace, security, and harmony prevail. Priests and theologians are here just as superfluous as politicians and statesmen."[63]

Man's nature is, therefore, problematic. Schmitt was sure of this based on the dogma of original sin,[64] which corresponds to a theological foundation. There is a direct relationship between this dogma and the possibility of enmity.[65] Original sin, in the same way as enmity, leads to a rift ("*Abstandnahme*")[66] or division of men that makes the undifferentiated optimism of a universal humanity, or the contemporary universal concept of man, impossible. The biblical story of Cain and Abel is continually repeated in human history:

> The other is my brother. The other shows himself to be my brother and my brother is my enemy. Adam and Eve had two sons, Cain and Abel, so the history of humanity begins. This piece contains everything; it is the dialectical tension that keeps world history in motion and world history is not yet finished.[67]

If history in someway repeats itself, then the phrase "politics is destiny" is undoubtedly true.[68] As long as man remains man, he cannot rid himself of enmity. As Schmitt himself recognized, there is a clear relationship between the anthropological question of man's good and evil and what seventeenth-century philosophers, including Hobbes, Spinoza, and Pufendorf, called the state of nature.[69] They defined it as a place where men lived in a constant state of danger, in which individuals were dangerous by nature—that is, beasts led by their instincts. Schmitt's political theory cannot be said to presuppose such a state,[70] and is differentiated on three points: First, the dogma of original sin does not refer back to a natural state of war, but to paradise. The natural state of man is freedom, not struggle. Schmitt merely intended to highlight the possibility of evil that is open to free men.[71] Second, in Schmitt's political conception, enemies are *hostes*, or public enemies. By contrast, Hobbesian enmity arises between individuals and only appears between states as a consequence of this radical enmity. And third, the Hobbesian state of nature is irreproachable because he denies the existence of sin there. The original fall, however, is not irreproachable because freedom—that is, decision—mediates there.

(2) The assumption that man is a free being. Schmitt barely wrote of human freedom. He referred to it in an allusion to Helmuth Plessner, for whom man is an "open question."[72] Schmitt's stance always appears in contrast to the bourgeois conception of freedom and individualism. However, although he did not subscribe to liberalism, the political concept outlined here is not deterministic; it presupposes freedom.[73] In a world without politics, that is, without the possibility of friend-enemy conflict, everything would function on its own and then, "for what would they be free?"[74] The possibility of enmity presupposes a concept of man as both free and problematic. Man is not determined and always has the possibility of deciding in any direction and, therefore, because man has a fallen nature, this problematic character can become particularly dangerous. With this thesis, Schmitt swapped the old phrase of Plautus (Asinaria, 2), "man is a wolf to man"; for another: "man is a man to man." Everything depends on how he decides to be a man.[75] As long as man remains a problematic being, nothing definitive can be said of his action.

(3) The friend-enemy distinction belongs to the human spirit. There is no such relationship between animals on the same level as the kind of intensification that the relationship between men acquires. True friendship and enmity are only possible between men.[76] Enmity has nothing to do with criminality or brutality, but rather with the human condition. First, enmity exists because human life is open to transcendence; it does not dissolve in the neutrality proper to natural life.[77] Second, enmity exists because the human spirit has dialogic nature—that is, human beings are constituted by their capacity to relate to the other.[78] Inasmuch as man needs this relationship, he is not indifferent to it and he establishes relationships with the other that can take on different forms according to the substance on which it is established.

The specifically political form of that relationship is called friendship-enmity.

(4) Enmity assumes friendship. A human group fights against a people with a different way of being, but they do so in favor of those who form part of their own group: "Now, the substance of the political is not enmity pure and simple, but the ability to distinguish between friend and enemy, and to presuppose both friend and enemy."[79] The question of a real enemy is also a question of true friendship, of the way of being that is defended in conflict—that is, of what caused it.

> Every war on two fronts always raises the question concerning who is to be considered the real enemy. Is it not a sign of inner conflict to have more than one real enemy? If the enemy defines us, if our identity is unambiguous, where does the doubling of the enemy come from? The enemy is not something that can be set aside for whatever reason, or that must be annihilated because of his absolute lack of value. The enemy is on the same level as I am. For this reason, I must deal with him on the course of a clash, in order to gain a measure of myself, my own limitation, and my figure. [80]

In one spot even Schmitt, shifting the weight to the other side, defines politics in a positive way, without mentioning the enemy, although it is assumed: "Only the political enumerates the intensity of a unity."[81]

(k) The friend-enemy distinction belongs to *nomos*, which is not to say that friendship and enmity are completely determined by space, but rather that, from a people's very first moments, the conditions of space and of their inhabitation decisively influence how the enemy is configured.[82] Later in the history of a people, space's mediation in this regard is forgotten. However, this requires a means, the perception of something in common with which an association or dissociation can be constituted. And that something is a common space, a *nomos*, whether it be economic, religious, or technical.

PHENOMENOLOGY OF THE ENEMY

At this point, it is important to explain why Schmitt primarily spoke of the enemy and not of the friend.[83] Indeed, he spent some pages specifying who the enemy is, while the meaning of a friend is left to be deduced as a counterpoint. The counterpoint of the political enemy is political unity—that is, the "friend" part of the distinction. But is this approach enough? Once politics has been defined from the extreme case, there can be no other approach. Friendship is also defined from its extremity, from the exception, from enmity. A friend is anyone who is not an enemy, anyone who does not pose a danger for political existence.

The enemy question is most certainly unavoidable for any political philosophy. Perhaps it would be better to omit it for educational reasons and pretend that there are no enemies; however, reality as we know it is important.[84] We must start from the truism that there is a real possibility of enmity. The tendency to eliminate this idea is a consequence of the fact that man generally prefers security to certainty and prefers to hide reality behind abstract words like *peace, law,* or *universalism.* Anything else is seen as a diabolical attempt. Thus, in this context, Machiavelli is considered the devil involved in political affairs. However, if Machiavelli had wanted to be truly Machiavellian, he "would sooner have written an edifying book than his ill-reputed *Prince.*"[85] In short, the increasing tendency to eliminate the concept of enemy is a deceptive and cowardly stance, given that lasting world peace has never been a reality:

> If and when this condition will appear, I do not know. At the moment, this is not the case. And it is a self-deluding to believe that the termination of a modern war would lead to world peace.[86]

An answer to the question of perpetual peace can only be given from metaphysical and theological assumptions, as already seen. Among other things, enmity is a real possibility in this state of affairs.

But who is then the enemy? To start, as a first approximation, Schmitt offered a very brief philological-historical analysis of what the word *enemy* means:[87] In German, in its original sense, *enmity* meant the same thing as *hostility.* An enemy is anyone against whom a complaint has been registered or against whom one harbors hostility. Over time, new forms of hostility developed that led to a change in the concept of enmity and, consequently, to the loss of the agonal sense it once had. In other languages, an enemy is only considered negatively as a non-friend, as seen in the words *amicus-inimicus, ami-ennemi, amico-nemico, Prijatelj-neprijatelj.* Thus, the idea of *hostis* was especially weakened in the Romance languages. In English, the word *enemy* has eliminated the use of the word *foe,* which is Germanic and originally denoted an adversary in a mortal struggle. This elimination has also weakened the idea of enemy. However, despite a weakening of these terms, three types of enmity can still be distinguished, namely conventional, real, and absolute.

A political enemy, unlike a conventional or absolute one, is a real enemy. He is not morally evil, aesthetically ugly, or an economic competitor with whom it may be advantageous to come to some agreement, all of which are more like conventional enemies. A political enemy is also not an absolute enemy—that is, he does not essentially negate the other, he does not reproach the other as inhuman, and, therefore, the other does not pose an absolute threat that must be destroyed at all costs. A political enemy is simply an "other" that is foreign:

> The possibility that specifically political relations exist is found in the fact that there are not just friends—those that have the same way of being (*Gleichgeartete*) and allies—but also enemies. An enemy is, in a particularly intense sense, an other, a stranger, with whom, in extreme cases, existential conflicts can arise. [88]

The "other" is not an individual subject, but rather a community of men fighting for their existence. A political enemy is only a public enemy. [89] A private enemy corresponds to someone who personally affects another, while public refers to acts that primarily affect the rest of the community, a people as a whole. To signal this nuance, Schmitt proposed a distinction between *inimicus* and *hostis*. [90] Schmitt noted that Plato already writes that only real wars are fought among the Hellenes and barbarians—that is, between natural enemies, which intend to form a new state. However, according to Plato, real wars are not fought between Greeks unraveling political unity. [91] On the other hand, the Gospels of Matthew (5, 44) and Luke (6, 27) say, "*diligite inimicos vestros*," but they do not say, "*diligite hostes vestros*." [92] Thus, Schmitt indicates the difference between *hostis* and *inimicus* and he gives an example of it by demonstrating how, in the struggle between Christianity and Islam, Christians have never thought that they must, for the sake of the Saracens or the Turks, give up Europe. [93] Loving an enemy only makes sense in the personal sphere. It does not say that the political enemies of a people must be taken as political friends and be defended against that people.

To define *hostis*, Schmitt turned to the *Forcellinis Lexicon totius Latinitatis III*, 320: "Hostis is est cum quo publice bellum habemus . . . in quo ab inimico differt, qui est is, quoquum habemus privata odia. Distingui etiam sic possunt, ut inimicus sit qui nos odit; hostis qui oppugnat." *Hostis* is a public, existential, and formal enmity. Public enmity has nothing to do with private hatred on account of some special interest. [94] In being public, it is also publicly known. It is existential [95] and can come from different areas of human life in which man acts and thinks. [96] It is a "formal" enmity and, therefore, remains within set, consensual limits. In being a known and determined enmity, it is possible to develop some restraint such that it is limited and contained. An enemy is so relatively, not absolutely.

Paradoxically, when one tries to remove the idea of enemy from vocabulary—and, therefore, obscure its reality—the possibility of absolute enmity emerges in full force. In neutralizing the idea of enemy, its criminalization appears: "The denial of real enmity paves the way for the destructive work of absolute enmity." [97] If the impossible existence of the enemy is declared beforehand, the need to develop some restraint of the enemy relationship will not be recognized and, therefore, the extreme case of war arrives. Thus, since total peace has never been achieved historically, when a conflict does break out, no limit will be set on destruction. Given this conception, Schmitt defended the thesis of "restraint" (*Hegung*) as necessary in any confrontation:

> This clearly demonstrates that the concept of enemy herein assumed does not make sense with the annihilation of the enemy; rather, it finds meaning in rejecting the enemy, in measuring their respective forces and in establishing a common border. It so happens that there is also an absolute concept of the enemy, which we expressly reject as inhumane. [98]

WAR

The concept of enemy defined by the extreme case has already been alluded to—that is, an enemy is he who, in said case, can annihilate me in the most physically radical way. That case is war. In what follows, war will be discussed, which, as an extreme, defines the political situation. In war, the enemy appears under a new guise: The enemy is he who, in extreme cases, can physically destroy my community. The concepts of the political and the enemy live in the shadow of the possibility of war. The real enemy is he who denies my very existence (not just physically) to the point that, in case of conflict, he can annihilate me physically. When mediation between enemies is not possible, the only option is war. [99] Political decision is tasked with finding a solution because war is not the most appropriate or the most desirable option. [100] But this mediation also remains in the shadow of the extreme case, the case in which no mediation is possible. That is, even a peaceful response to a conflict must take the extreme case into account in order to properly put it into practice.

Schmitt did not properly develop a theory of war, inasmuch as his considerations about it were intended to shed light on the political. [101] He also did not develop a theory of peace, although, in establishing limits for war, it can be somewhat outlined. The possibility of such mediation should only be considered for a concrete case and, therefore, it is "a field involving political self-determination and historical responsibility." [102]

A real enemy, then, is he who could become one in the extreme case. However, this still poses two questions: What is considered an extreme case? And is there a just cause for war? Schmitt did not understand war in the same way as Clausewitz—that is, as the continuation of politics by other means. He believed that it does refer to politics, but in a different way. For Schmitt, war breaking out means that politics has failed. War excludes the political situation and the political situation excludes war. However, both share one thing: the concept of enemy. War is an extreme concept in the shadow of which the friend-enemy distinction and, therefore, politics makes sense. Declaring someone an enemy makes sense if, in fact, one can lead an armed struggle against him and, if necessary, kill him. Thus, war is the most intense and, therefore, extreme case of the separation between friends and enemies:

> War as the most extreme political means discloses the possibility which under-lies every political idea, namely, the distinction of friend and enemy. This makes sense only as long as this distinction in mankind is actually present or at least potentially possible. On the other hand, it would be senseless to wage war for purely religious, purely moral, purely juristic, or purely economic motives. The friend-and-enemy grouping and therefore also war cannot be derived from these specific antitheses of human endeavor. [103]

Having considered the point of view of the interdependence between war and politics, we must specifically ask, what is war? "War is armed combat between organized political entities; civil war is armed combat within an organized unit. A self-laceration endangers the survival of the latter." [104] War's definition hinges on being an armed struggle, that is, in a war it must be possible to physically die. It thus differs from other types of fighting that are not strictly political, including: competition, intellectual argument, or the fight that each person has in their own life "for it is a fact that the entire life of human being is a struggle and every human being symbolically a combat-ant." [105] War follows from enmity and represents its extreme case: the existential negation of a mortal being. [106]

In Schmitt's definition of war, there are two main features: (a) War is an extreme case and turns up as a result of exception. (b) It concerns politics as a possibility and, because it involves exception, is related to it. If both of these points are not taken into account, one can fall into the mistake of thinking that Schmitt makes political life a continuous war or that war is the ideal of political life. This is not Schmitt's conception.

Consider the first point: War is an extreme case and turns up as a result of exception. [107] Positive law covers the possibility of war and how to act in case of it; however, it is generally not possible to determine, for all cases, situations of war. It comes in many different ways, for very different reasons and, therefore, always as an exception. This case is precisely characterized by the fact that war cannot be avoided. That it could be avoided assumes an impartial third party, an arbitrator. However, war implies the absence of third-party mediation for conflict and, therefore, the absence of an arbitrator. It is an exceptional case even for the state, that is, if war breaks out, the state itself is suspended. Who can decide on the case of exception? Or, who can decide if the case of enmity is extreme and, therefore, wage war? Anyone outside of the existential situation involving war—that is, a foreigner—cannot decide whether the separation between friends and enemies has become an extreme case, or what means should be implemented to end it and preserve their own existence. [108] Only the stakeholders themselves can decide and resolve an extreme case of conflict—that is, decide whether the existence of the foreign-er (in the sense of outside one's own people, its way of being) implies the denial of a particular mode of existence and how to act in its defense.[109] The existential nature of war makes the third objective, in its objectivity, unable to perceive what is essential to it.[110] One cannot decide, from outside of a contention, on its beginning and end.

Second, war concerns politics as a *possibility*. That is, the definition of the political as a situation of enmity would not be acceptable if the possibility of war were not really present. The equation "politics is equal to war"[111] is therefore untenable, as is a militaristic definition of the former, as if politics were always an armed struggle between conflicting people and, therefore, politically, it were not better to prevent wars. War is nothing more than the "*ultima ratio*" of the friend-enemy distinction. Schmitt explained it as fol-lows: "It does not have to be common, normal, something ideal, or desirable. But it must nevertheless remain a real possibility for as long as the concept of the enemy remains valid."[112] And later:

> War is neither the aim nor the purpose nor even the very content of politics. But as an ever present possibility it is the leading presupposition which deter-mines in a characteristic way human action and thinking and thereby creates a specifically political behavior.[113]

War is governed by its own rules, criteria, strategies, and tactics. It has its own logic, which differs from political logic, although political logic is pre-supposed, since it is the politician, not the soldier, who defines an enemy. From the definition of war nothing can be inferred about its content—that is, its motive, cause, or objective. These are diverse and have nothing to do with what war is. War occurs when there is a grouping of friends and enemies with the possibility of physical death. It does not matter whether this group-ing is based on religious, moral, economic, or juridical reasons in determin-ing war and its meaning.

The question of whether war could vanish is correlative to the question of whether enmity could vanish. The answer is no until now.[114] Even in a world that claims to be pacifist, war still appears as a possibility today:[115] the pacifist antiwar aversion may be so strong that it has the force to group men into friends and enemies (those in favor of and those against war in general). In that case, the will to prevent war would be such that war itself would not be feared, turning pacifism political too. A new kind of war arises from the pacifist claim, corresponding to wars raised in the name of humanity:

> Such a war is necessarily unusually intense and inhuman because, by transcending the limits of the political framework, it simultaneously degrades the enemy into moral and other categories and is forced to make of him a monster that must not only be defeated but also utterly destroyed.[116]

A permanent rejection of war would make sense only in the case of States where the possibility of enmity is excluded:

> The best will is impotent in regard to the concrete reality of different types of peoples and colliding interests and convictions. The existential distinctiveness of these peoples, interests, and convictions, find their political form in the state. Only if there is a substantial comparability, an existential relationship, as can be the case, for example, in states with a nationally comparable and similarly disposed population, is it reasonably conceivable to consider hostility permanently precluded even as a possibility. [117]

As we can see, *nomos* is ever present in Schmitt's theory. Peoples' "substantial homogeneity" implies the same structure as *nomos*. By sharing a common *nomos*, peoples exclude the possibility of enmity between them and vice versa. A people's way of being is configured by space, customs, and history and when fusing two peoples it is crucial. There must be homogeneity for this fusion to be possible. Otherwise, political decision can try it, but this forced fusion will almost certainly be precarious.

Since war is not good in itself, it must be justified with some defense. The question at this point corresponds to the following: To what extent is it legitimate to conduct war? This question has remained alive throughout the centuries and various responses have been offered. Indeed, in *The Nomos of the Earth*, Schmitt described the evolution of the concept of war from the sixteenth century to the eighteenth century—centuries that were decisive in the shaping of the present concept—and found that the above question was present throughout. [118] He identified three main forms for legitimizing war in this evolution. The first comes by way of the concept of *just war*; the main theorists that speculated to this effect included Augustine of Hippo, Thomas Aquinas, Bodin, Francisco de Vitoria, Baltasar Ayala, and Gentile, and they claimed that a war can only be undertaken when there is just cause to do so. The features of a just cause in an inter-State order can be summarized in the following points: (a) It must be fought between States, that is, between sovereign bearers of the *summa potestas*. (b) It must be undertaken against a just enemy, an *iustus hostis*, which is a sovereign State. (c) The decision of whether the cause is just is up to each sovereign state. Contention mainly arises around the last point, namely, who can clearly and objectively decide on the justice of a cause? Just war theory presupposes the existence of an absolute authority or, in Schmitt's words, a *"plenitudo potestatis spiritualis."* [119] Without this supposition, it makes no sense to speak of just war, because the aforementioned question will always reappear. From a theological standpoint, just cause is the only way to sanction conducting war. However, in many cases, although not necessarily so, this type of justification has led to the criminalization of the opposition. This criminalization was different, however, from the criminalization present in modern means of destruction.[120]

Bodin's emphasis on decision in his political writings gradually led to the neglect of just cause and to a new way of legitimizing war. Form, the process of war, eventually became the center of attention, where the important thing is to define *hostes iusti aequaliter*.[121] War then becomes a "war in form"— that is, fenced in. Its limit is found in the need for a relationship between organized, concrete entities in terms of space, and it involves military action by state-organized armies fighting against each other. In this case, the legitimization of war comes by way of formal perfection, not by way of material content. Zouch, Puffendorf, Bynkershoek, and Vattel all contributed to this idea in their work. With it, justice is reduced to pure form.[122] Subsequent historical progress termed war as always illegitimate. Thus, many began to argue that war is inhumane and, paradoxically, with it, the concept of "total war" appeared.[123] According to Schmitt, a war can be total for several reasons, including[124]: (a) because opponents fight using up their last reserves; (b) because absolutely destructive technical means are employed; (c) because of the geographical location; (d) because there is no distinction between combatants and noncombatants; (e) because, during the course of it, its intensity increases in an extreme way; (f) because it implies total risk for a nation. Schmitt attached the most important reason to the lack of a distinction between combatants and noncombatants, which converts other types of war— economic, propaganda, moral, etc.—into military wars and generates huge upsurges in enmity.[125]

> The core of things is found in war. By way of total war, the entire state's form and mode is determined; by way of particular weapons, war's peculiar form and mode is determined. Total war, however, finds its meaning in enmity.[126]

Total war opens up the concept of a total enemy, who is a criminal and unworthy of being included within humanity. Only such a characterization of enmity would permit the use of the technical means implemented in contemporary war.[127] Where is Schmitt situated in this evolution? Within his own tradition, on the side of "war in form." Now, in his consideration of the legitimacy of the war, an argument that differs from formal perfection becomes more important. Given that war moves in an existential logic, legitimacy must also be situated in this logic. It could be said that, for Schmitt, the justification of armed conflict is found in its authentic need. This has nothing to do with justice or "formality"—and, in this sense, it has nothing to do with what has traditionally been called legitimacy—but rather with the defense of one's own group.

There exists no rational purpose, no norm no matter how true, no program no matter how exemplary, no social ideal no matter how beautiful, no legitimacy nor legality which could justify men in killing each other for this reason. If such physical destruction of human life is not motivated by an existential threat to one's own way of life, then it cannot be justified. Just as little can war be justified by ethical and juristic norms. If there really are enemies in the existential sense as meant here, then it is justified, but only politically, to repel and fight them physically. [128]

The only justification for war is self-defense—that is, it is only permissible to kill in self-defense, in defense of one's own political unit and nation. Schmitt mentioned this literally, saying, "for a war receives meaning from being conducted in the interest of self-preservation against a genuine enemy." [129]

The following question can be asked once arriving here: Does Schmitt's theory of war correspond to warmongering? "No" is the only answer. [130] The ultimate goal of war has to be peace. We should not forget that the ultimate desire for a new organization of space appears *in Der Nomos der Erde* formulated as follows: "Historically speaking, new amity lines are on the agenda." [131] That is, new limits are needed for war. Peace cannot be sought directly, but only through the limitation or demarcation of war and, therefore, through the search for a measure of enmity, that is, through the friend-enemy distinction. [132] By normatively denying war or enmity, neither will disappear from historical reality. Schmitt explained this point as follows:

The solemn declaration of outlawing war does not abolish the friend-enemy distinction, but, on the contrary, opens new possibilities by giving an international *hostis* declaration new content and new vigor. . . . If a part of the population declares that it no longer recognizes enemies, then, depending on the circumstance, it joins their side and aids them. Such a declaration does not abolish the reality of the friend-and-enemy distinction. [133]

The only way to face such a distinction is to develop a measure for it. The concept of limiting war belongs to international law born during the inter-State age [134] and remains its only effective solution. [135] Given that the demarcation of war is linked to a relativization of the enemy—that is, the non-qualification of the enemy as criminal or as "unjust"—it is possible to claim that the concept of demarcating war assumes a kind of progress in "humanizing." [136] The concept of demarcating war parallels the non-criminalization of the enemy. The enemy is an *iustus hostis* because he is a member of a sovereign state—that is, he belongs to an orderly community. On the other hand, since the cause of war is always existential, it does not differentiate the enemy as criminal. The enemy is an "other" that must be retained at his borders, but he is not a criminal.

In Schmitt's political conceptualization there is place for a measure of war. The concept of demarcating war is seen as a logical consequence of the theory of *nomos* in two ways. *Nomos* supposes, as noted in the second chapter, a limit of space and, therefore, differentiation of spaces and the balance between them; *nomos* excludes the existence of a single space with singular power, which already represents a limitation of power. Limiting space makes indiscriminately applying power impossible; it also implies the demarcation of friendship and enmity, making it impossible to qualify an enemy as absolute.

In his analysis of post–World War I and II, Schmitt realized that the concept of peace should be lauded since then is nothing more than a political mask trying to disguise the difference between war and peace. [137] This mask concealed the reality of the Cold War, a topic that greatly interested Schmitt. [138] In this historical context, the question of the problematic definition of peace emerges. If military action is more clearly recognizable, then it could be said that everything that is not war is peace [139] and vice versa. War and peace reveal themselves as two relative and mutually exclusive concepts that negatively determine each other. With this definition, Cicero's ancient phrase finds new relevance: *inter pacem et bellum nihil est medium.* [140] However, in making these two realities mutually exclusive, this definition overlooks the real issue, namely, whether there is a third state between war and peace. [141] This question must be asked here because the concept of peace has become so problematic that peace determined negatively—that is, as that which is not war, is a fallacy. [142] To get to the heart of the matter, the question must be asked in different terms:

> Are measures of military force, including retaliation, compatible with peace or not? And if they are not, are they then war? This approach focuses on *peace as a concrete order.* [143]

If there were an intermediate situation between war and peace, it would be an abnormal situation, an exception. Nevertheless, an exceptional situation is closer to war than to peace since it is neither a normal situation nor a concrete order. It is a dangerous situation because nonmilitary action can be hostile in the most effective and intense ways and, vice versa, military action can be planned under the guise of peace. In such a situation, everything is false. [144] According to Schmitt, Germany lived this situation after both World Wars, and their resulting peace treaties only sought the continuation of war by other means. [145] With these references to the Cold War, Schmitt sought to highlight that the central problem is not so much to end war, but rather to achieve real peace, which should follow a path toward the creation of a concrete ordering of peace that corresponds to a real situation of peace [146] and not toward utopia or abstraction. The creation of a real state of peace ultimately depends on who makes political decisions:

We all want peace, but the question, unfortunately, is who decides what peace is, who decides what order and security are, who decides what should be regarded as a bearable or unbearable situation. [147]

Chapter Six

The Political Order

The political is a situation that goes through different phases, which can be summarized in the following two equivalent chains of events: (a) exception—conflict—political unity; (b) breakdown of the relationship between friends and enemies—friend and enemy opposition—sovereign decision.

Each of these three steps shapes the political situation. When we talk about the formation of a new order we are referring to the third moment of the political situation, which marks its end. The sovereign decision, which manages to end conflict, is able to secure a new and concrete order in which a normal situation and, consequently, a legal order are possible.[1] Here, the concept of the political and the concrete order of *nomos* are linked; conflict gives way to what, in contemporary terms, is called consensus. The conflict is mediated. Through the sovereign's political decision, representation is created, consensus is strengthened, and conflict is ended.[2]

LEGITIMATE SOVEREIGNTY

In passing from disorder and conflict to order, the sovereign emerges as the central figure. This topic was already addressed with reference to political decision and, in what follows, it will be briefly mentioned in relation to a newly instituted order in which a sovereign becomes a "legitimated" sovereign.

A sovereign decision is required for an exceptional situation to come to an end. The sovereign is he who decides on the exception and, therefore, on a political situation in ending it.[3] Precisely because the situation of exception is characterized by suspending the existing legal order, a decision to end said situation can be nothing more than the reestablishment (not necessarily the restoration) of a concrete order. The figure of the sovereign acquires its value from the realization of that action and his figure does not exist apart from it; therefore, it is closely related to the concrete order that it aims to create.[4]

The sovereign does not have a monopoly on power, but rather on sovereignty. It is not possible for a central power to decide on all exceptions and all conflicts that appear in social life. In order for the sovereign to be able to decide in the case of exception par excellence—that is, where the existing order is destroyed—he has to reserve his decision for that case. Even there, the sovereign must recognize the dialectical character of all human power, must also appreciate other powers in society, and must balance them such that, when an exceptional situation occurs, the sovereign is truly powerful.[5] The efficacy of power, without which it is meaningless, depends on the political *nomos*, on how political space has been divided and balanced. The sovereign, to be an effective power, must have a monopoly on political decision in the political situation; a monopoly on decision, as we saw, is not according to statute, but rather frames all statute. In this sense, the sovereign can be a dictator, as referred in chapters 3 and 4.[6]

Once here, two questions arise. First, how can the sovereign be introduced into an order of law that follows from the end of a political situation? In Schmitt's words, how can the highest power be related to the juristic form?[7] In principle and simply, one can say that decision again creates a positive juridical framework within which his sovereignty is framed as a representation of the people and, thus, acquires a specific legal form. The second question appears immediately upon discussing the sovereign as an invincible power in the political situation and refers to the legitimacy of that power.

The latter becomes problematic with Bodin's approach in this regard in his treatise, *The Six Books of the Commonwealth*. There, he claimed that whoever has power is sovereign in his own right and permanently and this statement supposedly answers any question about legitimacy. This represents the turning point that changed the course of classical theory and led toward modern political theory on legitimacy. The former was anchored in theology; the latter is based on the factual power. Ultimately, whoever can ensure peace and security is sovereign, that is, whoever can impose himself is sovereign. Hobbes seems to even differentiate the concepts of *auctoritas* and *potestas* in saying, "*auctoritas non veritas facit legem*." However, according to Schmitt, in fact it is one, since in this statement *auctoritas* means nothing more than *summa potestas* and, therefore, becomes the *summa potestas* in *summa auctoritas*.[8] Over time, the distinction between *auctoritas* and *potestas* has even been erased terminologically; however, reality remains the same and this difference continues to appear under a variety of names. Thus, for example, some of these distinctions include direct-*potestas* and indirect-*potestas*, or to reign and to govern, or the distinction between power and neutral power that appears in liberal theory.[9] Nevertheless, in his comments on Carl Schmitt's theory,[10] d'Ors noted that Schmitt does not seem to distinguish between the two either. Where is *auctoritas* in Schmitt's theory? An interpretive problem again emerges. He complained, if it can be said that way, that there is no authority and that there is no recognized *potestas spiritualis* able to legitimize a concrete sovereignty.[11] It is important to find a legitimation for power; now, be that as it may, power must be effective; it is not enough for it to be legitimate. *Auctoritas* and *potestas* must be coherent. This is a cardinal issue for all political thought.[12] One could speak of a third way of establishing legitimacy—beyond pure factuality or *potestas spiritualis*—through legalism, which Schmitt considered inauthentic.[13] Legality for the legislative State is a kind of legitimacy, despite the circularity of the argument in the case where the sovereign that has to be legitimized by the Law also creates the Law.

From the political point of view, the important thing is to know who decides, the basis of which he decides becomes clear once the previous question is addressed. That is, *potestas* is the most important question regarding practice. Since his theory aims to be practical, Schmitt was interested in seeing things from the point of view of *potestas* and, thus, transformed the distinction *potestas-auctoritas* into another, namely, *direct potestas—indirect potestas*. Schmitt, of course, claimed that the latter exists and is always a danger, a constant threat to the former.[14]

POLITICAL UNITY

Political unity appears as a result of overcoming the friend-enemy distinction in a political situation[15] and of a constitutional process in which the dialectic between identity and representation is settled.

The labeling of an enemy would make no sense without the existence of a kind of unity or a previous friendship. As Schmitt noted, "In this case, friendship means an intense group or association of persons and enmity corresponds to separation."[16] The development of the definition of political unity in Schmitt's writings is as follows:

> In any event, that grouping is always political which orients itself toward this most extreme possibility. This grouping is therefore always the decisive human grouping, the political entity. If such an entity exists at all, it is always the decisive entity, and it is sovereign in the sense that the decision about the critical situation, even if it is the exception, must always necessarily reside there.[17]

And in the 1933 edition as follows:

Political unity is always therefore, provided that it is present, the decisive, total and sovereign unity. It is total because everything is potentially political and, therefore, may be affected by political decisions; secondly, because it decisively influences the totality of the existence of those who take part in it. [18]

Some years earlier, in 1930, he had written *Staatsethik und pluralistischer Staat*:

Political unity can have and take on different content. However, it always characterizes the highest level of unity, whereby it has been determined the strongest distinction, the grouping into friends and enemies. Political unity is the highest unity, not because its dictates are omnipotent or because it levels the unities beneath it, but because it decides and because within itself, all other opposing groups can become a hindrance to the point of dissociation into extreme enmity (i.e., to the point of civil war). . . . The most intensive unity exists or it does not. It can be destroyed, but then normal order falls. [19]

Four characteristics of political unity appear in these descriptions, namely that it is unity, sovereign, total, and existential. It is unity because within it there is no division into friends and enemies and because it has arisen from the decision coming from the sovereign's will, a single will; it is sovereign because decision in the case of emergency falls to it; it is total because it can affect any area of human life and any person's life; and it is existential because it has its legitimacy, its rationale, in existence itself, as already noted in the last chapters. [20] Schmitt, however, was quick to resolve potential fears that such a definition might inspire. This can be seen in the following quote from the 1933 edition of *The Concept of the Political*:

None of the above two things means that every aspect of a person's life within a political unity has to be determined by the political sphere or subject to its commandments or that a centralist system is meant to annihilate any other institution or association within the political unity. [21]

A situation of political unity, with all of the aforementioned characteristics, is reached in the mediation of a political conflict through a decision that puts an end to it. With it, the enemy is moved to its boundaries and peace within one's own borders is achieved, as well as a resistance against the enemy. Political unity is different from other types of units—religious, economic, and so on—that are defined by an antagonism, a differentiation with respect to other political units. It is a political community. [22] The meaning that the word *community* acquires in this context does not come from contrasting with that of society. Schmitt does not go into depth about Hegel and Tönnies's distinction in which community appears as natural while society is a product of a contract and, therefore, can be formed and dissolved at any time. [23] His concept of community belongs to an earlier tradition regarding this distinction. For Schmitt, a community has profound existential and historical value. Thus, the connection between the community and the political spheres is stronger than the connection between the social and political spheres. The social sphere is closer to the strictly juridical sphere. In using this distinction, Schmitt intended to show that a people has an innate political capacity that is represented in the concept of political unity.[24]

Political unity essentially has two types of activity, namely normal activity and exceptional activity. "Normal" activity consists in creating and maintaining a normal situation within one's own borders,[25] that is, peacekeeping within one's own territory. This activity is based on the relationship between protection and obedience that the sovereign must maintain with his subjects.[26] This relationship is at the core of all power dynamics among men and is also at the core of all human order:

> On this principle rests the feudal order and the relation of lord and vassal, leader and led, patron and clients. This relation is clearly and explicitly seen here. No form of order, no reasonable legitimacy or legality can exist without protection and obedience.[27]

Schmitt referred to this relation as "eternal." It is a constant, a category of a type of ever-present human relationship. It corresponds to the actual way that power is manifested in a normal situation. The concrete way of establishing this relation must be defined in each concrete situation and appear in the constitution. Indeed, its "political element" refers to political power's normal activity.

Exceptional activity of the political unity involves identifying the enemy and, in case of conflict, confronting him. The enemy has been defined in previous pages as one who is existentially something different. Consequently, then, political unity includes those with the same way of being (*Artgleichheit*). This homogeneity, in which consensus is reached, makes political unity governable. When an enemy appears, homogeneity is threatened and, to defend it, the sovereign decides on *ius belli*. In deciding regarding the enemy, he is also called to decide in the extreme case—that is, war—for which he can also count on the lives of men to maintain the peaceful existence of political unity.[28] This power over the men's physical lives elevates the political community above other communities and associations.[29] A religious community, for example, may require its members to die for the faith, but not for the religious community itself. Here we find a deeper and different idea of the enemy than in the political sphere. An economic association cannot ask a man to die for a profit, which would be inconsistent with individualistic principles: The individual may die for that which he deems worthy. Economic associations have their own means to fight the enemy, for example, "letting him die of hunger." A purely civilizing cultural system would have no reason to count on men's lives, although it also has its own means to get rid of the enemy—in this case, the inept—for example, with euthanasia or by provoking suicide. In the political sphere, as stated, when speaking of war, there is only one reason why men can be ordered to die, and it is to defend the life of the political community.

Political unity is not a historical form, but rather a political category.[30] Historically, this category may appear in different ways—one of which is the Modern State—and may acquire different content. Schmitt theoretically discussed some of the political forms under which he lived[31]; thus he wrote of the following models: the National Socialist State, for which he proposed the well-known triadic arrangement of state, people, and movement[32]; the *Rechtsstaat*, mainly described in *Verfassungslehre*; and the *Gesetzstaat* (legislative State), characterized as a total State. Since this book seeks to narrate Schmitt's philosophical-political discourse and not his historical analysis, I will not stop to describe each of these State models and will only enter into his ambiguous position on the Modern State in the *Excursus*. Moreover, Schmitt wrote most about political unity.

POLITICAL PLURIVERSE: THE *GROSSRAUM* THEORY

Political unity is always formed by reference to an enemy. From this, it follows that the overall political framework must necessarily be composed of a plurality of political units. Political space, rather than a universe, is actually a pluriverse, which rectifies the very concept of the Modern State. Political entity is not universal and does not tend toward universality, but rather toward large space (*Großraum*).[33] In recent decades, there have been attempts to imagine a kind of world unity that includes the entire earth under a single center of power.[34] Claiming that a politically unified universe is possible is the same as maintaining that the enemy can disappear and that a peaceful world can emerge, a paradise without politics. But to maintain this stance is to ignore the world we live in. This would be a mere economic and communicatory union that would not let in anything outside of it. There would be no other and, therefore, no potential enemy.[35] However, Schmitt's political world is not monist, but rather pluralistic. It is not clear that absolute political unity is ideal for human order,[36] and even if it were, who would assume power over a centralized globe?[37] Schmitt warned against the danger to which a purely technical unity exposes itself, namely, the possibility of technical death.[38] Duality, nevertheless, is not ideal either.[39] Against the utopia of global political unity that seeks to ensure peace, Schmitt's pluralist theory can be found, which is always possible with the end of developing a measure for the relationship between various political units.[40] These relationships should be included in an international legal order.[41]

The Political Order   125

The question is: What kind of political units coexist in a political pluriverse that leads toward an order of peace? Here Schmitt introduces the notion of *Großraum*.[42] A *Großraum* has an order of peace only if it is not limited to being an enlarged State space—in the sense of the Modern State—that is, only if it does not correspond to outwardly closed State centralism, but rather allows for a decentralized order in which the independence and freedom of the various peoples within it are respected.[43]

Großraum (large space) is one of Schmitt's most famous and original concepts in the sense in which he used it. Like *nomos*, it was developed in the search for a principle of order, in this case to establish an international order. It is a spatial concept. More than an order, it is an ordering principle that gives rise to genuine international law[44] and that responds to the new mode of "global" thinking: "Wir denken heute planetarisch und in Großräumen."[45]

The horizon of this new ordering concept is global. We can talk about novelty since it is distinguished from both the order of space based on the existing national States from the sixteenth to the nineteenth centuries and from Western democracies' order with a universalistic tendency put into practice in the nineteenth century. The response to that call lies in a plurality of orders with a tendency toward large space:

> The task of German law currently consists of finding—between the contemporary interstate conservative position and the spread of a non-State and non-national universal world law determined by Western democracies—a specific concept of "large spatial order" that avoids classical representations of space that are no longer valid and that does justice to both the spatial measure of our current image of land and to new State and nation concepts.[46]

From a historical point of view, for the construction of a new order, it is necessary to rid ourselves of the concepts of Modern State and universal law. In *Völkerrechtliche Großraumordnung*, Schmitt clearly expressed the need for abandoning the idea of the State as the guiding principle of space.[47] The very idea of State precludes a thorough understanding of international law.[48] The State is simply a way of representing space that, in recent times, has been the most important, but it is neither exclusive nor definitive.[49] The first point of attack on the concept of State came from criticism of the principle of sovereignty. With the defeat of this principle, an era that tends toward humanitarian universalism with a pacifist end emerged.[50] However, it is also necessary to overcome the universalist conception of world order that is closely related to an individualist context in which the bourgeois State was born.[51] Small spaces are from an era that has already passed; universalism is, for many, the future. And it is against this future that the idea of *Großraum* stands.[52] The idea of universalism defends the thesis of a certain worldwide mixture of all borders and differences. The latter claim, which is presented as if it were free of ideology, reflects the intention of turning the world into an abstraction for the capital market.[53] Thus, Schmitt noted:

> We must overcome and put aside the dominant spatial representation of the nineteenth century, which even today determines juristic concepts and that, ultimately, viewed from the world of politics is ordered toward Anglo-Saxon universalism of dominion over the seas, which overcomes the distinctions of territory, spatial concepts and borders.[54]

Schmitt's theory of space cannot be well understood without considering its opposition to spatial universalism as a theory of interventionism, expansion, and imperialism.[55] One can only properly speak of universalism in reference to the religious sphere[56] precisely because, although the Church is a juristic structure in the same way as an empire, it is of a different nature.[57] As a juristic institution, it is visible, but at the same time it is invisible in as much as its foundation and end are beyond this world and, therefore, beyond time. This is a society that leaves nothing outside of itself; it is divine and eternal with its end fulfilled. Therefore, it can be said to be universal and thus lacking borders.[58] Any political formation, however, by not being ordered to spiritual ends, must necessarily have borders and limits. It is temporary and cannot aspire to being more than a large space and, as such, to have borders and certain possibilities. The unification of all mankind would entail an outcome foreign to humanity because every man should be able to escape a given power.

From a philosophical point of view, in order to leave behind both the State approach that is territorially closed and the universalistic approach, it is necessary to create a new order of space that definitively puts aside the concept of space deducted from modern mathematics.[59] Against an empty, neutral concept of space, one appears that is qualitatively and dynamically configured,[60] which Schmitt specifically called "*Leistungsraum*" (development space).

The Monroe Doctrine of 1823 constitutes the first historical example of a theory of *Großraum*,[61] which showcased the independence of all American States, as well as ensured the noncolonization of this space and banned intervention by non-American powers. This doctrine can be considered a principle of order driven by the exclusion of intervention by foreign powers in the space governed by a political idea.[62] This doctrine was so inspired by the idea of *Großraum* that Schmitt even saw the possibility of translating it to other countries and historical situations. Now, this is true in its original inspiration and not in its degeneration, namely, in Roosevelt and Wilson's capitalist imperialism, which later warped it and toward which Schmitt expressed utter contempt.[63]

But what exactly does *Großraum* mean for Schmitt? First it must be said that, although Schmitt came to the concept of *Großraum* in a particular historical moment, in the specific circumstances that Germany was living through, it goes beyond this moment to become a political category—that is, valid for any historical circumstance. Thus Schmitt did not abandon the theory of *Großraum* after the failure of the post-German Empire, as might be expected. Schmitt himself expressed the matter as follows: "Despite being well-liked in our day, the word (*Großraum*) is beyond the circumstances of daily journalism, politics and changes in trends, which otherwise affect all words."[64] It comes from the technical-industrial-economic sphere.[65] Thus, for example, after the First World War, the expression *Grossraumwirts-chaft*[66] was fashionable, which brought together the basic idea of new market trends. Schmitt proposed giving it a new meaning outside of that context, and the meaning it acquired in Schmitt corresponds to *Leistungsraum*, that of a "sphere of organization, planning and human activity originated from a global trend toward development."[67]

Schmitt got this word from the field of biology, namely from Viktor von Weizsäcker,[68] and it can be translated into our conceptual framework as "development space." It is a space that, compared to the conception of a vacuum in which bodies move from mathematics, is differentiated and qualitative—that is, it has an internal measure itself.[69] It would not be fitting, therefore, to talk about a world that is in a space, but rather of a space that is created in and with the world. Thus, a spatial order is not a given empty space in which certain elements are integrated; it is an order that corresponds to situations and events, and hence its configuration varies with the history and life developed by a community in that space in time.[70] In such a conception, words like *space*, *land*, *territory*, *country*, *parcel*, and so on are not equivalent or interchangeable. Each has its specific meaning, denoting distinctions about the earth that, over time, depend on the human life inhabiting it.[71] *Leistungsraum* denotes, like any *nomos*, the unity of *Ordnung* and *Ortung*. Therefore, it denotes a development space, just as *nomos* assumes the same: *nehmen, teilen, weiden*. Any *nomos* is a space for the development of human society in the different activities that pertain to it and, with this same meaning, *Großraum* was conceived.

There is a close relationship between the spatial concept herein described and the concept of empire, *Reich*. One can say that the spatial conception of *Großraum* belongs to the empire's juristic form.[72] To avoid any misconception, Schmitt differentiated the concepts *Imperium*, *Imperialismus*, and *Reich*. The term empire—*Imperium*—is often understood in a universal sense, that is, as a possible and desirable idea for a peaceful union of all men and of the whole world under one power. Part of nineteenth-century imperialism—*Imperialismus*—has been understood as the progressive colonization and expansion of the capitalist economy. Free from these misconceptions, Schmitt understood empire—*Reich*—as every political form that rests on the

principles that tend toward large space—*Großraum*—and nonintervention.
He himself defined it as follows:

> In this regard, empires correspond to guiding and propelling powers whose
> political idea emits in a given space and that in principle exclude intervention
> from other foreign powers. [73]

In the same way that "large space" is not an extension of "small" spaces, [74]
Großraum is not an extension of State spaces, but rather proposes a change in
spatial order where the order of the State is replaced by the order of the
empire. An empire is not identical to a *Großraum*, but every empire is a large
space in which its political idea radiates—that is, it marks the direction of
development and of the activity in that large space without undoing the
differences that can be found within it, for example, different peoples or
nations. [75] The concept of empire comprises three elements: a *Großraum*, a
people, and a political idea.

Neither empire nor *Großraum* are absolutely closed blocks, but rather
lend themselves to multiple relationships within international law that
Schmitt summarized as follows [76]: (1) the relationships between different
Großräume, which would come to constitute something like *Welthandel* or
international trade, (2) the relationships between the empires of those
Großräume, (3) the relationships between different peoples or nations within
a *Großraum*—that is, international relations, and (4) the relationships between peoples or nations of different *Großräume*, while respecting the principle of nonintervention of foreign powers in a *Großraum* that is not their
own. Ultimately, Schmitt expressed in his own words what he meant with
this new ordering concept as follows:

> The idea of *Großraum* mainly serves to overcome the conceptual monopoly of
> an empty State territory and to come into contact with the concept of empire in
> constitutional and international law as a key concept of juristic thought. This is
> linked to a renewal of the entirety of juristic thought, which returns to con-
> ceive, in relation to all institutions, the old and eternal connection between
> order and localisation (*Ordnung* and *Ortung*). This aims to give concrete con-
> tent back to the word "peace" and to give the character of an essential determi-
> nation to the word "homeland." [77]

This concept became important in Schmitt's texts after the Second World
War, and his lecture on "El orden del mundo después de la Segunda Guerra
Mundial" [The Order of the World after World War II] at the Institute of
Political Studies in Madrid is particularly relevant in this regard. On this
occasion, in 1962, [78] he was also appointed honorary member of the Institute
and, in May 1943, he gave another lecture there entitled "Cambio de estructura en el derecho internacional" [Changing Structure in International

Law].[79] What was the situation after World War II? The following text from *Der Nomos der Erde* answers this question:

> Today (1954), the world in which we live is divided into two parts, East and West, which confront each other in a cold war and, occasionally in also in hot wars. This is the present division of the earth.[80]

In this situation, where should the new *nomos* of the earth direct itself? There are three possibilities, of which Schmitt only considered the third valid.[81] The first possibility is that one of the blocs would triumph over the other and thus the anticipated unity of the world would be attained with a power that would plan and organize the world in a technical manner such that peace would be achieved. The second is to keep the world in balance with the two blocs, which would entail a heightened tension and a progressive development of the technical means for warfare. The third takes into account the global space of the planet and, therefore, concerns the new *nomos* of the earth and involves a new ordering of the entire earth. It represents a new way of understanding the relationship between unity and multiplicity beyond conquest and colonization. Herein, there is no new land to conquer, nor any free space. This new order, therefore, cannot come from the discovery of a new world as was the case with the conquest of America, nor can it emerge from technological discovery. As Schmitt concluded in the preface to *Der Nomos der Erde*, this new order must be born of a new approach to peace from the basic orders of man's earthly existence. From this new approach different spaces will emerge, among which a balance will exist that will make an order of the entire earth possible, a new order of peace.[82] In this regard, decision is needed, specifically political decisions to make a new world order possible.

With this in mind, Schmitt wondered what lines would draw the new world order. He answered with reference to three phenomena that constitute objective problems in the twentieth century, including anticolonialism, the conquest of space, and industrial development done by developed countries in underdeveloped areas.[83] Anticolonialism is mostly "anti-European, discriminatory propaganda"[84] that affects two conceptual distinctions, including war-peace and enemy-criminal. The solution to the problem of anticolonialism is found in preventing anti-Europeanism and, with it, the discrimination and criminalization of the opponent and thus a cold war, the intermediate state between war and peace, which, in Schmitt's words, is nothing more than "the liquidation of the historical past at the expense of European nations."[85] The gradual conquest of space is a future project that belittles history to date, giving increasing importance to technical progress. The conquest of space forces changes in power relations. Thus, whoever dominates new cosmic spaces will dominate the land with an effective power and, in turn, it will be easier for whoever dominates the earth to also dominate cosmic spaces. Third, the industrial development undertaken by developed countries in underdeveloped areas is conceived from the context of industrial progress. It involves an appropriation of the earth, namely, a settlement of industry, *Industrienahme*, which means "the taking of the means for industrial production,"[86] whose beginning Schmitt described, by changing up the old adage, as *cuius regio, eius industria*.[87] In an era of industrial and technical development, old religious disputes between Catholicism, Lutheranism, and Calvinism are no longer relevant. Today, it only makes sense to pursue grandiose scientific-technical-industrial development appropriate to the leading system, whether it be liberal-capitalist, socialist-communist, or liberal-socialist.

The progress of this industrial development brings its own idea of space.[88] Agrarian culture had its own land categories. Their settlements meant *Landnahmen*, appropriation of land. In the seventeenth and eighteenth centuries, England, where industrialization began, became a maritime country par excellence and gave birth to a new organization of space. Their new settlements were no longer "appropriations of land," but were "appropriations of the sea," or *Seenahmen*. Today we have reached another stage. In the new *nomos*, "appropriations of land" have become *Industrienahme*. Space is space for industrial development, *Leistungsnahme*. The world opens up to a single world space, *Weltraumnahme*, because the nature of industry and the market allow for it.[89] One could even think of a political unity of all mankind according to one industrial space. Along with this unity, it is also fitting to imagine more aggressive progress and new means for exercising power that radically separate mankind's ethical and moral progress from industrial and technical progress.[90]

In opposition to growing industrial development that tends toward *Großraum*, the earth is still divided into a multiplicity of States that claim to be sovereign. However, these States are dependent on extending industrial development and, in particular, on the balance of two world powers, especially because of atomic power, that, as such, need that "large space" (*Großraum*) so that they do not fall into political insignificance.[91] Thus, it can be said that the space of industrial development will determine the fate of all peoples on the earth.[92] On this point, the world is full of contradictions. On the one hand, it appears as a purely commercial environment for the progress of humanity, in which the most developed countries attempt to help less developed ones. On the other hand, it is clear that cold war is most intensely fought in this space.[93] Faced with these problems, there are two possible answers and decisions:

> Will the dualism of cold war worsen or will a series of large autonomous spaces (*Großräume*) form, thereby producing a balance in the world and, in this way, the condition for a stable order of peace? These two possibilities are

open. We therefore have a field for free political decision and historical responsibility.[94]

EXCURSUS: STATISM AND ANTISTATISM IN SCHMITT'S POSITIONS AND CONCEPTS

What was Schmitt's position regarding statist thought? This is a disputed question in scholarship. There are at least three possible interpretations: He was a statist thinker.[95] That is, he considered the Modern State as the essential and optimal political form, the archetype of political unity and, therefore, saw it as the definitive form beyond which nothing better can be built. There are many texts that contradict this interpretation, especially Schmitt's writings devoted to the State as a political form linked to the historical circumstances in which it arises. The second interpretation corresponds to Schmitt as a "nostalgic" thinker of the State. Therein, theoretically the State can no longer be maintained and belongs to an era that has ended. However, the State era has not been as dire as depicted because it has supported true law and true politics and the era that comes after it will probably not be much better.[96] Certainly, for Schmitt, the political State form is not philosophical or politically irrelevant, because it manifests relevant elements of the political sphere. Many texts confirm this position. The third interpretation sees Schmitt as an "ironic" theorist of the State. Schmitt was statist because existentially he belonged to the State era by tradition. However, he understood the State and its insurmountable internal problems, and this knowledge led him to proclaim the end of it. This latter statement is based on the criticisms he makes of the State, which intended to show its theoretical errors and their impossibility in practice. The State has been in decline and its own suppositions have led to his death.

In short, which position did Schmitt defend? In the first place, he argued that there be a State and that there be a clear political *nomos*. Second, he argued that the State must adjust as much as possible to historical circumstances. Each historical *nomos* calls for a kind of State. Thirdly, according to Schmitt, the Modern State located the specificity of politics better than other political forms that preceded it, thanks to the theological-political analogies he implies. Fourth, the State implements a philosophy of the people and some organizational techniques that, in both cases (parliamentarianism and democracy), are superior to previous historical forms. Fifth, some of the philosophical, technical, and political transformations of the State seriously threaten the Modern State's gains. This explains, in sixth place, his initial sympathy for the National Socialist State. He saw it as an attempt to synthesize the technical achievements of the Modern State with the actual presence of the people in politics. It appears as the Modern State without the liberal defect that belittles the people and without the "democratic" defect that ignores the true essence of politics. Schmitt shortly thereafter found out that this State model did not work and progressively distanced himself from it.

In my view Schmitt did not take the side of the State, but rather the side of concrete order. That is, he took the side of any political form capable of creating an order, not just any order, but rather that which corresponds to the situation of a people at a particular historical moment. In that sense, Schmitt's political philosophy includes a theory of the State, but it is not just that. It is more a theory of concrete order and, consequently, of the State and of political forms in as far as they are integrated into a concrete order.

Thus, he described Hobbes's State as an order that was designed from the specific historical circumstances of religious wars, the National Socialist State as an order that corresponded to the Weimar crises, or the parliamentary State as an order that corresponds to a pluralistic society. Does this mean that Schmitt changed his mind in each of his texts? No. Rather, his discourse, although it involves a permanent historical reference, tries to go beyond the historical realm. A political form represents an order that corresponds to the *Lebensordnung* (order of life) of a people and therefore varies. It would be contradictory to Schmitt's "historical thought" to anchor it in a particular theory of the State.[97] In many scholars' opinions, however, Schmitt's attitude toward the State is the thread that runs through his thought:[98] Both his juristic and political ideas are developed within the State framework. Moreover Schmitt defined himself as the last representative of the *ius publicum europaeum* and, in that sense, contextually, he is a 'statalist' thinker.[99] However, Schmitt proposed a political pluriverse whose units are *Großräume*, as discussed below.

For Schmitt, the concept of State is not a general idea, but a concrete concept, namely, that which refers to the political form that represents the order born in Europe in the sixteenth century and that endured until the twentieth century. It is true that its trajectory includes variations that go from the absolute State of the seventeenth and eighteenth centuries, through the neutral, non-interventionist State of the nineteenth century, up to the total State of the twentieth century.[100] The State is not an essential general concept valid for any time, but rather is bound to historical circumstances and may, therefore, end with them.[101] Its birth in the sixteenth century is due to two major historical events: First, the fight for the establishment of a new order in newly discovered lands. According to Schmitt, this revolution ushered in modernity more than individualistic ideology.[102] Second, Schmitt highlighted the struggle between Catholicism and Protestantism—that is, religious civil wars,[103] which appeared in response to these historical events and in the struggle with the already decadent form of the empire (*Reich*).[104] Indeed, the appearance of this new order resulted in overcoming the medieval feudal order. The State replaced the feudal order and proposed a new order of space driven by historical events.[105] Now, it seems that if the State were defined, in whatever form, in opposition to the previous political form and as a response to historical circumstances in favor of neutrality to achieve peace, it would be necessary that, under changing circumstances, this form of political unity would also undergo variations or even disappear. It would be necessary, therefore, to start thinking with non-State categories in response to the new historical moment. [106] However, reality has shaped up differently: The State still stands in the twenty-first century. No specific response has emerged in face of the new situation that differs from that which was born in the sixteenth century. [107] If the state as a political form can disappear, then it is not a political category and is only a historical-political form. When the State monopolizes the political realm, confusion surfaces. [108]

Now, does Schmitt clear up this confusion? On this point, there are two interpretations. There is first a negative answer, which most scholars who enter into dialogue with Schmitt adopt. [109] The other responds positively in asserting that there is a difference in levels between the political-philosophical realm—a subject of political unity—and the political-historical realm—a subject of the State—and accepts that Schmitt distinguished them. This is the position I take. On this point, there are certainly controversial texts, for example:

> The political element [of a constitution in a "constitutional State"] cannot be separated from the State, from the political unity of a people. And to render public law non political would mean nothing other than to deprive public law of its connection with the State. [110]

> Fleeing politics means fleeing from the State. [111]

In these texts, both of the above interpretations can be forced. It may seem that they confirm the first; however, as already noted, we must distinguish between the texts in which Schmitt tries to make a general theory and those in which, from the beginning, he takes the Modern State as a reference point, given that it was the political form contemporary to his writing. These last two citations are part of a constitutional theory that takes the Modern State as support and, therefore, it is logical that he identified politics and the State, since the State and political unity are circumstantially identified from the outset. [112] They refer to the spatial order or territory because its initial definition corresponds to spatial borders. The State concept is static, it is more the peaceful state of a people than a government function; it is also fundamentally a power. Being a power against any outside intervention is its main activity. The State is the absolute *status quo* that preserves the existence of a people on which the development of any other activity depends. But also Schmitt devoted numerous critiques to this State model, although they can largely be placed into two groups. One of them analyzes the very principles of the State form at its origin. The other analyzes the liberal *Rechtsstaat* as a decadent form of the State. The former mainly appears in *Der Leviathan des Thomas Hobbes* (1938), in *Der Staat als Mechanismus bei Hobbes und Descartes* (1937), and in *Der Status quo und der Friede* (1925). The latter appears in *Verfassungslehre* (1928), in *Die geistesgeschichtliche Lage des heutigen Parlamentarismus* (1923), and in *Staatsethik und Pluralistischer Staat* (1930). Looking at these publication dates, it can be said that Schmitt evolved from a critique of liberal *Rechtsstaat* to a critique of the State in any form—that is, a critique of the State form's very principles.

I start by synthetically presenting the critique of the state form's principles, considering how these principles appear formulated in State theorists' work, and then I will summarize the critique of the liberal State in its legal and political aspects. The first ironic critique is of de-theologization, which appears in *Ex Captivitate Salus*. It explains how the cry *Silete theologi!* that jurists proclaimed at the beginning of the State era turned against them, generating the great paradox of the State, which amounts to being a machine that turns against itself and that destroys itself. De-theologization was more of a bad remedy than any kind of solution. The State is the political paradigm of secularization and neutralization, and Hobbes is its first theoretical representative.[113]

The second critique is the conception of political unity as an artificial product of human calculation. Conceiving of the State as a contract—that is, considering arbitrary human decision as essential to the State's origin—represents the crucial step that leads to the disembodied technical machine that the State became over time.[114] The total State of the twentieth century was already prefigured there since it needed nothing more than the total development of technique, namely arms, nuclear power, and mass communication technology, to become total. Once thought of as an artificial human product, the State always tends toward greater perfection oriented at becoming a machine free of any glitches. The technical domain legitimizes the State as the supreme authority. This idea resulted in the nineteenth-century legalistic conception of the State and in the twentieth-century conception of the total State. The State as a technically perfect machine reached full neutrality.[115]

Schmitt's third fundamental critique of the concept of the State is the distinction and separation that it generates between individuals' inner and outer "jurisdictions." This is, in his opinion, the biggest flaw in the theory of the Modern State and is where the State's liberality originated.[116] In principle, there is no right of resistance against the Hobbesian *Leviathan*. In the Modern State, people are constituted as individuals against the State and are subjects. There is no intermediary instance of a stratified nature between individuals and the State. The State under its sovereignty determines its subjects' activity, even, to some extent, establishes the person in whom they are to believe. A sovereign power's decision-making ability is absolute. The

State as public reason, against subjects' private reason or conscience, can decide on what they should believe. But, in the nuance that Hobbes gives this statement, we find the seeds of the State's destruction; in his attempt to suppress all indirect power, he subjected moral and religious power to temporal power. However, he recognized that there are certain individual reserves that cannot be rooted out with which the seed of the indirect power of conscience appears and, therefore, dangerous forms of power, which cannot be reconciled with the sovereign power in any way. Historically, this change took place only after the religious wars. The State thus became neutral with respect to the inner sphere and a public confession materialized where every citizen is free to internally profess whatever he wants.[117] The aforementioned separation between the public and private spheres grows to the point that the *Leviathan* becomes an "an externally all powerful, internally powerless concentration of power."[118] Thus, coercion becomes the only means by which to execute this power. Schmitt claimed that this separation between the internal and external sealed the *Leviathan* figure's death,[119] which is wounded in an area proper to it, namely, the unity of its power. Despite this, it has been maintained for centuries. Schmitt remained in the strict Hobbesian tradition of the rejection of indirect powers,[120] while recognizing that there is an internal dialectic to human power, making it impossible to banish indirect powers from political reality.[121] However, even understanding this unavoidable dialectic intrinsic to all human power, he did not try for integration, but rather gave a one-dimensional solution: Whatever wields indirect power must be eliminated. Power can only be direct, but to my mind, this is not the option when dealing with Hobbes. The real option is found in integrating public and private, for which it is necessary to admit something that Schmitt does not acknowledge, namely that not everything that comes from individuals is necessarily private and not every State action is necessarily public.

The fourth critique deals with thinking about the State as the sole and ultimate form of political unity. The pure form of the Modern State has corroded and taken the form of the bourgeois *Rechtsstaat* because of the progressive fissures produced by its failures and theoretical errors.[122] This State model has only drawn out the consequences of the above mentioned principles, for which Schmitt offered another series of critiques that deal, on the one hand, with the legal element and, on the other hand, with the political element. Hence, I will now consider a synopsis of the critiques of the liberal State, which, in some way, have already been discussed in the previous pages.

In speaking of the Constitution, we have already seen the critiques of the "ideal" concept of constitution that is identified by the bourgeois *Rechtsstaat*. Such a constitution is liberal—that is, it contains the concept of liberty proper to bourgeois individualist liberalism, the *liberté* of the French Revolution, that defends citizens against abuses by public power.[123] The potential enemy of liberty is the State, and individuals must defend their freedom against it. [124] This concept of freedom and of the State poses serious problems for the realization of the democratic ideal. In this context, the constitution has to take responsibility for ensuring this guarantee and it does so mainly by attributing to the concept of statute certain characteristics that allow for the establishment of a clear distinction between a legal norm and a command or measure. [125] Statute's general character is its fundamental property that cannot be relinquished without the *Rechtsstaat* disappearing. Statute is based on preference for the general versus the singular and, therefore, on eliminating exception from the framework of State theory. It is also characterized by the requirement of equality before it, meaning equality for all of the issued statutes and protection against breaches, waivers, and privileges in whatever form they arise. However, it is impossible that this concept of statute be maintained without being accompanied by a "political" concept of statute because, if not, how can the question of its origin be resolved? [126] With regard to liberty, Schmitt mentioned two fundamental principles that must appear throughout the ideal constitution, namely, a distribution principle and an organizing principle. Under the former, the sphere of individual liberty is assumed as a pre-State notion and thus unlimited when compared to the State; therefore, the power of the State is, in principle, limited. [127] The latter refers to the practice of former. For the liberty of the State to be truly limited, its sphere of action must be reduced—that is, by dividing its power into an enclosed system of circumscribed powers. [128]

These two principles, hidden as such in the liberal constitution, are transparent in human rights and the separation of powers. Every modern conception of the State maintains these principles, thus ensuring a *status quo*, a *status mixtus* [129] in which "rights acquired" are more important than political existence and the security of the State. [130] There are also certain "organizational criteria" [131] derived from the principle of separation of powers. First, there is the prohibited disruption of the sphere of individual liberty except by law, such that the law itself becomes the ultimate guarantor of bourgeois freedom. Second, there is the measurability of all manifestations of state power, which means overall control. [132] And third, there is judicial independence. The constitution is a system of legal, closed, and sovereign norms, such that no one can break or influence it by needs of a political nature. The constitution is, to some extent, everything in such a system, because everything else refers to it. It is its own legitimacy in the form of legality. The judicial sphere is independent of all relation to the political sphere, but this is only possible provided that there are general norms that always oblige, essentially, the judge whose independence derives from the very independence with respect to political power. But if the judge had to decide beyond the law, his decision would be exceptional and would collide with the political sphere. The limit of judicial independence is therefore found in statute itself, in the existence of a community of moral ideas or equity that facilitates its application, and in a state of minor conflict. If this were not so, not even statute could be applied. According to Schmitt, every State experiences the judicial sphere's limit,[133] which is why no State can be just a judicial organization, a neutral body; rather, its essence lies in political decision.

These legal elements, which are proper to *Rechtsstaat*, do not imply a form of government[134] precisely because "freedom constitutes nothing."[135] Thus, when manifest in a particular State, they must be combined with political elements. The constitution of *Rechtsstaat* may appear in the form of monarchy or democracy, both in their moderate versions since they are as always, in principle, limited by individual freedoms. In this sense, the Modern Constitution of the bourgeois *Rechtsstaat* has mixed elements of *Rechtsstaat*, independent in itself, with strictly political and formal elements in order to constitute a form of government. Along with a critique of legalism, Schmitt posed a critique of the political element of the Modern State that, in advanced societies, has resulted over time in parliamentarianism. The theme of this critique comes to be the description of parallels and differences between democracy and parliamentarianism, for which he pitted parliamentarianism against democracy and vice versa.[136] Since democracy is an impossible way of governing given that it lacks a political-formal principle of representation, the parliamentary system becomes necessary. However, from the point of view of true representation, parliamentarianism is a cheap substitute at the same time that it is a denial of democracy because it lacks an authentic identity principle. Historically, there has been no other choice but to play between the two.

The democratic form of government is mainly based on the political and formal principle of the identity of people and the State, that is, on popular sovereignty. According to the "democratic doctrine,"[137] the people are the subject of both constituent and constituted power. The populace is always present and, therefore, cannot and need not be represented. This principle entails the minimization of representation. Political issues should be resolved thanks to an all-out popular homogeneity. Popular will in the democratic system is configured based on certain assumptions, the first of which is equality.[138] Schmitt's critiques this point by claiming that such uniformity lacks reality and is nothing more than a feigned assumption.[139] In addition, the remaining identifications that are deduced as corollaries of this principle, namely, identification between governors and the governed, between populace and representation, the State and statute, the quantitative and qualitative, suffer from a lack of reality. Its presumed validity is based on a mere postulate of such identifications such that there is always distance between intended equality and the identification's result.[140]

For a democracy to truly exist, an essence of equality is necessary, which can be found in different walks of life, or in the physical, economic, legal, moral qualities, and so on that make up a people. Depending on where it is found, the political sphere will be organized pivoting on one reference point or another. But it can even be raised, and indeed it so happens, as a result of the interference of democratic principles in liberal doctrine—that is, equality as apolitical. For example, equality of all human beings by virtue of "being human" amounts to nonpolitical equality since it lacks the correlate of inequality and it would be an unfair human equality since only taking communal aspects into account, as opposed to specific particularities, does not address the human dignity of each individual.[141] This equality is typical of a "religion of humanity," but never of political form. The democratic concept of equality, however, is political and, as such, must relate to a distinction. In democracy, all equality finds its meaning through the correlate of a possible inequality.[142] Therefore, it can in no way refer to humanity, but needs to be set to a particular people. In fact, the central concept of democracy is the people and not humanity. Within a people, all are equal with regard to a particular substance that changes according to the times. This substance is characterized by the absence of qualitative differences. Democracy thus moves, even though it does not want to, in a flat, immanent metaphysics.[143] From the point of view of government action, democratic equality has a fundamental problem in that it virtually excludes action. Once democracy has allowed a people's will to be obtained as the sum of homogeneity, it has to carry out another identification process between the winning majority and the losing minority to obtain the general will and not a mere sum of particular wills, for which the popular will must be educated. The defeated individual must understand that he was wrong in his vote. A program to educate people must therefore be established in order to recognize one's own will and express it correctly.[144] If this happens, democratic education is nothing more than a path toward dictatorship.[145]

He also criticized the failures of the democratic concept of a people as a constituent power. If the people's power is constituent it should come before and above the constitution, since constituent power is characterized by a lack of any kind of norm before it. However, the constitution also gives the people its political powers. And it cannot be otherwise because a people is properly inorganic, so much so that once organized, it is no longer a people. But to govern, organization must occur. The paradox is that, for a government of the people to emerge, the people can no longer exist as such. If a people, as such, has the power to elect and vote, we must suppose, if we want to stay within the democratic framework, that it remains an immediately present entity at all times.[146] Contradiction cannot help but follow, since it is unclear what a whole people that governs without being organized means. This cannot be so; to govern, it must be organized in a parliament, but parliament is not the same thing as the people. Now, in parliamentarianism, individual and secret ballot transforms the democratic "citizen" into a private, liberal man. In the decisive moment of surrendering the will, the link between a gathered people and voting is broken. The people do not vote and choose as a people such that voting's results do not reflect popular will, but rather the sum of private wills. This objection comes from Rousseau as well. There is thus a contradiction between it and the democratic concept of a general will since a people is necessarily no longer present as such through this method, as it dissolves into the particularity of each individual. If proportional representation is lauded instead of believing in the possibility of identifying a people in voting, then democratic principles become deformed, giving way to liberal ones.[147] One is left to believe in the assumption of substantial equality to apply the principle of equality of opportunity to exercise freedom. The people no longer exist as a constituent power, but rather a general opinion of the majority, but not of all. In order to keep the democratic idea alive, an inorganic public opinion must emerge, which, contrary to what it may seem, does not arise from nothing, but rather is elaborated by political parties and focus groups. This is consistent in parliamentarianism, which, with the application of liberal principles, puts the private sphere above the public one with the result that today we have a democracy without a people.[148] From a logical point of view, this system is nothing more than the degeneration of democracy, a degeneration that is, furthermore, impossible to avoid. Every democracy that wants to be a system of government has become a parliamentary system, such that the only justification for the latter is, many times, to be a "lesser evil" with regard to democracy.[149]

In the nineteenth century, with the spread of liberal ideas, the idea of democracy became definitively relegated in favor of parliamentarianism. The liberal idea of universal human equality and substantive equality was incorporated into democracy's formal identity. This equality is intended to be accomplished by the use of the idea of individual liberal freedom. The individual thus emerges as a sphere of unlimited freedom against the State.

Along with this principle, the conditions by which a parliamentary system works appear, namely, instruction and individual property. Instruction is seen as a personal quality, a faculty for exercising representation. Indeed, in nineteenth-century parliament, representatives were enlightened men, which led to the belief that only such people could distinguish between personal and public interest. Slowly, in conformity with democratic principles, universal suffrage was extended such that parliament ceased to represent a particular enlightened class and "learning."[150] It was initially understood rather as the place to which a commission of interests was brought and, although property is not a quality that can be represented, property owner interests began to be represented, which required a census suffrage. Later, it represented the means for expressing public opinion and thus fell into a functional dependence on voters. Ultimately, this system becomes an undefined government. It uses, on one hand, aristocratic ideas to build representation and, on the other hand, democratic

conceptions to put decision into the people's hands in case of conflict between parliament and government, such that the people appear as a superior,
third agent of balance. In Schmitt's words, "[but] it is a system that applies
and mixes different governmental and legislative forms in the service of a
pliable counterpoise."[151] It generates the following scale: Parliament is a
commission of the people, and government a commission of parliament.
With the unity of these two ideas, parliament appears as a democratic institution, without actually being so. Schmitt found this legitimation of parliament
insufficient. It ultimately aims, using a plurality of wills, to hide decision
and, above all, the responsibility that it brings with it.

The suppositions of parliamentarianism necessary for sustaining the principles set out above are as follows: rationalism, free competition, and pre-
established harmony. In this system, action is generated in the free competition of opinions, with harmony resulting from this competition.[152] Discussion is therefore essential to parliamentarianism and, for it to be possible up
to the last consequences, dissemination is also essential. For competition to
be fair in the struggle of opinions, all parties must be equally informed.

As already mentioned, since parliamentary principles are different from
democratic ones, how the popular will is shaped in these systems differs. The
universality of the right to vote here means that every adult person, by virtue
of being so, should be emancipated *eo ipso* on the same political level as
everyone else.[153] In this case, defeated minorities are not ignored; they do not
go through an identification process with the majority and a system of proportional representation is established.[154] The movement of popular will that
results from this technique puts private interest before public interest because
"upward movement"[155] leads from selfish interests and opinions through the
conduit of party will to a presumed homogeneous will of the State. In this
system, parties play an important role in channeling and forming the will of
the people. Schmitt claimed that the principle of parliamentarianism is not
effective because it does not give rise, in reality, to a government since the
wills within the parliament are so divided. He reinforced this point saying:
"How can the unity in which the violent antagonism of parties and special
interests is overcome and fused together come about in this situation?"[156]
Can a plurality of parties act as a government with conflicting interests?
Schmitt's answer, ultimately, was that parliament does not govern in the
strict sense; he set out a strong critique of pluralism, which was done with an
eye on the form that the Weimar Republic took.[157] His criticism of pluralism
is closely linked to that of *potestas indirecta*, to which reference has already
been made. Schmitt mainly fought liberalism and, therefore, pluralism with
the concept of order and political unity.

Despite all these critiques of the Modern State, Schmitt continued to
defend it as better than other political forms or, at least, better than any other
form that has been tested so far. His defense is historical: The Modern State

is the largest political and technical construction in history. However, this judgment is coupled with a rejection of certain aspects of the configuration of it, which, according to Schmitt, severely damages the specifically political character of the State. *Corruptio optimi pessima.*

The question here, then is, what kind of State would Schmitt get behind? Certainly not the multiparty State of the nineteenth and twentieth centuries, the *Rechtsstaat* to which he dedicated, as we have seen, numerous critiques. He also could not get fully behind the Hobbesian sovereign State, to which he also devoted some criticism, especially regarding its mechanistic configuration and its neutrality that empties the values proper to a ruler of all metaphysical and religious content, the decisionism it assigns to the sovereign, and, ultimately, its individualism. Was he really a supporter of the totalitarian State between 1934 and 1945, about which, after the war, he offered extensive commentary? The new *nomos* of the earth will guide political decision in order to shape new forms of political unity that can achieve peace for new historical challenges. The future is open to new possibilities. There is no sense, following Schmitt, in giving a normative response to the question of the State's best form.

Chapter Seven

Precedents of the Political Theology

According to some studies, ancient Asian theology can be found at the core of all other theologies and cosmologies and has its roots in very basic forms and explanations of the world and people. It contains awareness that the socio-cosmic universe, or social microcosm, and the physical macrocosm are not independent. This way of explaining the relationship between the cosmos and society implies a certain political theology since it considers that there is harmony between the transcendent and the historical, that is, between men in connection with the gods and men in relation with the processes of this world. Chinese culture was aware of this relationship in which the cosmos is socialized and politicized. Humans are medial between religious transcendence and the physical world. In this way, the three levels—the religious, the sociopolitical, and the physical—are interrelated. [1]

In the Greco-Roman world, the interrelationship between the state and the divine, politics and religion, is evident. It was a world in which the state and the divine belonged together, in which a non-divine state and a stateless divinity were not possible (*Gottlose Staat–Staatslose Gottheit*). Both the *polis* and *civitas* were understood in antiquity as religious ideas. [2] Marcus Terentius Varro named this formula "civil theology," as defined in Saint Augustine's criticism in the *City of God*. [3]

The break between the divine, political, and cosmic spheres emerged with Christianity precisely because stressing divine transcendence alongside society and the world caused a certain rift between the spiritual and the material. Consequently, an immediate suspicion against astral theology emerged and, on the other hand, the union of theology and the political signified to Christianity, in principle, the impermissible theologization of existing state and social forms. [4] However, a distinction between these three spheres did not mean a separation or total rupture.

One of the best testimonies of the practical vision of medieval political theology, not necessarily Christian but within a Christian cosmos, is Eusebius of Cesarea's "Life of Constantine."[5] The bishop Eusebius glorifies divine monarchy as a model for Constantine's government, which consolidates the *pax Augusta* (an eschatological sign of redemption), because it coincides with Christ's incarnation. In "Monotheism as a Political Problem,"[6] Peterson explains how Eusebius follows the idea of the connection between monotheism and monarchy.[7] The idea of monarchy was initially essential in order to differentiate Judaism from the poliarchy of paganism, and Christianity unconsciously adopted this concept. In Peterson's view, the integral formula "kingdom, peace and monotheism" was the Christian construction that, at that time, was opposed to the pagan political theology that defended the national gods against the Roman Empire. To elucidate this Christian political formulation was perhaps the theo-political intention of Eusebius of Caesarea in his *Life of Constantine*. In contrast, Saint Augustine rejected absolutely the analogy between the Roman Empire and the Kingdom of Christ. According to Augustine, the Kingdom of Christ is limited to the Church alone.

In fact, Augustine offers a new perspective, whereby the proposed Christian definition of the relationship between these two realms is that the civil state cannot be identified with the sacred realm, nor a prince with a minister of Christ. The only sacred institution in the world is the Church and its head, the pope. A prince's power can attain legitimacy under the power of God only if he identifies himself with the doctrine and with the way of life professed by Christ and his ministers. In this view, religion and politics are mixed in the arena of earthly life but they have two distinct and separate spheres of jurisdiction, viz. the political and the spiritual. Augustine believes that, in historical terms, there is a *res mixta*: a theological-political arena in which men should conduct their lives, although they have clear references that guide their judgment in the minister of the Church, the pope, and in the representative of the principality, the prince.[8]

In this context, political theology frequently is adjusted to a scheme whereby the political head should seek the benediction of the spiritual power in order to legitimize his power. Conversely, the spiritual power seeks political influence in order to achieve its own ends, for example the growth of Christianity through evangelization. This relationship was the believed praxis of the so-called political Augustinism: Political persecution of heretics was a common practice in the Middle Ages, even if the legitimacy of this practice was highly controversial within the Church.[9] Likewise, within the Christian empire there is a current that operates against the absolute power of the pope according to the political-theological thesis of Ockham. Before 1337, Ockham tries to demonstrate by means of biblical exegesis that Pope Benedict XII, and John XII before him, were heretics.[10] When such a situation occurs, it is important that the Christian prince should have more authority over the population than the pope. Indeed, not only must the political powers be independent from the ecclesiastical hierarchy, but the government of the Church should also be aristocratic, or even democratic. Although papal rule is divine because of Christ's prescription, many aspects are also human: There is no need for a monarchical government in the Church. All these considerations follow his metaphysical distinction between *potentia absoluta Dei* and *potentia ordinata*, as established by Albertus Magnus, Thomas Aquinas, and definitively, by himself.[11]

The very expression "growth of Christianity," as opposed to that of "increase of Christians or Christianity," tells us many things about how to understand the relationship between religion and politics in the medieval era. The medieval mentality considers the religious uniformity of the political community to be desirable—one community, one religion. However, the religious uniformity of the Commonwealth is not specifically Christian but "pagan." This idea of uniformity maintains the tradition of the civil theologies of antiquity, while mixing it with Christian views. The only specific Christian-Catholic criteria for the relationship between the Church and State is that political and spiritual power should not reside in the same hands; in other words, absolute power is illicit even if it is the pope who holds it.[12]

Early modernity opens new perspectives for theo-political practices. The expression itself already appears in Spinoza's *Theological-Political Treatise*, published in 1670, although Hobbes had already made use of the theo-political strategy in his *Leviathan* published in 1651. It is argued that for Christianity to permit a purely secular policy, a theological reformation must be achieved; and that such a reformation cannot be effective without a shift in the interpretation of sacred history. Both authors undertake the task of interpreting the scriptures in order to secularize politics and free themselves from the pope's power (in the case of Hobbes) and from that of the Calvinist theologians (in the case of Spinoza). The former defends the English monarchy, the latter republicanism against the Orangists. In both cases, different as they may be, the result is that the *suprema potestas*, the sovereign, should have the *potestas spiritualis* as much as the *potestas civilis* for the sake of the *salus publica*.[13] This conclusion is the anti-Catholic thesis and it is the revival of a kind of "civil theology" in Christianity. This approach drives a separation between public confession and private faith, which tends to preserve freedom. In the course of time, the pope would be a private interpreter of faith and a private governor, with no political relevance whatsoever. Far from being secularized, early modern politics, then, refounds the unit of power, spiritual and political, on a single head.

In 1922, with reference to this context and history, Carl Schmitt first coined the term "political theology" to describe some aspects of this problem.[14] The term *"politische Theologie"* first appeared that year, but interest in the subject can be found in his earliest writings.[15] Consequently, it does not emerge from predictions or from a normative study, but rather, it emerges from the recognition of an object of study: the conceptual transfer between theological and political spheres. Schmitt looked at that relationship with interest and tried to think about its content.

Thus, from the first time he wrote on the topic, political theology appears not as a method to do politics or as a good mode of legitimizing the political, but rather as a method of knowledge that allows one to distinguish the deep structure of a political context. For Schmitt, therefore, political theology is an area of knowledge initially discovered within research on jurisprudence and, therefore, by no means a proposal for concrete action in the sphere of the political.[16] The main interest in this book is to study the meaning that political theology, in the sense that Schmitt coined, may have for a political philosophy and *not* to identify the place this concept holds in our day in relation to, for example, the life of the Church,[17] to some political regimes,[18] or to academia.[19] In this chapter I will address the precedents and related topics of Schmitt's political theology.

THEOLOGY OF HISTORY

If the concept of the political always depends on conceptions that are held about human beings and history, political theology must also be related to a particular interpretation of history that envisions history from the perspective of theological events. This kind of history has been called the theology of history, and it has been undertaken since Augustine's *City of God.* Carl Schmitt also followed this path in one of his reflections on history.

Reflection on history makes its appearance at different stages in the development of Schmitt's discourse. It appears in the first period as an ironic essay on diary writers, *Die Buribunken* (1918), and later in *Land und Meer* (1942), *Drei Stufen historischer Sinngebung* (1950), *Der Nomos der Erde* (1950), *Existentielle Geschichtsschreibung: Alexis de Tocqueville* (1950), and in *Die Einheit der Welt* (1952). There are two kinds of approaches to history: One is what I have called here, in chapter 2, a "geo-interpretation of history" that is centered on *nomos* and narrated in *Land and Sea*; the second one is a "theology of history" that it is not just one of the many narratives of history that can be attempted, but rather provides the ultimate meaning of history.

In Schmitt's approach, to answer the question on history is to expose the meaning of history for historical thought—that is, that which refers to history and not to a philosophy of history,[20] or that which is capable of taking on unique and unrepeatable situations that, therefore, are only true once. As Schmitt liked to say, "a historical truth is only true once."[21] This statement is not indicative of a historicist approach, against which Schmitt took a clear stand in *Die Buribunken* in describing those diary authors who wished to be an objective will to power in the face of history.[22] What Schmitt meant to say on this point is that the truth of "each" response refers to "a" question raised by history such that there are no general valid responses in history.[23] Each situation is somehow unique:

> Every human word is a response, every response receives its meaning from the question to which it responds and it is pointless for anyone ignorant of the question. The meaning of the question rests, in turn, on the concrete situation in which it arises.[24]

On this point, Mohler related how, in a letter dated December 4, 1948, Schmitt commented on the importance of dialogue as the appropriate way of expressing what we can call "thought on the unique."[25] A dialogue never knows where it leads, even though the dialogue is on something that has already been thought over many times. That which is said or thought cannot be separated from the concrete situation in which it was said or thought.[26] Hence the importance that Schmitt attached to dialogue as a method of knowledge. History's structure is also conceived dialogically.

Schmitt rejected the philosophy of history in the sense that the term acquired in the Enlightenment. As knowledge, it emerged in opposition to the theology of history.[27] Theology of history is an interpretation of history as a history of perfection and revelation. Along with the concepts illustrated in the philosophy of history, such as those of Voltaire, Comte, or Hegel, another possibility is raised: the Christian idea of history.[28] Only from there, according to Schmitt, is it possible to achieve a unity of all historical events in the uniqueness of each from the conception of Providence. The Christian era was a milestone. Until then, the events of history were like that of nature, a cycle that repeats continuously. With the beginning of the Christian era— that is, with the concrete fact of Christ's birth—another way of understanding history appeared. The concrete event of Christ's birth is the concrete point of a beginning. His death was the concrete point of an end. The eternal burst into time. Transcendence and history became one in this incident. The concrete story of a life makes and symbolizes the history of all humanity, of which it is only possible to be aware through Revelation.[29] History finds its meaning, then, in reference to those events in Christian history with which the concept of history is properly born.

> Christianity, in its essence, is not a morality or a doctrine, or any kind of penitential preaching, or religion in the sense in which this term is used in the field of comparative religion, but rather a historical event of endless, irreplaceable and incorruptible uniqueness. It is the incarnation of the Virgin. The creed speaks of historical events.[30]

This involves a happening and not just pure facticity,[31] that is, a historical event that reveals the meaning of history.[32] There is no present that is no longer because it has passed; it is rather a present that makes perfect sense at all times because it can be contemplated from the central events of Christian history such that it is never a mere passing by. The present, then, is not a will for power over history. In accordance with this, Schmitt defined history as follows:

> We dare to tell a story that is not just a record of what happened, nor a humanistic, reflective image of personality, and even less so a portion of nature that revolves around itself, but rather one that is the incarnation— through the impotence and misery, hope and honor of our existence—of the eternal in the course of time, one that is rooted in the place of the spirit.[33]

History is mainly revealed as a present, a present oriented toward the future, not just toward a historical future, but rather a future beyond time, that is, toward eternity.[34] In history, things happen. It is a happening over time that "makes its way," but this is not just any road. In history human beings have chosen some possibilities and left others behind. The fact that they have followed one road and not another makes each historical happening an event—that is, it makes every happening relevant, meaningful in itself, that it not be occasional and replaceable. The singularity of historical events leads the rationalist philosophies of history to stumble, precisely because they seem to open the door to unintelligibility. However, the intelligibility of these happenings is captured in a Christian view of history. Each event is referred to a plan, which is the work of the person, Christ, who has the power to bring about significant events in history.[35] It may be objected that this reference to the past seems more like a retention of events than a projection of the future for history.[36] For this, Schmitt relied on Konrad Weiss's conception, who—in the order of understanding the historical past—claimed that it is not enough to take "retentive forces" into account. Historical circumstances can always more easily acquire than retain. The past is more than a museum and is rather the succession of significant events that acquire their meaning and unity in an eternal history. Eschatological power is the real governing power in history. The central facts of the Christian era—Christ's birth, crucifixion, and resurrection—remain alive throughout time with an "unaltered presence."[37] With the Christian interpretation of history, we dive into an eschatological way of thinking that does not negate immediate ends, but rather gives them a foundation and meaning. The medieval era attempted to synthesize this conception of history in the concept of *Katechon*, which is the reality of a historical force that in some way represents the eschatological one and that stops the end of time by repressing the spirit of evil. It also gives meaning to history, especially political history. The Old Testament prophets are an example of that kind of force.

In accordance with Löwith, Schmitt observed how there was a need in the nineteenth century to devise a historical parallel with the Roman and early-Christian period of civil wars to understand itself.[38] This parallelism started with Saint-Simon's *New Christianity*, which supposes that the Christian era has ended and that a new *potestas spiritualis* has emerged, in which social-ism is the new religion. From a logical point of view, Saint-Simon was not far off, since contrasting with Christian history is always necessary for achieving ultimate meaning in history.[39]

In short, Christianity provides a true picture of history, but certainly there are many Christian views of it. Anti-utopianism is common to all of them, as well as having in mind the end of time considered as something more than the end of a cycle.[40] Schmitt proposed three possibilities in this regard: (1) to design parallelisms as commented above, (2) to recover a conception of political action as a *Katechon*—that is, as a force that holds back the power of evil, prevents the coming of the Antichrist, and (3) the consideration that the Christian doctrine, by being embodied in a true story, supersedes any philosophy of history.

Of these three possibilities, Schmitt emphasized the second, that is, the *Katechon*—a concept that he repeatedly referred to throughout his works.[41] He assigned a great deal of importance to it and even presented it as a theological-historical category. The concept of *Katechon* refers to Saint Paul's famous passage in II Thessalonians, verses 3–9.[42] There, Saint Paul related how, before the coming end of the world, an Adversary would come to try to remove God from His throne: "*Et nunc quid detineat scitis, ut revelatur in suo tempore. Nam mysterium iam operatur iniquitatis: tantum ut qui tenet nunc, tenent, donec de medio fiet.*" History, which began as such with the coming of Christ, will end with the coming of the Antichrist. Saint Paul assumed something that has not been revealed to us when he said, "you all know" what has held him back until now, preventing his coming until it is time. The mystery of iniquity is really already at work; he who is holding the Antichrist back just needs to be removed from the middle.[43] This force that stops the Antichrist plays a historical role in transcendence; that is, it is providential. It is, therefore, a political-theological figure that connects his-torical and political events with the great beyond. That is, it makes transcen-dence relevant in the course of history.

Interpreters from every era, as d'Ors noted, have seen the Roman Empire as the figure of that force.[44] The political is incarnated within a theology of history as a function of *Katechon* and that is where it acquires its legitimacy. Legitimacy in this case is found in the opposition to an absolute foe: the devil. It is not a historical foe, but is incarnated in historical powers. Within this context, we can better understand Schmitt's assertion that, for the Christian conscience, salvation is the meaning that decides the world history. [45] The force that stalls evil is the real ruler of history. [46] As d'Ors interprets, [47] we can say that eschatological power, the Final Judgment of every man's salvation and damnation, governs history in two ways: One that is properly historical, the effective force of events, Providence, and the other that is fundamental, giving meaning to history—that is, making a moral judgment on it. However, the meaning of each historical event can only be clearly seen when the history of salvation is complete. Meanwhile, historical and moral judgments are not necessarily linked in the course of history and, hence, the transcendent meaning of historical events in time is always an open question until the end. If we accept that this interpretation is contained in the concept of *Katechon*, it can be recognized as the theological-historical category par excellence—that is, as a concept that describes history's true modus operandi. [48]

Some general reasons for establishing a relationship between theology and politics can be enumerated as derivatives of this conception of history. First, precisely because God is somehow in history, both the theological and political spheres are essentially measured by an ontological-existential way of thinking. [49] In connection to these spheres, man's existence can be fully understood. Both situate him in the extreme case: theology facing possible spiritual death, salvation, or damnation; the political facing physical death. It can be said that theology is measured by a concrete existence, which is God's existence. If—as a science—theology distances itself from this existence, it loses its true object of study. It only makes sense, therefore, to the extent that it refers to said existence. With regard to humans, theology has an existential sense in as much as it refers to the absolute possibility of human life understood in the fullest sense. The political is also measured by an ontological-existential way of thinking in as far as its object of study corresponds to a principal aspect of existence: the relationship between people and communities. As it moves away from that existence's conditions, it becomes abstract. And in relation to each particular man, it has an existential sense because, in a concrete case, political decision can call upon the life of one or more men. Both areas of knowledge correspond to modes of recognizing an existence of what characterizes it as such. Second, for the immediate relationship between theology and politics, it must be said that both spheres make an immediate reference to power. Both include the exception within the scope of the reality of their power, which, in jurisprudence and the political, is analogous to miracle and theology. [50] In both cases, "normal" rules may be suspended.

To conclude what has been argued above, it can be said, as Schmitt claimed, that there is a theological-political *res mixta*. This statement historically engages with the question of Augustine's two cities. Since then, the relationship between them emerges as a concrete problem for any political theory. This involves establishing the correct relationship between the following three pairs: the spiritual sphere–worldly sphere, religion-politics, and the church-state.[51] Understanding these pairs as united or separated in concrete political reality is not a problem solved once and for all in history, but rather always involves a decision.

Schmitt's thesis consisted in defending the separation of Church and State as government agencies, but in denying the full autonomy—even if acknowledging a clear distinction—between the religious and political spheres, the spiritual and the earthly spheres, in concrete political life: There is a theological-political *res mixta*. Ignoring the problematic nature of the complete separation between the two spheres, contrary to what may seem to be the case, does not resolve the problem, but rather worsens it: The question of the autonomy always reappears in different forms.[52] Schmitt gives the example of the Council of Nicaea, which did not intend to just solve a dogmatic problem concerning the Father-Son relationship, but also to solve a series of intrigues between the Church and the Emperor Constantine, which had concrete political consequences. With the question of how to articulate the relationship between the Father and the Son, another political topic, along with a theological one, was brought into play.[53]

The question is then: How are both spheres related? Schmitt's response is as follows: They are not "substantially" different; the two realms do not have different material bases.[54] Their diversity comes from a certain formal difference. On the side of the earth, the political is potentially ubiquitous, which is grounded in the fact that any aspect of men's lives can become political. The theological also acts in the same way. On the side of the spiritual sphere, there is ubiquitous reference to God, which could present itself in different ways.[55]

When the theological, or religious, spheres—Schmitt used these terms interchangeably—are not uniquely identifiable with the Church and the political is not uniquely identifiable with the State, then it is no longer possible to maintain a strict separation between the two Augustinian kingdoms and the borders that separate the two spaces begin to blur. Augustine did not do this either since the city of God and the earthly cities remain mixed in history until the final judgment.[56] What we have then is a *res mixta*, where the claim to "theological purity" is inconsistent with faith.[57] Notwithstanding this overlap, a formal conflict is possible between the two kingdoms in history precisely because a formal difference always remains possible, a difference not of substance, but rather of bodies, institutions, and formal competencies.[58] A conflict of competencies is a clash of organizations and institutions as specific orders. Such a conflict can only end in two ways: either with a response to the question of who decides in each case or with a definition of the field or the space occupied by each party in the sense found in the famous phrase, *cuius regio, eius religio*. We are well acquainted with the consequences of the latter solution. The former could be even better defined in the question:

Who in specific decides what is earthly and what is spiritual, and how is this related to the intermediate situation that occurs in the time between the first coming of Christ and his final return,[59] a space in time that Schmitt called the "Christian eon"? Only there does a political theology make sense.[60] Political theology as a knowledge sphere remains with this argument situated in *nomos*, in space-time history.

THE LOSS OF *POTESTAS SPIRITUALIS*

Schmitt was obsessed by the famous exclamation, "Be silent, theologians!" "'Silete theologi!' is still in force, which was launched at the beginning of the State era by an international lawyer against theologians of both confessions."[61] Schmitt masterfully described legal science's path in the last two centuries in his small study *Die Lage der europäischen Rechtswissenschaft*,[62] which clarifies how the aforementioned crisis deals directly with the loss of legitimation.

The crisis of European legal science began in 1848 with the triumph of legal positivism, which ignored the natural law and the "illusion of reality."[63] Legal science then became a mere commentary on and interpretation of State Statutes. Statute appeared as closed, impersonal, objective, and outside of surrounding circumstances, while motive acquired a personalist hue linked to the legislator. In the twentieth century, a new step was taken, which Schmitt called the "motorization of the law," through which the legislation process became ever easier and faster. The last step emerged with the economic order of a single market where the law became an elastic means that is formed or de-formed depending on all kinds of interests. In this process, the separation between legitimacy and legality that destroys law arose.

Since becoming a science, the law has been situated between two fires: on the one hand, theology and philosophy and, on the other hand, the technical sphere. Dependence on the former—at a time when theology had become a secular natural law (seventeenth and eighteenth centuries) and philosophy had become idealism—was as terrible as the rationalist technicality in whose arms it now finds itself.[64] In abandoning theology, jurists were trying to form their own tradition to avoid the problem contained in just war. However, in separating from dogma, they did not get the autonomy they sought, but rather took on a commitment to rationalism and progress.[65] With this call to silence theology, the State era began, signifying a process of secularization and the jurist age.[66] Thus, the legal concepts that had been supported by theology were transfused to the theory of the State. Taking a long view, one can see that legal science went from depending on theology and philosophy to being a part of a technical sphere of norms.[67] It could be said that this transformation came about in a struggle with theology and theological faculties.[68]

The price of this autonomy is, however, the loss of legitimation. Since then, jurists have been searching for a foundation for their science, for legitimacy. When written constitutions emerged—as Schmitt noted—legislatures sought to institute their identity through solemn declarations, for example, by appealing to God or some other moral or ideological formula, in order to sanction them.[69] A theologized and moralized natural law, as well as general propositions within a theory of values, were also attempts to overcome the legalism that legal positivism entails.[70] Many jurists, in recent times, have favored a theory of values because it seems more scientific than the old Thomistic natural law theory. But, according to Schmitt, value and a theory of values are not capable of establishing legitimacy.[71] Ultimately, the loss of theological legitimation has brought with it a move from transcendence to immanence in the foundation of legal science.

DETERMINING THE CONCEPT OF SOVEREIGNTY

The relationship between theology and politics was initially raised through the topic of sovereignty.[72] To define sovereignty, Schmitt referred to the theological and political analogy between miracle and exception. Schmitt did not consider himself a theologian; he did not intend to offer a theological argument or enter into a theological dispute—and this is one of the ways in which he differs from Juan Donoso.[73] His words are those of a modern-era jurist, an heir to Bodin and Hobbes and, therefore, "necessarily" cast-off theology.[74] However, from his own position as a jurist, he found himself methodologically required to look to theology to explain certain legal and political phenomena.[75]

Political theology is not a postulated science; rather, it is the recognition of a relationship between two spheres of knowledge and, ultimately, between two realities, which is helpful in legal and political research. Now, how is the leap from political theology to the concept of sovereignty made possible? Or, as Schindler asked, "Why does Schmitt entitle his four chapters on the theory of sovereignty 'political theology?'"[76] His definition of the sovereign is well known.[77] Power is in the hands of whoever can decide the exception. There is a direct relationship between sovereignty and decision and, therefore, between theological and political power. Ultimately, the critical question is "who decides,"[78] both in the establishment of a specific statute and in the determination of a political situation to decide what is right and wrong or what is earthly and what is spiritual? Any definition of the concept of sovereignty has to radically consider this question. That is, it must question what it means to be able to decide absolutely. Absolute decision raises the question of absolute power and, with it, the relationship between God and the sovereign is justified.

The sovereign is vested with power and can absolutely decide as to when an exception is present, only because power exists in an absolute sense.[79] God is primarily presented as well, in the eyes of political theology, as power, that is, as having absolute power of decision and, therefore, as the sovereign par excellence.[80] Schmitt would say that whoever believes in an almighty and loving God cannot claim that power is bad or neutral, and on this point he cited Gregory the Great.[81] In fact, statements like "God is dead" and "power is in itself evil" come from the same era and the same situation, namely one that is marked by the assertion that a human is a man for humans—that is, an era of total humanization. Schmitt's political theology begins with the belief that, even if all that can really be affirmed is that a human is a man for humans and that a human being, by virtue of his power, is never a god to other men, even if there is a connection between human and divine power. There are, in any case, powerful men, and in every society directly exercised political power exists. The Church, despite representing an absolute competence, must never be realized as a political *potestas* and, according to Schmitt, should not even attempt it indirectly.[82] If so, precisely because it is an absolute competence, the Church would control the sovereign's power such that he would cease to be the decisive instance in politics. This would deprive him of the character that underlies his effectiveness— that is, the exclusivity of mediation.[83] The theological-political connection here addressed is made of realities rather than competences.

HOBBES'S INFLUENCE

In this regard, it can be said that Hobbes served as Schmitt's greatest inspiration.[84] Schmitt devoted a full written analysis to their theses and he considered this topic so relevant in Hobbes that he defined the author's State theory in *Leviathan* as a political theology.[85] The great monster, as Schmitt claimed, is an image of both political theology and theological politics.[86] For Hobbes, this symbol was not simply a metaphor; as good nominalist, he thought it was a reality created by speech.[87]

According to Schmitt's analysis, the interplay between theology and politics appears in Hobbes's theory in several ways: First, the meaning and purpose of his political thought is to develop an idea of peace that will end religious civil wars. His political theory is directed at earthly peace, especially within the Christian community.[88] Secondly, despite attempting to neutralize religion, his State theory leaves a door open to transcendence since he positions truth on the top of his State theory structure: Hobbes maintained that Jesus is the Christ. Absolute truth appears to remain intact. However, therein lies the crux of the matter. In practical philosophy, the problem of "who interprets?" "who decides?" and "who can coin the truth with validity?" remains.[89] Hobbes responded to these questions with the famous statement, *Auctoritas non veritas facit legem*. The true neutralization that the Hobbesian system opens up corresponds to the interchangeability of the highest thesis in his system: "Jesus is the Christ." The system would remain intact if instead of that statement another appeared that invoked, "Allah is great."[90] The key is that the truth is not instated by itself and instead must be interpreted. It requires a decision or, as Schmitt claimed, it requires the existence of an *auctoritas interpositio*. Whoever decides, including on theological truth, is sovereign. Third, it can be said that theology reappears on the other side in Hobbes's system, namely, as the foundation of obedience. By deciding, the sovereign determines the relationship between protection and obedience. What is interesting for political theology at this point is that the true foundation of sovereignty, of the relationship between protection and obedience, is for Hobbes in the natural commandments, which are not simple dictates of reason, but rather correspond to God's commands and words from scripture. Thus, the foundation of obedience is not just found in the human sphere itself, but rather in the existence of an absolute power that is God. One last feature that Schmitt highlighted in Hobbes's work in relation to political theology, and for which he praised Hobbes, corresponds to Hobbes's realization that any struggle between the spiritual-ecclesial sphere and the earthly-political sphere is a political struggle. The solution to this struggle cannot be reached by physically separating the two spheres or diluting an intermediate realm, but rather can only be reached formally with an answer to the question: *Quis iudicabit*? And the response is clear: The sovereign is a lieutenant of God.[91] Contemporary political theology offers an *Entweder-Oder* that is resolved in favor of the here and now.[92]

COUNTERREVOLUTIONARY INFLUENCE

Among the counterrevolutionary philosophers—Bonald, de Maistre, and Donoso Cortés—Schmitt especially stopped to consider Juan Donoso Cortés. He also inspired Schmitt's political theology. Like Hobbes, he realized that "their era demanded a decision."[93] That ultimate decision can only involve categories with decisive alternatives like, for example, good-evil, God-Satan, life-death. Between these categories, synthesis and resolution by a third party is not possible. An alternative that does not allow for compromise is imposed. Therefore, according to counterrevolutionary thinking, elucidating the ultimate alternative, which involves a final political decision, does not belong to the State, but rather to the Church. The value of the State, as Maistre claimed, is found in the fact that it poses a decision; the value of the Church is found in the fact that it represents a final decision that is not subject to appeal.[94] Each of these authors expressed the theological-political analogy differently. Schmitt devoted special attention to the analogy as established by Donoso Cortés where it corresponds to the result of the conviction that reality is constituted in God's image. Thus, he can claim that "theology is the light of history."[95] Moreover, Donoso used political theology to legitimize the concept of dictatorship against liberalism. The legitimacy of dictatorship follows from the dogma of original sin. Because of sin, the human being is something of a beast. Order can only be restored through a political decision made by one who seeks the truth and the good. But ultimately, he who seeks the truth and the good lets himself be guided by God's commands. Donoso's theory of dictatorship implies a theistic metaphysics, in the same way that, as he himself points outs, anarchist theory contains an atheistic metaphysics, and liberalism supposes deism. Donoso's thought also contains a characterization of bourgeois political theology.

Even if Schmitt didn't share the idea of the Church's direct political power, he was influenced by the counterrevolutionary critique of liberalism and of the centrality of decision, both of which were crucial ideas for shaping his political theology.

Chapter Eight

Political Theology

Political theology is a field of knowledge of political reality that makes sense in a period of historical time, which corresponds to the age between the coming of Christ to earth and the end of the world, the coming of the Antichrist and the second coming of Christ. It corresponds to an "intermediate state" in the history of humanity.[1] Political theology is an extremely polymorphous field of knowledge. However, we can distinguish two different parts of it, one that is theological and one that is political, that are respectively aimed at their specific concepts. In principle, politics is not done from theology and politics does not work with theological concepts.[2] That is, the object of theology never stops being God and Revelation in order to be political. Nevertheless, Schmitt specified that any discussion, each statement, each question, and each answer related to the political must be defined and specified within the "theo-political" framework.[3]

POLITICAL THEOLOGY AS A FIELD OF KNOWLEDGE

Political theology intends nothing more than to first of all explore this hypothesis: the recognition of the affinity between the systematic structure of theological and juridical concepts and the political consequences that this resemblance or analogy entails.[4] This is not meant to postulate the existence of a science that has immediate practical effects; rather, it means to recognize a relationship between two regions of man's life in society. This analogy is significant because all significant concepts of the theory of the Modern State are secularized theological concepts: This is the second implicit historical hypothesis of Schmitt's political theology.[5]

Many examples of this relationship can be found; however, Schmitt offered a paradigmatic one in his first *Political Theology*: The state of exception in jurisprudence has the same meaning as the miracle in theology.[6] This observation represents the key to understanding the development of philosophical ideas about the State in recent centuries. The theory of the Modern State implies a Deist theology, which denies the possibility of miracles and therefore any intervention involving a violation of natural laws or statutes. In consequence, political theory excludes the possibility that the sovereign may perform any action that imposes an exceptional intervention in the legal order.

Throughout his works, Schmitt gave many examples of the structural similarities between theological and juridical concepts. Through them, he attempted to find the tradition behind that relationship and, finally, he tried to account for it.[7] Explaining the proof of the analogy, in his book *Political Romanticism*, Schmitt strove to show the connection between occasionalist metaphysics, its idea of God, and the political theory and practice of the Romantics, which is ultimately characterized by an inability to decide. Another example is found in his book *Dictatorship*, in which he showed how the concept of exception is a historical-political constant. He analyzed the different ways in which exception has presented itself throughout history and the political conceptualization ascribed to it at each of these historical moments.

Thus, political theology can be summarized in two statements, one historical and the other logical, which I will analyze below: (a) There has been a historical development in jurisprudence, during which theological concepts have been translated to those of the theory of the State. Schmitt conceptualizes this process with the term "secularization." (b) Because of this, it is possible to establish a systematic structural analogy between theological and political or juridical concepts.

SECULARIZATION

The transfer of theological concepts to the theory of the State must be understood in the broader context that Schmitt called the "secularization process."[8] Schmitt did not read the same meaning into the secularization process as Vico and Comte—a landmark law or a similar rational construction. Schmitt also did not see it as establishing a meaning of progress or decline. On the other hand, he did not mean that at every historical moment of this process the dominant mind-set—in line with secularization—becomes the exclusive mind-set. The proper function of this concept is to find a specific explanation for the origin of contemporary concepts in the theory of the State.

Schmitt was convinced that different moments can be discerned in the development of the European spirit according to the different ways of conceiving human existence that occur in each. He studied this process starting from the dominant conceptions of each era. It can even be said that they recreate reality.[9] The ideas that dominate any age change gradually; Schmitt referred to this change as the "stages of changing central domains."[10] Displacement has one direction and meaning and is realized in four steps corresponding to four centuries and moves from theology to humanitarian morality, going through metaphysics until flowing into economics and technique. This does not mean that only one kind of thinking took place in any given century or that one type of science has developed, but rather that, in every century, all ideas and all sciences are tinged by a specific hue that colors everything and allows for the application of an overall qualifier that is theological, metaphysical, and so on. On this point, Schmitt offered the example of the gradual transformation of the concept of progress, which, according to the historical moment is permeated with different nuances. For example, improvement in the eighteenth century centered on training, autonomy, and education, that is, on moral perfection; in the nineteenth century, however, progress was considered a breakthrough in economic or technical fields, where moral improvement appeared to be subordinate.[11]

As a sphere becomes dominant, a society's principal problems become those that arise within it; others are secondary and are always resolved from the dominant sphere. For example, in the sixteenth century, which was dominated by theology, when theological questions were clear everything else was supposed to follow easily. After that, a transition from the theological thought of the sixteenth century to the metaphysical thinking of the seventeenth century occurred. The latter is characterized by intellectual construction of large systems. The eighteenth century brought on the displacement of rationalist metaphysics toward a deist philosophy corresponding to a process of popularization, enlightenment, humanization, and "rationalization." The specific *pathos* of the eighteenth century corresponds to "duty," and a characteristic expression therein is that of the Kantian idea of God, a God as a "parasite of ethics." Each word in the title of his famous work, *Critique of Pure Reason*, is polemically oriented against the dogma-ontology-metaphysics series. The nineteenth century is a hybrid constructed with a romantic-aesthetic part and an economic-technical part. First came an aesthetic stage that completed the change over from eighteenth-century moralism to economicism. Romanticism opened this road up through the deployment of aesthetic enjoyment and consumption.[12] The end of the nineteenth century can be characterized by industrialism, a union between the technical and the economic spheres. The most common intellectual construction at the moment corresponds to Marxism, which analyzed all intellectual and spiritual phenomena through economic infrastructure. At this time, rapidly changing technical progress affected all other areas such that it became the dominant factor in the development of all social spheres. A religion of technical progress was born, according to which all social problems can be automatically solved. Finally, as a consequence of this, the twentieth century emerged as the era of religious belief in the technical sphere.

These changes did not happen by magic, but rather are consequences of concrete historical events and decisions. Ruling elites change; the evidence of their convictions and arguments continually transforms, as do the content of their intellectual interests, the moral principles of their actions, and the secret of their political success. All of the spiritual representations that a person makes of his life and world pertain to the existential, not normative, sphere, such that, to the extent that the existence of men varies, their intellectual and spiritual representations and vocabulary also transform.

In this change there lies a danger; the biggest mistake possible is a consequence not of the evolution of a concept or of a vision of the world, but rather of the confusion of the planes or spheres of life—that is, of the fact that a concept that belongs to one sphere crosses over to another that does not belong to it. This is how many theological concepts became part of the theory of the State. The political has an important role in explaining this process; it offers a reason for its movement and orientation. One cannot historically speak of a specifically political age. Rather, all eras have been political in as much the friend-enemy conflict has always appeared in one area of human activity or another. It is certain that conflict emerges more fiercely with issues that are central to a society's life at each historical moment and, therefore, it is logical that "a center of spiritual attraction" eventually becomes a political stage. Mankind always flees controversial spaces to move to ones of peace. Unable to give a concrete solution to a problem within the sphere in which it arises, man moves to another one where the problem is meaningless and, therefore, is solved. This peace is always momentary because, ultimately, new points of dissension will be found in the new sphere and will lead to a new conflict and on and on. Modern thought conceives of moving centers of interest as a kind of progress in which the "where" is marked by an indicator of neutralization that, by being the absence of any dispute, signifies depoliticization. [13]

The relevant question here is as follows: Is there really an absolutely neutral ground on which humanity can rest at long last? Is there such a thing as an absolutely secular ground? The evidence that progress offers suggests that this ground is found in pure technique. On this point, all nations, classes, faiths, ages, and generations seem to come together, since each one can take advantage of the conveniences and luxuries offered by technical "comfort." [14] It seems that we've reached the end of our rope and that we've finally found this anticipated place where peace is possible. If we have really found this neutral space, the question then becomes: For how much longer? How long will this state of peace last? Schmitt's answer is that it is a provisional state and will only last a limited time. [15] Technique, not man, is neutral precisely because the spiritual realm is pluralistic and conflict can always emerge; the human character does not know absolute homogeneity or automatism. Whoever expects perpetual peace and the ushering in of man's moral progress from a neutral, technical sphere forgets the essence of the technical, namely that of being an instrument and, therefore, a means to an end that it lacks in itself. No decision can be derived from it, not even a decision in favor of neutrality. Technique is neutral because it is instrumental, but, precisely for that reason, it cannot use itself to bring about peace, because, ultimately, the only thing it can do is promote war or peace and it is equally prepared for either road.

At the end of his book *Politische Theologie II*, Schmitt described this concept of the world that supposes scientific de-theologization.[16] For scientism, theology does not exist as a science with specific categories. There is also no new scientific, democratic, or revolutionary theology. It is no longer possible to construct a political theology from the beginning, *ab ovo*, precisely because no *ovo* exists any longer; rather, there is only a *novum*. In its human-earthly, scientific formulation, novelty is the process-progress that comes from infinite human curiosity. The new person who emerges from this process is not a new Adam, nor a new pre-Adam, nor indeed a new Christ-Adam, but rather he is a product that depends on the process. Process-progress produces itself, the new man, and even the conditions for novelty's possibility, which is opposite of a creation out of nothing in the traditional sense. It simply means creation from nothing as a condition of possibility for the self-creation of a new world. Here, personal freedom emerges as the highest value; it is conditioned by the freedom of scientific values and human knowledge, which rests on the condition that men are free to use its fruits to freely produce. The rationale for the freedom to utilize production is the freedom of assessment (evaluation) found in free consumption. There is an irreversible syndrome of value-use and evaluation in the progressive, technical-industrial society that is characterized by scientism. The new man carries progress's ferocity within himself; however, he denies the concept of the enemy and any secularization or replacing of old representations of the enemy. It "overcomes" whatever is worn out with scientific-technical-industrial novelty and old things annihilate themselves in the scientism-technical-industrial process-progress. This kind of de-theologization only allows, in Schmitt's words, one type of eschatology:

> This kind of eschatology is a utopia on the principle of hope, the content of which is a *homo-homini-homo* eschatology. At most this eschatology is a utopia on the principle of hope, the content of which is a *homo absconditus* who produces himself and, moreover, produces the conditions for his own possibility.[17]

Secularization, in Schmitt's view, is nothing more than the historical distancing of genuine legitimacy; it loses sight of the real structural analogy that is found between theology and the theory of the State.

POLITICAL THEOLOGY AS STRUCTURAL ANALOGY

There is a possible analogy between theological and political concepts; here we find the main thesis.[18] Hans Blumenberg critiques Schmitt in his *Die Legitimität der Neuzeit*,[19] arguing that to defend theo-political analogies it is not necessary to accept the secularization thesis. This idea seems to be clear in Schmitt's *Politische Theologie II*, where he insists that all he has said on the topic of political theology can be reduced to jurists' sentences on the systematic structural affinity between theological and juridical concepts involved in juridical and political practices.

Even if the analogical method is open to the possibility of transferences between political and theological concepts and functions in both senses, Schmitt's secularization thesis postulated in the first *Political Theology* and in "Age of Neutralizations and Depoliticizations" obliges him to consider transfers in only one direction, from the theological to the political, only in Early Modernity, and only as a historical explanation of a single functional process. This unidirectional manner of considering the theo-political relationship makes it necessary to adopt the so-called "process of secularization" as a way of explaining historical changes. In my view, all of these assumptions are not sufficiently justified in Schmitt's writings.[20] Certainly in *Politiche Theologie II* Schmitt no longer insists on the secularization thesis, not even in his criticism of Blumenberg's first edition of the *Legitimität der Neuzeit*. Rather, he only focuses on the analogical aspect of the method, although it is also true that he does not retract his earlier opinions.

In effect, as Hans Blumenberg points out, for the simple analogy to be a feasible method it is only necessary to recognize the shared absoluteness of the theological and political phenomena, with no historical derivation. Even if there were transference of roles, for example in the case of sovereignty applied to God and to the political representative, this does not imply the transformation of a single substance in that God disappears in the sovereign's countenance. In this sense Blumenberg affirms that political theology could only be a metaphorology.[21] The progressive worldliness of humanity as a metamorphosis of one identical substance that transforms itself to acquire new forms is a false assumption, affirms Blumenberg, and Schmitt got caught in this trap.[22] The identity that remains permanent in this process of transformation is not an identity of substance but rather of function. The content of this function is quite different in the distinct steps of the process, depending on the diverse interpretations of the world and of humankind.

Even if, contrary to Blumenberg's assumption, Schmitt thinks in terms of a transformation of function and not of substance, he assumes a process of secularization and, accordingly, he limits the method to the historical research of the Early Modernity, even though it would otherwise be perfectly possible to apply it to the Middle Ages[23] or to the supposed postmodern age, as many contemporary intellectuals have shown. The dogma of secularization, interpreted as an "expropriation" and involving the idea of "historical injustice,"[24] is a construction of the philosophy of history. According to Blumenberg this characterization is ideological and it misinterprets the very concept of history. History should not be defined in relation to the past or to an origin of substance that it betrays in each moment. On the other hand, Modernity claims its own legitimacy through a discontinuity with the Middle Ages.[25] The Modern Age is the moment in which reality is justified because of its very existence and not because there is a transcendental or precedent order, a reference that justifies this order. Immanence is the modern category par excellence, argues Blumenberg, and Modernity affirms its autonomy and its authenticity through science and technology.[26] Even if this were the case, counterattacks Schmitt, it is very naive to think that the negation of all political theology is not in itself a political-theological thesis: that of the continued rejection of God. Otherwise politics would no longer exist, and all human things would be arranged in functions of science, technology, and economy. In a radically immanent world, the preeminence of the political sphere cannot be considered. In pure immanence, the very concept of politics fades away and is substituted by a purely economic and technological organization.

In my view, what is interesting about political theology as a method is not the study of historical causes or historical explanations, but rather its focus on structural parallels, from the transference of meanings between two different spheres that aspire to be absolute and that share the same contexts of meanings in a given age. In this sense political theology is a kind of genealogical thinking.[27] It should not assume historical derivations or theological-political intentions in the political actors. Moreover, if we take the method's structural analogy aside from the secularization thesis, the true interest of the enquiries derived is not related to the determination of historical processes from one age to another, transporting meanings from one field to another. Rather, it centers on the exhibition of the structural affinity between theology and politics, grounded in a shared concept of power.

Schmitt does not refer to an analogy of attribution—that is, God's faculties, qualities, or power cannot be attributed to the sovereign; rather, it is an analogy of proportionality: the systematic structure of theology is similar to that of politics. For example, just as God rises above things with his power, so too in the earthly realm, there is a qualitative difference by which whoever represents qualitatively rises above the represented. This structural similarity is reflected in a sociological analysis of juridical concepts, which presupposes what Schmitt called a radical ideology,[28] that is, a final foundation that does not imply any kind of causality.

The sociology of juridical concepts forces us to go beyond the juridical *praxis* sphere that is oriented toward immediate practical interests alone and to turn to investigating the last, and therefore radical, systematic structure of juridical concepts and to compare it with the conceptual articulation of a particular era's social structure. Schmitt understood radical ideology as a radical conceptualization—that is, analyzing a concept until one finds its ultimate theological and metaphysical roots. With these methodological tools, he showed how the metaphysical concept that a given era forges of the world and of God is similar in structure to the type of political organization that becomes apparent in it.[29]

In *Political Theology*, Schmitt gave a glaring example of how political theology operated in the seventeenth and eighteenth centuries.[30] In the seventeenth century, the monarch occupied the same place in the theory of the state that God did in Cartesian metaphysics. Just as one God ruled the world, one king established laws. This conviction was so deeply ingrained in the collective consciousness that even Hobbes, despite adopting scientism and being an individualist and nominalist, retained the sovereign's personalism and assigned him a final task whose function was to make final decisions and create a state in the form of a monstrous person. From that moment, scientism progressively penetrated the theory of the State even before it had changed the concept of the relationship between God and the world. The protagonist of these new constructions became the god of deism, who is at the base of the mechanical state that works automatically. Similarly, Leibniz and Malebranche's metaphysical constructions are found at the base of Rousseau's concept of *volonté général*. Just as God is only manifested in general acts and his will is also general, so too the democratic general will has the people as its subject; it is a "depersonalized" will, so to speak.[31] With the passage of time, metaphysics became obsolete and movements emerged that offered not only immanent political construction, but also that openly combated transcendence. This is in line with Comte, Proudhon, and Bakunin, who suggested that humanity must take the place of God, which became their motto and their claim.

In short, all this research into relationships is political theology. This line of research is missing a continuation; however, to the extent that this analysis provides insights into political reality, it should prospectively be made use of. The perhaps excessive moderation of Schmitt's approach and the heuristic richness of his formulations have led to a discussion of political theology that lasts to this day. Schmitt brought together the core of the discussion that the first volume of political theology sparked in his text *Politische Theologie II*.[32]

POLITICAL THEOLOGY IN PRAXIS

Even if Schmitt conceived of political theology as a mere field of knowledge that is not specifically oriented to political or juridical praxis, it is admissible to question how this analogy works in praxis. There are at least three ways of distorting Schmitt's idea in *praxis*: The first is to defend specific decisions and concrete political forms with theological categories. This is an application of theology in the service of politics.[33] The second lies in the attempt to legitimize a ruler's actions as God's direct action through him, which corresponds to theocracies. The third inverts the analogy such that the main analogue becomes political reality and, thus, it assigns some features of political reality to God.[34]

Following the exegesis of Peter Koslowski and Ernst Wolfgang Böckenförde, we can also consider three ways of carrying out theological-political *praxis* nowadays within Christianity. In Koslowski's opinion there are three ways of understanding political theology.[35] First, political theology can be seen as an immediate deduction of politics from theology. In this regard, it must be noted that any political deduction of the dogma of the Trinity is impossible, as Erik Peterson had argued against Schmitt's *Political Theology*, as we will see.[36] This way of interpreting political theology can be found in what Böckenförde called institutional theology, which he understood as the set of assertions made from faith on the political order, legitimation, task, and, eventually, structure.[37]

Second, political theology can be seen as a deduction of politics from theology mediated through non-theological arguments. Given that an immediate deduction from theological dogmas is impossible, precisely because their implicit political content is little to none, a hypothesis is then drawn up, namely that a deduction is possible with the alleged correspondence between the religious and political spheres. If it were considered legitimate, the law that would govern deductibility would be something like the following: If a theological text contains no political statement, one proceeds in political *praxis* in the same way as one proceeds in religious *praxis*.[38] For example, what the Pope is for the Church should be what the ruler is for the State. This method should not be called political theology, but rather "Christian political theology."[39] Böckenförde called it "labeled political theology" and described it as an interpretation of Christian revelation made by Christians and the Church in which they remain involved in the political and social order.[40]

The third possibility corresponds to conceiving political theology within a Christian context—which Böckenförde called juridical political theology[41] and Koslowski described it as an analogy.[42] For both authors, this is the only possibility compatible with Schmitt's views. In this case, political theory is founded on theological analogies,[43] which do not claim to have exegetical authority: "They do not deduce political forms from religious content; rather, they further base them on reflection about theological claims."[44] This consists of introducing theological arguments into the context of political theory without mixing assumptions from both spheres. These analogies do not intend—by reference to the political sphere—to be dogmatic; rather, they intend to formulate political theory through the help of intelligent theological reflection.[45] The problem, as Schmitt himself once pointed out, is hitting upon the right "attunement of the instrument," [46] but as Koslowski noted,[47] there is no systematic approach to finding this balance. One cannot know to what extent these analogies are appropriate. In any case, Koslowski attempted to find a way to systematize the mode in which they can be used correctly. He called them *analogiae Dei* or *analogiae theologiae.*[48] This method unfolds in three steps:[49] (1) enunciating a current relationship in the sphere of theology, for example, the relationship between God and the world by virtue of his omnipotence; (2) establishing a relationship between different relationships, for example, the relationship between God's power with respect to the world and that of the sovereign with the respect to a people; (3) defining the kind of relationship as a similitude or dissimilitude.

The difficulty with such political-theological analogies is that one side of the relationship depends on the other. That is, in addition to a *per analogiam theologiae* relationship, a *per analogiam entis* can emerge.[50] This is a relationship between interdependent terms and not between correlative terms— that is, terms that vary at the same time. However, in Koslowski's view, at this point it is necessary to make a restriction: Christian political theology is possible provided that the relationship between theology and politics remains in one sense and not both—that is, as long as theology remains as an independent variable and politics as a dependent variable and not otherwise.

Only ignorance of Schmitt's theory on political theology would lead to the claim that this analogy implies a direct implementation of theological conceptions into political reality.[51] Schmitt certainly recognized that this has happened during some historical moments, but it is not at all what he intended. The fact that it can happen shows yet again that there is a structural relationship between the theological and political world. The only thing that can be said using Schmitt's political theology is that theological reflections can enter as an additional argument in political debate. Only in this way can it be significant for *praxis*.

THE SCHMITT-PETERSON DISCUSSION
ON POLITICAL THEOLOGY

Erik Peterson declares, in *Monotheism as a Political Problem*,[52] first published in 1935, the end of any legitimate kind of Christian political theology, be it ancient, medieval, or modern. In this book, Peterson aims to show the illegitimate way in which political theology had been practiced in ancient and medieval times. He calls for the abolition of all kinds of political theologies in order to preserve the Christian essence. His polemical last footnote states:

> To my knowledge, the concept of "political theology" was introduced into the literature by Carl Schmitt, *Politische Theologie* (Munich, 1922). His brief arguments at that time were not systematic. Here we have tried to show by a concrete example the theological impossibility of a "political theology."[53]

He also directly quoted Schmitt in his previous article from 1933, "Emperor Augustus in the Judgement of Ancient Christianity," in which he attributes the appropriation of the field to Schmitt and clarifies that "Political theology is not a part of theology, but a part of political thinking." [54]

Peterson and Schmitt were close friends and they never stopped being friends, in spite of having lost contact between 1933 and 1936 for political reasons. Indeed, Schmitt was an important influence in Peterson's conversion to Catholicism.[55] Thus, Schmitt probably perceived the cited "last footnote" in Peterson's *Monotheism* as Peterson's desire to keep distance from him in order to preserve political correctness since Schmitt was allied with Nazism[56] or since political correctness demanded conformity with the Protestant atmosphere, as can be seen in his correspondence with Álvaro d'Ors years later.[57]

Leaving aside personal affairs, let us move on to the realm of reasoning. Peterson shows the theological unviability of political theology by following two arguments. The first one is highly developed in his writings and amounts to the idea that the Christian God is a trinity and a trinity cannot be represented as such on Earth. The second argument appeals to Saint Augustine's criticism of the *pax romana* as representing the *pax christiana*. The Jewish tradition identifies the idea of "divine monarchy" with the first Christian Greek apologists through their supposition of the world's theocratic government, which supposes that God governs his people through a king. Peterson argues that the idea of the monarchy was essential for Judaism in order to differentiate monotheistic peoples from the polyarchy of paganism. Christianity, as a monotheistic religion, has unconsciously and illegitimately borrowed the "divine monarchy" of God as a political idea.

His thesis claims that since Trinitarian dogma was accepted, the tendency to transfer the idea of divine monarchy to emperors and kings can only eventually fail. Every political or juridical translation of the Trinity is necessarily subordinationist. For developing this argument, Peterson appeals to texts from the Cappadocian Fathers, Gregory of Nisa, and Gregory of Nazianzus, quoting the same *oratio* that Carl Schmitt later includes in his own interpretation in *Politische Theologie II*, the Third Theological Oration.[58]

Peterson deems Eusebius of Cesarea's *Life of Constantine* to be the main inheritor of medieval political theology's practical vision, which was not necessarily Christian, but fell within a Christian cosmovision.[59] Eusebius glorifies Constantine's government as a model of divine monarchy, which consolidated the *pax Augusta*, and as an eschatological sign of redemption. We have to take into account that even if Eusebius had signed the Nicene Creed, his Arian convictions were present in his writings, perhaps because of his rationalist theological beliefs that attenuated the idea of a Trinity. Confronted with the imperial *pax*, every national state was polytheistic, a fact that influenced the Patristics. In Peterson's view, the integral formula "kingdom, peace, and monotheism" was a Christian construct that opposed the pagan political theology, but it was not specifically Christian. Augustine of Hippo rejected such an analogy between the Roman Empire and the Kingdom of Christ in *City of God*. According to him, the Kingdom of Christ limits itself to the Church alone.

Álvaro d'Ors, was one of the participants in the Peterson-Schmitt debate. He was a close friend to Schmitt and challenged him on many topics, as seen in the correspondence between them. He builds on Carl Schmitt's defense by showing how part of the flourishing political theology of the Middle Ages did not perceive any contradiction with the Trinitarian dogma.[60] He mentions as an example the projection of the Trinitarian dogma in the co-reign of the Byzantine Emperor Constantine IV Pogonatus with Heraclius and Tiberius until 681.[61] What is more, d'Ors asserts—in opposition to Peterson—that it is perfectly valid to speak of a concrete derivation from Christian theological concepts to juridical-political life. He ultimately describes Peterson's criticism as follows, "Based on an ancient consideration of the world, he wanted to deduce a previous conclusion about political theology in the modern age."[62]

Political theology can only be pagan or heretic, Peterson concludes, and it seems to follow that it is an illicit research field. Thus, theo-political research can only lead to confusion in a Christian cosmos. The impossibility of a "divine monarchy" closes off the possibility of any other analogy following Christian realities. Schmitt published *Political Theology II* in 1970 mainly in order to clarify his own thesis against Peterson's misunderstandings, but also to present a separate one against Blumenberg's criticism on the topic. Schmitt concludes that if Peterson's critique of political theology is not valid for pagan or medieval political theologies, then it is even less so for the early modern era. The political realm in Early Modernity was dependent on a Christian theological reform without which it could not have come into being. In addition, he attests to the possibility of new forms of political theology emerging from the Trinitarian dogma, as can be perceived in Goethe's motto "nemo contra deus nisi deus ipse." A political theology dependent on the Trinitarian dogma is also alive in his friend-enemy criterion of the political.[63] In contemporary theology, this can also be seen in Henry de Lubac's[64] political theology of the Eucharist and W. T. Cavanagh's later developments a propos.[65]

The core of Schmitt's thesis remains untouched because he does not affirm the orthodoxy or heterodoxy of the different ways of understanding political theology as theology or as a model for constructing the political realm.[66] Rather, this criticism seems to be the sole concern of Peterson's writings against Schmitt.[67] But it also remains untouched because Schmitt affirms the possibility of political theology in Early Modernity and Peterson does not analyze his examples in any way.[68] Peterson only criticizes the idea of divine monarchy as an orthodox Christian political theology, while he presumes that he has criticized every possible political theology, whether ancient, modern, or contemporary. Moreover, Schmitt insists that Peterson misunderstands him:

> Everything I have said on the topic of political theology is statements of a jurist upon the obvious theoretical and practical legal structural resemblance between theological and juridical concepts. These belong to the research area of the history of law and sociology. . . . I will not dare, as a non-theologian, to enter a discussion on theological aspects of the doctrine of Trinity with theologians.[69]

The only way to understand the Peterson's dislocation is to accept Nichtweiss's thesis that Peterson's main concern is not with criticizing Schmitt's political theology, but rather with criticizing the *Reichstheologie*.[70]

Schmitt mainly argues that there is a shared world of meanings and representations between the religious and the political spheres that always implies some kind of transference.[71] In this sense we can speak of a "metaphorological political theology" more than a "substantial political theology" in Schmitt's works, as Blumenberg and d'Ors, have pointed out. The only metaphysical presupposition involved in political theology is the shared absoluteness of theological and political phenomena. In the end, Schmitt agrees with Peterson on the idea that political theology is not theology and thus neither orthodox, nor heterodox. Given this, Schmitt's main thesis remains untouched by Peterson's criticism.[72]

I am persuaded that, from the theological point of view, Schmitt would agree with Peterson and "catholic orthodoxy" on the idea that the public representation of the kingdom of God is only found in the Church and any secular political community can aspire to identify with it. Schmitt would clearly agree with this based on his hermeneutic of Saint Augustine in *Political Theology*.[73]

If, from the theological point of view, there is nothing to say about a "correct analogy," then the possibility of multiple theo-political analogies emerging after the breakdown of the Roman Empire's political theology should exist. They could be called Christian, as they were inspired by Christian dogmas. In the same way we could speak about Christian art by looking at images of the Virgin, even though none of them represent her real face. This amounts to Schmitt's criticism of Peterson.

Schmitt attempted to answer Peterson's objection according to which "divine monarchy" became impossible once the dogma of the Trinity was defined, developing a political theology dependent on the Trinitarian dogma.[74] The theme of the Trinity in Schmitt's work came, therefore, by way of a critique aimed at Peterson,[75] who converted from Evangelicalism to Catholicism in 1930 and who saw the mixture of political and theological concepts, according to Christianity itself in the fourth century, as a serious error on the part of the Church.[76] He therefore used Gregory of Nazianzus's formulation of the Trinitarian dogma as a key feature of his attack on political theology.

Schmitt's response to Peterson's objection aimed to show that a political theology based on a theology that includes the Trinitarian dogma among its dogmas is also possible.[77] According to Schmitt, no political theory can be deduced directly or immediately from the Trinitarian dogma, but, and this is the most controversial question in Schmitt's political theology, can a political theory be *indirectly* deduced from the dogma of the Trinity? Or asked in a more Schmitt-like formula: On what political relationship does the Trinitarian dogma shed light? Schmitt was therefore faced with showing how political theology can also be undertaken from the dogma of the Trinity.[78] If this were possible, then Peterson's position could also be argued against with the claim that there is in fact a Christian political theology, even from the same point of view that Peterson himself held.

Contrary to what might appear at first sight, Schmitt claimed that precisely the formulation of this dogma made it clear that it is impossible to separate the theological and political spheres, which would only be possible from an abstract reading of the dogma of the Trinity. Theology and politics cannot be separated because the second person of the Trinity has two natures, divine and human, in one effective unit. Mary gave birth to a divine creature in historic time and on a particular day. Taking Peterson's example, Schmitt explains that according to Gregory of Nazianzus, there are three possibilities regarding the consideration of God relative to the power: anarchy, polyarchy, and monarchy. Christians defend the unity of government, but this unity does not mean that the government must to be carried out by a single person since, for them, divine unity always brings plurality. The unity that it conceives of is Trinitarian and is capable of overcoming duality. Thus, the Trinitarian monarchy is a return to unity of that which comes from itself—that is, a return to unity from multiplicity. In this analysis, Schmitt forced Gregory of Nazianzus's thesis to save his own concept of the political.[79] He insisted in showing that the heart of this Father of the Church's argument is the following statement: "*to Hen stasiatzon pros heauton,*" which he translated as: "The One is always in uproar against itself."[80] There is no doubt that, when Schmitt chose this thesis in his argument, he had in mind his own criteria for the political: the friend-enemy distinction. This shows that not only is political theology possible from the dogma of the Trinity, but also that precisely in analogy is where the criteria for what is specifically political is found.[81]

The key to this is found in the interpretation of the word *stasis*. To explain this concept, Schmitt cited a passage from Plato[82] where he argues, on the one hand, the impossibility of life where there is calm and, on the other hand, the necessity of unity where there is life. The apparent paradox of the movement-unity dialectics is implicit in the term *stasis*, which first means *Ruhe*, rest, *status*, quiet, place; as well as the opposite, *Unruhe*, movement, uproar, *kinesis*, "*politische Unruhe,*"[83] political unrest, civil war, enmity in unity, politics. A "politico-theological *stasiology*" appears in the heart of Trinitarian life, in which the problem of the enemy does not hide itself.[84] The unity of God appears damaged by a certain division.

At this point, political theology can take three paths to explaining the rupture in the divine unity, a rupture that is found in the origins of the political. One path is Christian and monotheistic, which finds one of its representatives in Augustine, whom Schmitt studied and whose ideas he described in the text herein discussed.[85] The theory of the Trinity does not completely dissolve the identity of God the Creator and God the Redeemer. They are not identical, but they are still one. The duality of natures, God and man, is turned into unity through the action of the third person. Schmitt's thesis, which sees in divine diversity the condition of possibility for plurality and, therefore, with the addition of human freedom and evil, turns out to be fully consistent and a keen observation.[86]

The second path is the dualistic or Gnostic one.[87] From this point of view, god the creator and god the redeemer have always been enemies. This idea, according to Schmitt, is common to both the properly Gnostic movement as well as to the philosophy of modernity.

> The main structural power with Gnostic dualism, that is, with the problem of the God of creation and the God of salvation, dominates not only every religion of salvation and redemption. It exists inescapably in every world in need of change and renewal, and it is both immanent and ineradicable.[88]

This enmity, which is discussed in the cited text, is addressed by both Goethe's old aphorism: "*nemo contra deum nisi deus ipse,*"[89] which in itself does not contain a theological reference since Goethe used it more in a political sense to refer to Napoleon's power.[90] It was also used in Jakob Michael Lenz's fragment, "Catherine of Siena,"[91] which Schmitt mentioned at the end of *Politische Theologie II*[92] and connected with Gregory of Nazianzus's previously mentioned argument, which interprets the latter from Gnosticism. If the relationship between God the Father and God the Son is interpreted in a dualistic way, as happens in some of the cited texts—that is, as a relationship of insurrection or revolution, one enters into a sociology of political theology where the problem of enmity stands out.

There is a third path and it is the pluralist one, which is not regarded as political theology, but rather as "politheology." Blumenberg[93] implements the clearest form of this approach, especially in his text *Arbeit am Mythos*.[94] It does not exclude Schmitt's dualistic interpretation of Goethe's phrase and extends it in a polytheistic-pantheistic version.[95] He argued that there is a difference between writing *Nemo contra Deum nisi Deus ipse* and *Nemo contra deum nisi deus ipse*. Goethe writes god in lowercase. This does not involve a struggle within one God, but rather a struggle between gods. A god can only balance its power in a struggle with other gods. This statement belongs to a polytheistic context and, therefore, mythological, not to a theo-logical context in the strict sense. It involves the complete rejection of theol-ogy through dissolution in paganism.

Now, where can Schmitt be found among these three paths? How is it possible that "Catholic" Schmitt gives a Gnostic interpretation of the Trini-tarian dogma as he seems to do at the end of *Politische Theologie II*? How is it possible that, contrary to his method, he makes theological politics a "de-monic parody" that consists in applying his concept of the political to the theology of the Trinity, thus instituting enmity within God himself?[96] If this were so, he would have chosen to easily escape from a difficult problem and he would have fallen prey to a circular argument: once the Trinity has been interpreted in political terms, the political relationship of enmity is deduced from it according to the theological-political method. That is, in strict politi-cal theology, the theological statement "nothing against God but God him-self" leads to the political statement "nothing against man but man himself" or *homo homini homo* in Schmitt's formulation. However, if theological dogma had been previously determined politically, there would be a distor-tion in the theological-political method, making it into a mere theological politics of the worst kind—that is, a political manipulation of theology. This approach would in itself suppose de-theologization:[97] the theological-politi-cal method can only deduce political enmity from a possible enmity in God through the de-theologization of God.

There are several places where it seems clear that Schmitt takes the side of a dualistic interpretation. One is in the "Guideline for the Reader" in *Political Theology II*, which clearly states that he continued the 1922 publi-cation of *Political Theology* in the direction of a political *Christology*.[98] This term refers to a dualistic interpretation of Goethe's aphorism. That is, it seems that research on political theology has led to a political Christology and to the affirmation of a divine-human contradiction in God himself. This contradiction leads, in turn, to an opposition between God and the world with which the path of secularization begins. With another, he confirmed the friend-enemy thesis as a distinction present in reality and it is here that he approves of Gnostic dualism as immanent in every salvific religion, as I have already mentioned. Much earlier in the *Schattenrisse*, he had taken the side of dualism, but there it is clear that it is a stand against the monotheistic-scientism-causal explanation of the world—that is, against the materialistic interpretation of the world that is monistic.[99]

Now, how does Schmitt make these claims? Are they as categorical as those made in *Politische Theologie* when positively defining political theology from his own position, or are they rather thrown out there as hypotheses, as possible interpretations of a political theology? How is the latter idea reached? First there is the comment he once made about his principal thesis on the Trinitarian dogma just as Gregory of Nazianzus conceived of it. He seemed to understand the Catholic interpretation well and did not contradict it.[100] Here Schmitt seems to imply the opposite of what he claimed at the end according to the literal tone: if *stasis* is not possible in the Trinity, then neither a political *stasiology* nor a dualistic interpretation are possible. Second, when Schmitt commented on *stasiology* he does not seem to do it with his own thoughts, but rather explained the fate of the Trinitarian dogma just as it has been historically interpreted, that is, the interpretive possibilities for said dogma.[101] Political theology has always been considered possible in the monotheistic account, but Schmitt tried, without claiming to hold this posture personally, to show that even in a non-monotheistic account—that is, a dualistic account of the Trinity—political theology is possible, and even the very criterion of the political is found there. Third, he attempted to analyze if in a de-theologized reality, the "new reality,"[102] the concept of enemy still appears. De-theologization, which has its greatest advocate in Blumenberg, aims to overcome Gnosticism. However, Schmitt noted that in Blumenberg's interpretation, far from distancing himself from Gnostic dualism, he necessarily maintained it. His description of the new world as permeated with a volt of constant change (*erneuerungsbedürftigen*), in which the need for progress, change and novelty is constitutive, necessarily maintains duality, a dialectic: such a world—despite believing that theology has been substituted by science—has a theology in which god the creator and god the redeemer are enemies because the lord creator of the world and the lord liberator, the executor of a new world, cannot be close allies. Although it tries to hide itself, this is the enmity that appears in the de-theologized world of science. This world that seeks total de-theologization and total depoliticization is also, paradoxically, one that absolutely finds the enemy. Once it reaches the earth, the statement "*nemo contra deum nisi deus ipse*" transforms into, "*nemo contra hominen nisi homo ipse*," no one is against man except man himself.[103]

Finally, in other writings, Schmitt disregarded Gnostic thought. For example, in *Ex Captivitate Salus*, Schmitt refers to Däubler's text, *Das Nordlicht*, as follows:

> "Today I know that the aurora borealis shines in the pale glow of a gnosis of humanity. It is the sign of a humanity that wants to save itself, a native radiation that the Prometheuses of the earth emit to the cosmos."[104]

> "Hence, the dim light of Stoic suicide comes from the origin of our aeon. It is nothing more than moonlight; similar to all the attempts of humanist religion and is incapable of building sacramental forms."[105]

Previously I pointed to two reasons that could lead to the belief that Schmitt's interpretation of the Trinity is dualistic in a gnostic mode. Now, I have outlined some of the details that give us reason to think that it is not. Thus one cannot say that Schmitt took the side of the technical mode of conceiving reality and, with it, favored a dualistic interpretation of the Trinity. Rather, on the contrary, as we have seen, political Christology or theological stasiology of politics belongs to a world conceived of technically and scientifically that aims toward de-theologization and depoliticization. Nothing is further from Schmitt's position.

While God and the world still exist, neither politics nor political theology will disappear from the human horizon. In this sense, what Schmitt wants to demonstrate through the proposition of the "structural analogy" is that the relationship between politics and religion will always remain open, and that each historical moment has had to find an answer in a specific manner. The way in which each moment finds such answers may generate new means to interpret history, philosophy, jurisprudence and politics.

CARL SCHMITT'S POLITICAL THEOLOGIES

Schmitt not only theorizes that political theology constructs a matrix for research into the history of ideas but he also writes theological-political genealogies. Despite the common assumption of the contemporary critics, Schmitt did not write only one theo-political genealogy, but at least three, viz. a "political theology of the sovereign," a "political theology of representation," and a "political theology of revolution." Each of them is based on a different analogy. As we have seen, the first of these is based on the analogy between God and the modern sovereign, while the second focuses on the analogy between representation in the Church and in the Modern State. Finally, the third is based on the analogy between the Trinitarian relationship and the criteria of the political, the friend-enemy relationship. The three analogies presuppose the modern construction of the State and consequently, they are valid only in the context of modernity.

As already mentioned, the "political theology of the sovereign" supposes the functional analogy between God and the political sovereign. We can find this political theology—the best known—in the first *Politische Theologie*, and through this analogy Schmitt tries to discover the potentiality of the political decision in modern political construction. The analogy offers him the perspective to understand the sovereign as a supreme power, *legibus solutus*, as Bodin characterizes the supreme power in the *Six livres de la république*. The Modern State was born under the auspices of that kind of political power—that is, an absolute one. It is this State that decides in the case of exception, which is a situation where there is no law. Historically, nobody at that time had experienced such absolute political power, and even if theorists like Bodin or Hobbes could imagine such power, it had to be due to the kind of transference from the theological power of God. Also in *Dictatorship* and *Political Romanticism* we find examples of their kind of political theology.

Through political theological research, Schmitt discovers the fictional character of the modern *Rechtsstaat* that hides under the formal legal finery, the absolute decision making of a person who decides. Such a fiction is also the case of the Kelsenian paradigm or of Krabbe's construction. In fact, each modern political order depends upon a political decision. This idea shows in the distinction between *pouvoir constituant* and *pouvoir constituée*. However, power and law are two different dimensions of the same political reality and they are not completely derived the one from the other, as the decision of the sovereign precedes statute law in modern constitutional States.

The "theology of representation" highlights a second analogy, an analogy between juridical representation in both institutions: Church and State. Following the specific Christian theological-political idea, Schmitt wrote the small booklet titled *Roman Catholicism and Political Form,*[106] which was first published in 1923, the year after his *Politische Theologie*, and, even before that, in 1917, he published "The Visibility of the Church: A Scholastic Consideration." His thesis was that the Church is a supernatural institution, the head of which is Christ himself, but whose representative is the pope. Yet as a historical institution the Church has a political form and its own public law. This supernatural institution, in historical times, has to exist together within the specific form of the political community, Kingdom, State, and so on. Here Schmitt puts the theological-political problem in Augustinian terms.

In the first pages of his short essay on *Roman Catholicism*, he notes that there is no specific political idea of Catholicism but rather, as history has shown, Catholicism could combine with almost every political idea. There is a risk, in his view, on account of the Catholic Church's almost perfect bureaucracy and its universal organization. It is the political fear of the potential

usurper. Carl Schmitt recognizes that there is an "antirömiches Affekt"—that
is the persecution of the Catholic Church from different political interests
over the last centuries. This supposedly perfect organization is the consequence, in Schmitt's view, of the force of its representation. The Church's
representatives are not mere civil servants but rather individuals with a personal remit coming from an interrupted chain from Christ himself. There is a
personal relationship coming from above that spreads to the lowest members
of society through these representatives. For authentic representation to exist
implies that the inner and the outward being in the action of a representative
cannot be separated. In the case of the Church, the inner sense consists of
personifying Christ. [107] As Ernst Kantorowicz showed years later, in my view
clearly inspired by Schmitt, in his theological-political treatise on the Middle
Ages, [108] the theological doctrine on the Church as a *corpus mysticum*, the
head of which is Christ, has been taken by the jurists to consolidate the idea
of a State in which the head is the King. That was the juridical praxis in
England's Tudor age, when the State was "embodied" around 1300. As Kantorowicz shows, the parallels with the Church gravitate around the body and
not the person. Unlike its head—for the case of the State—the body does not
die, although the continuity must be a fiction built for the State, thanks to the
theological intermediation of the eternal constitution of the Church, whose
head and body does not die.

Even if Schmitt were not aware of Kantorowicz's research, which was—
published in 1957, thirty four years after Schmitt's tractate—when he wrote
the short essay on Catholicism, his intuition was that in the transfer from the
juridical configuration of the Church to the State, "embodiment" was at the
cost of "personifying" and hence, its representation is not authentic. In comparison to the authentic representation of the Church, the representativeness
constituted by the State's apparatus is merely technical-instrumental. In the
State, the personal relationship disappears and it is merely functional: the
civic servant does not compromise his inner self and it is sufficient for him to
act outwardly as a servant of the State. Beyond the patent differences, the
Modern State is analogous to the Church in its institutional construction. It is
clear that Schmitt has nostalgia of this authentic representation. Indeed, he
prefers the aesthetics of form to the techniques underlying the processes.

There is still a third theological-political analogy. This third one was
developed years later, in 1970, in his second *Politische Theologie II*. This
analogy was explicated in the context of his response to Erik Peterson's
criticism of his *Politische Theologie* in his treatise *Monotheismus als politisches Problem*. As we have already mentioned, Peterson proposes that every
political theology should be eliminated based on the impossibility of God's
monarchy following the definition of the Trinitarian dogma. His main thesis
is that if the Trinitarian dogma is accepted, then God can have no parallel
figure within the political world. God is one but a Trinity cannot be translated

into a political analogy. Political theology could only be pagan or heretic, concludes Peterson.

As a response to Peterson, Schmitt develops the "political theology of the revolution" in his *Political Theology II*, already commented on here. The worldly transfer of the unity of the one God being three on the earth can be considered as a *stasiology*, a continued possibility of revolution between parties. So the friend-enemy relationship, which for him defines a specific political criterion, must be understood as a secularization of the Trinitarian theological premise. He has not further developed this analogy.

Consistent with the methodological presuppositions, Schmitt has tried to show that many of the core concepts in the modern theory of the State are secularized theological concepts: that is the case of the sovereign, of political representation and of the friend-enemy relationship.

Epilogue

In what sense can we speak of a political discourse of Carl Schmitt? There is an internal logic to all of Schmitt's production, articulated through certain original categories. For a discourse to be built, it is inherent to find formal elements that capture reality. Schmitt certainly sketched formal categories that express political reality's consistent ways of being. In his multiple discourses, he tries to grasp multiple historical contexts and events. Schmitt is a critical thinker. In any case he also tries to understand and analyze the political in itself. Carl Schmitt's discourse is a discourse on the political. Furthermore it is a political discourse, because he positions himself through it.

Although human life is quite variable because it depends on time, space and circumstances, certain categories can be theoretically uncovered for analysis, even though they themselves are rooted in history. The formal categories that traverse his discourse refer mainly to order. Schmitt's discourse invokes a certain mystic of order. These categories can be gathered into three main groups that match the dialectical logic of interiority-exteriority. These categories include: *order*, which corresponds to interiority aspects; *exception*, which involves an externality; and *power*, which supersedes the previous two when the order is renewed. There are many signifiers alluding to these formal categories. The first category is evoked with signifiers such as *nomos*, land, people, law, constitution, norm, and *Großraum*. The second group of signifiers refers to exception and includes the various oppositions that breathe life into it, such as friend-enemy, war-peace, and land-sea. Finally, the genesis of a new order is expressed in words like decision, sovereign, representation, political unity, and political pluriverse. Schmitt's logic advances with a scheme that involves an *in-out* dynamic and resolution through a higher third party, to which the—again spatial—scheme of an *up-down* dynamic is also added to resolve the dialectical movement.

179

These three formal categories refer to space. If we temporarily project them, we find that order is a starting point; the first point is always a *nomos* and the order that it sets out. Conflict comes later, since it is also defined with relation to an order. The expansion of different land appropriations and scarcity give way to conflict. And the exercise of *power* always involves a conquest. Conflict is resolved through the exercise of political power, which conquers new areas of peace. However, it must be reiterated that Schmitt's logic is predominantly spatial, despite the author's interest in the diachronic aspects of political reality.

The logic of Schmitt's political discourse is configured from the experience of *nomos*. *Nomos* is to praxis as *logos* is to theory. The main categories of common life are, according to Schmitt: *nehmen, teilen, weiden* (to take, to divide, to cultivate). The first thing that man does is appropriate land and inhabits it, and then he differentiates its parts and makes them public, later he cultivates them and makes them economically productive. Man's life, both personal and in community, is constituted in relation to space, being physical, cultural, political, virtual or spiritual.

The key areas of man's life in society—economics, law, politics—cannot ignore *nomos*. The categories each one of them works with are implicitly rooted in *nomos*. Schmitt shows this with the signifiers he uses: *Nahme, Maßnahme, Abstandnahme, Ausnahme, Machtnahme*.

Nahme indicates that Schmitt developed a philosophy of having, which is a philosophy of existence, of concreteness and of particularity. Man cannot live on mere abstractions. The first purely material particularization, from an objective point of view, that Schmitt recognizes is *Nahme*, the appropriation of land. All *Nahme* is now a basic exercise of power, and an elemental power, and therefore potentially has to do with the political. Man, as an existing being, appropriates land. Man does not just materially appropriate land; rather, in formally appropriating it, he measures it—*Maßnahme*—and formalizes, in turn, the measure in law—*Gesetz*. *Nahme* thus becomes more universally *Maßnahme*. To the extent that all *Maßnahme* and *Nahme* refer to a social or material space, and the space available to man is limited, it always leaves something out of it; measured space is always placed against other possible measures and formalizations. This means that all *Maßnahme* or *Nahme*, by being particular, involve a possible *Abstandnahme* or distancing and, therefore, the added possibility of conflict. The friend-enemy relationship arises primarily as a mine-yours relationship. In the case of conflict, measures are "disordered" and cannot recognize each other. A new adjustment becomes necessary and the need to implement a new *nomos* emerges. This is a moment of crisis, of *Ausnahme*. In this moment, a *nomos* proper does not exist and is in a state of doubt. Decision is then required to establish a new *nomos* that is in line with a people's new situation. This decision is not simply aimed at a new appropriation of land, but rather at apprising and resolving conflict, a new *Nahme*, which can only be undertaken through a *Machtnahme*.

This structure, this "space," which is expressed in historical cycles, logically and ontologically depends on an absolute *Nahme*, which is absolute power because final decision rests in its hands. The *structural analogy* between the theological and the political, which makes the latter assertions possible, is crucial in Schmitt's thought. It has a profound purpose: all political realism, and that which is derived from the political, is ultimately explained by recourse to God. Thus, the political *indirectly* brings God to the fore and, for his part, man—a political being—cannot be explained from the material alone.

Carl Schmitt pursued the essence of the political in a way that has hardly been matched in the history of Western thought. This was his principal goal and, in pursuit of it, he created new signifiers and new significance along the way and, without him much realizing it, he established an original political discourse that evokes a mystic of order.

Notes

INTRODUCTION

1. "Wer von Politischen spricht, kann von Carl Schmitt nicht schweigen." *Frankfurter Allgemeine Zeitung*, May 8, 1993.

2. Günter Maschke, *Der Tod des Carl Schmitt* (Wien: Karolinger Verlag, 1987).

3. Ilse Staff, *Staatsdenken im Italien des 20. Jahrhunderts: Ein Beitrag zur Carl Schmitt-Rezeption* (Baden-Baden: Nomos Verlagsgesellschaft, 1991).

4. Montserrat Herrero, *Carl Schmitt und Álvaro d'Ors Briefwechsel* (Berlin: Duncker & Humblot, 2004).

5. Schmitt himself found this book especially interesting, although he reproached the author since he would not have made reference to the central question of political theology. See Herrero, *Carl Schmitt und Álvaro d'Ors Briefwechsel*, 168, 174–77.

6. Carl Schmitt, "Das Problem der Legalität," *Die neue Ordnung* 4, no. 3 (1950), 270–75. In the same vein William E. Scheuerman argues that Schmitt's political choices "were intimately related to his critique of liberal jurisprudence." William E. Scheuerman, *Carl Schmitt: The End of Law* (Lanham, MD: Rowman & Littlefield, 1999), 2.

7. Carl Schmitt, *Ex Captivitate Salus: Experiencias de los años 1945–1947*, transl. A. Schmitt (Santiago de Compostela: Porto y Cia., 1960), 80. Benito Cereno is one of the literary figures that Schmitt used throughout his life. The metaphor refers to the protagonist of Herman Melville's novel of the same name in which Cereno is a ship captain detained by his crew for pretending to direct the ship's course without any hope of salvation.

8. Schmitt, *Ex Captivitate Salus*, 80.

9. Ingeborg Villinger, *Verortung des Politischen: Carl Schmitt in Plettenberg* (Hagen: v. d. Linnepe, 1990), 3: "I am a Catholic as a tree is green. . . . For me, the Catholic faith is the religion of my fathers. I am a Catholic not only by belief, but also by historical origin, if I can say so, by race."

1. BIOGRAPHICAL SKETCH

1. There are two main Schmitt's biographies David Cumin, *Carl Schmitt: Biographie politique et intellectuelle* (Paris: Cerf, 2005) and Paul Noack, *Carl Schmitt. Eine Biographie* (Berlin: Propyläen Verlag, 1993). There are also some notes on the life of Carl Schmitt in Ernst

Hüsmert and Ingeborg Villinger, *Verortung des Politischen: Carl Schmitt in Plettenberg* (Hagen: v. d. Linnepe, 1990) and in Paul Gottfried, *Carl Schmitt* (London: The Claridge Press, 1990).

2. This "Tu, quis es" evokes Saint John the Baptist, in the book of John 1:19.

3. By identifying with Epimetheus, he saw himself as intellectual defeated by the political "Prometheuses" that he suffered at different times in his life.

4. "ΚΑΙ ΝΟΜΟΝ ΕΓΝΩ." This phrase is attributed to Homer, but Homer didn't actually use the word *nomos*; rather, he wrote in the Odyssey, book 1, verse 3: "Many were the men whose cities he saw and whose mind he learned." Schmitt repeated this phrase frequently and he even etched it into a wood column at the Otero-Schmitt home in Santiago, Spain.

5. Noack, *Carl Schmitt*, 46–47.

6. Gottfried, *Carl Schmitt*, 7–10.

7. Carl Schmitt, "Berlin 1907," *Schmittiana I: Eclectica* 17, nos. 71–72 (1988), 14–20.

8. There are many notes and writings that make reference to words and phonemes in Düsseldorf's *Nordrhein Westfälischen Hauptstaatsarchivs*. See, for example, RW 265–34, Mt. 10 (in the archive's nomenclature).

9. Noack, *Carl Schmitt*, 48.

10. From a conversation with Anni Stand, Schmitt's secretary starting in 1938, in Plettenberg, December 7, 1992.

11. "Anima" is the Latin translation of the Slavic name Duschka, which was also given to one of his granddaughters, born from the marriage between Anima and a Spanish Professor from Santiago de Compostela, Alfonso Otero.

12. Günther Krauss, "Erinnerungen an Carl Schmitt," *Criticon: Konservativ heute* 95–96 (1986), 127–30 and 180–86, 128.

13. Villinger, *Verortung des Politischen*, 16.

14. Alexander Schmitz und Martin Lepper ed., *Hans Blumenberg: Carl Schmitt. Briefwechsel* (Frankfurt: Suhrkamp, 2007).

15. Joseph W. Bendersky, *Carl Schmitt: Theorist for the Reich* (Princeton, NJ: Princeton University Press, 1983), 136.

16. About the relationship between both see Samuel Weber, "Taking Exception to Decision: Walter Benjamin and Carl Schmitt," *Diacritics* 22, nos. 3–4 (1992), 5–18.

17. José A. Estévez, *La crisis del Estado de derecho liberal: Schmitt en Weimar* (Barcelona: Ariel, 1989), 53.

18. This is treated extensively in Andreas Koenen, *Der Fall Carl Schmitt: Sein Aufstieg zum "Kronjuristen des dritten Reiches"* (Darmstadt: Wissenschaftliche Buchgesellschaft, 1995).

19. "Institut für Zeitgeschichte" of Munich (IfZ), Archiv Fa 503, November 19, 1936 report.

20. The omitted part was illegible in the newspaper I was able to access. "The suppression of" is likely missing.

21. Schmitt, *Glossarium: Aufzeichnungen der Jahre 1947–1951* (Berlin: Duncker & Humblot, 1991), 159–60.

22. Thus, Barbara Nichtweiß, *Erik Peterson: Neue Sicht auf Leben und Werk* (Freiburg: Herder, 1992), 727–36.

23. Ingeborg Villinger and Ernst Hüsmert, *Verortung des Politischen: Carl Schmitt in Plettenberg* (Hagen: v. d. Linnepe, 1990), 24.

24. Badly or half-educated; semi-literate.

25. The *Führer* protects the law. "Der Führer schützt das Recht: Zur Reichstagsrede Adolf Hitlers vom 13. Juli. 1934," *Deutsche Juristen Zeitung* 39 (1934), Sp. 945–50.

26. IfZ Fa 503.

27. German jurisprudence fighting against the Jewish spirit. Carl Schmitt, "Die deutsche Rechtswissenschaft im Kampf gegen den jüdischen Geist," *Deutsche Juristen Zeitung* 41, no. 20 (1936), 1193–99.

28. Carl Schmitt, *On the Three Types of Juristic Thought*, trans. by J. W. Bendersky (Westport, CT: Praeger Publishers, 2004).

29. Montserrat Herrero, *Carl Schmitt und Álvaro d'Ors Briefwechsel* (Berlin: Duncker & Humblot, 2004), 63–64.

30. Robert M. W. Kempner, *Ankläger einer Epoche: Lebenserinnerungen* (Frankfurt a. M.: Ullstein, 1983).

31. RW 265–92, Mt. 9.

32. The content of the responses was edited by Helmut Quaritsch, *Antworten in Nürnberg* (Berlin: Duncker & Humblot, 2000).

33. Carl Schmitt, "The Question of Legality," in *State, Movement, People*, transl. S. Draghici (Washington, DC: Plutarch Press, 2001), 55–81.

34. RW 265–93, Mt. 6.

35. Ingeborg Villinger and Dirk van Laak, *Bestandsverzeichnis zum Nachlaß Carl Schmitt* (Siegburg: F. Schmitt-Verlag, 1993).

36. See Herrero, *Carl Schmitt und Álvaro d'Ors Briefwechsel*, letters 143 and 144.

2. SPACE AND *NOMOS*

1. On Schmitt's linguistic expressionism, see Ingeborg Villinger's edition of Carl Schmitt's Schattenrisse, *Carl Schmitts Kulturkritik der Moderne: Texte, Kommentar und Analyse des "Schattenrisse" des Johannes Negelinus* (Berlin: Akademie Verlag, 1995), 301–25.

2. Carl Schmitt, *The Nomos of the Earth in the International Law of the Jus Publicum Europaeum*, transl. G. L. Ulmen (New York: Telos Press Publishing, 2006), 38. Schmitt seals the close relationship between law and history in a letter to Alfonso Otero, where he writes the following: "You and I both know that all history is the history of law. . . . My topic is not the history of law, but rather state law and international law, two disciplines that are loaded with history and whose concrete scientific representation, in a simple piece of research without historical examples, that is, without case law, necessarily cannot be understood." Cited in Gary L. Ulmen, *Politischer Mehrwert: Eine Studie über Max Weber und Carl Schmitt* (Weiheim: V C H, Acta Humaniora, 1991), 304–5.

3. "Wir suchen das Sinnreich der Erde [We look for the profound meaning of the earth]." Carl Schmitt, *Der Nomos der Erde* (Köln: Greven Verlag, 1950), *Vorwort*. He uses Konrad Weiss's expression, who was one of his favorite poets and for which one of his books is named: *Das Sinnreich der Erde* (Insel Verlag, 1939). The English translation does not fit in this meaning: "We seek to understand the normative order of the earth." Schmitt, *The Nomos of the Earth*, 39. When possible, we will follow the English translation.

4. Schmitt, *The Nomos of the Earth*, 80–83.

5. The English edition of *The Nomos of the Earth*, 324–57, includes "Three Concluding Corollaries" that were not consider as such by Schmitt. The editor of the English translation has not respected the number scheme of the Corollaries established by Schmitt in his re-edition of "Nehmen, Teilen, Weiden" in: Carl Schmitt, *Verfassungsrechtliche Aufsätze aus den Jahren 1924–1954: Materialen zu einer Verfassungslehre* (Berlin: Duncker & Humblot, 1958). The five introductory Corollaries are included in the Part I of *The Nomos of the Earth*. Number six is "Raum und Rom" and number seven is "Nehmen, teilen, weiden." Many of these articles were collected by Günter Maschke, *Staat, Grossraum, Nomos: Arbeiten aus den Jahren 1916–1969* (Berlin: Dunker and Humbolt, 1995).

6. Carl Schmitt, "El Orden del Mundo después de la Segunda Guerra Mundial," *Revista de Estudios Políticos* 122 (1962), 19–38. Original in Spanish. The text appeared in German in *Schmittiana II: Eclectica* 19, no. 79–80 (1990), 11–30. After in Maschke, *Staat, Grossraum, Nomos*, 592–618.

7. C. Schmitt, *On the Three Types of Juristic Thought*, trans. by J.W. Bendersky (Westport, CT: Praeger Publishers, 2004), 49. Here, Pindar's concept of *nomos basileus* appears as one of the most beautiful and ancient creations of legal thought in all of humanity. And here he marks out the concept of *nomos*, separating it from the meaning that Pindar gives it: *nomos* does not mean decree, rule, or norm, but rather law, which is as much norm and decision as it is, above all, order.

8. Although no doubt Schmitt, following Bachofen, would not discount mythology, see Johann J. Bachofen, *Mutterrechts* (Dortmund: Karl Schwalvenberg Verlag, 1947), 12.

9. Schmitt, *The Nomos of the Earth*, 45.

10. The influence that anthropological geography has on this fundamental point should be kept in mind and, concretely, the work of Friedrich Ratzel. For example, whole paragraphs in *Erdenmacht und Völkerschicksal: Eine Auswahl aus seinen Werken* (Stuttgart: Kröner, 1940), treat land and space similarly to Schmitt.

11. Schmitt, *The Nomos of the Earth*, 45.

12. "Appropriation, distribution, and production are the primal processes of human history, three acts of the primal drama." Schmitt, "The New Nomos of the Earth," in *The Nomos of the Earth*, 351. In a small foot note in his book *Land und Meer*, he notes "Appropriation, distribution and production are, following this sequence, the three fundamental concepts of every concrete order." Günter Maschke edition, *Land und Meer* (Köln: Hohenheim, 1981), 71. It is the most complete edition of the text. Here it is worth comparing Jean L. Feuerbach's opinion: "*Nomos* is the genealogical process in which a complete judicial, historical and political order emerges." Jean L. Feuerbach, "La theorie du 'Großraum' chez Carl Schmitt," in *Complexio Oppositorum: Über Carl Schmitt*, ed. H. Quaritsch (Berlin: Duncker & Humblot, 1988), 416.

13. Carl Schmitt, *Land and Sea*, transl. S. Draghici (Washington, DC: Plutarch Press, 1997), 1.

14. Schmitt, *The Nomos of the Earth*, 42. He describes the relationship with the land that comes with the development of agriculture. He also refers to winemaking in *Roman Catholicism and Political Form*, trans. G. L. Ulmen (Westport, CT: Greenwood Press, 1996), 11.

15. Schmitt, *The Nomos of the Earth*, 42.

16. Schmitt, *Land and Sea*, 5.

17. Schmitt describes this idea as follows: "It is the reproductive root in the normative order of history," *The Nomos of the Earth*, 48. The original version is: *Der Nomos der Erde*, 19: "Sie ist das Wurzelschlagen im Sinnreich der Geschichte." The English translation uses "normative" instead "profound meaning of history."

18. Carl Schmitt, "Raum und Rom," *Universitas* 6, no. 9 (1951), 963.

19. Ulmen points to the possible influence of François Perroux on the spatial conception of Schmitt's thought, whom Schmitt cited in "The Legal World Revolution," transl. G. L. Ulmen, *Telos* 72 (1987), 76. See Ulmen, *Politischer Mehrwert*, 441. It is not easy to determine this influence, but it can be said that it largely comes, in addition to Bachofen's indicated lectures, from his favorite poets: Theodor Däubler and Konrad Weiss. Concerning the influence that these poets had on Schmitt, see: Ernst Hüsmert, "Die letzten Jahre von Carl Schmitt," *Schmittiana I. Eclectica*, 53. Precisely because of this spacialization of concepts, a kind of cubism, from an esthetic interpretation, is attributed to Schmitt. See Villinger, *Carl Schmitts Kulturkritik der Moderne*, especially the last chapter: "Expresionismus oder Kubismus?" 316–25.

20. Schmitt, "Raum und Rom," 965. Schmitt's description of the consonant *R* can be found in the archive labeled RW 265–34/Mt.10.

21. Schmitt, "Raum und Rom," 965. Schmitt repeated this idea many times, as we will later see. In *Völkerrechtliche Großraumordnung mit Interventionsverbot für raumfremde Mächte: Ein Beitrag zum Reichsbegriff im Völkerrecht* (Berlin/Wien/Leipzig: Deutscher Rechtsverlag, 1941), 65 he points out that he takes the idea from biological research. Stephen Legg speaks of the "radical indeterminacy" of Schmitt's spatial ontology. Stephen Legg, "Introduction: Geographies of the nomos," in *Spatiality, Sovereignty and Carl Schmitt: Geographies of the nomos*, ed. S. Legg (Abingdon, UK: Routledge, 2011), 16.

22. Carl Schmitt, "Der Aufbruch ins Weltall," *Christ und Welt* 25 (1955), 9: "The sea is a strange and threatening place for men. Only dry land is habitable or, more clearly, man's home."

23. On this point, the reference Konrad Weiss described is important. In the first pages of *Der christliche Epimetheus* a spatial conception appears with reference to being: "God works historically not through humans, not through humanity, but through 'space-time' dispositions within humanity, that is, these dispositions are the plan's creations and mediations and, at the same time, the arrows that mark the plan's path." Konrad Weiss, *Der christliche Epimetheus* (München: Edwig Runge, 1933), 3.

24. This does not mean that Schmitt lacked diachronic perspective. He had an extensive sense of historicity, but precisely because of his spacialization of concepts, that is, the translation of time into space, history is, for Schmitt, essentially present. The past is tradition that is

present in every historical moment and the future depends on the present answer to the question that history itself asks of us.

25. On this point, it is worth noting the citation that Schmitt makes of Friedrich Ratzel's *Der Lebensraum* cited in *Völkerrechtliche Großraumordnung*, 64. "The expiration of space is the sign of every life."

26. On this point it is worth noting the assertion that he takes from Otto Weininger, cited in *Rom und Raum*, 967: "Space is Paradise; time is Hell." He also cites this phrase in *Glossarium. Aufzeichnungen der Jahre 1947–1951* (Berlin: Duncker & Humblot, 1991), 171.

27. Schmitt, *Glossarium*, 55 and 60. This assertion is repeatedly used in *Glossarium*.

28. Schmitt, *Glossarium*, 60 and 63. Also Schmitt, *Glossarium*, 171: "Here in the Plettenberg, in the mountains at the foot of the Lenne, I lose time, but I gain space. Time detaches itself from me, while space approaches me and embraces me. It contains me. Wouldn't you like to ask me questions as if I were a 'primitive' person and make me an object of study on magical thinking?" Also in Carl Schmitt, *Ex Captivitate Salus: Experiencias de los años 1945–1947*, transl. A. Schmitt (Santiago de Compostela: Porto y Cia., 1960), 95: "This is the wisdom of a cell. I lose my time, but I gain space. The peace that maintains the meaning of words suddenly comes over me. *Raum* and *Rom* are the same word." There is an English translation of the Poem included in this book in "Ex Captivitate Salus: A Poem," transl. G. L. Ulmen, *Telos* 72 (1987), 130, but not a translation of the entire book.

29. In a letter to Pierre Linn, he says it as follows: "I see myself in Westphalia, in my paternal home. . . . Our economic situation has changed, it's true that we are 'ruined' and Mrs. Schmitt is knee high in the tribulations of having enough money to eat. Either way, it affords a certain spatial continuity and even *loci* stability in a time of terror and general nihilism." Schmitt, *Glossarium*, 80. Spatial continuity seems to liberate the spiritual void signified by nihilism. Insecurity was a sign of postwar life. Kramme points out how intellectuals of the period responded to this insecure and nihilistic environment with a return to *Lebenswelt* and he included Schmitt in this group. See Rüdiger Kramme, *Helmuth Plessner und Carl Schmitt: Eine historische Fallstudie zum Verhältnis von Anthropologie und Politik in der deutschen Philosophie der zwanziger Jahre* (Berlin: Duncker & Humblot, 1989), 7.

30. Cited in Friedrich Nietzsche, *Werke*, Kröner Ausgabe, Bd. 7, II, 58. Schmitt, *Raum und Rom*, 967. He repeats the same assertion in *Glossarium*, 317.

31. Schmitt, *Glossarium*, 187.

32. Álvaro d'Ors was critical with regard to this question in "El 'Glossarium' de C. Schmitt," in *Estudios sobre Carl Schmitt*, ed. Dalmacio Negro (Madrid: Fundación Cánovas del Castillo, 1995), 23: "This exchange of time for space goes beyond a diachronic sensibility as admirable as Schmitt's and ultimately is not well understood."

33. On this same note Ratzel claims: "If temporal events are attributed to historical research, if the spatial being is attributed to geographical research, the following should not be forgotten: all events take place in space, all history, therefore, has its setting." Ratzel, *Erdemacht und Völkerschicksal*, 9. Schmitt himself cited him in the same way: "Friedrich Ratzel, the great founder of political geography, claimed that 'history becomes geographic and territorial with each generation." Schmitt, "Raum und Großraum im Völkerrecht," *Zeitschrift für Völkerrecht*, 24 (1941), 149.

34. Schmitt, "Raum und Rom," 963. Schmitt, *Ex Captivitate Salus*, 95. Schmitt, *Glossarium*, 317.

35. Schmitt, *Glossarium*, 317. This is another frequent idea in Schmitt's work. It also appears in *Political Theology II: The Myth of the Closure of Any Political Theology*, transl. M. Hoelzl and G. Ward (New York: Polity Press, 2014); and *Roman Catholicism and Political Form*, transl. G. L. Ulmen (Westport CT: Greenwood Press, 1996), 3. Tomissen ventures that it is very possible that Hans Urs von Balthasar took the title of one of his famous books from Schmitt: *Der antirömische Affekt* (Freiburg i. Br.: Herder, 1974). Piet Tomissen, "Carl Schmitt metajuristisch betrachtet," *Criticon* 30 (1975), 184.

36. D'Ors, "El 'Glossarium' de Carl Schmitt," 21.

37. Carl Schmitt, "Illyrien. Notizen von einer dalmatinischen Reise," *Hochland*, 23, no. 3 (1925), 293.

38. In this sense, Schmitt ironically affirms the following: "Schmitt allows himself the incredible assertion that everything respectable that remains on earth was inherited from medieval Christians, compared to whom we are apprentices, whose foundations we have misappropriated by living in 'dulci jubilo' during a few centuries, while later finding out how a de-Christianized world really thinks about the arts and sciences." Carl Schmitt, "Die Buribunken," *Summa. Eine Vierteljahresschrift* 4 (1918), 91.

39. Schmitt, *Glossarium*, 34: "Man in space" and "Man and Men."

40. Schmitt, *Glossarium*, 46.

41. Schmitt, *Glossarium*, 47.

42. Schmitt, *Glossarium*, 46: "This loss of spatial perspective and position, this dislocation, is an abstraction of the relationship between order and position (for the eternal ancient man)."

43. Schmitt, "Illyrien," 294: "The original population of Illyria—Greek, Kelt, Roman, German, Slavic and Mongol, was a fantastic mix of languages and religions, an air filled with demons, ancient paganism, Roman and Greek Christianity, Gnosticism and Islam."

44. Schmitt, "Illyrien," 294: "But land, the mountains, the sea and the sun seem to ignore all of this origin."

45. Schmitt, "Illyrien," 296.

46. Schmitt, "Illyrien," 294: "The land, not blood, gives man, the son of the earth, his figure and face. All of the races situated in Illyria obtained something new from this land and became bearers of the Illyrian spirit."

47. Schmitt, "Nomos-Nahme-Name," in *The Nomos of the Earth*, 338. The discovery of *nomos* expresses Schmitt's "passion for the object." From his first writings, especially *Schattenrisse*, Schmitt always bet against all forms of subjectivism—die *Ich-Bezogenheit* (reference to the self)—in favor of the object; It could be said that Carl Schmitt is *Sach-bezogen* (referred to the object). See the *Schattenrisse*: "Richard Dehmel" and "Herbert Eulenberg," in Villinger, *Carl Schmitts Klturkritik der Moderne*.

48. Schmitt, "Nomos-Nahme-Name," in *The Nomos of the Earth*, 342. On this point, Schmitt relied on d'Ors's argument in his book dedicated to Carl Schmitt, *De la Guerra y de la Paz* (Madrid: Rialp, 1954), 160 as follows: "Cicero's translation of the Greek term *nomos* for the Latin word *lex* represents one of the heaviest burdens in Western conceptualization and linguistic culture."

49. Schmitt, "Appropriation/Distribution/Production: An Attempt to Determine from Nomos the Basic Questions of Every Social and Economic Order," in *The Nomos of the Earth*, 326.

50. Schmitt, "Nomos-Nahme-Name," in *The Nomos of the Earth*, 345: "However, just as division precedes production, so appropriation precedes division; it opens the way to apportionment. It is not division—*divisio primaeva*—but appropriation that comes first. Initially, there was not basic norm, but a basic appropriation."

51. Schmitt, "The New Nomos of the Earth," in *The Nomos of the Earth*, 351.

52. Schmitt, "Nomos-Nahme-Name," in *The Nomos of the Earth*, 344.

53. Schmitt, *The Nomos of the Earth*, 70. In Schmitt's discourse, historical reason is distinguished from theological reason, which is the absolute, transcendent foundation, as we will see in the last chapters.

54. Schmitt, "Nomos-Nahme-Name," in *The Nomos of the Earth*, 345; "Nehmen, Teilen, Weiden," in *Verfassungsrechtliche Aufsätze*, 504 in note number four. There is no English translation of this part of the last edition by Carl Schmitt of this article. Also see *The Nomos of the Earth*, 71.

55. Schmitt, "Nehmen, Teilen, Weiden," in *Verfassungsrechtliche Aufsätze*, 503 in note number three. There is no English translation of this part of the last edition by Carl Schmitt of this article. He cites a reference from Marx's *Capital*, note 2 of chapter 24, to Goethe's *Lehrgespräch* and that manifests *nomos*'s originating character.

56. Schmitt, "Appropriation, Distribution, Production," in *The Nomos of the Earth*, 325. On this point Schmitt cites paragraph 247 of *Grundlinien der Philosophie des Rechts* and says: "I leave the attentive reader to develop from this attempt that I start with a quote in paragraph 247 in the same way as Marxism has developed paragraphs 243–246." It is the text of a 1981 annotation published in the Maschke edition of *Land und Meer* as *Nachbemerkung*.

57. Schmitt, *The Nomos of the Earth*, 48. And also 78: "Such constitutive processes are certainly not everyday occurrences, but neither are they simply matters of bygone times and only of archeological or antiquarian interest today. As long as world history remains open and fluid, as long as conditions are not fixed and ossified; in other words, as long as human beings and peoples have not only a past but also a future, a new *nomos* will arise in the perpetually new manifestations of world-historical events."

58. Schmitt, *The Nomos of the Earth*, 48.

59. Schmitt, "The New Nomos of the Earth," in *The Nomos of the Earth*, 351. Christian Graf von Krockow was referring to this configured space when describing *nomos* as follows: "*Nomos* means something like the metaphysical substance of space." *Die Entscheidung: Eine Untersuchung über Ernst Jünger, Carl Schmitt und Martin Heidegger* (Frankfurt: Campus Verlag, 1990), 104.

60. Schmitt, *The Nomos of the Earth*, 42.

61. Erich Przywara, *Mensch* (Nürnberg: Glock und Lutz, 1958), 211–13.

62. Przywara, *Mensch*, 213: "through a pluriverse of a plurisovereignty."

63. Further clarification in Peter Schneider, *Ausnahmezustand und Norm. Eine Studie zur Rechtslehre von Carl Schmitt* (Stuttgart: Deutsche Verlagsanstalt, 1957), 32.

64. Schmitt, *Glossarium*, 31.

65. Schmitt, *The Nomos of the Earth*, 45.

66. These categories are contained in the concept of *nomos* and are a part of it. Schmitt uses the term, *enthalten*, that is, "contain" or "imply." "Appropriation, Distribution, Production," in *The Nomos of the Earth*, 335 and 328: "Land was the precondition of all subsequent economy and law." In a note contained in the German edition of the book *Land and Sea*, Schmitt gives the following definition of *nomos*: "The Greek word *nomos* comes from the adverb *nemein* and also has three meanings: First, *Nemein* is primarily the same as 'to take.' Consequently, *nomos* corresponds to 'that which is possessed.' The Greek *legein-logos* is similar to German's *sprechen-Sprache*. That which is possessed is, firstly, the earth, then the sea, about which much has been said in our universal history and, in the industrial sector; it is the appropriation of industry, that is, possession of the means of production. Secondly, *Nemein* means division and distribution of that which is possessed. In this sense, *nomos* corresponds to the division and fundamental distribution of the land and the respective ordering of property. The third meaning is 'to cultivate,' that is, the economization, taking advantage of and assessment of the land given to it in division, production and consumption. Possession, division and cultivation are, in this sequence, the three categories of every specific order." Schmitt, *Land und Meer*, 71. Schmitt basically repeats this in "The New Nomos of the Earth," in *The Nomos of the Earth*, 351. On this matter, see also Hermann Schmidt, "Der Nomosbegriff bei Carl Schmitt," *Der Staat* 2 (1963), 81–108.

67. Schmitt, "Appropriation, Distribution, Production," in *The Nomos of the Earth*, 325: "To deal with this problem, we will attempt first to apprehend the original meaning of the word *nomos* and then to ascertain elementary and true categories that are both basic and inclusive." Also, in the *Theory of the Partisan* he reiterates the point saying: "In fact, the new spaces can and must be conquered by men. Old-style land- and sea-appropriations that human history has known up to now would have a sequel: a new type of space-appropriation. *Appropriation*, however, will be followed by *distribution* and then *production*. In this respect, despite all progress, everything remains as before." Schmitt, "Theory of the Partisan: Intermediate Commentary on the Concept of the Political," transl. G. L. Ulmen, *Telos* 127 (2004), 68.

68. In this regard, Hugo Fischer discusses Schmitt's realist metaphysics: "Zur neueren realist-metaphysischen Staatstheorie," *Archiv für Rechts und Wirtschaftsphilosophie* 23 (1929–1930), 196–99. He believes Schmitt to be a realist based on the relevance that he gives to existence without disregarding essential aspects, thus avoiding historicism. This opinion always finds a place in Przywara's line of thought focused on "the return to objects." Przywara knows Schmitt's work well. This is more in line with existential realist thought than with positivist or materialist thought. As seen in the *Schattenrisse*, which defines his existential position well, from his first writings, Schmitt fought against both naturalism—a paradigm of the first way of conceiving reality here mentioned—and romanticism—a paradigm of subjectivism. Another interpretation brings the Schmittian "existential fact" in line with Nietzschean

philosophy. For example, Pattloch's book in which he identifies Schmitt's Nietzscheism in his theory of space. See Peter P. Pattloch, *Rechts als Einheit von Ordnung und Ortung: Ein Beitrag zum Rechtsbegriff in Carl Schmitts "Nomos der Erde"* (Aschaffenburg: Pattloch Verlag, 1961), 11. But as found in one of Schmitt's letters from September 13, 1961, Schmitt was somewhat annoyed by Pattloch's interpretation: "Nietzsche was amazing; I am not. The Christian Epimethians shut their mouth like the dead and you have not taken into account the fact that there is a non-perspectivist space." Cited in Armin Mohler, "Carl Schmitt und die konservative Revolution," in Quaritsch ed., *Complexio Oppositorum*, 131. In addition, von der Heydte frames it within this line of thinking; however, he finds any likeness more in decisionism. Friedrich August von der Heydte, "Heil aus der Gefangeschaft? Carl Schmitt und die Lage der europäischen Rechtswissenschaft," *Hochland* 43 (1951), 289: "In many ways, Carl Schmitt is the executor of Nietzsche's will concerning the theory of the State: he is heir, an authentic representative of German romanticism that injects a Nietzschean spirit into the theory of the State." In this group we may also include Karl Löwith, especially as outlined in his brief text, "Politischer Dezisionismus." A chapter of his book *Der Mensch inmitten der Geschichte: Philosophische Bilanz des 20. Jahrhunderts*, (Stuttgart: J. B. Metzler Verlag, 1990), 19–48. He has similarly been treated in public opinion as well. In a small article published in *Corriere della Sera* (April 17, 1985), Claudio Magris called Schmitt a "lucid Nietzschean." The list is endless; however, others, such as Maschke clearly argue that Schmitt's greatest enemy was nihilism. See Günter Maschke, *Der Tod des Carl Schmitt* (Wien: Karolinger Verlag, 1987), 34. This can also be seen in Schneider, *Ausnahmezustand und Norm*, 290. Schmitt conceives of true nihilism as the separation between *Ordnung* and *Ortung*, as he himself says in *The Nomos of the Earth*, 6. On the other hand, the *Schattenrisse*, especially those entitled "Mein Bruder" and "Eberhardt Niegeburth," show his consistent opposition to Nietzscheism, which Schmitt interpreted technically, as did Ernst Jünger. Villinger characterizes Schmitt's position on Nietzsche as follows: "Nietzsche is the philosophical guarantor, who Schmitt introduced as the founder of the 'great individual' and remains present in all of the *Schattenrisse*. His *Zarathustran* 'Superman' is not just the model for pedagogical reform efforts and for the industry of literary training, but in Schmitt's representation, he is also related to technique. Correlation of the technical Schattenrise Superman appears in the modern labor organization, which Schmitt associated with Darwin." Villinger, *Carl Schmitts Kulturkritik der Moderne*, 304–5. There are also existentialist interpretations like the one sustained by Graf von Krockow in *Die Entscheidung*, which tries to relate Schmitt's ideas on decision with those of Heidegger and Jünger. He cites his existentialism in a "practical connection to circumstance." *Die Entscheidung*, 5. Hasso Hofmann, in *Legitimität gegen Legalität: Der Weg der politischen Philosophie Carl Schmitts* (Neuwied/Berlin: Luchterland, 1964), writes of a "political existentialism." There is no doubt that regarding Schmitt it is possible to speak of a certain existentialism and historicism, in the sense that "immediacy" is superior in his approach. This "immediacy" refers to the most profound parts of conscience, not to anything exterior. The most real is that which is the most immediate to the conscience. For this reason as well, Schmitt's supposed historicism is nothing more than a fight against utopia.

69. Schmitt, *Land and Sea*, 4–5.

70. Schmitt, "Nomos-Nahme-Name," in *Nomos of the Earth*, 345.

71. Schmitt, "Appropriation, Distribution, Production," in *The Nomos of the Earth*, 328.

72. Georg W. F. Hegel, *Elements of the Philosophy of Right* (Cambridge: Cambridge University Press), §§ 41, 42, 44, and 71.

73. Schmitt, "Nomos-Nahme-Name," in *The Nomos of the Earth*, 347.

74. Schmitt, "Nomos-Nahme-Name," in *The Nomos of the Earth*, 348.

75. This appropriation precedes any division. As Schmitt says, "When great philosophers like Thomas Aquinas and Hobbes intuit that a first division constitutes the beginning of all legal order—a *divisio primaeva*—this historical fact needs one more thing added to it: possession of the measurement of that which is distributed, thus an *occupatio* or *appropiatio primaeva*, precedes division and distribution, that is, the *suum cuique*." Schmitt, " Nomos-Nahme-Name," in *Verfassungsrechtliche Aufsätze*, 502–3 in note number 2. There is no English translation of this note.

76. Schmitt, "Appropriation, Distribution, Production," in *The Nomos of the Earth*, 326.

77. Schmitt, "Appropriation, Distribution, Production," in *The Nomos of the Earth*, 327.
78. Schmitt, "Nomos-Nahme-Name," in *Nomos of the Earth*, 345: "appropriation precedes division." Schmitt, *The Nomos of the Earth*, 70. And again Schmitt, "Nomos-Nahme-Name," in *The Nomos of the Earth*, 342. In "Nomos-Nahme-Name" Schmitt refers to d'Ors' treatment of this point in "La función de la propiedad en el ordenamiento civil" ("Property's function in the history of civil legislation"), in *Historia del Derecho Privado: Trabajos en Homenaje a Ferrán Valls i Taberner* (Barcelona: PPU, 1989), 2841–65. Schmitt, "Nomos-Nahme-Name," in *Nomos of the Earth*, 342: "A first-rate expert, the Spanish Romanist Álvaro d'Ors, rightly stated that the translation of *nomos* with *lex* is one of the heaviest burdens that the conceptual and linguistic culture in the Occident has had to bear. Anyone familiar with the further development of the law-state and with the present crisis of legality knows this to be true."
79. Schmitt, *The Nomos of the Earth*, 46–47. See Álvaro d'Ors, *Una introducción al estudio del Derecho* (Madrid: Rialp, 1963), 27–28. See also Schmidt, "Der Nomosbegriff bei Carl Schmitt," 93–94.
80. Schmitt, *Glossarium*, 46. Schneider speaks of this relationship in terms of a foundational relationship. Schneider, *Ausnahmezustand und Norm*, 33. However, Schmitt speaks more of a presupposition, of a condition, than of a foundation.
81. Schmitt, *The Nomos of the Earth*, 73: "In its original sense, however, *nomos* is precisely the full immediacy of a legal power not mediated by laws; it is a constitutive historical event— an act of legitimacy, whereby the legality of a mere law first is made meaningful."
82. Schmitt, *Land and Sea*, 37: "Every basic order is a spatial order. To talk of the constitution of a country or a continent is to talk of its fundamental order, of its nomos."
83. Schmitt, "Appropriation, Distribution, Production," in *The Nomos of the Earth*, 327. See also: Schmitt, "Nomos-Nahme-Name," in *The Nomos of the Earth*: "*Nomos is an nomen actionis of nemein*, and *nemein*. By common consent, *nemein* means both *teilen* (to divide) and *verteilen* (to distribute). Oddly enough, it also means *weiden* (to pasture). Thus nemein can be used both intransitively and transitively."
84. Schmitt, "Appropriation, Distribution, Production," in *The Nomos of the Earth*, 328.
85. Schmitt, "Nomos-Nahme-Name," in *The Nomos of the Earth*, 345: "The unity of the *nomos* is only the unity of *oikos*."
86. Schmitt's description is relevant in "Nomos-Nahme-Name," in *The Nomos of the Earth*, 347: "Everything on earth based on progress and development, in both East and West, now contains at its core a concrete and precise creed, whose principles of belief proclaim that the industrial revolution leads to an immeasurable increase in production. As a consequence appropriation becomes outmoded, even criminal, and division is no longer a problem given the abundance. There is only production, only the problem-less fortune of pure consumption. . . . Things govern themselves; man confronts himself; wandering in the wilderness of alienation has ended. In a world created by man for himself—a world of men for men (and unfortunately sometimes against men)—man can *give* without *taking*."
87. On this point, it is important to highlight that, according to Ulmen, Schmitt did not banish liberalism with economic arguments; he did not dismiss it as an economic system, but rather as a political one. See Gary L. Ulmen, in "Politische Theologie und politische Ökonomie—Über Carl Schmitt und Max Weber," in H. Quaritsch, ed., *Complexio Oppositorum: Über Carl Schmitt* (Berlin: Duncker & Humblot, 1988), 351. Also in Ulmen, *Politischer Mehrwert*, 2 and 165. In this regard, Helmut Kuhn also highlights the antiliberal effect of the friend-enemy distinction, "Besprechung des Buches Carl Schmitt-Der Begriff des Politischen," *Kantsstudien* 38 (1933), 191–93. Leo Strauss argued against this argument. Even if the position of politics in Schmitt is, fundamentally, a position against liberal culture, Schmitt is not free of liberal suppositions. Leo Strauss, "Anmerkungen zu Carl Schmitt, 'Der Begriff des Politischen,'" in Heinrich Meier, *Carl Schmitt, Leo Strauss und "Der Begriff des Politischen": Zu einem Dialog unter Abwesenden* (Stuttgart: Metzler Verlag, 1991), 100. Strauss gives two fundamental reasons for arguing this. One is circumstantial: if Schmitt himself admits that liberalism reigns in Europe and Schmitt's thought is concrete, Strauss concludes, "his reflections are necessarily influenced by elements of liberal thought." Strauss, "Anmerkungen," 101. The other concerns the very principles of his political theory, namely, his last word is not the position of politics, but rather 'the order of human affairs.' This order must come from an

integral knowledge, but this kind of knowledge is not polemical and is not found in specific situations, but rather by returning to the origin, to uncorrupted nature. Ultimately, the position of politics suffocates. Strauss, "Anmerkungen," 124. Strauss was not the last to hold such an opinion; Helmut Schelsky also describes Schmitt as a liberal in his brief study "'Der Begriff des Politischen' und die politische Erfahrung der Gegenwart," *Der Staat* 22 (1983), 322.

88. Carl Schmitt, "The Age of Neutralizations and Depoliticizations," in *The Concept of the Political*, transl. G. Schwab (Chicago: Chicago University Press, 2007), 80–95.

89. Carl Schmitt, *Political Romanticism*, transl. G. Oakes (Cambridge, MA: MIT Press, 1986); Carl Schmitt, "Romantik," *Hochland* 22 (1924–25), 157–71 and Carl Schmitt, "On the Counterrevolutionary Philosophy of the State," in *Political Theology: Four Chapters on the Concept of Sovereignty*, transl. G. Schwab (Chicago: University of Chicago Press, 2005), 53–67, 62–65. Also Schmitt, *Political Theology*, 53–66.

90. On the critique of liberalism, I follow in some points Günter Maschke's approach in his study on "Drei Motive im Anti-Liberalismus Carl Schmitts," in *Carl Schmitt und die Liberalismuskritik*, ed. Klaus Hanser and Hans Lietzmann (Leske + Budrich: Opladen, 1988), 55–79. For a further account of the critique of liberalism see John P. McCormick, *Carl Schmitt's Critique of Liberalism: Against Politics as Technology* (Cambridge: Cambridge University Press, 1997).

91. Günther Krauss, "Erinnerungen an Carl Schmitt," *Criticon. Konservativ heute* 95–96 (1986), 127–30 and 180–86.

92. Carl Schmitt, *Theodor Däublers "Nordlicht": Drei Studien über die Elemente, den Geist und die Aktualität des Werkes* (München: Georg Müller, 1916), 64–65: "Men have become poor demons; they know everything and believe in nothing. . . . They want heaven on earth, heaven as a result of the market and industry, which should surely be here in Berlin, Paris, or New York, a heaven with swimming pools, cars, and club chairs, whose sacred text corresponds to a highway map." Also on liberalism and de-politicization see Schmitt, *The Concept of the Political*, 68–79.

93. Schmitt analyzes this governing system in his study on *The Crisis of Parliamentary Democracy*, transl. E. Kennedy (Cambridge, MA: MIT Press, 2000).

94. Schmitt, "Appropriation, Distribution, Production," in *The Nomos of the Earth*, 328: "The major problem is the sequence of these processes, which has changed often in accord with how appropriation, distribution, and production are emphasized and evaluated, both practically and morally, in human consciousness."

95. Schmitt, "Appropriation, Distribution, Production," in *The Nomos of the Earth*, 331: "Here is where socialism falls in with classical political economy and its liberalism. The core of liberalism, both as a science of society and a philosophy of history, also is concerned with the sequence of production and distribution. Progress and economic freedom consist in freeing productive powers, whereby such an increase in production and in the mass of consumer goods brings appropriation to an end, so that even distribution becomes an independent problem."

96. Schmitt, "Appropriation, Distribution, Production," in *The Nomos of the Earth*, 335. As we will later see, Schmitt often asks himself this question. See Carl Schmitt, *La Unidad del Mundo*, transl. A. Truyol y Serra (Madrid: Ateneo, 1951). It was first published in Spanish. One year later in German, "Die Einheit der Welt," *Merkur* 6 (1952), 1–11. Also *The Concept of the Political*, 57. An attempt to update Schmitt's *nomos* theory to contemporary geopolitical conditions is Stephen Legg, ed., *Spatiality, Sovereignty and Carl Schmitt: Geographies of the Nomos* (Abingdon, UK: Routledge, 2011).

97. Schmitt, *The Nomos of the Earth*, 45: "Externally, the land-appropiating group is confronted with other land-appropriating or land-owning groups and powers."

98. Schmitt, *Glossarium*, 187. It is interesting to note that, in parallel, Ernst Jünger argues the following: "All rhythmic things are weapons against time; and, in the end, we fight against time. Human beings always fight against the power of time." Ernst Jünger, *Radiaciones. Diarios de la Segunda Guerra Mundial* (Barcelona: Tusquets, 1992), I, 88.

99. Schmitt, *The Nomos of the Earth*, 78.

100. Schmitt, *Glossarium*, 187.

101. Carl Schmitt, "Die Monroedoktrin als der Präzedenzfall eines Völkerrechtlichen Grossraumsprinzips," in *Völkerrechtliche Großraumordnung*, 19–20: "For us, there are neither a-

local political ideas nor spaces or spatial principles without ideas. On the other hand, a specific political idea always requires that a specific people set it off and that it has a specific opponent in mind, from which it obtains a political character."

102. Erich Pryzwara, *In und Gegen: Stellungnahme zur Zeit* (Nürnberg: Glock und Lutz, 1955), 224: "the authentic and archaic origin of power that only acquires full power within the State."

103. He follows the relationship between space and power set forth by Przywara, especially in his *Humanitas: Der Mensch gestern und morgen* (Nürnberg: Glock und Lutz, 1952), even though this position on power is also related in the cited book *In und Gegen*.

104. Schmitt, "Nomos-Nahme-Name," in *The Nomos of the Earth*, 336: "secret sinister end."

105. Schmitt, "Nomos-Nahme-Name," in *The Nomos of the Earth*, 338: "Nomos penetrates archy and cracy. Neither can exist without *nomos*."

106. Schmitt, "Nomos-Nahme-Name," in *The Nomos of the Earth*, 347: "What one today calls world history in the West and in the East is the history of development in the objects, means and forms of appropriation interpreted as progress. This development proceeds from the land-appropriations of nomadic and agrarian-feudal time to see appropriations of the 16th to the 19th century. Over the industry-appropriations of the industrial-technical age and its distinction between developed and underdeveloped areas, and, finally, to the air-appropriations and space-appropriations of the present."

107. Schmitt, *Glossarium*, 63–64.

108. Schmitt, *Glossarium*, 187.

109. Schmitt, "Nomos-Nahme-Name," in *The Nomos of the Earth*, 348: "A land-appropriation is constituted only if the appropriator is able to give the land a name." Schmitt, "Nomos-Nahme-Name," in *The Nomos of the Earth*, 349: "As soon as a true name appears, the solely economic *nomos* ceases to exist, having been exhausted in economy and administration."

110. Enemy considered as *hostis* not as *inimicus* as we will see in chapter 5. In this regard, see Schmitt, *The Concept of the Political*, 28–29.

111. See Jean Luis Feuerbach, "La Théorie du Grossraum chez Carl Schmitt," in H. Quaritsch, ed., *Complexio Oppositorum*, 408.

112. This last point, namely, the interdependence between changing space and the variation of the concept of enmity and war is spelled out in Georg Schwab, "Enemy oder Foe" in *Ephirrosis: Festschrift für Carl Schmitt zum 65. Geburtstag* (Düsseldorf, 1953), II, 665–82. The description of the different legal stages that *nomos*'s variations contain, from the pre-global juridical order to the juridical order of the State, are also explained in detail in Schneider, *Ausnahmezustand und Norm*, 41–221.

113. Schmitt, *Land and Sea*, 5–6. See also *The Leviathan in the State Theory of Thomas Hobbes: Meaning and Failure of a Political Symbol*, transl. G. Schwab and E. Hilfstein (Westport, CT: Greenwood Press), 6–15.

114. Schmitt, *The Nomos of the Earth*, 50: "There was no concept of a planet, of human compass and orientation common to all peoples. In this sense, there was no global consciousness and thus no political goal oriented to a common hope."

115. Schmitt, "The New Nomos of the Earth," in *The Nomos of the Earth*, 351–52.

116. Schmitt, *The Nomos of the Earth*, 56.

117. Schmitt, *The Nomos of the Earth*, 59 onward and 87. This is a key concept in Schmitt's discourse. It is related to the meaning of history, to politics and definitively to political theology. It was coined by Saint Paul in his Second Letter to the Thessalonians. We will come back to this concept in chapter 7.

118. Schmitt, *The Nomos of the Earth*, 63: "But, Caesarism is a typically non-Christian form of power, even if it concludes concordats. Both as a term and a spiritual problem, this Caesarism is a modern phenomenon. It began with the French Revolution of 1789, and belongs historically to the time of the great parallel between the situations of early Christianity and that of the 19th century."

119. Schmitt, *The Nomos of the Earth*, 65.

120. Schmitt, *The Nomos of the Earth*, 101 onward. Also Schmitt, *Cambio de Estructura en el Derecho Internacional* (Madrid: Instituto de Estudios Políticos, 1943), 4–5. Published only in Spanish. Also Schmitt, *The Nomos of the Earth*, 49: "The originally terrestrial order was altered in

the Age of Discovery, when the earth first was encompassed and measured by the global conscious-ness of European peoples. This resulted in the first *nomos* of the earth. It was based in a particular relation between the spatial order of firm land and the spatial order of free sea, and for 400 years it supported a Eurocentric international law: the *jus publicum Europaeum.*"

121. Schmitt, *Land and Sea*, 35–36.

122. Schmitt, "The New Nomos of the Earth," in *The Nomos of the Earth*, 352: "The Euro-centric structure of nomos extended only partially, as open-land appropriation, and otherwise in the form of protectorates, leases, trade agreements, and spheres of interest; in short, in more elastic forms of utilization."

123. At this stage, the sea's relationship with man has changed: "Naturally, the oceans are free and should remain so. But the sea is no longer just an 'element' for us; it has become a space that is accessible to human governance, development and power distributions." Carl Schmitt, "Raum und Großraum in Völkerrecht," *Zeitschrift für Völkerrecht* 24 (1941), 169.

124. Schmitt, *The Nomos of the Earth*, 90.

125. Schmitt, *The Nomos of the Earth*, 172. See also Schmitt, *Land and Sea*, 47–48. This topic can also be found in "Staat als ein konkreter, an eine gechichtliche Epoche gebundener Begriff," in Schmitt, *Verfassungsrechtliche Aufsätze*, 375–86. See also Schmitt, "The New Nomos of the Earth," in *The Nomos of the Earth*, 352.

126. Schmitt, *Land and Sea*, 19–22. See also Schmitt, "The New Nomos of the Earth," in *The Nomos of the Earth*, 353: "Land war was not conducted between peoples, but only between the armies of European States. The private property of civil populations was not booty according to international law. Sea war was trade war. In sea war, the enemy war any state with which the opponent had commercial dealings."

127. Schmitt, *The Nomos of the Earth*, 88.

128. Schmitt,, "Cambio de estructura en el Derecho Internacional," 5. Also in Schmitt, *Völkerrechtliche Großraumordnung*, 13–23.

129. Schmitt, "The New Nomos of the Earth," in *The Nomos of the Earth*, 352.

130. This line assumed that two sovereigns who acknowledge a common authority—that is, a common order—would reach an agreement on the acquisition of heterodox land. It did not entail a delimitation between Christian and non-Christian territories, but rather an internal boundary between two Christians sovereigns holding land or sea occupations. Amity lines first emerged in a secret clause added to the treaty of Cateau-Cambresis and pertained to the era of religious wars between maritime powers and Protestants occupying land. The demarcation line marked where law was in effect. What was beyond the line was outside of moral, legal, and political assessments of space itself. The freedom that delimited this line was found in the fact that beyond it a free use of violence opened up. Ultimately, these lines divided the state of nature and the civil state. There was no conception of a common ordering.

131. Schmitt, *The Nomos of the Earth*, 140–41.

132. Schmitt, *The Nomos of the Earth*, 128.

133. Schmitt, *The Nomos of the Earth*, 249: "The declaration of war was based on the desire for juridical form, and on the premise that there is no third party in matters of war and peace: *Tertium non datur*. In the interest of belligerents and neutrals, and in order to avoid the intermediate situation of what today is called 'cold war,' international law clearly distinguished between two distinct *statuses*."

134. Schmitt, *The Nomos of the Earth*, 227. The following text is important in this regard: "As a result of World War I, this Eurocentric *nomos* of the earth was destroyed. Today (1954), the world in which we live is divided into parts East and West, which confront each other in a cold war and, occasionally, also in hot wars." Schmitt, "The New Nomos of the Earth," in *The Nomos of the Earth*, 353.

135. Schmitt, *The Nomos of the Earth*, 231–32.

136. Schmitt, *The Nomos of the Earth*, 241: "[T]his world conference in no sense created a new world order. It left the world in its earlier disorder, eliminated only two European Great Powers—two pillars of the former spatial order—and undertook a redivision of the European territory. Whereas European conferences in preceding centuries had determined the spatial order of the earth, at the Paris Peace Conference, for the first time, the reverse was the case: the world determined the spatial order of Europe. This means that a complete disorganized world

attempted to create a new order in Europe." When he speaks of a disorganized world, he refers to a world without a clear ordering of space, which has even destroyed the concept of war.

137. Schmitt, *The Nomos of the Earth*, 230.

138. Schmitt, *The Nomos of the Earth*, 241–58. Schmitt thoroughly discusses the Geneva Conference in his book *Das politische Problem der Friedenssicherung* (Leipzig: Teubner, 1930).

139. Schmitt, *The Nomos of the Earth*, 235. "In short: over, under, and beside the state-political borders of what appeared to be a purely political international law between states spread a free, i.e., non-state sphere of economy permeating everything: a global economy. In the idea of a free global economy lay not only the overcoming of state-political borders, but also, as an essential precondition, a standard for the internal constitutions of individual member states of this order of international law. . . . This minimum standard consisted of the freedom—the separation—of the state-public sphere from the private sphere, above all, from the non-state sphere of property, trade and economy."

140. Schmitt, "Totaler Feind, totaler Krieg, totaler Staat," in Carl Schmitt, *Positionen und Begriffe im Kampf mit Weimar-Genf-Versailles, 1923–1939* (Hamburg: Hanseatische Verlagsanstalt, 1940), 235–40. Also Schmitt, *The Nomos of the Earth*, 246.

141. Schmitt, "The New Nomos of the Earth," in *The Nomos of the Earth*, 354: "Development of modern technology has robbed the sea of its elemental character. A new, third dimension—air space—has become the force-field of human power and activity." Also Schmitt, *Land and Sea*, 56–59.

142. Schmitt, *The Nomos of the Earth*, 319. See also Schmitt, "Cambio de estructura en el Derecho Internacional," 3.

143. Schmitt, *The Nomos of the Earth*, 320: "With air bombardment, the lack of relation between military personnel in the air and the earth below, as well with inhabitants thereon, is absolute. Not even the shadow of the relation between protection and obedience remains. Independent air war allows neither the one nor the other side a possibility to establish a relation. The airplane flies over and drops its bombs; low-flying pilots dive down and then fly up and away; both execute their destructive function, then immediately leave the scene, with all that has befallen men and materials on the ground, whose fate is in the hands of the sovereign of the surface State."

144. Schmitt, *The Nomos of the Earth*, 321. "Given the fact that war has been transformed into a police action against trouble makers, criminals and pests, justification of this 'police bombing' must be intensified. Thus, one is compelled to push the discrimination of the opponent into the abyss."

145. He uses the phrase "a clean break between the land and sea" in "Gespräch über den neuen Raum," in *Estudios de Derecho Internacional en homenaje a Barcia Trelles*, ed. C. de Miguel (Zaragoza: Universidad de Santiago de Compostela, Zaragoza, 1958), 267.

146. Schmitt, *Land and Sea*, 5. See also Schmitt, "Gespräch über den neuen Raum," 266.

147. Schmitt, "Gespräch über den neuen Raum," 264: "According to the Bible, God has assigned dry land to men as a habitable place, while he reduced the sea to the limit of that habitable space. The sea lurks as a continuous danger and threat. God's goodness involves the sea, such that it does not devour us in a flood. The sea is strange and an enemy of the people. It is not a habitable space. According to the Bible, the only habitable space is dry land."

148. Schmitt, "Gespräch über den neuen Raum," 265: "You heard him: the sea shall cease to exist! In the new earth, there are no oceans. The sea disappears with sin and evil. This is the end of the New Testament. From the story of the creation of the first book of Moses until the end of St. John's Revelation, the Bible contains a contrast between the land and sea."

149. Carl Schmitt, "Die geschichtliche Struktur des heutigen Weltgegensatzes von Ost und West," in *Freundschaftliche Begegnungen: Festschrift für Ernst Jünger zum 60. Geburtstag*, ed. Armin Mohler (Frankfurt, Vittorio Klostermann, 1955), 139. See also Schmitt "Gespräch über den neuen Raum," 268–69.

150. Schmitt, "Die geschichtliche Struktur des heutigen Weltgegensatzes von Ost und West," 137.

151. Jean Gottmann, *La politique des Etats et leur Geographie* (Paris: Armand Colin, 1952).

152. Schmitt, *La Unidad del Mundo*, 22.

153. Schmitt, "Die geschichtliche Struktur des heutigen Weltgegensatzes von Ost und West," 137–138: "Earth has a North and South Pole, but not an East and West one. Geographically speaking, in our terraqueous globe the East/West opposition is fluid and indeterminate; it merely represents 'the ebb and flow of a little night and a little day.' In geographical relation to America, for example, China and Russia are the Occident. In relation to China and Russia, Europe represents in its turn the Occident. From a purely geographical point of view, there is no such thing as a polar tension, much less a reasonable explanation for world conflict expressed in global terms, which renders moot the possibility of understanding its particular structure." Also Schmitt, "Gespräch uber den neuen Raum," 268.

154. Schmitt, "Die geschichtliche Struktur des heutigen Weltgegensatzes von Ost und West," 139.

155. Schmitt, *Land and Sea*, 6.

156. Schmitt, *Land and Sea*, 7. Also Schmitt "Gespräch über den neuen Raum," 264. Also Schmitt, *The Leviathan in the State Theory of Thomas Hobbes*, 5–11.

157. Schmitt, *Land and Sea*, 8.

158. Schmitt, *Land and Sea*, 49. Also Schmitt "Gespräch über den neuen Raum," 273.

159. Schmitt, *Land and Sea*, 54.

160. Schmitt, "Die geschichtliche Struktur des heutigen Weltgegensatzes von Ost und West," 148: "The nomos of the earth would be deprived of its specific here and now if land and sea elements are speaking of which should be understood only as a piece of nature and natural tensions."

161. Schmitt, "Gespräch über den neuen Raum," 267.

162. Schmitt, "Die geschichtliche Struktur des heutigen Weltgegensatzes von Ost und West," 12. Also Schmitt, "Gespräch über den neuen Raum," 267.

163. Schmitt, "Die geschichtliche Struktur des heutigen Weltgegensatzes von Ost und West," 150: "In comparison to animal relations, enmity among men involves a tension that goes far beyond the natural sphere. Among men, the transcendent sphere is always close by. This supplement or 'bonus' can be called 'spiritual' and, if you will, illustrated with Rimbaud's phrase: *Le combat spirituel est aussi brutal que la bataille d'hommes*. In any case, enmity among men is capable of particular levels and upsurges."

164. Schmitt, "Die geschichtliche Struktur des heutigen Weltgegensatzes von Ost und West," 151.

165. Schmitt, "Gespräch über den neuen Raum," 274.

166. Robert G. Collingwood, *An Autobiography* (Oxford: Oxford University Press, 1939), 29–43. Also Robert G. Collingwood, *The Idea of History* (Oxford: Clarendon Press, 1946), in the last part where he discusses the evidence for historical knowledge. Also Robert G. Collingwood, *The New Leviathan, or Man, Society, Civilisation and Barbarism* (Oxford: Clarendon Press, 1942). Cited in Schmitt, "Die geschichtliche Struktur des heutigen Weltgegensatzes von Ost und West," 151.

167. Arnold Toynbee, *The World and the West* (Oxford: Oxford University Press, 1953). Cited in Schmitt, "Die geschichtliche Struktur des heutigen Weltgegensatzes von Ost und West," 152.

168. Schmitt, "Die geschichtliche Struktur des heutigen Weltgegensatzes von Ost und West," 152–53. Also Schmitt, "Gespräch über den neuen Raum," 277.

169. Schmitt, "Die geschichtliche Struktur des heutigen Weltgegensatzes von Ost und West," 151.

170. Schmitt, "Die geschichtliche Struktur des heutigen Weltgegensatzes von Ost und West," 153: "Hegel's dialect of history holds the promise of reaching the true uniqueness of historical occurrence. . ... But, unity becomes easily lost in the grand systematic and historical occurrence becomes a purely rational process."

171. Schmitt, "Die geschichtliche Struktur des heutigen Weltgegensatzes von Ost und West," 160.

172. Schmitt, "Die geschichtliche Struktur des heutigen Weltgegensatzes von Ost und West," 157: "It is true that unleashed technique produces an immense potential for impetus. But impetus and call are not the same things. . . . I have observed that unleashing technique closes man in rather than opening up new spaces for him. Modern technique is useful and necessary,

but it is still far from being an answer to a call. It always meets new needs, which technique itself partly induces. Otherwise, it is always in doubt and, thus, cannot be a response. . . . To dominate unleashed technique would be, for example, the work of a new Hercules. It is here that I expect to find the new call, today's *Challenge*." And also Schmitt, "El orden del mundo después de la Segunda Guerra Mundial," 36: "Only when new spaces have found the immanent measure that corresponds to those requirements, will the balance of the great new spaces function. Then we will see which nations and peoples had the strength to engage in industrial development and stay true to themselves and, secondly, which nations and peoples were not able to save face because they sacrificed their human individuality to the idol of a technified land."

173. Schmitt, "Gespräch über den neuen Raum," 279: "Where is the cosmos' call or challenge? I only hear and see that desperate humanity with the means and methods of a free technique call upon cosmic spaces and try with all their might to penetrate them. But I neither hear a call nor a challenge."

3. THE LEGAL SCIENCE

1. Karl Löwith, "Der okkassionelle Dezisionismus von Carl Schmitt," in, Karl Löwith, *Sämtliche Schriften* (Stuttgart: J. B. Metzlersche Verlagsbuchhandlung, 1984), VIII, 37.

2. Karl Löwith, "Politischer Dezisionismus," in Karl Löwith, *Der Mensch inmitten der Geschichte: Phi losophische Bilanz des 20. Jahrhunderts* (Stuttgart: J. B. Metzler Verlag, 1990), 47: "changing thought."

3. On this point, there are many different opinions. Certain commentators say that Schmitt's thought changes according to circumstance, such as the above cited author, Löwith. Others, the majority, distinguish periods in Schmitt's work, for example, Christian Graf von Krockow in *Die Entscheidung: Eine Untersuchung über Ernst Jünger, Carl Schmitt und Martin Heidegger* (Frankfurt, Campus Verlag, 1990) or Helmut Quaritsch, *Posittionen und Begriffe Carl Schmitt* (Berlin: Duncker & Humblot, 1989). Others try to give unity to Schmitt's thought, for example, Peter Schneider, *Ausnahmezustand und Norm: Eine Studie zur Rechtslehre von Carl Schmitt* (Stuttgart: Deutsche Verlagsanstalt, 1957), Reinhard Mehring, *Pathetisches Denken: Carl Schmitts Denkweg am Leitfaden Hegels: Katholische Grundstellung und antimarxistische Hegelstrategie* (Berlin: Duncker & Humblot, 1989), or Mathias Kaufmann, *Recht ohne Regel? Die philosophischen Prinzipien in Carl Schmitt Staatsund Rechtslehre* (Freiburg: Alber, 1988).

4. Schmitt himself indicated this in the prologue to the 1969 edition of *Gesetz und Urteil* (München: C. H. Beck'sche Verlag): "The 1912 treatise 'Gesetz und Urteil' involves a judicial decision and its autonomy against norm, to which judicial-material content appeals for its foundation. I later formulated a subsequent reflection on the proper meaning of decision as such ('*Die Diktatur*' 1921, '*Politische Theologie*' 1922, *Der Hüter der Verfassung*' 1931, *Über die drei Arten des rechtswissenschaftlichen Denkens*' 1934) in which it is general knowledge that the total sphere of law is not structured by norms, but also by decisions and institutions (concrete orders)." As will be seen, my thesis is continuist, precisely because I think that it is possible to find a unified political discourse in Schmitt's theoretical thought.

5. Both in this chapter and those that follow, I have made a distinction between the following terms: *state* and *State*. The first, I have designated the status of a political unit, whatever its form. The second designates the political unit that corresponds to the Modern State. This distinction is in line with that of Otto Brunner, Werner Conze, and Reinhart Koselleck. See: Reinhart Koselleck, *Staat*, in *Geschichtliche Grundbegriffe: Historisches Lexikon zur politischsozialen Sprache in Deutschland* (Stuttgart, Klett-Cotta, 1990), VI, 1-154. Schmitt thus argues in *On the Three Types of Juristic Thought*, trans. by J. W. Bendersky (Westport, CT: Praeger Publishers, 2004), 74: "With him appears the great *Leviathan*, which devoured completely the other orders. He sets aside or relativizes the traditional feudal legal, *ständischen* and ecclesiastical communities, hierarchical stratification and inherited rights. He sets aside every right of resistance based on such prestately orders, gives the lawgiver a monopoly on *Recht*, and seeks

to construct the civil order from the individual." In addition, see the following texts from Schmitt: *Staat als ein konkreter, an eine geschichtliche Epoche gebundener Begriff*, 1941, in Carl Schmitt, *Verfassungsrechtliche Aufsätze* (Berlin: Duncker & Humblot, 1958), 375–86; Carl Schmitt, *Glossarium: Aufzeichnungen der Jahre 1947–1951* (Berlin: Duncker & Humblot, 1991), 19; Carl Schmitt, *Völkerrechtliche Großraumordnung mit Interventionsverbot für raumfremde Mächte: Ein Beitrag zum Reichsbegriff im Völkerrecht*, (Berlin/Wien/Leipzig: Deutscher Rechtsverlag, 1941), 53.

6. The latter is also the case in the book *Staat, Bewegung, Volk* (1933). Carl Schmitt, "State, Movement, People: The Triadic Structure of Political Unity" in *State, Movement, People: The Triadic Structure of Political Unity*, S. Draghici, trans. (Washington, DC: Plutarch Press, 1993), 3–54.

7. Schmitt himself made this distinction in Carl Schmitt, *Political Theology: Four Chapters on the Concept of Sovereignty*, transl. G. Schwab (Chicago: University of Chicago Press, 2005), 30. The legal form is governed by the legal idea and by the necessity of applying a legal thought to a factual situation, which means that it is governed by the self-evolving law in the widest sense. Because the legal idea (*Rechtsidee*) cannot realize itself, it needs a particular organization and form before it can be translated into reality. That holds true for the formation of a general legal norm (*Rechtsgedanken*) into a positive law (*positives Gesetz*) as well as for the application (*Rechtsanwendung*) of a positive general legal norm by the judiciary or administration.

8. Schmitt, *Political Theology*, 31: "Thus a transformation takes place every time. That the legal idea cannot translate itself independently is evident from the fact that it says nothing about who should apply it. In every transformation there is present an *auctoritatis interpositio*. A distinctive determination of which individual person or which concrete body can assume such an authority cannot be derived from the mere legal quality of a maxim." This feature is clearly expressed in Alfred Schindler und Frithard Scholz, "Die Theologie Carl Schmitts," in *Der Fürst dieser Welt: Carl Schmitt und die Folgen*, ed. Jacob Taubes (München/Paderborn: Finck/Schöningh, 1983), 161: "The gap between law and juristic order or juridical reality must be overcome in another 'state' through transformation (from the legal idea) for which an 'auctoritatis interpositio' is necessary." As Mariano Croce and Andrea Salvatore assert, Schmitt was the first in framing the issue of "legal indeterminacy." At least he formulates it in the most radical terms. Mariano Croce and Andrea Salvatore, *The Legal Theory of Carl Schmitt* (Abingdon, UK: Routledge, 2013), 144. This issue has given rise to a broad discussion. On this topic see William E. Scheuerman, *Carl Schmitt: The End of Law* (Lanham, MD: Rowman & Littlefield, 1999).

9. Carl Schmitt, *Dictatorship: From the Origin of the Modern Concept of Sovereignty to Proletarian Class Struggle*, transl. M. Hoelzl and G. Ward (Cambridge: Polity, 2014), 168: "the fundamental juridical problem in political science—that is, the opposition between right (*Recht*) and the exercise of right (*Rechtsverwirklichung*)." This idea is consistent in his legal theoretical writings and is present until the end. Also in: Carl Schmitt, *Gesetz und Urteil: Eine Untersuchung zum Problem der Rechtspraxis* (Berlin: Otto Liebman, 1912), 51; *Der Wert des Staates und die Bedeutung des Einzelnen* (Tübingen: J. C. B. Mohr/Paul Siebeck, 1914), 69–70 and 78–81; *Politische Theologie*, 29–32; *On the Three Types of Juristic Thought*, trans. J. W. Bendersky (Westport, CT: Praeger Publishers, 2004), 51: "For a law cannot apply, administer, or enforce itself."

10. Michele Nicoletti describes the intellectual environment at the time in the following manner: "In the late nineteenth and early twentieth centuries, dualism was characterized as the only perspective that seemed possible for preserving 'the value of the spirit,' for combating the triumph of empirical objectivity, as positivism had proclaimed, for fighting the relativism that had fractured European culture and threatened to destroy it. With this perspective in mind, Schmitt's Catholicism and the neo-Kantian environment in which he grew up came together and harmonized. The affirmation of this dualistic construction is as strong in Schmitt as the attempt to find a bridge, mediation, between the two sides of dualism." "Die Ursprünge von Carl Schmitts 'Politischer Theologie,'" in *Complexio Oppositorum: Über Carl Schmitt*, ed. H. Quaritsch (Berlin: Duncker & Humblot, 1988), 109.

11. I conducted this study in "Posiciones ante el derecho de Carl Schmitt," in Carl Schmitt, *Posiciones ante el derecho*, ed. and transl. Montserrat Herrero (Madrid: Tecnos, 2012), which contains translations of Schmitt's *Gesetz und Urteil*, *Über die drei Arten des rechtswissenschaftlichen Denkens*, and *Freiheitsrechte und institutionelle Garantien der Reichsverfassung*.

12. Carl Schmitt, "Appropriation, Distribution, Production," in *The Nomos of the Earth*, in Carl Schmitt, *The Nomos of the Earth in the International Law of the Jus Publicum Europaeum*, transl. and annot. G. L. Ulmen (New York: Telos Press Publishing, 2006), 324.

13. Schmitt, *Völkerrechtliche Großraumordnung*, 65: "Space as such is not a concrete order. However, each concrete order and every community has concrete places and spatial contents. In this sense, it can be said that every juristic institution contains a spatial conception within it and carries with it an internal measure and internal limit."

14. Schmitt, *Völkerrechtliche Großraumordnung*, 65–66.

15. Schmitt, *The Nomos of the Earth*, 42.

16. Schmitt, *The Nomos of the Earth*, 42.

17. Schmitt, *The Nomos of the Earth*, 48.

18. Carl Schmitt, *Land and Sea*, transl. S. Draghici (Washington, DC: Plutarch Press, 1997), 37.

19. Hermann Schmidt, "Der Nomosbegriff bei Carl Schmitt," *Der Staat* 2 (1963), 94.

20. Carl Schmitt, *Der Wert des Staates und die Bedeutung des Einzelnen* (Tübingen: J. C. B. Mohr/Paul Siebeck, 1914).

21. Isensee notes how, in the early days of his career, Schmitt was trapped not only in decisionism, but also in legal normativism. Josef Isensee, "Ausprache," in Joseph Kaiser, "Konkretes Ordnungsdenken," in Quaritsch ed., *Complexio Oppositorum*, 338. In the same way, Mathias Schmitz, *Die Freund-Feind-Theorie Carl Schmitts: Entwurf und Entfaltung* (Köln, Opladen: Westadt Verlag, 1965), 79. See also, Lutz-Arwin. Bentin, *Johannes Popitz und Carl Schmitt: Zur wirtschaftlichen Theorie des totalen Staates in Deutschland* (München: Beck, 1972), 81–85.

22. For a similar opinion see Paul Noack *Carl Schmitt: Eine Biographie* (Berlin: Propyläen Verlag, 1993), 31.

23. Schmitt, *Der Wert des Staates*, 78–79: "Between the concrete and the abstract there is an insurmountable gap, which cannot be settled by any gradual step. Hence, it becomes necessary that in every statute law there is a moment where mere positivity becomes valid such that, in certain circumstances, the fact that a positive determination is made is more important than its specific content." The text mainly describes a hiatus between the abstract and the concrete regarding the stating of the law, which solves decision. At no time is the very mode of juristic thinking raised—that is, how reality is thought of legally—although the necessity of going back to that stage is assumed. Thus he says, "Juristic thought that accompanies the transposition of reality to rule should become statuted." Schmitt, *Der Wert des Staates*, 78. This transformation, which is here only assumed, will be referred to years later in On the Three Types *of Juristic Thought* , and in *The Nomos of the Earth*. Certainly, inconsistencies are present, which are a consequence of the fact that Schmitt's theory on law was not merely complete from the beginning, but rather was qualified as it developed.

24. Schmitt, *Der Wert des Staates*, 53: "To use an expression from St. Augustine (*Civ. Dei* II 11. c. 24), for the State the law is 'origo, informatio, beatitude.' Thus, the state is nothing more than *Rechtsstaat* and every empirical State receives its legitimacy from being the first server of the law."

25. In the same way, Hans-Georg Flickinger ed., *Die Autonomie des Politischen: Carl Schmitt Kampf um einen beschädigten Begriff* (Weinheim: V. C. H., Acta Humaniora, 1990), 2. Also see the work of Noack, *Carl Schmitt*, 31. Therefore, this text is not comparable—and in this sense a contradiction between them cannot be established—with others that either refer to other moments in the development of the law—for example the source of law or juristic thinking—or they refer to another juridical context, which is outside of the framework of *Rechtsstaat*.

26. This is shown by Gary L. Ulmen, *Politischer Mehrwert: Eine Studie über Max Weber und Carl Schmitt* (Weinheim: V C H, Acta Humaniora, 1991), 276–77. He argues: "His work on the value of the State is a response to the pluralist challenge." 278. Also Ulmen, *Politischer*

Mehrwert, 282: "Just as Schmitt asserted the priority of the State (in the ethos of the law), he was critical on the comparisons between law and statute, law and the state in the passing from *Rechtsstaat* to a legislative State, which freed the way for an absolute, neutral value and a representation of legality free from qualities, without content, form or function."

27. Schmitt, *Der Wert des Staates*, 2, 52, 55 and 68.

28. Schmitt, *Der Wert des Staates*, 8: "the law (*Recht*) precedes the State." Also Schmitt, *Der Wert des Staates*, 46–48, 50, and 54 contain significant texts.

29. Schmitt, *Der Wert des Staates*, 2–3.

30. Schmitt, *Der Wert des Staates*, 10: "By contrast, this book is interested in the question of the State, while law is only addressed as it applies to that which is derived from a legal philosophical definition of the State." In the same sense, see Schmitt, *Der Wert des Staates*, 14.

31. Schmitt, *Der Wert des Staates*, 10: "the law as norm cannot be deduced from the facts." Here we must distinguish between "being" and "fact" so as not to make Schmitt fall into contradiction. This thesis also appears in Savigny. In *Vom Beruf unserer Zeit für Gesetzgebung und Rechtswissenschaft*, he writes that law can only be known and described in its being, in its objective origin, but it cannot be made subjectively or as a derivation of a given sociological conjuncture. A ruling as a duty cannot be done at all. Quoted in Wolf's *Nachwort* in Savigny, *Grundgedanken der Historische Rechtsschule*, 37.

32. Schmitt, *Der Wert des Staates*, 38.

33. Schmitt, *Der Wert des Staates*, 35.

34. Schmitt, *On the Three Types of Juristic Thought*, 55–56. Here Schmitt contrasts the concepts of concrete figure and "attribution point."

35. Schmitt, *Der Wert des Staates*, 56. Also: "If there must be some law, it cannot be deduced from power since the difference between law and power cannot just be overcome." Schmitt, *Der Wert des Staates*, 30. And also: "law cannot be explained by power; rather law explains power." Schmitt, *Der Wert des Staates*, 24.

36. Below I list some of the important texts that show the distinct nuances regarding this point in various works: Schmitt, *Gesetz und Urteil*, 3: "That which should happen does not certainly follow from that which happens." Schmitt, *Political Theology*, 18: "The connection of actual power with the legally highest power is the fundamental problem of the concept of sovereignty." Schmitt, *On the Three Types of Juristic Thought*, 53: "Normativity and facticity are 'completely different planes': the ought lies outside of the is and, according to normativist thought, retains its own inviolable sphere, while in concrete reality, all distinctions between right and wrong, order and disorder, normatively seen, are transformed into the material basis for the application of norms." Also Schmitt, *On the Three Types of Juristic Thought*, 66. Also Schmitt, *On the Three Types of Juristic Thought*, 68: "Now a fact, a 'pure fact,' is naturally not a source of law." Here, a distinction between the 'real'–concrete order–and 'factual' should be made. Reality has, within itself, an order, that is a law expressed in concrete figures (*Recht*). The factual, however, is a pure position of power. When speaking of law as a concrete order, Schmitt notes that the concrete *nomos* precedes law. Nevertheless power precedes legal order and its implementation. Each happens at distinct stages.

37. Ingeborg Villinger, *Carl Schmitts Kulturkritik der Moderne: Texte, Kommentar und Analyse des "Schattenrisse" des Johannes Negelinus* (Berlin: Akademie Verlag, 1995), particularly the chapter "Wilhelm Oswald."

38. Schmitt, *Der Wert des Staates*, 27.

39. On this point, both works are comparable because both cases refer to the moment of the transformation of law into statute in the case of a positive constitution. Additionally, both are in the contextual framework of the *Rechtsstaat*, even if *Constitutional Theory* considers this kind of State in a broader framework.

40. Carl Schmitt, *Constitutional Theory*, transl. J. Seitzer (Durham, NC: Duke University Press, 2007), 77. Emphasis made by Schmitt.

41. Schmitt, *Der Wert des Staates*, 56 and 83.

42. Schmitt, *Der Wert des Staates*, 38 and 78.

43. To see this, compare the following: Schmitt, *Der Wert des Staates*, 81 and 78. Schmitt, *Constitutional Theory*, 64. Schmitt, *Political Theology*, 31. The need for transformation through decision also appears connected to judicial decision: Schmitt, *Gesetz und Urteil*, 51.

Schmitt, *On the Three Types of Juristic Thought*, 51. Schmitt establishes the supremacy of law over power until his last writings. Here considered as law (*Recht*), in other writings as *nomos*.

44. Schmitt, *Constitutional Theory*, 64.

45. Schmitt, *Dictatorship*, 118: "The contradiction between legal norm and law-implementing norm, which governs all understanding of the law, becomes (in commissary dictatorship) a contradiction between legal norm and a specific guideline for action."

46. A long reference to Kantian and post-Kantian theory of law is made in this work. Schmitt, *Der Wert des Staates*, 56–67.

47. Schmitt, *Der Wert des Staates*, 80.

48. As we shall see he does make a more extensive reference to the relationship between man's inner and outer spheres in Carl Schmitt, *The Leviathan in the State Theory of Thomas Hobbes: Meaning and Failure of a Political Symbol*, transl. G. Schwab and E. Hilfstein (Westport CT: Greenwood Press, 1996), 56–57.

49. Schmitt, *Der Wert des Staates*, 11-12.

50. Michele Nicoletti, *Trascendenza e Potere: La teologia politica di Carl Schmitt* (Brescia: Morcelliana, 1990), 63–64, points out how in Schmitt's very first writing, his doctoral thesis, *Über Schuld und Schuldarten: Eine terminologische Untersuchung* (Breslau: Schletter'sche Buchhandlung, 1910), a dualistic view of reality can be seen, which requires consideration. The inner is not the outer and vice versa; the world of consciousness is not identified with the world of external reality. However, while establishing said distinction, analysis of the concept of guilt emerges, which is a more articulate vision that overcomes dualism: External action is not completely separated from the inner process. Nicoletti points out that this issue poses an anthropological problem for Schmitt. It seems problematic to recognize the subjective capacity at the religious-ethical level, as occurs in *Über Schuld und Schuldarten*, and deny it in the legal-political field. Nicoletti, *Trascendenza e Potere*, 61. It seems to me that there is not a negation, but rather a clear differentiation between the two spheres.

51. Schmitt, *Der Wert des Staates*, 67.

52. Schmitt, *Der Wert des Staates*, 20: "If law is faced with autonomous and independent power, then a dualism follows, which corresponds to that which is found between 'is' and 'ought,' between the normative and the genetic, between critical thinking and naturalistic reflection." Also Schmitt, *Der Wert des Staates*, 31: "No law can be deduced from reflection on nature, to which human coexistence also pertains, insofar as it is an opportunity to observe and explain the social sciences."

53. Schmitt, *On the Three Types of Juristic Thought*, 52. Also Carl Schmitt, "Die Rechtswissenschaft als letztes Asyl des Rechtsbewußtseins," *Universitas* 5, no. 5 (1950), 524. And in relation to *nomos*, Schmitt, "*Nomos-Nahme-Name*," in *The Nomos of the Earth*, 342–43. On this issue, see Schneider, *Ausnahmezustand und Norm*, 272.

54. Schmitt, *Constitutional Theory*, 64.

55. See Carl Schmitt, "The Plight of European Jurisprudence," transl. G. L. Ulmen, *Telos* 83 (1990), 35–70.

56. Schmitt, *Constitutional Theory*, 181. Here Carl Schmitt describes the character of the law and statute in the bourgeois *Rechtsstaat*.

57. Schmitt, *Constitutional Theory*, 154.

58. Carl Schmitt, *The Crisis of Parliamentary Democracy*, transl. E. Kennedy (Cambridge, MA: MIT Press, 2000), 39–42.

59. Schmitt, *Constitutional Theory*, 155.

60. Ernst-Wolfgang Böckenförde, "Aussprache" in Kaiser, "Konkretes Ordnungsdenken," 336.

61. Carl Schmitt, "The Question of Legality," in *State, Movement, People*, transl. S. Draghici (Washington, DC: Plutarch Press, 2001), 60.

62. Schmitt, "The Question of Legality," 59-60. See also Carl Schmitt, "Besprechungen der Bücher von Herbert von Borch: 'Obrigkeit und Widerstand. Zur politischen Soziologie des Beamtentums' and von F. J. P. Veale: 'Der Barbarei entgegen' und von Georg Schwarzenberger: 'Machtpolitik'," in *Das Historisch-Politische Buch* 3, no. 3 (1955), 72.

63. Schmitt, "The Question of Legality," 62.

64. Schmitt, *On the Three Types of Juristic Thought*, 64–66.

65. Carl Schmitt, "Von der TV-Demokratie: Die Aggressivität des Fotschritts," *Deutsches Allgemeines Sonntagsblatt*, June 28 (1970), 8: "The law is an instrument of power and whoever comes to have that instrument on hand is stronger than anything that could be legitimately done against him."

66. Carl Schmitt, "The Legal World Revolution," transl. G. L. Ulmen, *Telos* 72 (1987), 73–89.

67. Schmitt, "The Legal World Revolution," 73.

68. Carl Schmitt, "Recht und Macht," *Summa: Eine Vierteljahresschrift* 1 (1917), 37–52.

69. Schmitt, *Der Wert des Staates*, 39.

70. Schmitt, "Recht und Macht," 52.

71. In most of his works, it appears, above all, in the form of State-Law. For example, in the second part of Schmitt, *Der Wert des Staates*, primacy is given, on a theoretical level, to law over power. This can be seen in the texts listed here: pp. 39, 46–48 and 50–54. In *Constitutional Theory*, however, when he refers to the time when the Constitution is born, importance is given first of all to the *nomos*, when speaking of the absolute concept of constitution, Schmitt, *Constitutional Theory*, 59–60 and 184: "That which is directly lacking (in the *Rechtsstaat* legal idea) is the *nomos*"; but importance is given to the making-law power of the State, when speaking of the positive concept of constitution. Schmitt, *Constitutional Theory*, 75 and 97.

72. Carl Schmitt, "Zu Friedrich Meineckes 'Idee der Staatsräson,'" *Archiv für Sozialwissenschaft und Sozialpolitik* 56, no. 1 (1926), 227.

73. Schmitt, "Zu Friedrich Meineckes 'Idee der Staatsräson,'" 231: "[H]e confesses with personal determination through a general moral commandment."

74. Schmitt, "Zu Friedrich Meineckes 'Idee der Staatsräson,'" 232.

75. Hans Kelsen, *Pure Theory of Law*, transl. M. Knight (Berkeley: University of California Press, 1967).

76. A sample of these dialogues can be seen in Kelsen's book *Wer soll der Hüter der Verfassung sein?* (Berlin-Grunewald: Rothschild, 1931), which was a response to Schmitt's 1931 publication *Der Hüter der Verfassung* (Tübingen: Mohr/Siebeck , 1931).

77. In the same vein, Kaiser, "Konkretes Ordnungsdenken", 323. With this connection between law and *nomos*, Schmitt places himself in a realist position. Ulmen, *Politischer Mehrwert*, 79: "Conceptual realism, for Schmitt, is a presupposition of jurisprudence and Roman law. To him, it is the quintessential conceptual jurisprudence."

78. This is the opinion of Friedrich August von der Heydte, "Heil aus der Gefangeschaft? Carl Schmitt und die Lage der europäischen Rechtswissenschaft," *Hochland* 43 (1951), 292.

79. Kaiser shares this affirmation. It is expressed in *Konkretes Ordnungsdenken*, 319: "The rich 1934 concept that Schmitt used describes a way of juristic thinking and a juristic-philosophical position."

80. Schmitt, *On the Three Types of Juristic Thought*, 66–67.

81. Carl Schmitt, *La defensa de la Constitución*, transl. M. Sánchez (Barcelona: Labor, 1931), 32ff.

82. Schmitt, *On the Three Types of Juristic Thought*, 43.

83. Schmitt, *Der Wert des Staates*,18.

84. Schmitt, *On the Three Types of Juristic Thought*, 45.

85. On this point, Schmitt becomes an heir to the historical school of law (*Historische Rechtsschule*). There is a relationship between law and the essence and character of different peoples. Schmitt repeatedly acknowledged his admiration for Savigny. So, for example, in Schmitt, "The Plight of European Jurisprudence," 54, he regards him as the paradigm of the first distancing from the legality of the legislative State. This relationship with Savigny's theory does not mean Schmitt should be qualified as a historicist. Schmitt's theory is neither reactionary nor "restorative" because it is based on the conviction that each historical era has its own forms of manifestation: "We know that there is not such a thing as a restoration of past situations. A historical truth is true only *once*." Schmitt, "The Plight of European Jurisprudence," 59. What interested him was not Savigny's "reaction," just as he was not interested in Hegel's "revolution." His concern is that both represented a *Katechon* as he notes in "Die legale Weltrevolution: Politischer Mehrwert als Prämie auf juristische Legalität und Superlegalität," *Der Staat* 17 (1978), 328–29. The last notes of this article were not translated

into English, for which I quote the German edition. In this sense, the importance of Savigny for Schmitt rests in the fact that he is an alternative to legal positivism. However, as noted by Kaiser, *Konkretes Ordnungsdenken*, 319, Schmitt also had other sources of inspiration with respect to this point, as in the case of Santi Romano and Maurice Hauriou.

86. Schneider described this stance in *Ausnahmezustand und Norm*, 267: "Decisionism as a type of thought is for those times when you have to move from a chaotic state to an order through decision, where factional fighting must be overcome by a decision that establishes order. Thought on a particular order, however, belongs to those times in which the concrete may be assumed. Legitimacy rests with this or that legal form, in correspondence with the situation."

87. Schmitt, *On the Three Types of Juristic Thought*, 45.

88. Schmitt, *On the Three Types of Juristic Thought*, 56–57. With respect to this, Schneider, *Ausnahmezustand und Norm*, 262: "The distinction between order and legal order is of great significance. It holds the distinction between exceptional and normal states. In an exceptional situation, order applies; in a normal situation, legal order applies."

89. This philosophical position is spelled out years later in Schmitt, "The Plight of European Jurisprudence," where he describes his position on the meaning of the philosophy of law to legal theory as opposed to that of Johannes Popitz, who felt that the fundamental concepts with which the science of law worked, such as individual or reciprocity, are originally philosophical, and therefore philosophy is necessary for legal science. As Schmitt claimed, "I find, however, that legal science freed from the impasse of general concepts would make philosophy reflect. To me, Socrates, Plato and Aristotle were primarily lawyers and not what are today called philosophers. It naturally follows that what I understand for lawyers or legal science is not a series of enlightened teachers that pertain to the Taylorist industry of exams and classes. Philosophy of law, for me, is not a philosophical vocabulary of an available system applied to legal issues, but the development of specific concepts from the immanence of a particular law and particular social order." Schmitt, "Die Lage der europäischen Rechtswissenschaft," 427. There is not English translation of this note. Juristic analysis, by contrast: "Runs along a concrete path of observation, which probably leads to a better result than general methodological digressions, or along theory of knowledge of pure, logical possibility or the pure legal conditions of a science in general." Schmitt, *On the Three Types of Juristic Thought*, 47–57. And he also indicates in a concrete mode, *On the Three Types of Juristic Thought*, 44: "Whether for example, as I suspect, genuine juristic thought, at least in public law, is conceptually realistic, while a consistent nominalism endangers or destroys good jurisprudence and at best could have certain latitude in civil traffic law." See also Ernst-Wolfgang Böckenförde, "Konkretes Ordnungsdenken," *Historisches Wörterbuch der Philosophie*, ed. J. Ritter/K. Gründer (Basel: Schwabe Verlag, 1984) VI, 1312 "Particular order does not see—in a legal-philosophical way—the law based on an abstract duty of regulatory mandates, but does see it in the dualist combination of being and duty in the orders of life and suprapersonal institutions of socio-historic reality."

90. Schmitt, *Political Theology*, 13.

91. Schmitt, *On the Three Types of Juristic Thought*, 51. Schmitt, "Zu Friedrich Meineckes 'Idee der Staatsräson,'" 233: "That *status* signifies the fundamental and comprehensive unity of an essential and substantial public order that is measured by being; it has the inner rationality of being and wants, therefore, 'in suo essere' to endure. Through this, it remains related to (said today in a false antithesis) a static concept of order." In relation to this point, Schmidt, "Der Nomos Begriff bei Carl Schmitt," 81: "[I]t is not necessary that decisionism be the last word to mediate space and law. It is rather in the *nomos* where the true nature of the universal is the Law, beyond decisionism (act) and normativism (potential)." Also Schneider, *Ausnahmezustand und Norm*, 269: "The 'concrete' gets its name from the contraposition of itself and abstract individualism. The concrete does not mean the specific person in the sense that Martin Buber employs, but rather the community as opposed to the abstraction of an individual."

92. When internal order and external structure do not correspond, a mismatch is produced that can result in an exceptional situation. The Weimar Constitution serves as an example: "The Constitution of the German Empire, the legal bourgeois element of the new democracy, is the Weimar Constitution. It has been shown that the Weimar Constitution, much to the dismay of

its creators and advocates, is not very alive in the consciousness of the German people." Carl Schmitt, "Der bürgerliche Rechtsstaat," *Abendland* 3 (1928), 201.

93. Schmitt, *On the Three Types of Juristic Thought*, 55. The place of the law is not, therefore, the general legal norm, although, in part, it is formed by norms. The place of law is in juristic substance, a concrete people's order, the *nomos*. On this point, Schmitt's inheritance from the historical school appears again. As Friedrich C. von Savigny stated: "It has already been stated above that the proper place of law is the common conscience of a people." *Grundgedanken der Historischen Rechtsschule* (Frankfurt: Vittorio Klostermann, 1965), 5.

94. Therefore, legal science that focuses its attention on solving dispute cases should be qualified as decisionist. Schmitt, *On the Three Types of Juristic Thought*, 60–62. The decision on a case of conflict pertains to the political sphere. Thus, when society wants to regulate everything legally, and even the political sphere cannot escape this legalization, the law becomes an area of constant change, a political weapon.

95. Schmitt, *On the Three Types of Juristic Thought*, 89. This defense of the institution does not detract from the importance of the political institution *par excellence*, the state. Although the incorporation of institutions is necessary in society, the representative sphere has a formal superiority. He praises Hegel for his clarity on this point.

96. Schmitt himself does not define institution. He expresses the difficulty of doing so from the point of view of the German language. The concept of institution resembles those of "Einrichtung," "Anstalt," "Organismus." But none of them are completely suitable for the reality to which they refer. The Latin word *institution* has a conservative tint to it because of the nuances it entails. Therefore, to avoid difficulty, he employs the phrase "concrete order thinking" instead of "institutional thinking." See Schmitt, *On the Three Types of Juristic Thought*, 89. However, we cannot forget the connection between Schmitt's *Ordnungsdenken* and institutional juristic thought, particularly that of Maurice Hauriou, to whom Schmitt refers multiple times. Croce and Salvatore, *The Legal Theory of Carl Schmitt*, 2 speak of "institutional turn" in Schmitt's way of thinking. Their book argues that after the 1930s Schmitt adopts an institutional perspective inspired by Maurice Hauriou and Santi Romano. They analyze similarities and differences between these thinkers, also Mortati, and Schmitt. See also Böckenförde, "Konkretes Ordnungsdenken," 1312–14. The juridical theory of the institution is in the current of the historical school of law, to which we have previously referred. A close adherence to historical reality can only be understood outside the context of contractarian thought. The institution, for institutionalist thinking, involves the idea of undertaking, or putting something to work, that is performed and remains in a social environment; for this idea to be realized, power comes from an organized body. It represents, both in law and in history, the category of duration, continuity, and the real. See Maurice Hauriou, "Aux sources du droit: Le Pouvoir, l'Ordre et la Liberté," *Cahiers de la nouvelle journée* 23 (Paris: Librairie Blond & Gay, 1933).

97. Schmitt, *On the Three Types of Juristic Thought*, 51. And also an example of the family as institution see Schmitt, *On the Three Types of Juristic Thought*, 55.

98. Schmitt, *Constitutional Theory*, 381. This text shows that his thought on the concrete order already took shape in 1928. Also see Villinger, *Carl Schmitts Kulturkritik der Moderne*, 136.

99. Because of that Cristi can compare Schmitt with thinkers addressing a "spontaneous order" of society, as is the case of Hayek. Renato Cristi, *Le libéralisme conservateur. Trois essais sur Schmitt, Hayek et Hegel*, transl. N. Burge (Paris: Ed. Kimé, 1993).

100. Schmitt, *Constitutional Theory*, 77.

101. Schmitt, "Staat als ein konkreter, an eine geschichtliche Epoche gebundener Begriff," 379–80.

102. Schmitt, *On the Three Types of Juristic Thought*, 50. Also Schmitt, "Die Lage der europäischen Rechtswissenschaft," 429. For the relationship between Hegel and Carl Schmitt's thought see Mehring, *Pathetisches Denken* and Jean-François Kervégan, *Hegel, Carl Schmitt: Le politique entre spéculation et positivité* (Paris: PUF, 1992).

103. This is what Schmitt said in one of his first books about the unbridgeable gap between the abstract and the concrete if it were not for the mediation of decision. Schmitt, *Der Wert des Staates*, 79 he noted: "[A]bstract legal thinking must become positive law as soon as the State is capable of doing so."

104. Bentin wrote along these same lines in *Johannes Popitz und Carl Schmitt*, 86.

105. Schmitt, *On the Three Types of Juristic Thought*, 56–57.

106. And he does not realize this because: "All valid norms, so long as they are valid, are naturally always 'in order'; the 'disorder' of the concrete situation, in contrast, does not interest the normativist who is only interested in the norm." Schmitt, *On the Three Types of Juristic Thought*, 52. See also Schmitt, *Political Theology*, 12–13. In this text, it is clear how, even in 1922, Schmitt was aware of the distinction between order and legal order.

107. Carl Schmitt, "Der Spiegel," *Die Rheinlande* 22 (1912), 62.

108. This is how Schmitt describes it in "Raum und Großraum in Völkerrecht," 153 speaking about the relationship between land and sea: "Oceans, however, are 'free' and this freedom is in its essence, not in its State. Intermediate formations such as the coast are not understood as limits, because the spatial thought of States only knows a lineal border; these areas are subordinated to the logic of "either . . . or," which is characteristic of statehood decisionism."

109. This proposal of order has its origin in Hobbes or so claims Schmitt, *Völkerrechtliche Großraumordnung*, 63: "At their core, these theories of space and their manifestation are always the same: the law is legally mandated; mandates can only direct people; the government exercises its power not over things, but over people. Hence, the State government can only be determined personally and all of the determinations have legal significance because the objects are regulated by the standard, as with any event, in this particular space and time. That which is specifically juristic, the concrete order, in this way is converted into a form that is void of content." This particular order based on the modern idea of space is empty of content, not the specific order proposed by Schmitt. And Schmitt, *On the Three Types of Juristic Thought*, 69: "Decisionist thinking, on the other hand, permits the positive connection to a definite factual point in time, in which from a previous absence of norm or absence of order springs forth the positive sole noteworthy positive law, which then however, is supposed to have additional value as positive norm."

110. Carl Schmitt, "A Pan-European Interpretation of Donoso Cortes," transl. M. Grzeskowiak, *Telos* 125 (2002), 100–115.

111. Schmitt, *On the Three Types of Juristic Thought*, 61. In this same sense, Schneider, *Ausnahmezustand und Norm*, 273.

112. Schmitt, *Political Theology*, 17. This position was a constant for Schmitt. Starting with his first systematic work on legal science, this claim was constant: the normative power of the factual is impossible. It appears in *Gesetz und Urteil*, 3; *Der Wert des Staates*, 9–10 and 56.

113. Schmitt frequently repeated: "A statute, for Schmitt, is an attempt to ratify the law." Conversation with Ernst-Wolfgang Böckenförde, Freiburg, August 30, 1993.

114. "No norm applies in a vacuum or in an abnormal situation (in relation to the norm)." Carl Schmitt, "Staatsethik und pluralistischer Staat," *Kantstudien* 35, no. 1 (1930), 32. What is interesting here is that he says that an abnormal situation is one without legal order, but not without any order whatsoever.

115. As noted by Kaiser, "Konkretes Ordnungsdenken," 328, Schmitt's decision is not incompatible with order in the following way: "Thought on concrete order is not just the given order and the institutions that constitute this order . . . , it also tests juristic strength in its application to new orders, which are generated from disorder through acts of will and juristic acts."

116. Schmitt, *On the Three Types of Juristic Thought*, 59. An apt description of this appears in Pattloch's book, although the central thesis of the book—as I have already mentioned—was openly rejected by Schmitt. See Pattloch, *Recht als Einheit von Ordnung und Ortung: Ein Beitrag zum Rechtsbegriff in Carl Schmitts "Nomos der Erde"* (Aschaffenburg: Pattloch Verlag, 1961), 28.

117. Schmitt, *On the Three Types of Juristic Thought*, 59. In this sense Schmitt speaks of a "totale Planung" in *Glossarium*, 47.

118. Schmitt, *Gesetz und Urteil*, 57: "The application of the law is neither legislation nor interpretation, although it is always preceded by interpretation." And also Schmitt, *Gesetz und Urteil*, 69: "[T]he question of the law's justice is a completely different problem from the justice of a decision, because the latter always rests on the context of a valid legal order."

119. Schmitt, *Political Theology*, 5.

120. Schmitt, *Political Theology*, 17.

121. Hasso Hofmann underlines this point in *Legitimität gegen Legalität: Der Weg der politischen Philosophie Carl Schmitts* (Neuwied/Berlin: Luchterland, 1964), 136, that: "Schmitt's decision is certainly not a theory of pure decisionism, which he would describe as arbitrary, but it presupposes substantial concepts such as unity and concrete order."

122. With regard to this see Schneider, *Ausnahmezustand und Norm*, 266–67. Schneider thinks that at this point there is some ambiguity in Schmitt's thought such that the position I have just outlined is not always so clearly expressed. In my view with some distinctions, this ambiguity can be undone: juridical decision is not the same, whether legislative or judicial, as political decision. In addition, within political decision a difference can be made between a decision that puts an order into place—in this sense, order is a consequence of decision—and that which references a preexisting order—in this sense, order is the cause of the decision. In the previously mentioned conversation with E.-W. Böckenförde (Freiburg, August 30, 1993), Böckenförde replied to the question of whether order is the cause or consequence of decision in Schmitt's thinking saying, "Political decision creates an order, but when there is chaos, it is not possible to make a decision."

123. Schmitt, *Constitutional Theory*, 65. The English translator uses here instead of normative element of the law, "the normative element of justice"; in my view this translation is not accurate inasmuch as Schmitt always avoids using the word *justice* because this word opens the door to subjective conceptions or values. Instead he uses the word *correctness*. See Carl Schmitt, *Gesetz und Urteil: Eine Untersuchung zum Problem der Rechtspraxis* (Berlin: Otto Liebman, 1912).

124. Adam writes similarly in *Rekonstruktion des Politischen: Carl Schmitt und die Krise der Staatlichkeit, 1912–1933* (Weiheim: V. C. H. Acta Humaniora, 1992), 125.

125. Schmitt, *Dictatorship*, 6.

126. Schmitt, *Dictatorship*, 118–19.

127. So says Schmitt, *Dictatorship*, xliii: "Any dictatorship that does not make itself dependent on pursuing a concrete result, even if one that corresponds to a normative ideal (and hence does not aim to make itself redundant) is an arbitrary despotism."

128. Schmitt, *Dictatorship*, 8.

129. Schmitt, *Constitutional Theory*, 151.

130. Schmitt, *Constitutional Theory*, 76–79 and 125.

131. Schmitt, *Dictatorship*, 118–19.

132. Schmitt, *Constitutional Theory*, 145.

133. Schmitt, *Constitutional Theory*, 125.

134. Because of the clarity with which Schmitt expresses this point, Ulmen in *Politischer Mehrwert*, 225–57, calls his theory one of "Lückentheorie." The "jump" in the decision reveals the "legal gap" that all legality has. And it is this gap that demands decision.

135. Schmitt fought against subjectivism, as I have pointed out several times, from his earliest writings, even subjectivism in relation to the will. See Villinger, ed., *Carl Schmitts Kulturkritik der Moderne*.

136. In the same way, Adam, *Rekonstruktion des Politischen*, 38: "Decision is morally demanding because it must break the iron shell of legality."

137. Carl Schmitt, "Coloquio sobre el poder y el acceso al poderoso," *Revista de Estudios Políticos* 52, no. 78 (1954), 3–20, 20.

138. Carl Schmitt, *Political Romanticism*, transl. G. Oakes (Cambridge, MA: MIT Press, 1986), 116.

139. This is a question he asked when referring to himself: "I am a surprisingly passive person. That I have acquired a reputation as a decisionist is incomprehensible to me. I think one must distance oneself from taking joy in decision as such, as I have, to develop a theory of decisionism." Ingeborg Villinger and Ernst Hüsmert, *Verortung des Politischen: Carl Schmitt in Plettenberg* (Hagen: v. d. Linnepe, 1990), 5.

140. Emphasizing Schmitt's decisionism, von Krockow dedicated his work, *Die Entscheidung* to making a parallel between decision in Heidegger, Jünger, and Schmitt. He considered decisionism reduced to a period in Schmitt's texts.

141. Schmitt, *Dictatorship*, 8; Schmitt, *Constitutional Theory*, 59; Schmitt, *Political Theology*, 31.

142. Schmitt, *Political Theology*, 31. This conviction is a constant in his work. It appears from his earliest writings. See *Gesetz und Urteil*, 48 and 55. Also Schmitt, *Der Wert des Staates*, 79.

143. Schmitt, *Constitutional Theory*, 76.

144. Schmitt, *Constitutional Theory*, 64.

145. Schmitt himself points this out in "Zu F. Meinecke 'Idee der Staatsräson,'" 228: "The question of normality or abnormality of a particular situation seems to me to be of the utmost importance. Whoever infers that we are in an abnormal situation—whether that be because the world is in a radically abnormal situation or because it is just a situation—will find a different way to solve any problem in the political, moral or legal fields than he who thinks that the situation is one of simply unclear or disordered normality."

146. Schmidt does not refer to different periods here, but rather to nuances and to a comprehensive development of Schmitt's thought. Schmidt, "Der Nomos Begriff bei Carl Schmitt," 81. Moreover, as previously mentioned, Schmitt never acknowledged himself as a decisionist. See the preface to the 1969 (second edition) version of *Gesetz und Urteil* (München: C H Becksche Verlagsbuchhandlung).

147. In support of affirming the progressive development of his theory, see the prologue of the second edition of *Politische Theologie* written in November of 1933. Adam, *Rekonstruktion des Politischen*, 125, holds an opinion close to mine.

148. Schmitt, *Gesetz und Urteil*, 5 and 85.

149. Schmitt, *Gesetz und Urteil*, 1.

150. Schmitt, *Gesetz und Urteil*, 1.

151. Schmitt, *Gesetz und Urteil*, 72: "That the 'legality' of the decision can no longer be identified with its justice does not mean to abandon objective measure and allow everything to depend on the judge's subjectivity."

152. Schmitt, *Gesetz und Urteil*, 69: "Hence, it has been inferred that the sentence should be able to be logically deduced from the law, while it can be seen that in the determination of this dependence, the problem rests in its foundation and limit."

153. Schmitt, *Gesetz und Urteil*, 91: "A government of interpretative methods is a real power and it creates juridical concepts that are just as effective as formal laws."

154. Schmitt, *Gesetz und Urteil*, 32.

155. Schmitt, *Gesetz und Urteil*, 26.

156. Schmitt, *Gesetz und Urteil*, 32: "The manifested content is the only thing that remains of the law."

157. Although both issues—the question of justice of interpretation and the justice of decision—are not exactly the same. See Schmitt, *Gesetz und Urteil*, 11 and 29.

158. Schmitt, *Gesetz und Urteil*, 17–18.

159. Schmitt, *Gesetz und Urteil*, 73.

160. Schmitt, *Gesetz und Urteil*, 100. Also Schmitt, *Gesetz und Urteil*, 62: "This was also our foundation, denying the legality, or the 'subsumption' as criterion of a fair decision, and the search for impeccable judgment."

161. Schmitt, *Gesetz und Urteil*, 42: "It would be a trivial misunderstanding to fear that the judge will now do whatever he pleases, since he does not decide 'legally.' The law is still the rule for the judge; the individual cannot be run over; but to provide specific criteria for the legal practice of justice from the decision which comes from the praxis, legality is not enough, as has been demonstrated."

162. Schmitt, *Gesetz und Urteil*, 100 and 98.

163. Schmitt, *Gesetz und Urteil*, 55. Álvaro d'Ors referring to the idea of "abstract justice" in *Introducción al estudio del Derecho*, 111, claimed: "I think this is a tempting path that seems to lead to the truth, but actually it is a dead-end." See also Montserrat Herrero, "Posiciones ante el derecho de Carl Schmitt," in Carl Schmitt, *Posiciones ante el derecho*, ed. and transl. M. Herrero (Madrid: Tecnos, 2012).

4. THE LEGAL ORDER

1. "Bonald was the first to answer this in his great work, 'Récherche de la vérité': The truth is in society and history." "Der Gegensatz von Gemeinschaft und Gesellschaft als Beispiel einer Zweigliedrigen Unterscheidung: Betrachtungen zum Schicksal solcher Antithesen," *Estudios Jurídico Sociales* (Zaragoza: Universidad de Santiago de Compostela, 1960), I, 167.Also Carl Schmitt, *Political Rom anticism*, transl. G. Oakes (Cambridge, MA: MIT Press, 1986), 60: "As of 1796, the reproach that Bonald raises against Descartes and Malebranche runs as follows: They do not see what is essential, human society. Society and history, that is reality." Also *Political Theology II: The Myth of the Closure of Any Political Theology*, transl. M. Hoelzl and G. Ward (New York: Polity Press, 2014), 53, he refers to the philosophers of the restoration as fathers of sociology.

2. Louis-Gabriel-Ambroise de Bonald, *Legislation primitive I*, in *Oeuvres complètes de Bonald*, ed. l'abbé Migne, 3 vols (Paris: Migne ed., 1859), 1170.

3. Louis-Gabriel-Ambroise de Bonald, *Essai Analitique I*, in *Oeuvres complètes*, 968.

4. Louis-Gabriel-Ambroise de Bonald, *Pensées III*, in *Oeuvres complètes*, 1275.

5. Louis-Gabriel-Ambroise de Bonald, *Observations II*, in *Oeuvres complètes*, 609.

6. Carl Schmitt, *Political Romanticism*, 60–62.

7. Carl Schmitt, "Illyrien: Notizen von einer dalmatinischen Reise," *Hochland* 23, no. 3 (1925), 294.

8. Schmitt never adopted said distinction. Within his own theory he always spoke of community or coexistence (*Gemeinschaft* or *Zusammenleben*). The concept of society (*Gesellschaft*) applies to a liberal-pluralist context and, therefore, is the opposite of the State. Schmitt found the best definition of this concept in Eduard Spranger. For him, society consists of different forms of human associations that are neither the Church nor the State. Quoted in Carl Schmitt, "Die Wendung zum totalen Staat," *Europäische Revue* 7, no. 4, 246.

9. Carl Schmitt, "Appropriation, Distribution, Production," in *The Nomos of the Earth in the International Law of the Jus Publicum Europaeum*, transl. G. L. Ulmen (New York: Telos Press Publishing, 2006), 328. Also Carl Schmitt, *Constitutional Theory*, transl. J. Seitzer (Durham, NC: Duke University Press, 2007), 59 and 77.

10. Schmitt, *Constitutional Theory*, 74.

11. Schmitt, *Constitutional Theory*, 76.

12. Schmitt, *Constitutional Theory*, 239.

13. Schmitt, *Constitutional Theory*, 60.

14. Schmitt, *Constitutional Theory*, 67.

15. Schmitt, *Constitutional Theory*, 75.

16. Schmitt, *Constitutional Theory*, 89.

17. A distinction must be made in using the term "ideal." In the first case, when Schmitt ironically mentions it to refer to the bourgeois constitution of the *Rechtsstaat*, he uses the term ideal in a romanticized way, in order to signify perfect utopia. A constitution that is valid for any people cannot be anything but abstract. When he uses "idea" as true meaning, it acquires the same meaning as in Plato's theory. That is, the ideal is the form of any reality. For each particular people there is also a particular idea of constitution.

18. Schmitt, *Constitutional Theory*, 89.

19. Carl Schmitt, "Staatsethik und pluralistischer Staat," *Kantstudien* 35, no. 1 (1930), 36.

20. Schmitt, *Constitutional Theory*, 173.

21. Carl Schmitt, *The Crisis of Parliamentary Democracy*, transl. E. Kennedy (Cambridge, MA: MIT Press, 2000), 33–50.

22. Schmitt, *Political Theology*, II, 45.

23. Schmitt, *La defensa de la Constitución*, 114.

24. Schmitt, *Constitutional Theory*, 169.

25. Schmitt, *Constitutional Theory*, 75. As noted by Ernst-W. Böckenförde in "Der Begriff des Politischen als Schlüssel zum Staatsrechtlichen Werk Carl Schmitts," in *Complexio Oppositorum: Über Carl Schmitt*, ed. H. Quaritsch (Berlin: Duncker & Humblot, 1988), 288, this does not mean that the constitution is a decision placed over the establishment and longevity of

the State, but rather is only placed over its form. But it is through the constitution that the State acquires its permanent form.

26. Schmitt, *Constitutional Theory*, 75–76. In this regard, the way that Böckenförde in "Der Begriff des Politischen," 289, refers to this should be noted: "The constitution is not a contract, but rather a decision and certainly a decision regarding the type and form of political unity. The constitution as a contract is only possible—in constitutional theory this is explicit—between political units, which create an organism or interstate relationship." Indeed, Schmitt mentioned an authentic constitutional pact as a federal pact in the chapter dedicated to federal constitutional theory in Schmitt, *Constitutional Theory*, 379–409. I will not discuss this here as it is a special case. For Schmitt, the quintessential constitution is one of political unity and is not fundamentally a pact, but rather a decision.

27. Schmitt, *Constitutional Theory*, 145: "Every constitutional rule based on the constitution and that proceeds in the context of constitutional competencies is essentially of a different nature than an act of the constitution-making power."

28. On this point there is a noticeable difference between Rousseau, Hobbes, and Schmitt. The first two do not differentiate between constitution-making power and constituted power. However, in Schmitt's theory, this is a fundamental distinction. See Pasquale Pasquino, "Die Lehre vom 'pouvoir constituant' bei Emmanuel Sieyès und Carl Schmitt: Ein Beitrag zur Untersuchung der Grundlagen der modernen Demokratietheorie," in Quaritsch, ed., *Complexio Oppositorum: Über Carl Schmitt*, 371–85. Pasquino draws a parallel between Schmitt and Sieyès in relation to this distinction. This distinction is only possible if one distinguishes between subject and form. The constitution-making power is subject—not form—and, as such, creates decision. Form is created in decision itself. Also Peter Schneider, *Ausnahmezustand und Norm: Eine Studie zur Rechtslehre von Carl Schmitt* (Stuttgart: Deutsche Verlagsanstalt, 1957), 380.

29. This problem is one of the first that Schmitt refers to. It is already in *Dictatorship* (1921). Before the appearance of the concept of representation as described in his theory of the constitution, the concept of sovereign dictatorship was coined. Armin Adam, *Rekonstruktion des Politischen: Carl Schmitt und die Krise der Staatlichkeit, 1912–1933* (Weiheim: V. C. H. Acta Humaniora, 1992), 89.

30. Schmitt, *Constitutional Theory*, 76.

31. Carl Schmitt, *On the Three Types of Juristic Thought*, trans. J. W. Bendersky (Westport, CT: Praeger Publishers, 2004), 51: "For a law cannot apply, administer, or enforce itself. It can neither interpret, nor define, nor sanction itself; it cannot without ceasing to be a norm even designate or appoint the concrete men who are supposed to interpret and administer it."

32. On this point Schmitt quotes Guizot in *Constitutional Theory*, 63: "Guizot, a classic representative of liberal commitment to the *Rechtsstaat*, speaks of the 'sovereignty of reason,' of justice, and of other abstractions, in the proper knowledge that a norm can be called 'sovereign' only to the extent that it is not positive will and command but is the rationally correct will, reflects reason, and constitutes justice, and therefore has particular *qualities*; for otherwise only those who exercise will and command are sovereign." The nuance of the question is found in the expression "otherwise." Speaking in absolute terms, what Guizot claimed is true, but not in concrete situations.

33. Schmitt, *On the Three Types of Juristic Thought*, 56. In the same vein, see Schmitt, "Staatsethik und pluralistischer Staat," 32.

34. Schmitt, *Constitutional Theory*, 136.

35. Schmitt, *Constitutional Theory*, 239.

36. Schmitt, *Constitutional Theory*, 240.

37. In order to clarify the following, one must recognize Schmitt's distinction between parliamentarianism and democracy as different political forms; even if, in practice, the only way to accomplish democracy is the parliamentarian form of government.

38. Böckenförde in "Der Begriff des Politischen," 297: "Representation is first described—as we have heard here—in 'Römischer Katholizismus und politische Form,' then in a long note in 'Geistesgeschichtlichen Lage des Parlamentarismus' and lastly in 'Verfassungslehre.'"

39. Adam, *Rekonstruktion des Politischen*, 99: "Representation is like visible presenciality, personification of political unity."

40. Schmitt, *Constitutional Theory*, 247.

41. Schmitt, *Roman Catholicism and Political Form*, transl. G. L. Ulmen (Westport, CT: Greenwood Press, 1996), 30–31. Carl Schmitt, "The Visibility of the Church: A Scholastic Consideration," in *Roman Catholicism and Political Form*, transl. G. L. Ulmen (Westport, CT: Greenwood Press, 1996), 53.

42. In this expression, there is an underlying idea that the living unity of a plurality can only be achieved by an active unity, and not from a summation of wills.

43. Alvaro d'Ors draws a clear distinction between different types of representation: juridical, abbreviated, aesthetic, symbolic, and conceptual. Although each has different nuances, there is a characteristic common to all: a tension of presence-absence. To represent is to replace what is absent with something present. Álvaro d'Ors, *Ensayos de Teoría Política* (Pamplona: Eunsa, 1979), 224–29.

44. Schmitt, *Constitutional Theory*, 242.

45. Schmitt, *The Crisis of Parliamentary Democracy*, 97.

46. Schmitt, *Constitutional Theory*, 242.

47. Schmitt, *Constitutional Theory*, 242.

48. Schmitt, *Constitutional Theory*, 243. This existential concept of representation has been recognized by Hauriou, claiming that for a government to be representative, it cannot be solely representative in a constitutional sense (the primary type of representative institutions), but that it must also be representative in the existential sense of the word, which gives the institution real meaning. Also Voegelin in *The New Science of Politics* (Chicago: The Chicago University Press, 1987) dedicates considerable space to the concept of existential representation.

49. Schmitt, "Nehmen, Teilen, Weiden," 92–93.

50. Schmitt, *Roman Catholicism and Political Form*, 19.

51. On this point, Schmitt admired Hobbes's ability to conserve the idea of personality of representation, despite his nominalism. See Carl Schmitt, "Die vollendete Reformation. Bemerkungen und Hinweise zu neuen Leviathan Interpretationen,, *Der Staat* 4 (1965), 53. Also, see Adam, *Rekonstruktion des Politischen,* 97.

52. Adam speaks of "Pathos der Würde" (sense of dignity), when referring to representation. Adam, *Rekonstruktion des Politischen*, 102.

53. Thus as Erich Przywara notes, in *Mensch* (Nürnberg: Glock und Lutz, 1958), 11, referring to Schmitt: "Representation is the over-ordered element in this desired union (identity and representation) through which a popular, purely vital unity is possible, 'which has an elevated and superior way of being,' such that identity and representation are related to each other as the immanence of God in the world and the transcendence of God to the world."

54. Schmitt, *Constitutional Theory*, 243.

55. Schmitt, *Constitutional Theory*, 245.

56. Adam, *Rekonstruktion des Politischen*, 98: "The representative does not even represent the people in their 'natural existence'; he represents what would be unseen were it not represented, namely: its political unity."

57. Schmitt, *Constitutional Theory*, 243.

58. On this point, the influence of cubist aesthetics can be seen in Schmitt's early years, making him realize the importance of form, which appeared in the dialectic of representation. See: Ingeborg Villinger, ed., *Carl Schmitts Kulturkritik der Moderne: Texte, Kommentar und Analyse des "Schattenrisse" des Johannes Negelinus* (Berlin: Akademie Verlag, 1995), 165. This book clearly explains the meaning of form and Schmitt's conceptualization, as well as to what extent there is an aesthetic in his thought and how it can be referred to.

59. Joseph H. Kaiser, "Die Dialektik der Repräsentation," in *Festschrift für Carl Schmitt zum 70. Geburtstag*, ed. H. Barion, E. Forsthoff, and W. Weber (Berlin: Duncker & Humblot, 1959), 72.

60. Hans Barion, "Weltgeschichtliche Machtform? Eine Studie zur Politischen Theologie des II. Vatikanischen Konzils," in *Epirrosis: Festschrift für Carl Schmitt zum 65. Geburtstag*, Düsseldorf, 1953, II, 13.

61. Schmitt, *Roman Catholicism and Political Form*, 21. On this point, Michele Nicoletti, "Die Ursprünge von Carl Schmitts 'Politischer Theologie,'" in *Complexio Oppositorum: Über Carl Schmitt*, ed. H. Quaritsch (Berlin: Duncker & Humblot, 1988), 127: "Political theology is,

accordingly, the inner theologicity of all the political mediations, which, in order to be effective, come 'from above,' then it ought to be a 'secularization' of a transcendent instance, a 'representation' of itself."

62. Carl Schmitt, *Political Theology: Four Chapters on the Concept of Sovereignty*, transl. G. Schwab (Chicago: University of Chicago Press, 2005), 31. Also Schmitt, *Constitutional Theory*, 122, he states: "The thorough change or transformation remains the essential process because the legal foundation (*auctoritatis interpositio*) for the validity of the State is thereby created."

63. Some clarity arises with regard to the idea of form when it is related to that of "figure" in Ernst Jünger's thought. Coincidentally, he knew Schmitt and was influenced by him. Jünger defines the concept as follows: "[F]igures are those bodies presented to the eyes which capture the world's articulation of its structure according to a more decisive law than that of cause and effect, despite the fact, however, that the unity by which this articulation is not visible." Ernst Jünger, *El Trabajador: Dominio y figura* (Barcelona: Tusquets, 1990), 38. Thus, with figure it is typical to evoke the whole, which is more than the sum of its parts and, therefore, it is formed—it is not built, but becomes—qualitatively. He offers the following examples: "A friendship is more than two men; a people are more than that which can be expressed by the result of a census of the population or a sum of political votes." Jünger, *El Trabajador*, 39. Specifically, he refers to politics, stating: "Also in politics, everything depends on fighting with figures, not with concepts." Jünger, *El Trabajador*, 39.

64. Schmitt, *Constitutional Theory*, 264, Schmitt, who described democracy as a political form that only applies the formal principle of identity—since he did not distinguish between the rulers and the ruled—defined identity as: "the existential quality of the political unity of the people in contrast to any normative, schematic, or fictional types of equality. On the whole and in every detail of its political existence, democracy presupposes a people whose members are similar to one another and who have the will to political existence."

65. Schmitt, *The Crisis of Parliamentary Democracy*, 26–27; *Constitutional Theory*, 78 and 257–67; Carl Schmitt, "Der bürgerliche Rechtsstaat," *Abendland* 3 (1928), 201.

66. Carl Schmitt, "State, Movement, People: The Triadic Structure of Political Unity,"in *State, Movement, People: The Triadic Structure of Political Unity*, transl. S. Draghici (Washington, DC: Plutarch Press, 2001), 36–37. Carl Schmitt, *Der Begriff des Politischen* (Hamburg: Hanseatische Verlagsanstalt, 1933), 8. This edition is not identical with that of 1932, from which translation into English was made.

67. Schmitt, "Staatsethik und pluralistischer Staat," 35.

68. Carl Schmitt, "Volksentscheid und Volksbegehren: Ein Beitrag zur Auslegung der Weimarer Verfassung und zur Lehre von der unmittelbaren Demokratie," *Beiträge zum ausländischen öffentlichen Recht und Völkerrecht* 2 (1927), 50: "In this regard, no constitution can clearly assure who might be a people. A people can be any group that irrevocably appears as such and decides who specifically, that is, who in the given political and social reality, acts as a people." Also see Adam, *Rekonstruktion des Politischen*, 100.

69. Schmitt, *Constitutional Theory*, 271.

70. Schmitt, *Constitutional Theory*, 272.

71. To avoid falling into a contradiction with what has been stated thus far, a distinction between the existence of a people (with political capacity) and the political existence of a people (politically active) must be made.

72. Schmitt, "Staatsethik und pluralistischer Staat," 35: "Power produces consensus . . . and vice-versa: consensus produces power." This idea also appears in "Coloquio sobre el poder y el acceso al poderoso," *Revista de Estudios Políticos* 52, no. 78 (1954), 7: "[C]onsensus determines power, this is true, but power also determines consensus and, in all cases, this is an irrational or immoral consensus. . . . A modern man with power has infinitely more means to promote a consensus of his power than Charlemagne or Barbarossa."

73. Schmitt, "Machtpositionen des modernen Staates," 369.

74. Schmitt, "Machtpositionen des modernen Staates," 370: "Here, various important concepts of juridical and State theory come into consideration, such as: popular acceptance, recognition, goodwill, support, acclamation and trust of the people. If we summarize these as 'consensus of the people,' a series of simple formulas can be created. . . . These two (power and

consensus) are, truly, inseparable. Authentic power produces authentic consensus and authentic consensus produces authentic power. Above all, stable power holds the most authentic and secure acceptance of the people." Also interesting is this quote in Schmitt, *On the Three Types of Juristic Thought*, 74: "The sovereign is omnipotent through the consent that he himself produced and made possible through the omnipotence and decision of the state." Another enlightening text is Schmitt, "Machtpositionen des modernen Staates," 368 which states: "Therefore, next to weapons and the development of technical means, the technical methods by which the public opinion and general will of the people are formed is of great importance to the Modern State's position of power."

75. Schmitt, "Machtpositionen des modernen Staates," 368: "The exasperated struggle over schooling, which has been carried out, for example, in the typically Modern State of France, was a political struggle for positions of political power."

76. Schmitt, "Machtpositionen des modernen Staates," 368: "For both, in all Modern States in the world, one can see that no State can simply let go of these new technical means. All modern States have the obligation, despite serious proclamations regarding fundamental rights and freedom, despite the abolition of censorship, despite the fundamental parity and neutrality, to exercise a vast control over radio and television."

77. Carl Schmitt, "Volksentscheid und Volksbegehren," 31: "A widespread and superficial interpretation of the word democratic calls for letting a people do anything it can."

78. In Gary L. Ulmen's opinion, expressed in *Politischer Mehrwert: Eine Studie über Max Weber und Carl Schmitt* (Weinheim: V C H, Acta Humaniora, 1991), 383: "Schmitt was not against the general right to vote; he simply wanted to show its limitations."

79. Schmitt, "Der bürgerliche Rechtsstaat," 202: "What is curious is that in our democratic constitution, a united people never appears, there are only representatives that assemble, the individual extracted from the masses. Also, in Schmitt, "Volksentscheid und Volksbegehren," 33–34: "The secret, individual vote, which is not preceded by any regulated, public, or legal procedure, actually annihilates the specific possibilities of there being an assembled people."

80. In Schmitt, "Volksentscheid und Volksbegehren," 7–8, he distinguishes between two terms: "Volksentscheid" and "Volksbegehren." Ulmen describes the difference between the two in *Politischer Mehrwert*, 383: "The emphasis, for him, is on the decision of the people (*Volksentscheid*), which is essentially 'ante legem,' this differs from a referendum, which is essentially 'post-legem.'"

81. Schmitt, *Constitutional Theory*, 240. Rüdiger Kramme, *Helmuth Plessner und Carl Schmitt. Eine historische Fallstudie zum Verhältnis von Anthropologie und Politik in der deutschen Philosophie der zwanziger Jahre* (Berlin: Duncker & Humblot, 1989), 215, says that with this difference, Schmitt acquires another, that of *Staatsbürger* and *Privatman* (citizen and private man).

82. Schmitt, *The Crisis of Parliamentary Democracy*, 39: "Freedom of opinion is freedom for private people; it is necessary for that competition of opinions in which the best opinion wins." And also Schmitt, *The Crisis of Parliamentary Democracy*, 16: "The unanimous opinion of one hundred million private persons is neither the will of the people nor public opinion."

83. Schmitt, "Der bürgerliche Rechtsstaat," 203.

84. Schmitt, "Der bürgerliche Rechtsstaat," 203: "Every democracy presupposes the total homogeneity of a people. Only one such unity can possess political responsibility. If it is, as in the current State, of a heterogeneous people, then the task is the integration of this mass to a unity. The authentic democratic method is not one of integration of a heterogeneous mass. The current state of a people, however, is divided into many different aspects: cultural, social, class, race, religion. Therefore, a solution ought to be sought outside of these democratic-political methods or parliament will simply become a tribune, which must allow these nuances to exist."

85. Schmitt, *The Crisis of Parliamentary Democracy*, 27: "The ancient dialectic in the theory of the will of the people has still not been resolved: The minority might express the true will of the people; the people can be deceived, and one has long been familiar with the techniques of propaganda and the manipulation of the public opinion."

86. Schmitt, *The Crisis of Parliamentary Democracy*, 28: "The consequence of this educational theory is a dictatorship that suspends democracy in the name of a true democracy that is still to be created."

87. Schmitt, *The Crisis of Parliamentary Democracy*, 27.

88. Schmitt, *The Crisis of Parliamentary Democracy*, 34.

89. Schmitt, *The Crisis of Parliamentary Democracy*, 39: "Public opinion protected through freedom of speech, freedom of the press, freedom of assembly, and parliamentary immunities means freedom of opinion in liberal thought, with all the significance which the word *freedom* has in this system."

90. Schmitt, "Volksentscheid und Volksbegehren," 49: "In terms of historical experiences, States with political life have an inaccessible magistracy, by which any attempt to put it aside results in a people becoming judges and, thus, lose its popular character, or, on the contrary, anarchy emerges in the absence of the State. The immediacy of democracy cannot be organized without ceasing to be immediate." Also Schmitt, "Volksentscheid und Volksbegehren," 35: "For the juridical knowledge of the democratic *Rechtsstaat*, one may deduce that a determined constitutional procedure of expression of a people's popular will limits the content of the expressible to certain possibilities."

91. Schmitt, *Constitutional Theory*, 272. Also Schmitt, *The Crisis of Parliamentary Democracy*, 16: "The people exist only in the sphere of publicity."

92. Schmitt, *Constitutional Theory*, 131.

93. Schmitt, "Volksentscheid und Volksbegehren," 33: "The very meaning of the word people rests on its opposition to both government and any fixed 'form' of magistracy. Also, in a democracy in which a people itself would need to govern, the meaning of the word people ought to always retain its meaning: a people are that which does not have any function of authority, that which does not govern."

94. Schmitt, "Volksentscheid und Volksbegehren," 48: "(a people) decide, called on from outside of itself and in a state of capture, without having constitutionally established specific legal procedures." Schmitt, "Der bürgerliche Rechtsstaat," 202: "Where can the people be found according to the constitutional text and the reality of the bourgeois State? Where is there space for acclamation, which can only take place when dissemination is created through the assembled people? There is no dissemination without a people, and there is not a people without dissemination." Also Schmitt, "Volksentscheid und Volksbegehren," 33: "A people that appears to actually be united in the market . . . is no more than a magnitude, recognized both sociologically and politically; it has a common will and expresses itself differently from the people, whose will is expressed, without assembling, as the result of a summation of secret, individual votes." In the same way, Schneider, *Ausnahmezustand und Norm*, 157, writes: "The popular will always subsists; but it can make itself present, current, in the state of 'being assembled.'"

96. Schmitt, *Constitutional Theory*, 131.

97. Schmitt, *Constitutional Theory*, 131. Adam identifies three sources of inspiration for this concept in Schmitt: roman state law, German conservatives and the role of acclamation in the Church. See Adam, *Rekonstruktion des Politischen*, 79–83. Barbara Nichtweiss points out, with regard to the last source of inspiration mentioned, that there is a possible influence in what relates to the term *acclamation* of Erik Peterson in Schmitt, specifically in his work, 'Heis Theos' (1920) in which Peterson studied the concept of acclamation in ancient and medieval Christianity. See: Barbara Nichtweiß, *Erik Peterson: Neue Sicht auf Leben und Werk* (Freiburg: Herder, 1992), 740.

98. Schmitt, *The Crisis of Parliamentary Democracy*, 16. Also in Schmitt, "Volksentscheid und Volksbegehren," 34: "Because the appropriate activity, capacity and function of the people, the nucleus of all popular expression, the original democratic phenomenon—what Rousseau saw as democracy in the strictest sense—is an acclamation, a cry of approval or condemnation from the assembled mass." Because of expressions such as this one, Schmitt's work has been said to have an element of democratism. For example, in Adam, *Rekonstruktion des Politischen*, 78, the following statement can be found: "Acclamation fills the void that democratic thought believes to fill with the right to general, free and secret voting. . . . It is the true articulation of the political under democratic conditions because it is the public articulation." Similarly Kramme, expresses this idea in *Helmuth Plessner und Carl Schmitt*, 215–17. What interests the author in this work is not to determine if Schmitt is democratic or not, but to attempt to understand in what sense the following is true: that rigorous democracy is the same

as a sovereign dictator. Schmitt had read this thesis in Donoso Cortés's discourse on dictatorship.

99. Schmitt, "Volksentscheid und Volksbegehren," 34: "[Y]ell high and low, cry with joy or complaint, strike shields with weapons, say 'Amen' to a pact of any kind or avoid this acclamation with silence."

100. This can be seen in the papers and notes found in Schmitt's legacy. He refers over and over again to the notion of charisma and charismatic legitimacy. Thus in *Nachlaß*, RW 265-K 16; RW 265-K 173; RW 265-K 180. The following brief entry in his 1972 diary is noteworthy: "Gesetz & Gnade/Nomos & Charisma" (law and grace/nomos and charisma). RW 265-K 131.

101. On this point, he provides two examples: "All of Napoleon's plebiscites resulted in an absolute 'yes' majority. Therefore, in 1799, 1804, 1814, and also in 1851 and 1852; after each coup, the people acknowledged the power he had created with a 'yes.' And, conversely, in Switzerland new laws are generally voted against with a 'no.' The basis for this is the same as in France: no one wants to vote against the *status quo*." Schmitt, "Der bürgerliche Rechtsstaat," 202–3.

102. Schmitt, "Volksentscheid und Volksbegehren," 36

103. Schmitt, *The Crisis of Parliamentary Democracy*, 26–27. The democratic character of modern democracies is limited by the process of expression of the will of the people. Schmitt, "Volksentscheid und Volksbegehren," 36: "The inevitable limit that corresponds to the nature of this procedure rests, as has just been said, on a dependence on the fact that any question must be formulated in an easy and simple way."

104. Schmitt, "Volksentscheid und Volksbegehren," 34: "Truly, no State can renounce these acclamations." Also Schmitt, "Volksentscheid und Volksbegehren," 34: "Acclamation is an eternal phenomenon of the whole political community. No State without a people, no people without acclamation."

105. Schmitt, *Constitutional Theory*, 132.

106. In the last years of his life, Schmitt's imagination was opened to the possibility of a direct democracy, without mediation, due to technological advances. He discussed this in an article published in *Deutsches Allgemeines Sonntagsblatt*, on June, 28, 1970, in an article entitled "Von der TV-Demokratie. Die Aggresivität des Fortschritts," 8: "Our representations of democracy depend on historical images from antiquity. Then, ancient democracy was clear and simple: the people were only those assembled and summoned by the magistrate in the forum or other adequate places. Such are a people. In another case, a people do not subsist. A people is only present if it assembles. This results in making argument, acclamations, cries, and a common will unnecessary. Can this be considered, keeping in mind our optical and acoustic means of communication? That would be a technical problem. There is no longer representation in the ancient sense. Neither as political nor as state form, nor as parliament or something of that nature, because modern technology appears to develop the means and compelling and evident methods that allow for a specific, permanent, evident means to identify social and political groups."

107. Adam, *Rekonstruktion des Politischen*, 89: "Because the people cannot speak, it selects a person capable of speech, of making the political form visible."

108. Schmitt, *Constitutional Theory*, 107.

109. Álvaro d'Ors, *De la guerra y de la paz* (Madrid: Rialp, 1954), 42–43: "Both in the case of the dictator's decision—and the very institution of a dictatorship implicates this—and in the case of a Senate decree, and even in the case of a senior judge declaring so on his authority, the *iustum*, or exceptional disruption of legality is found, which would last as long as the circumstance that provoked it did. The Treasury closed. Senate sessions were interrupted. Public events of all kinds ceased. All types of business, procedural and public auctions were suspended; all acts of jurisdiction were put on hold. All legal life was paralyzed for the duration of the 'iustum': laws remained silent during this period."

110. Álvaro d'Ors, "Cicerón, sobre el estado de excepción," in *Ensayos de Teoría Política*, 153–75.

111. d'Ors, *De la Guerra y de la Paz*, 43.

112. Schmitt was well versed in Cicero, as we can read in "Berlín, 1907," *Eclectica* 17, nos. 71–72 (1988), 17–19.

113. Schmitt, *Political Theology*, 6–14.

114. Carl Schmitt, *Dictatorship: from the origin of the modern concept of sovereignty to proletarian class struggle*, transl. M. Hoelzl and G. Ward (Cambridge: Polity, 2014). Also, "Ausnahmezustand und Bürgerkriegslage," in *Verfassungsrechtliche Aufsätze* (Berlin: Duncker & Humblot, 1958), 233-371.

115. Schmitt, *Political Theology*, 6.

116. Álvaro d'Ors, "La pérdida del concepto de excepción a la ley," in Álvaro d'Ors, *Escritos varios sobre el derecho en crisis* (Roma: Consejo Superior de Investigaciones Científicas, 1973), 149–53.

117. Schmitt, *Political Theology*, 12ff.

118. Schmitt, *Political Theology*, 5.

119. Schmitt, *Political Theology*, 14.

120. Schmitt, *Political Theology*, 14–15.

121. Schmitt, *Political Theology*, 36. This example appeared already in Donoso Cortes's "Essay on Catholicism, Socialism and Liberalism."

122. Carl Schmitt, *Theodor Däublers "Nordlicht": Drei Studien über die Elemente, den Geist und die Aktualität des Werkes* (München: Georg Müller, 1916), 77.

123. And he did, quoting Anschütz in his *Staatsrecht*: "There is not only a gap in the law, that is, in the text of the constitution, but moreover in law as a whole, which can in no way be filled by juristic conceptual operations. Here is where public law stops." Quoted in Schmitt, *Political Theology*, 15. During 1925–1926, Erik Peterson addressed the definition of this concept outside of the legal sphere in his "Lessons on Saint Luke." These years corresponded with his friendship with Schmitt in Bonn. Barbara Nichtweiss concluded, in her study *Erik Peterson: Neue Sicht auf Leben und Werk*, 760, that it is very likely that these two thinkers influenced each other on this point.

124. Schmitt, *Political Theology*, 7: "But whether the extreme exception can be banished from the world is not a juristic question. Whether one has confidence and hope that it can be eliminated depends on philosophical, especially on philosophical-historical or metaphysical, convictions."

125. Schmitt, *Political Theology*, 15.

126. Schmitt, *Political Theology*, 15: "The exception explains the general and itself. And if one wants to study the general correctly, one only needs to look around for a true exception. It reveals everything more clearly than does the general. Endless talk about the general becomes boring; there are exceptions. It they cannot be explained, then the general also cannot be explained. The difficulty is usually not noticed because the general is not thought about with passion but with a comfortable superficiality. The exception, on the other hand, thinks the general with intense passion." Schmitt only took a part of *Repetition* and quoted it from memory. In the French edition, *La répetition, oeuvres complètes* (Paris: Éditions de l'Orante, 1972) V, 93. There is no doubt that Kierkegaard was a source of inspiration and ideas for the configuration of Schmitt's concept of exception. As shown by Ellen Kennedy, "Politischer Expressionismus: Die Kulturkritischen und Metaphysischen Ursprünge des Begriffs des Politischen von Carl Schmitt," in *Complexio Oppositorum: Über Carl Schmitt*, ed. H. Quaritsch (Berlin: Duncker & Humblot, 1988), 244, Schmitt read Kierkegaard in 1918, the year he wrote *Politische Romantik*. Karl Löwith, "Politischer Dezisionismus," in Karl Löwith, *Der Mensch inmitten der Geschichte. Philosophische Bilanz des 20. Jahrhunderts* (Stuttgart: J. B. Metzler Verlag, 1990), 25, also made a long reference to Kierkegaard in relation to Schmitt's work and specifically to the present concept. Kramme, *Helmuth Plessner und Carl Schmitt*, 174–78, analyzed the parallelism between Schmitt and Kierkegaard on the concept of exception.

127. Just as Löwith also believed, see Löwith, *Politischer Dezisionismus*, note 25, 25.

128. Søren Kierkegaard, *La répetition*, 93.

5. THE CONCEPT OF THE POLITICAL

1. Schmitt claimed that there is an "inevitable order from the mindset of international law to a particular mode of political existence." Carl Schmitt, *Völkerrechtliche Großraumordnung mit Interventionsverbot für raumfrem de Mächte: Ein Beitrag zum Reichsbegriff im Völkerrecht* (Berlin/Wien/Leipzig: Deutscher Rechtsverlag, 1941), 29.

2. Carl Schmitt, *Political Theology: Four Chapters on the Concept of Sovereignty*, transl. G. Schwab (Chicago: University of Chicago Press, 2005), 6.

3. Quoted in Ernst Hüsmert, "Die letzten Jahre von Carl Schmitt," *Schmittiana I: Eclectica* 17, nos. 71–72 (1988), 43: "After World War I, I said: 'The sovereign is he who decides the state of exception.' After World War II, facing my death, I now say: 'The sovereign is he who controls the waves in space.'" These statements are of a paradigmatic nature, as the words can be changed without changing the formal structure and the meaning is maintained. The terms of this assertion must necessarily change with the change of *nomos*. The most important space is not so much the land as it is the air and the new way of 'appropriation' is not so much cultivation as the configuration and arrangement of waves in space (*Wellen*). The concept of *Wellen* is recurrent in *Glossarium*. I cite two places that show a change in the concept of sovereignty, while at the same time the impossibility of stopping it can be perceived in actual politics: "I have earned my space. Is this not pride? Friendly sound waves whistle, impertinent in my space." Carl Schmitt, *Glossarium: Aufzeichnungen der Jahre 1947–1951* (Berlin: Duncker & Humblot, 1991), 63. "The pervasiveness of limitless waves is no longer power, but influence." Schmitt, *Glossarium*, 187.

4. This text was published a number of times. Throughout the various editions, changes were made. In quantitative terms, the major difference is between the 1932 and 1933 editions, which have been taken into consideration in this book. From a qualitative point of view, Schmitt considered these variations irrelevant in terms of content and meaning. The different editions of *Der Begriff des Politischen* are: *Archiv für Sozialwissenschaft und Sozialpolitik* 58 (1927), 1–33; *Probleme der Demokratie* 5 (1928), 1–34; *Der Begriff des Politischen: Mit einer Rede über das Zeitalter der Neutralisierungen und Entpolitisierungen* (München: Duncker & Humblot, 1932); *Der Begriff des Politischen* (Hamburg: Hanseatische Verlagsanstalt, 1933); *Der Begriff des Politischen: Text von 1932 mit einem Vorwort und drei Corollarien* (Berlin: Duncker & Humblot,1963); *Der Begriff des Politischen: Text von 1932 mit einem Vorwort und drei Corollarien* (Berlin: Duncker & Humblot, 1979). The1963 edition has been reissued in Duncker & Humblot. Regarding the history of this work, see Mathias Schmitz, *Die Freund-Feind-Theorie Carl Schmitts: Entwurf und Entfaltung* (Köln, Opladen: Westadt Verlag, 1965), 157–60. Heinrich Meier's analysis of the differences between the 1932 and 1933 editions is also very interesting, Heinrich Meier, *Carl Schmitt, Leo Strauss und "Der Begriff des Politischen": Zu einem Dialog unter Abwesenden* (Stuttgart: Metzler Verlag, 1991). To explain the changes made to the 1933 edition, Meier proposes that they were responses to objections that Leo Strauss expressed to Schmitt in letters he wrote, but never received a reply.

5. The political theory of Schmitt is known in Italy as political "conflict theory." Quoted in Pasquale Pasquino, "Bemerkungen zum 'Kriterium des Politischen' bei Carl Schmitt," *Der Staat* 25 (1986), 385. The concept of the political as *Konfliktstheorie* (conflict theory), appears usually contrasted with that of *Integrationstheorie* (integration theory). This is an idea of the political situation as a break against a concept of politics as order. However, as we have seen in Schmitt, there is also a theory of order, for which the concept of the political is not a contradiction but its complement. In line with this, Pasquino, "Bemerkungen zum 'Kriterium des Politischen' bei Carl Schmitt," 386: "Secondly, there is no argument about the fact that Schmitt's thought has revolved around the topics of order, cohesion, homogeneity and political unity."

6. Schmitt himself emphasized what I have just explained in his prologue to the 1963 reprint of the 1932 *Der Begriff des Politischen*, *Der Begriff des Politischen: Text von 1932 mit einem Vorwort und drei Corollarien* (Berlin: Duncker & Humblot, 1979), 16: "so that an authentic document is saved from mythological falsehood and a true declaration can be made of its original informative purpose."

7. Pasquino, "Bemerkungen zum 'Kriterium des Politischen,'" 391, pointed out that it is possible that the fact that Schmitt's thought on politics revolves around a criterion might be motivated by his study of Max Weber's "politischer Verband" (political association) in his work *Wirtschaft und Gesellschaft*. Moreover, he notes that it is quite possible that the use of the expression, *das Politische*, could have been taken from Rudolf Smend in *Die politische Gewalt im Verfassungstaat und das Problem der Staatsform en Staatsrechtliche Abhandlungen*, 1968. However, the expression *das Politische* (the political) had already been used before Schmitt employed it. For example, it appeared in an article by Rudolf Manasse, "Struktur der Politik," *Summa* 3 (1918), 99–131, a magazine with which Schmitt worked closely.

8. Carl Schmitt, *Der Begriff des Politischen*, 9–19. This prologue is not included in the English translation. Carl Schmitt, *The Concept of the Political*, transl. G. Schwab (Chicago: Chicago University Press, 2007). Schmitt's response to Julien Freund in a 1961 letter affirms the statement I have just made. "I thank you warmly for the good advice of not changing anything in the 'Begriff des Politischen' text. I am going to take your advice. One cannot cross the same river twice. I have said this in the foreword to my collection of articles: 'Positionen und Begriffe' (1940) and it is good that you have reminded me of it." *Schmittiana II, Eclectica* 19 nos. 79–80 (1990), 52.

9. Schmitt, *The Concept of the Political*, 26.

10. Schmitt asks the following: "What is the criterion, the 'specific difference,' the great sign of differentiation?" Carl Schmitt, "Die Buribunken," *Summa: Eine Vierteljahresschrift* 4 (1918), 91.

11. Schmitt, *Begriff des Politischen*, 9, Vorwort: "Das beziehungsfeld des Politischen ändert sich fortwährend." For this reason, a substantial definition of the political is not possible.

12. The way Schmitt defines politics is not an isolated case in his writings, but rather can be found in the larger context of a method of knowledge that Schmitt tries to develop. Ingeborg Villinger, *Carl Schmitts Kulturkritik der Moderne: Texte, Kommentar und Analyse des "Schattenrisse" des Johannes Negelinus* (Berlin: Akademie Verlag, 1995), 140, describes this in the following way: "Schmitt opposes a method that relates to a specific linguistic (and extraordinarily modern) concept. Basing it on grammar and logic, he reaches a form of rhetoric that no longer refers to the subject or nature, and, thanks to the particular way of positioning it, it is as conceptually clear as the rhetoric of intuitive language. This method allows him to return to relationships, structures and correspondences within a conceptual field and specify the inherent contours in a subject area." Uwe-Justus Wenzel, "Die Dissoziation und ihr Grund," in *Die Autonomie des Politischen: Carl Schmitt Kampf um einen beschädigten Begriff*, ed. Hans-Georg Flickinger (Weinheim: V. C. H., Acta Humaniora, 1990), 24, refers to this way of forming concepts in his reference to limit as a "knowledge that theoretically favors the most extreme possibility." And he compares Schmitt's "orientation toward the borderline case" with Walter Benjamin's "Logik des Zerfalls" (logic of disintegration). Pasquino in "Bemerkungen zum 'Kriterium des Politischen' bei Carl Schmitt," 393, points out how this way of forming concepts is characteristic of many authors from the 1920s, including Max Weber, Walter Benjamin, and Siegfried Kracauer. Odo Marquard, referring to the same idea, includes Schmitt's concept of the sovereign, which he calls a "Grenzbegriff" (limiting concept) because it is oriented toward an extreme case. In *Historisches Wörterbuch der Philosophie*, ed. J. Ritter and K. Gründer (Basel: Schwabe 1971–2007), I, 871, he described the *Grenzbegriff* in the following way: "A limiting concept is a concept of something that must make itself known and validated in human knowledge and should be thought of for this negative end." This explanation opens a new perspective on the concept of politics at the epistemological level. The fact that the political situation is oriented toward the exception presupposes that human knowledge cannot fully explain it, and, therefore, it can neither be explained completely nor predicted.

13. Schmitt, *The Concept of the Political*, 29.

14. Schmitt, *The Concept of the Political*, 19–25.

15. Schmitt, *The Concept of the Political*, 28.

16. Schmitt, *The Concept of the Political*, 19. As can be seen, while Schmitt tried to get rid of this confusion, he was nonetheless criticized for not doing so. Volker Gerhardt argued this in "Politisches Handeln: Über einen Zugang zum Begriff der Politik," in *Der Begriff der Politik:*

Notes

Bedingungen und Gründe politischen Handelns, ed. Volker Gerhardt (Stuttgart: J. B. Metzlersche Verlagsbuchhandlung, 1990), 292.

17. Schmitt, *Der Begriff des Politischen*, 12, Vorwort.

18. Schmitt, *The Concept of the Political*, 20. Also *Political Theology II: The Myth of the Closure of Any Political Theology*, transl. M. Hoelzl and G. Ward (New York: Polity Press, 2014), 45. Also, Carl Schmitt, Von der TV-Demokratie: Die Aggressivität des Fortschritts," *Deutsches Allgemeines Sonntagsblatt* 26–28 (1970), 8, returns to the same point: "'The Concept of the Political' begins with a statement that I once crossed out because it seemed too difficult to be the first phrase in this work, so I decided to begin with the phrase, 'The concept of State presupposes the concept of the political.' This sounds very abstract, but it is a summary of what I have experienced. With this phrase, I can relate my whole life history of constitutional law. Up to now in each manual for International Law, State Law and Constitutional or Administrative Law, the concept of the political is defined from the concept of State. Politics is what concerns the State. I shift this and say that the State should be defined by politics. This is an amazing change."

19. Schmitt, *The Concept of the Political*, 31, footnote 12.

20. Schmitt, *The Concept of the Political*, 30–31. Schmitt's intuition partly influenced the *Begriffsgeschichte* School that was represented by Reinhart Koselleck, who was influenced by Schmitt.

21. Schmitt, *Der Begriff des Politischen*, 84, corresponding to "Das Zeitlater der Neutralisierungen und Entpolitisierungen."

22. Schmitt, *The Concept of the Political*, 30.

23. Schmitt, *The Concept of the Political*, 32.

24. There is a certain parallelism, although influence cannot be strictly established, on this point between the political criterion and tacitist theories. One of the most famous tacitists, Baltasar Álamo de Barrientos, stated, in his 1614 work, *Tácito español ilustrado con aforismos*, the following: "[T]he political is the distinction between friends and enemies." quoted in Enrique Tierno Galván, *Escritos, 1950–1960* (Madrid: Tecnos, 1971), 62. He also references this in *Cabos sueltos* (Barcelona: Bruguera, 1982), 167: "In the Spanish Golden Age, Spaniards said this in a very explicit way and it was repeated, henceforth, at other times." This reference to tacitists regarding the friend-enemy distinction is also cited in Günter Maschke, *Der Tod des Carl Schmitt* (Wien: Karolinger Verlag, 1987), 80. Another Spaniard, Eugenio d'Ors, with whom Schmitt remained friends, described the political situation in the same way, though in this case no one knows for sure whether there is an influence between the two or simply a parallel. There are two places where it becomes clear: "It is inevitable that business is always done against someone. Politics are carried out in the same way." "First the intellectual," in Eugenio d'Ors, *Nuevo Glosario II* (Madrid: Aguilar, 1947), 616. And speaking of the pan-European project in *Nuevo Glosario II*, 616–17.

25. Schmitt wanted to make it clear that this is an independent criterion and it cannot be manipulated so that it becomes something else, for example, as Julien Freund does in his book, *L'essence du politique* (Paris: Sirey, 1965). Schmitt makes a claim against this interpretation in Carl Schmitt, "Clausewitz als politischer Denker: Bemerkungen und Hinweise," *Der Staat* 6 (1967), 501.

26. Wenzel, "Die Dissoziation und ihr Grund," 18; he refers to this as the "modal character" of the concept of the political.

27. Schmitt, *The Concept of the Political*, 27.

28. Quoted in Meier, *Carl Schmitt, Leo Strauss und 'Der Begriff des Politischen*, 102. The content of the political situation is what Leo Strauss in his criticism of *The Concept of the Political* refers to as *Genus*, the genus by which Schmitt refuses to define the political. Meier, *Carl Schmitt, Leo Strauss und Der Begrif des Politischen*, 102–3. Also Hermann Hefele "Zum Problem des Politischen," *Abendland* 3, no. 7 (1928), 204: "Politics is power, not object. In principle, there are no political objects; the only political object is the person in the totality of his existence and references."

29. Dolf Sternberger, *Drei Wurzeln der Politik* (Frankfurt am Mainz: Suhrkamp, 1995), 22. Also, Ernst Vollrath, *Grundlegung einer philosophischen Theorie des Politischen* (Würzburg: Königshausen & Neumann, 1987), 317. With respect to this, Helmut Kuhn, "Besprechung des

Buches Carl Schmitt-Der Begriff des Politischen," *Kantsstudien* 38 (1933), 193 explains: "[F]or him, it is not about the essential content of the political, but the test of political existentiality." And he calls that existentiality "nothing." Additionally, Peter Schneider, *Ausnahmezustand und Norm: Eine Studie zur Rechtslehre von Carl Schmitt* (Stuttgart: Deutsche Verlagsanstalt, 1957), 250, shows the contradiction to which we have referred: "The concept of the political is either materially determined or not. But it cannot be both at once."

30. José María Beneyto, *Politische Theologie als Politische Theorie: Eine Untersuchung zur Rechts und Staatstheorie Carl Schmitts und ihrer Wirkungsgeschichte in Spanien* (Berlin: Duncker & Humblot, 1983), 93–101. Also in Wenzel, "Die Dissoziation und ihr Grund," 13–36.

31. Confirmation of my position on this can be found in Ernst-Wolfgang Böckenförde, "Der Begriff des Politischen als Schlüssel zum Staatsrechtlichen Werk Carl Schmitts," in *Complexio Oppositorum: Über Carl Schmitt*, ed. H. Quaritsch (Berlin: Duncker & Humblot, 1988), 285: "Politics within the State—as Carl Schmitt has indicated (*Der Begriff des Politischen*, 30)—is only politics in a secondary sense. It is in the classic sense of policing, caring for and maintaining the community's order, through which politics does not override peace and unity."

32. Quoted in Heinz W. Schmidt, "Vom Geistesgrund und der Feindschaft im Begriff des Politischen bei Carl Schmitt," in *Epirrosis: Festschrift für Carl Schmitt zum 65. Geburtstag* (Düsseldorf, 1953), II, 656. Also Wenzel, "Die Dissoziation und ihr Grund," 20.

33. Carl Schmitt, "The Age of Neutralizations and Depoliticizations," in Schmitt, *The Concept of the Political*, 80–96.

34. Schmitt, *The Concept of the Political*, 37.

35. Schmitt, *The Concept of the Political*, 38–39. Also in Carl Schmitt, "Weiterentwicklung des totalen Staats in Deutschland," in *Verfassungsrechtliche Aufsätze* (Berlin: Duncker & Humblot, 1958), 359: "According to these experiences of total 'non-politics,' knowledge should realize that any problem can be a potential political problem." In reality, the only thing necessary for a political conflict to emerge is a common space—it does not matter which kind—and various positions in that space. Because of the separation between areas of life, alluded to in this text, Schmitt was branded a liberal. In this vein Helmut Schelsky, "Der Begriff des Politischen und die politische Erfahrung der Gegenwart," *Der Staat* 22 (1983), 322–23.

36. Similarly, Julien Freund recognized this in *L'essence de la politique*, 539. Schmitt noted Hegel's dialectic as an example here. Specifically the concrete form of conversion of quantity to quality. This way of arguing expresses the fact that any sphere of life can experience a change in quality. Through this kind of change, for example, a situation can become a political one: "[H]is dialectic of concrete thinking is also explicitly political." Schmitt, *The Concept of the Political*, 62–63.

37. Carl Schmitt, *Der Begriff des Politischen* (Hamburg: Hanseatische Verlagsanstalt, 1933), 30: "[I]ts holy war and crusades are actions that allude to the friend-enemy distinction in a particularly authentic and profound way."

38. Carl Schmitt, *Roman Catholicism and Political Form*, transl. G. L. Ulmen (Westport, CT: Greenwood Press, 1996), 25.

39. What Schmitt considered total politicization is the liberal State which, in trying to eliminate the State, converted society itself into State, whereby any activity becomes political. See Schmitt, *The Concept of the Political*, 24. Also see Carl Schmitt, "Die Wendung zum totalen Staat," in *Positionen und Begriffe im Kampf mit Weimar-Genf-Versailles, 1923–1939*, (Hamburg: Hanseatische Verlagsanstalt, 1940), 147–57.

40. Schmitt, *The Concept of the Political*, 24.

41. Schmitt, *The Concept of the Political*, 27.

42. Schmitt, *The Concept of the Political*, 27.

43. With regard to this, see Reinhart Koselleck, *Futures Past* (New York: Columbia University Press, 2004), 155–91, particularly 191. It is interesting, when clarifying the concept of absolute enemy as it appears in Schmitt's criteria, to consider Koselleck's distinction between contrary symmetric concepts and contrary asymmetric concepts, already mentioned here. He describes the relationship of contrary asymmetric concepts "Aryan and non-Aryan" as follows: "The term 'Aryan' was constituted as a political term by the conceptual field which it negated

and to which any opponent could be consigned at will. The non-Aryan is merely the negation of one's own position, and that is that. Who might be Aryan cannot be deduced from the concept of the Aryan, nor from that of the non-Aryan. This then defined an elastic figure of negation whose actual arrangement was at the disposal of whoever had the power to fill linguistic vacancies or empty concepts. The concept itself did not indicate that the Jews were specifically identified, but they found, by falling under the category of non-Aryan, that they were destined for potential non existence. The conclusion was drawn as soon as the Aryan as Über-mensch felt himself legitimated in the removal of the non-Aryan as Unter-mensch." Koselleck, *Futures Past*, 190. The non-Aryan is an example of absolute enmity. On the contrary: "The conceptual couple Friend and Foe is characterized by its political formalism, delivering a frame for possible antitheses without identifying them. In the first place, because of its formal negation, this concerns purely symmetrical counterconcepts, for, in the case of Friend and Foe, there exists a definition of oneself or of one's Foe that is open to simultaneous use by both sides. These are epistemological categories whose substantial content (determined through historical experience) can serve to asymmetrically load both linguistic fields. However Schmitt might have concretized this contrast from his own position, he has coined a formula that cannot be outstripped as a condition of possible politics. This is a concept of the political, not of politics." Koselleck, *Futures Past*, 191. Schmitt's concept of enemy is not absolute and does not suppose its negation.

44. Schmitt, *The Concept of the Political*, 35.

45. It is not always about imposing *Entweder-Oder*, but being aware that there are different ways of being that may come into conflict. See Schmitz, *Die Freund-Feind Theorie Carl Schmitts. Entwurf und Entfaltung*, 151.

46. Schmitt, *The Concept of the Political*, 27. The friend-enemy distinction, given its absence of normativity and normality is considered to have an irrational side. This can be seen in Heinz Laufer, *Das Kriterium des politischen Handelns: Versuch einer Analyse und konstruktiven Kritik der Freund-Feind-Unterscheidung auf der Grundlage der Aristotelischen Theorie der Politik* (Frankfurt: Johann Bernecker, 1962), 17. Similarly, Hefele, "Zum Problem des Politischen," 203: "The concepts of friend and enemy should not be understood in a metaphorical way, but concretely."

47. Schmitt, *The Concept of the Political*, 54.

48. Schmitt, "The Age of Neutralizations," in Schmitt, *The Concept of the Political*, 95: "Today we even recognize the secret law of this vocabulary and know that the most terrible war is pursued only in the name of peace, the most terrible oppression only in the name of freedom, the most terrible inhumanity only in the name of humanity."

49. Carl Schmitt, "Die andere Hegel-Linie: Hans Freyer zum 70. Geburstag," *Christ und Welt* 10, no. 30 (1957), 2. This Cartesian formulation was transformed by Schmitt with different content. In a manuscript note, among diverse notes about *nomos*, he wrote: "I think, therefore I possess, I possess therefore I exist." *Nachlaß* RW-265-K. 61, Mt. 9, n. 2. These are not completely unrelated statements.

50. "Gleichgeartete und Verbündete" (same way of being). Schmitt, *Der Begriff des Politischen*, 8, 1933 edition.

51. "Andersgeartete" (different). Schmitt, *Der Begriff des Politischen*, 8, 1933 edition. This term continues to have certain national-socialist connotations and Schmitt used it at the time against the Jewish spirit, which appeared as "artfremdes Geist" (a foreign spirit). See Carl Schmitt, "Die deutsche Rechtswissenschaft im Kampf gegen den jüdischen Geist," *Deutsche Juristen Zeitung* 41, no. 20 (1936), 1193.

52. Löwith made the same observation in Löwith, "Politischer Dezisionismus," in Karl Löwith, *Der Mensch inmitten der Geschichte: Philosophische Bilanz des 20. Jahrhunderts* (Stuttgart: J. B. Metzler Verlag, 1990), 32.

53. Schmitt, "Von der TV-Demokratie: Die Aggressivität des Fortschritts": "A people can be identical to itself when it has a very clear enemy. Where there are clear distinctions between friend and enemy, as in the Near East today, identity is nothing but clearer."

54. On the contrary Kuhn saw enmity as irrationality and lacking in content in Kuhn, "Besprechung des Buches Carl Schmitt-Der Begriff des Politischen," 195.

55. Schmitt, "The Age of Neutralizations," in Schmitt, *The Concept of the Political*, 95–96. Kuhn, "Besprechung des Buches Carl Schmitt-Der Begriff des Politischen," 195: "The end of the book reads: 'the order of human things comes from the strength of integral knowledge. 'Ab integro nascitur ordo.' But the contemporary individual who bears this distinction is 'per definitionem' unable to join an order." Kuhn interprets Schmitt's thought as contradictory, although it seems that something went wrong in his own interpretation. Schmitt takes the expression "Ab integro nascitur ordo" from the IV Virgilio's Ecloge: "Ultima Cumaei venit iam carminis aetas; / magnus ab integro saeclorum nascitur ordo / iam redit et Virgo, redeunt Saturnia regna, / iam nova progenies caelo demittitur alto." After human decadence, Jesus's birth would usher in a new era of peace, a new order of ages. The figures of the Mother and the Child are essential representations of historical hope. A possible definitive achievement of peace, in Schmitt's view, also depends on the integral knowledge symbolized by these two figures. And because of this, definitive peace cannot be achieved on a purely historical level.

56. Strauss claims, in this vein, that politics is "fundamental." See Meier, *Carl Schmitt, Leo Strauss und 'Der Begriff des Politischen,'* 105. The term "determinant" seems more appropriate to me.

57. Carl Schmitt, *Theodor Däublers "Nordlicht": Drei Studien über die Elemente, den Geist und die Aktualität des Werkes* (München: Georg Müller, 1916), 63 and 65–66. Carl Schmitt, *Ex Captivitate Salus: Experiencias de los años 1945–1947*, transl. A. Schmitt (Santiago de Compostela: Porto y Cia., 1960), 35 and 36. Carl Schmitt, "Coloquio sobre el poder y el acceso al poderoso," *Revista de Estudios Políticos* 52, no. 78 (1954), 14. Also Schmitt, *Glossarium*, 30. A rather significant phrase appears in the latter citation: "Who today is the *Katechon*? . . . His place has never been deserted; otherwise we would no longer be around." Schmitt, *Glossarium*, 63. This argument also appears in Meier, *Carl Schmitt und Leo Strauss und der Begriff des Politischen*, 64: "The inseparability of the decision between friend and enemy in the political sphere corresponds to the urgency of the decision between God and Satan in the theological sphere."

58. Leo Strauss sustains this referring to a point in Schmitt's writing: "The affirmation of the political is nothing more than the affirmation of the moral." "Anmerkungen zu Carl Schmitt 'Der Begriff des Politischen,'" in H. Maier, ed., *Carl Schmitt, Leo Strauss und "Der Begriff des Politischen": Zu einem Dialog unter Abwesenden* (Stuttgart: Metzler Verlag, 1991), 115–19. Certainly, Schmitt would have qualms about moral arguments with regards to the political. Schmitt, *The Concept of the Political*, 58–59.

59. This thesis is in the Catholic tradition of political thought. It is a fundamental point in Konrad Weiss's writings, which, as noted, Schmitt deeply admired. This same idea appears in Helmuth Plessner, a contemporary anthropologist of Schmitt, from whom Schmitt borrowed the concept of "Abstandnahme" (distancing). In this regard, see Kramme, " *Helmuth Plessner und Carl Schmitt: Eine historische Fallstudie zum Verhältnis von Anthropologie und Politik in der deutschen Philosophie der zwanziger Jahre* (Berlin: Duncker & Humblot, 1989), 157, and of course it appears in Donoso Cortés's writings, which he also so admired.

60. Schmitt, *The Concept of the Political*, 58. Also Schmitt, "Zu Friedrich Meineckes 'Idee der Staatsräson,'" 228.

61. Carl Schmitt, "On the Counterrevolutionary Philosophy of the State," in *Political Theology: Four Chapters on the Concept of Sovereignty*, transl. G. Schwab (Chicago: University of Chicago Press, 2005), 56.

62. Many commentators on Schmitt's works have regarded him as a pessimistic thinker because he starts from an anthropological pessimism that he never overcomes. It is the case, for example, of Schmitz, *Die Freund-Feind-Theorie Carl Schmitts*, 115 and 152; Heinz Laufer, "Homo homini homo: Das anthropologisches Glaubensbekenntnis eines Doktrinärs," in *Politische Ordnung und menschliche Existenz: Festgabe für Erich Voegelin zum 60. Geburtstag*, ed. A. Dempf, H. Arendt und F. Engel-Janosi (München: C. H. Beck, 1962), 327. These critiques can be responded to by arguing that he does not begin with the worst state of nature, but rather with its possibility. See Schmitt, *The Concept of the Political*, 68. The example that Schmitt placed there is sufficiently graphic.

63. Schmitt, *The Concept of the Political*, 65.

64. In this regard Meier, *Carl Schmitt, Leo Strauss und Der Begriff des Politischen*, 66; Alexander Demandt, "Staatsform und Feindbild bei Carl Schmitt," *Der Staat* 27 (1988), 23–29; Helmut Quarischt, *"Positionen und Begriffe" Carl Schmitts* (Berlin: Duncker & Humblot, 1989), 38.

65. In this vein, Erik Peterson claimed in a text of the "Vorlesung zu Römerbrief": "The fact that politicians are more interested in Adam's case than moral theologians is part of its nature." and referring to the latter, he continues, "[T]hey cultivate observation of the events in private life, the former of public life." Referred in Barbara Nichtweiss, *Erik Peterson: Neue Sicht auf Leben und Werk* (Freiburg: Herder, 1992), 747.

66. Schmitt, *The Concept of the Political*, 59. As already mentioned, this concept comes from Plessner. Kramme, *Helmuth Plessner und Carl Schmitt*, 198: "Distancing oneself does not just mean separating from something, but rather, in addition, it means conserving something from those who are separated or, understood in an existential way, conserving oneself is the same as defending one's identity."

67. Schmitt, *Ex Captivitate Salus*, 94.

68. Schmitt, *Der Begriff des Politischen*, 21, in the 1933 edition. The following affirmation, "Die Politik ist das Schicksal," appears in Johann Wolfgang Goethe, *Paralipomena zu den Annalen,* Jubiläums-Ausgabe *Sämtliche Werke*, ed. E. von der Hellen (Stuttgart: J. G. Cotta 1902–1907), XXX, 412. Goethe spoke this phrase to Napoleon. Walther Rathenau paraphrased it as follows: "Die Wirtschaft ist das Schicksal," cited in Schmitt, *The Concept of the Political*, 78. With this affirmation, he has been accused of reducing social life to politics, as Vollrath claimed in *Grundlegung einer philosophischen Theorie des Politischen*, 289–90. Also is the case of Strauss, "Anmerkungen zu Carl Schmitt, 'Der Begriff des Politischen,'" 111–13.

69. Schmitt, *Der Begriff des Politischen*, 41–42, in the 1933 edition. In Schmitt's opinion this pessimistic view of human beings allows Hobbes to remain alive in the political imagination, despite man's individualism. Schmitt, *The Concept of the Political*, 52.

70. The affirmation that formulations of the political presuppose a state of nature is common in critiques of Schmitt. Hence, Strauss, "Anmerkungen zu Carl Schmitt, 'Der Begriff des Politischen,'" 121 and 106. However, Strauss acknowledges some differences between the two conceptions. First, while Hobbes makes his theory from the denial of that state of nature, Schmitt makes it by affirming it. Secondly, Schmitt's theory does not deal with individuals, but rather with groups of men. Another interpretation redirects him to Rousseau's, rather than Hobbes's, state of nature, as in Kuhn, "Carl Schmitt, Der Begriff des Politischen," 194. Hasso Hofmann also follows this line in his study, *Legitimität gegen Legalität: Der Weg der politischen Philosophie Carl Schmitts* (Neuwied/Berlin, Luchterland, 1964), 163–65. Armin Adam, *Rekonstruktion des Politischen: Carl Schmitt und die Krise der Staatlichkeit, 1912–1933* (Weinheim: V. C. H. Acta Humaniora, 1992), 85–86, argues that Schmitt himself makes a particular interpretation of Rousseau that allows him to assimilate both views.

71. In this regard, Strauss, "Anmerkungen zu Carl Schmitt 'Der Begriff des Politischen,'" 121: "The affirmation of the state of nature does not mean affirming war, but rather entails renouncing the safety contained in 'status quo.'"

72. Schmitt, *The Concept of the Political*, 60, citing Helmuth Plessner, *Macht und Menschlicher Natur* (Berlin: Ernst von Hippel, 1931). Another interesting text in this regard is Helmut Plessner, *Die Stufen des Organischen und der Mensch: Einleitung in die philosophische Anthropologie* (Berlin: de Gruyter, 1975), 291. Kramme, *Helmuth Plessner und Carl Schmitt*, 17, maintains the thesis that Schmitt needed an anthropology similar to that of Plessner to found his theory.

73. In the same sense, Adam, *Rekonstruktion des Politischen*, 59.

74. Schmitt, *The Concept of the Political*, 57.

75. Schmitt, "Coloquio sobre el poder y el acceso al poderoso," 20.On the story of this phrase see Montserrat Herrero, ed., *Carl Schmitt und Álvaro d'Ors Briefwechsel* (Berlin: Duncker & Humblot, 2004), 117–18, Letter 2, Sept., 1951, footnote 9.

76. Schmitt, *Der Begriff des Politischen*, 42, 1933 edition. The same idea is repeated in *Land and Sea*, transl. S. Draghici (Washington, DC: Plutarch Press, 1997), 4–5.

77. Carl Schmitt, "Die geschichtliche Struktur des heutigen Weltgegensatzes von Ost und West," in Armin Mohler, ed., *Freundschaftliche Begegnungen: Festschrift für Ernst Jünger*

zum 60. Geburtstag (Frankfurt, Vittorio Klostermann, 1955), 149–50. When speaking here of nature he is referring to nature as naturalism and not as ancient philosophy understands it. That is the concept of the natural sphere that Schmitt struggles with and not any another teleological character. This is clearly seen in the *Schattenrisse*.

78. Carl Schmitt, "The Visibility of the Church: A Scholastic Consideration," in *Roman Catholicism and Political Form*, trans. G. L. Ulmen (Westport, CT: Greenwood Press, 1996), 51.

79. Carl Schmitt, *Theory of the Partisan: Intermediate Commentary on the Concept of the Political*, transl. G. K. Ulmen, *Telos* 127 (2004), 75. This even happens in the case of a partisan outside of any formal war. In this case, it is very important to understand the figure of the "interested third-party," who establishes relations with the regular sphere, which is necessary for the partisan if he wants to remain within the framework of the political. The interested third-party is on the side of the partisan. This being "on the side of" has the sense of a political friendship that is equivalent to political recognition, although it is not public. The partisan has an authentic, but not absolute, enemy.

80. Schmitt, *Theory of the Partisan*, 71–72. Also in Schmitt, *Glossarium*, 213: "'The enemy is the figure who questions our own. He will harass us or we will harass him until the last' (*Sang an Palermo*). What do these verses mean and where do they come from? A test of intelligence for each reader of this small text: *The Concept of the Political*. Anyone who cannot answer the question from his own spirit and knowledge should decline to discuss the difficult subject of this small text."

81. Carl Schmitt, "Staatsethik und pluralistischer Staat," *Kantstudien* 35, no. 1 (1930), 36.

82. Schmidt, "Vom Geistesgrund und der Feindschaft im Begriff des Politischen bei Carl Schmitt," 652.

83. It has almost always been thus interpreted. See Strauss, "Anmerkungen zu Carl Schmitt, 'Der Begriff des Politischen,'" 104. Pier Paolo Portinaro, *La crisi dello jus publicum europaeum: Sagio su Carl Schmitt* (Milano: Ed. di Communità, 1982), 249, speaks of "l'ostilità come concetto primario." Otto Brunner, *Land und Herrschaft: Grundfragen der territorialen Verfassungsgeschichte im Mittelalter* (Brünn/München/Wien: Rudolf M. Rother Verlag, 1943), 2.

84. Schmitt, *Der Begriff des Politischen*, 9, in the 1933 edition: "[O]ne could think it just and useful to be silent on these awkward matters for reasons of education or tactic and act as if there were no longer enemies. None of this comes into question here. Here there are no fictions or normativities, but rather the existing reality and the real possibility of such a distinction."

85. Schmitt, *The Concept of the Political*, 66.

86. Schmitt, *The Concept of the Political*, 54. This "I do not know" stated in Schmitt's work is another of conflicting points repeated throughout the criticism Schmitt has received. In this description, it seems that Schmitt has no other remedy but to hold on to some positivism, which makes his position highly vulnerable since it is left without any basis. If, in the future, a peaceful world were possible, his theory would be invalidated. The "weiß ich nicht" seems to leave that possibility open. However, this is only possible to believe if one has not read chapter 7 of the same work. There Schmitt justifies why that situation will never come to pass. So the phrase "weiß ich nicht" is ironic. In this regard, Strauss, "Anmerkungen zu Carl Schmitt, 'Der Begriff des Politischen,'" 113–14. He asks: If politics is threatened, why does Schmitt sustain it, what reason would he have for doing that.

87. Schmitt, *Begriff des Politischen*, Corollarium 2, 104ff. The three Corollarium of *The Concept of the Political* have not been translated into English.

88. Schmitt, *Der Begriff des Politischen*, 8, in the 1933 edition.

89. The idea of the common good is implicit in the concept of the enemy as a public "other," which was key in classical definitions of politics. It can be read between the lines in his thesis as follows: when a group faces another that seeks to destroy its existence, it is fighting for the good of the group itself. This is so much so that, in this concept of "common good" inherent to Schmitt's enemy thesis, the private enemy is not justified. Thus, it is understandable that Schmitt claimed that there is no reason to declare war on an enemy outside of a political situation—that is, outside of a showdown to the death with a public enemy and, therefore, in favor of one's own community. See Schmitt, *The Concept of the Political*, 49–50. It has been suggested that Schmitt would not admit the assimilation of a theory of the common good

because it seemed suspicious. Schmitt's aphorism is well-known: "Wer 'bonum commune' sagt will betrügen." Quoted in Josef Pieper, *Noch wußte es niemand: Autobiographische Aufzeich-nungen 1904–1945* (München: Kösel Verlag, 1976), 197. Also quoted in Josef Pieper, "Notiz-en," *Hochland* 46 (1954), 344.

90. According to Leo Strauss, this point is where Schmitt differs from Hobbes: "According to Schmitt, the subjects of the state of nature are not individuals, but rather totalities." Strauss, "Anmerkungen zu Carl Schmitt, 'Der Begriff des Politischen,'" 110.

91. Schmitt, *The Concept of the Political*, 29.

92. Schmitt, *The Concept of the Political*, 29. It is not in vain that Schmitt supports the Gospel of Saint Matthew. It is as if he wanted to give a hint that the friend-enemy criterion has a theological foundation. Nichtweiss expressed this, in light of Peterson and Schmitt's relation-ship. See Nichtweiss, *Erik Peterson: Neue Sicht auf Leben und Werk*, 762. Löwith, "Politischer Dezisionismus," 40, criticized Schmitt's use of this Gospel passage: "Schmitt reduces, in a typically liberal way (and in contradiction with his thesis in '*Roman Catholicism and Political Form*' . . .), an absolute claim of the Christian religion to a relative private matter." Erik Peterson differed with Schmitt on this matter: "Surely he meant by this the religious and political enmity that the rulers of this world had against Christians, not an inherent enmity between political units, and, when faced with the unique way that Christ is eschatologically driven, took on an apocalyptic intensity." Quoted from Nichtweiss, *Erik Peterson: Neue Sicht auf Leben und Werk*, 762.

93. Schmitt, *The Concept of the Political*, 29.

94. This does not involve a private or total enmity—that is, Schmitt did not propose a theory of general distrust. He thus explained it in *Ex Captivitate Salus* speaking of Max Stirner, 93: "As every solipsist sees the enemy in everyone that is not himself, so the whole world becomes his enemy and he believes that the world must fall into his trap if he obligingly offers a brotherly kiss. . . . I wonder who can be my enemy and who can be so in such a way that I recognize him as an enemy and even have to acknowledge that he considers me an enemy? The greatness of this is found in a recognition of this mutual recognition."

95. I insist on this point. Keep in mind the distinction: matter (content)/form (a way of having content) or the symmetrical one, essence/existence. I speak in terms of the latter be-cause, when talking about the existentiality of enmity, Schmitt referred to it. What does it mean to say that the enmity proper to the political is existential? Existence adds to essence a relation-ship to the other. Thus, in a political situation, that enmity is existential means that for a people to be classified as an enemy, as well as perceiving that this people has a certain way of being (an essential determination), it must be shown to have a particular way of being that is different from mine (an existential determination). And these determinations do not refer to individuals, but rather to peoples or human groups. A particular mode of being that is manifested toward me as a different existence with regard to my own is not "without essence." That Schmitt leaves it undetermined does not mean that it is "nothing" or an irrational or "purely" existential content. As I mentioned, the concept of enemy is considered, in the terminology of Koselleck, as a contrary symmetrical concept. In describing this concept, the relative nature that was just mentioned is implicitly considered. Thus, the historian's description in Koselleck, *Futures Past*, 155, is useful here: "The simple use of 'we' and 'you' establishes a boundary and is in this respect a condition of possibility determining a capacity to act. But a 'we' group can become a politically effective and active unity only through concepts which are more than just simple names or typifications. A political or social agency is first constituted through concepts by means of which it circumscribes itself and hence excludes others, and therefore, by means of which it defines itself."

96. He cited Hegel here, highlighting the clarity of his definition of the enemy, which other contemporary philosophers avoided. For Hegel, the enemy is "ethical difference" in the sense of ethics not of morality, that is, in the sense of the concrete life of a people. See Schmitt, *The Concept of the Political*, 62.

97. Schmitt, *Theory of the Partisan*, 78.

98. Schmitt, *Der Begriff des Politischen*, in the notes to the 1963 edition, 119. The text, "Hinweise" (indications), has not been translated into English.

99. Pasquino, "Bemerkungen zum 'Kriterium des Politischen' bei Carl Schmitt," 395. He thinks that given that the political situation is always oriented at the extreme case, mediation can only come through power.

100. Thus in Carl Schmitt, *The Nomos of the Earth in the International Law of the Jus Publicum Europaeum* (New York: Telos Press, 2003), 322, Schmitt wrote that new amity lines are historically possible. And in the prologue to the German edition he notes, "The earth has been promised to the peaceful. New thought on the '*nomos* of the earth' will also be open to them." Carl Schmitt, *Der Nomos der Erde im Völkerrecht des Jus Publicum Europaeum* (Köln: Greven Verlag, 1950), Vorwort. This prologue has not been translated into English.

101. Schmitt, *The Concept of the Political*, 33.

102. Carl Schmitt, "El Orden del Mundo después de la Segunda Guerra Mundial," *Revista de Estudios Políticos* 122 (1962), 35.

103. Schmitt, *The Concept of the Political*, 36.

104. Schmitt, *The Concept of the Political*, 32.

105. Schmitt, *The Concept of the Political*, 33.

106. Schmitt, *The Concept of the Political*, 33.

107. Schmitt, *The Concept of the Political*, 35: "extreme case taking place."

108. Schmitt, *Der Begriff des Politischen*, 8, in the 1933 edition: "A foreigner cannot ask the question of whether the 'extreme case' is present or the follow-up question of what extreme means are necessary for life in order to defend existence and preserve one's self—'in suo esse perseverare.'"

109. Schmitt, *The Concept of the Political*, 27.

110. Schmitt, *Der Begriff des Politischen*, 8, in the 1933 edition. Christian Graf von Krockow, *Die Entscheidung: Eine Untersuchung über Ernst Jünger, Carl Schmitt und Martin Heidegger* (Frankfurt, Campus Verlag,1990), 58–59, qualifies this reasoning as "devaluing objectivity" and notes that "it implies a disconnect between all rational argument in the political sphere and becomes a stain of prejudice in the name of 'existential judgment.'"

111. Carl Schmitt, "Die Raumrevolution: Durch den totalen Krieg zu einem totalen Frieden," *Das Reich* 19 (29 Sept. 1940): "The meaning of every war that is not meaningless is found in the peace that ends it." See also Schmitz, *Die Freund-Feind-Theorie Carl Schmitts. Entwurf und Entfaltung*, 151.

112. Schmitt, *The Concept of the Political*, 33. Gianni Vattimo notes in this regard that Schmitt's friend-enemy distinction does not imply dictatorial or military politics. Gianni Vattimo, "Inventò la politica di amico-nemico," in *La Stampa*, April 17, 1987.

113. Schmitt, *The Concept of the Political*, 34.

114. Schmitt, *The Concept of the Political*, 36. The following text from Carl Schmitt, *Die Wendung zum diskriminierenden Kriegsbegriff* (München/Leipzig: Duncker & Humblot, 1938), 1, is also crucial: "Starting some years ago, bloody wars have been conducted in different parts of the earth in which a more or less general agreement on the concept and description of the war is prudently avoided."

115. Schmitt, *The Concept of the Political*, 36.

116. Schmitt, *The Concept of the Political*, 36.

117. Carl Schmitt, *Constitutional Theory*, transl. J. Seitzer (Durham, NC: Duke University Press, 2007), 394.

118. Schmitt, *The Nomos of the Earth,* 140–68.

119. He thus recognized Hobbes's change in perspective as a change, above all, on this point. Schmitt noted at the end of his copy of the *Politische Theologie* manuscript: "Hobbes's decisionist sovereignty is the classic case of secularization through the appropriation of a synthetically formed, conceptual political position: absolute spiritual power."

120. Schmitt, *Ex Captivitate Salus*, 94: "Theologians tend to define the enemy as something to annihilate." Carl Schmitt, *The Leviathan in the State Theory of Thomas Hobbes: Meaning and Failure of a Political Symbol*, transl. by G. Schwab and E. Hilfstein (Westport, CT: Greenwood Press, 1996), 48: "only the just war is the true 'total' war." Also Schmitt, *The Concept of the Political*, 49: "That the justice does not belong to the concept of war has been generally recognized since Grotius. The notions which postulate a just war usually serve a political purpose."

121. Schmitt, *The Nomos of the Earth*, 157: "European state war thus became an armed struggle between hostes aequaliter justi. How should the question of just war be decided otherwise, if there is not spiritual authority? Should one of the subjects of one of the belligerent states decide on the justice or injustice of his government? That would produce only civil war and anarchy. . . . It must be remembered that the historical significance of the Modern State consists in its having ended the whole struggle over justa causa, i.e., concerning substantive right and substantive justice understood in the early feudal-legal, estate-legal, or creedal-theological sense."

122. Schmitt, *Begriff des Politischen*, Corollarium 2, 102–11. Also Schmitt, *The Nomos of the Earth*, 152–68. Also Schmitt, *The Nomos of the Earth*, 143–45

123. The antecedent concepts of total war that might have influenced Schmitt are as follows: the "global war" proclaimed by the French Revolution and that appears in French literature as "guerre totale"; Clausewitz's concept of "absoluter Krieg", see Robert Hepp, "Der harmlose Clausewitz," *Zeitschrift für Politik* 25, no. 3 (1978), 303–18; and no. 4, 390–429; and Ernst Jünger's *"totale Mobilmachung,"* or total mobilization, which can be seen in Carl Schmitt, *Die Wendung zum diskriminierenden Kriegsbegriff*, 242–43: "A superb representative of the German infantry, Ernst Jünger, has introduced an expressive formulation that is unprecedented: total mobilization. Regardless of the content and the justice that corresponds to that particular formulation of potential weapons or total mobilization, one must attend to and value the important knowledge that is contained in it."

124. Carl Schmitt, "Totaler Feind, totaler Krieg, totaler Staat," in *Positionen und Begriffe im Kampf mit Weimar-Genf-Versailles, 1923–1939*, ed. C. Schmitt (Hamburg: Hanseatische Verlagsanstalt, 1940), 234–40, 235–36.

125. Schmitt, *Begriff des Politischen*, Corollarium 2, 102–11.

126. Schmitt, "Totaler Feind, totaler Krieg, totaler Staat," 236.

127. Schmitt, *The Nomos of the Earth*, 320–21. On this point, Carl Schmitt, "Besprechungen der Bücher von Herbert von Borch: 'Obrigkeit und Widerstand: Zur politischen Soziologie des Beamtentums,' von F. J. P. Veale: 'Der Barbarei entgegen' und von Georg Schwarzenberger: 'Machtpolitik,'" *Das Historisch-Politische Buch* 3 (1955), 201: "[T]he terrible problem of modern warfare, whose way of understanding justice leads to blindly destroying one of the great discoveries of reason and human culture, the achievement of the development of the distinction between enemy and criminal and, in its place, establishes the disastrous path of criminalizing the political enemy."

128. Schmitt, *The Concept of the Political*, 49.

129. Schmitt, *Constitutional Theory*, 394. Two more texts from *Constitutional Theory* shed light on this point: Schmitt, *Constitutional Theory*, 76: "Every existing political unity has its value and its 'right to existence' not in the rightness or usefulness of norms, but rather in its existence. Considered juristically, what exists as *political* power has value because it exists. Consequently, its 'right to self-preservation' is the prerequisite of all further discussions; it attempts, above all, to maintain itself in its existence, 'in suo esse perseverare' (Spinoza); it protects 'its *existence*, its *integrity*, its *security*, and its *constitution*,' which are all existential values."

130. Meier, *Carl Schmitt, Leo Strauss und der Begriff des Politischen*, 73: "Schmitt's last word is not to affirm the political in the sense of affirming war as such, but rather of affirming 'the order of human matters.'" There are numerous opinions against this interpretation: Schmitz, *Die Freund-Feind Theorie Carl Schmitts*, 101; Laufer, *Das Kriterium des politischen Handelns*, 155.

131. Schmitt, *The Nomos of the Earth*, 322. Also Schmitt, *The Nomos of the Earth*, 94: "The characteristic feature of amity lines consisted in that, different from 'rayas', they defined a sphere of conflict between contractual parties seeking to appropriate land, precisely because they lacked any common presupposition and authority. In part, however these parties still shared the memory of a common unity in Christian Europe. But the only matter they could agree on was the freedom of the open spaces that began 'beyond the line.' This freedom meant that the line set aside an area where force could be used freely and ruthlessly."

132. Koselleck's argument on this topic is insightful. Koselleck, *Futures Past*, 191: "Whoever places peace as a concept overlaying Friend and Foe has to presuppose that, for peace, at

least two parties exist who are willing and able to arrive at a settlement. *Non ergo ut sit pax nolent sed ut ea sit quam volunt.* Not that one shies from peace, but that each seeks his own peace. As long as human agencies exclude and include, there will be asymmetric counterconcepts and techniques of negation, which will penetrate conflicts until such time as new conflicts arise."

133. Schmitt, *The Concept of the Political*, 51.

134. Schmitt, *Völkerrechtliche Großraumordnung mit Interventionsverbot für Raumfremde Mächte*, 55: "We should remember again and again that international law is a law of war and peace, 'ius belli ac pacis.' In different historical periods, the concrete and specific reality of war and peace linked to space and time and the interaction of these two states form the core of each international order and the coexistence of all peoples organized in space that is distributed in some way." And in Schmitt, *Die Wendung zum diskriminierenden Kriegsbegriffs*, 1: "What has always been valid shows itself, that the history of international law is a history of the concept of war. International law is primarily a 'law of war and peace,' 'ius belli ac pacis,' and so it will be as long as there is a right of self-governing peoples, organized at the State level—that is, as long as war is conducted between States and not as an international civil war. All dissolution of old orders and new configurations pose this problem." Also Schmitt, *Die Wendung zum diskriminierenden Kriegsbegriffs*, 3: "A hierarchy of simple norms is clearly not enough; in its place, there must either be a hierarchy of institutions and concrete authorities of international law or the concept of discriminatory war must be imposed in any way." And also, Schmitt, *Die Wendung zum diskriminierenden Kriegsbegriffs*, 52: "We know that the concept of war in the eighteenth and nineteenth centuries cannot remain unchanged, that new orders and communities of international law are inevitable and, above all, that a real community of European peoples is the condition for a real and effective international law." I agree with Schmidt; even though the concept of "Hegung des Krieges" (limit of war) belongs to a certain era—international law from the State era—it is valuable in itself and is operative in any historical moment. It is even a key concept in understanding the war-peace relationship. See Schmidt, "Vom Geistesgrund und der Feindschaft im Begriff des Politischen bei Carl Schmitt," 656. This is also seen in Dolf Sternberger, *Schriften IV: Staatsfreundschaft* (Frankfurt am Mainz: Insel Verlag, 1980), 317–18.

135. Schmitt, *Begriff des Politischen*, 19, Vorwort.

136. Schmitt, *Begriff des Politischen*, 11, Vorwort. Julien Freund spoke in this vein of a distinction that might be useful in better understanding what Schmitt intended to say. This involves a distinction between combat war and fighting war. Freund, *L'éssence de la politique*, 541.

137. Schmitt, *Völkerrechtliche Großraumordnung,* 55–56: "What kind of peace could be found in international European law between 1648 and 1914, which assumed sovereign States? How can peace be achieved and, with it, an international law among sovereign States that claim for themselves a free sovereign decision on war abandon law? It is natural that the coexistence of these power formations proceeds not from real peace given substantially, but rather from the progressive lawfulness of war."

138. On this point, see Carl Schmitt, "Der Status quo und der Friede," *Hochland* 23, no. 1 (1925), 1–9.

139. Carl Schmitt, "Inter pacem et bellum nihil medium," *Zeitschrift der Akademie für deutsches Recht* 6, no.18 (1939), 594. Also, Schmitt, *Begriff des Politischen*, Corollarium 2, 105. And Schmitt, *Völkerrechtliche Großraumordnung*, 56. The following text from "Die Raumrevolution" is quite graphic: "The essence of peace is not just about getting guns to stop firing, planes to stop dropping bombs or about diplomats speaking their bit at the feasts of peace held in Geneva. There, war would simply be the absence of peace and we know what that entails from experience with the instrument of Versailles and with these twenty years of an intermediate state between war and peace that came from there. Peace does not depend on just any peace treaty, but rather on the foundation of a new order, which it is time for in the development of the historical present."

140. Schmitt, "Inter pacem et bellum nihil medium," 595. Also Schmitt, *Begriff des Politischen*, Corollarium 2, 106.

141. "Dieses nihil medium ist aber gerade die Situationsfrage." Schmitt, *Begriff des Politischen*, Corollarium 2, 106. This is also cited in Schmitt, "Inter pacem et bellum nihil medium," 595.

142. Schmitt, "Inter pacem et bellum nihil medium," 594.

143. Schmitt, *Begriff des Politischen*, Corollarium 2, 106.

144. Schmitt, *Begriff des Politischen*, Corollarium 2, 109.

145. Schmitt, *Begriff des Politischen*, Corollarium 2, 107. This is also cited in Schmitt, "Inter pacem et bellum nihil medium," 595.

146. "The real problem is found in regard to authentic peace, not to the concept of war." Schmitt, "Inter pacem et bellum nihil medium," 595. Another text that clarifies this is Carl Schmitt, *Der Völkerbund und das politische Problem der Friedenssicherung* (Leipzig: Teubner, 1930), 1: "The powerful issue of pacification in Europe and the earth rests in large historical relationships. Its very content cannot be otherwise recognized. It cannot be addressed from the changing tactics of everyday political groupings and it is even less a simple juridical question about the content of written peace treaties. Rather, it is necessary to ignore legal constructions or, even better, the fictions with which 'right' to an objectively unsatisfactory state is opened up." Also Schmitt, "Die Raumrevolution": "In the great history of mankind all true peace is only true once. The peace that truly puts an end to war by the order of space can only be the peace of the order of space." There are surprisingly many authors that do not recognize Schmitt's attempt in this regard, for example Dolf Sternberger claimed: "The author doesn't launch the question of peace anywhere." Sternberger, *Schriften IV: Staatsfreundschaft*, 317. See also Rüdiger Altmann, "Der Feind und der Friede," *Merkur: Deutsche Zeitschrift für europäisches Denken* 22, no. 9 (1968), 781.

147. Carl Schmitt, "Völkerrechtliche Formen des modernen Imperialismus," in *Positionen und Begriffe im Kampf mit Weimar-Genf-Versailles, 1923–1939*, ed. C. Schmitt (Hamburg: Hanseatische Verlagsanstalt, 1940), 176. And also Schmitt, "Der Status quo und der Friede," 5: "Here we see that in all peace attempts, the difficult question does not concern peace—since all agree that they want peace—but rather the question is who decides what an obstacle or a danger to peace 'concretely' means and what specific means there are for protecting peace in danger or how hampered peace can be restored. The same question always remains, who judges?"

6. THE POLITICAL ORDER

1. In this vein, Odo Marquard, *Aussprache*, in *Complexio Oppositorum: Über Carl Schmitt*, ed. H. Quaritsch (Berlin: Duncker & Humblot, 1988), 335: "The concept of concrete order is the response to the political in the form of the intensity of the relationship between friend and enemy."

2. According to this interpretation, one cannot speak of three concepts of the political, namely, (1) one that is within consensus theory and mainly outlined in *Verfassungslehre*, (2) another within a theory of conflict in which there are two acting subjects, (3) a third, also in the framework of the theory of conflict, but in which, once the sovereign comes into play, there are three main actors involved in the conflict. In my opinion, this is not about three different concepts of the political, but rather three successive moments of the political situation, to which I have alluded in the text. See Vilmos Holczhauser, *Konsens und Konflikt: Die Begriffe des Politischen bei Carl Schmitt* (Berlin: Duncker & Humblot, 1990), 86–89.

3. Carl Schmitt, *Political Theology: Four Chapters on the Concept of Sovereignty*, transl. G. Schwab (Chicago: University of Chicago Press, 2005), 5.

4. Gary L. Ulmen expresses the relationship to order with the term "actuality" in Gary L. Ulmen, *Politischer Mehrwert: Eine Studie über Max Weber und Carl Schmitt* (Weinheim: V C H, Acta Humaniora, 1991), 242.

5. This appears more clearly in the following text, Carl Schmitt, "Staatsethik und pluralistischer Staat," *Kantstudien* 35, no. 1 (1930), 36: "Political unity is the highest unity, not because it dictates in a powerful way or because it is superior to other types of unity, but because it decides."

6. Regarding this point, we must remember the description of the sovereign dictator that Schmitt laid out in Carl Schmitt, *Dictatorship: from the Origin of the Modern Concept of Sovereignty to Proletarian Class Struggle*, transl. M. Hoelzl and G. Ward (Cambridge: Polity, 2014), 119.

7. Schmitt, *Political Theology*, 18.

8. Carl Schmitt, *The Leviathan in the State Theory of Thomas Hobbes: Meaning and Failure of a Political Symbol*, transl. G. Schwab and E. Hilfstein (Westport, CT: Greenwood Press, 1996), 45.

9. Carl Schmitt, *La defensa de la Constitución* (Barcelona: Labor, 1931), 168.

10. See Álvaro d'Ors, *De la guerra y de la paz* (Madrid: Rialp, 1954). Also Álvaro d'Ors, "Teología Política, una revisión del problema," *Revista de Estudios Políticos* 205 (1976), 41–79.

11. The note in chapter 3 of *La defensa de la Constitución*, 168 is of particular interest on this point.

12. Schmitt, *La defensa de la Constitución*, 166.

13. Carl Schmitt, *Legality and Legitimacy*, transl. J. Seitzer (Durham, NC: Duke University Press, 2004), 4: "The final, actual meaning of the fundamental 'principle of legality' of all State life lies ultimately in the fact that there is no longer any government or obedience in general because only impersonal, valid norms are being applied. In the general legality of all State exercise of power lies the justification of one such State type. A closed system of legality grounds the claim to obedience and justifies the suspension of every right of resistance. In this regard, the specific manifestation of the law is the statute, while legality is the particular justification of State coercion."

14. Thus, in the first note to chapter 8 of *Constitutional Theory* he states: "Concepts such as sovereignty and majesty by necessity always correspond only to effective power. Authority, by contrast, denotes a profile that rests essentially on the element of continuity and refers to tradition and duration. Both power and authority are, combined with one another, effective and vital in every state." Carl Schmitt, *Constitutional Theory*, transl. J. Seitzer (Durham, NC: Duke University Press, 2007), 458–59.

15. There is no doubt that the force with which this thesis appears in Schmitt stems from the controversy he cites regarding pluralism within the State.

16. Carl Schmitt, "TV-Demokratie: Die Agressivität des Fortschritts," *Deutsches Allgemeines Sonntagsblatt* 23, no. 26 (1970), 8.

17. Carl Schmitt, *The Concept of the Political*, transl. G. Schwab (Chicago: Chicago University Press, 2007), 38.

18. Carl Schmitt, *Der Begriff des Politischen*, edition of 1933, 21.

19. Schmitt, "Staatsethik und pluralistischer Staat," 36–37.

20. Hence, political unity is not identical to the written Constitution. The latter is a consequence of the former. On this point, see H. Quaritsch, *"Positionen und Begriffe" Carl Schmitts* (Berlin: Duncker & Humblot, 1989), 36. Ulmen, with respect to this, stated: "All philosophers of the state, from Plato to Hegel, have recognized political unity as the state's ultimate value. Schmitt follows this; however, he goes further, basing political unity on political existence." Ulmen, *Politischer Mehrwert*, 325.

21. Schmitt, *Der Begriff des Politischen*, edition of 1933, 39.

22. Carl Schmitt, *The Concept of the Political*, 43–45.

23. Carl Schmitt, "Der Gegensatz von Gemeinschaft und Gesellschaft als Beispiel einer Zweigliedrigen Unterscheidung: Betrachtungen zum Schicksal solcher Antithesen," *Estudios Jurídico Sociales* (Zaragoza: Universidad de Santiago de Compostela, 1960), I, 166. Schmitt shows he is skeptical of dualistic distinctions.

24. Political unity is a political category, not a historical form, as is the State. It is more in the tradition of what was thought of as a state before the sixteenth century. See Carl Schmitt, "Zu Friedrich Meineckes 'Idee der Staatsräson,'" *Archiv für Sozialwissenschaft und Sozialpolitik* 56, no. 1, (1926), 233. The concepts of political unity and order were already present in this 1926 text.

25. Carl Schmitt, *Hugo Preuss: Sein Staatsbegriff und seine Stellung in der deutschen Staatslehre* (Tübingen: J. C. B. Mohr, 1930), 26: "The normal activity of a State is that of

relativizing opposing groups within itself and preventing the ultimate consequence: war. If a State is no longer able to perform this activity, the responsibility of politics is transferred from the outside to the inside. Internal political oppositions become groups that are defined by the friend-enemy distinction, meaning civil war, be it large or small."

26. Carl Schmitt, *The Concept of the Political*, 52. His reflection on this point is also interesting in Carl Schmitt, "Coloquio sobre el poder y el acceso al poderoso," *Revista de Estudios Políticos* 52, no. 78 (1954), 3-20, 6-7: "Very true. But why do you obey? Obedience is not at all arbitrary, but is somehow motivated by something. Why, then, do men give their consent to power? In some cases, they do it out of trust, in others out of fear, sometimes out of hope, other times out of desperation. But what they need is protection, and they seek such protection from power. From man's point of view, there is no reason other than the relationship between protection and obedience. He who does not have the power to protect someone does not have the right to demand obedience. And conversely, he who seeks and accepts protection is not entitled to disobedience."

27. Carl Schmitt, *The Concept of the Political*, 52.

28. Carl Schmitt, *The Concept of the Political*, 46.

29. Carl Schmitt, *The Concept of the Political*, 47. Alexander Demandt, "Staatsform und Feindbild bei Carl Schmitt," *Der Staat* 27 (1988), 23, highlights this idea, but in this case he considers political unity in the form of the State.

30. Therefore, the concepts of State and political unity cannot be equated. The State is the form of political unity, and can be so in many ways. The Modern State is one of these ways. In this regard, see Armin Adam, *Rekonstruktion des Politischen: Carl Schmitt und die Krise der Staatlichkeit, 1912–1933* (Weiheim: V. C. H. Acta Humaniora, 1992), 85.

31. He commented on this in an interview with the newspaper *La Noche* on Saturday, April 7, 1962: "Throughout my life I have observed six changes of regime: Empire, the Spartacist Republic, the Republic of Weimar, Hitler's regime, the American occupation and the current Federal Republic. I am accused of being accommodating, but, can a man choose the regimes of the country in which he resides? It is much easier to say this while exiling oneself and only later return to the Motherland."

32. This is more clearly described in Carl Schmitt, "State, Movement, People: The Triadic Structure of Political Unity," in *State, Movement, People: The Triadic Structure of Political Unity*, transl. S. Draghici (Washington, DC: Plutarch Press, 2001), 3–54. The interpretations or explanations given of Schmitt's work are diverse. In general, there are two. Either it is taken as a theoretical description of a new political reality that attempts to legitimize a system, which at a determined moment assumes a concrete order—this is the most common opinion—or others see that in this work, similar to others published in the National Socialist era, Schmitt attempted to "moderate" the totalitarian State that the Nazis attempted to build and his writings, therefore, are nothing more than a diagnosis of the situation. An example of this can be seen in the text by Holczhauser, *Konsens und Konflikt*, 181.

33. See Ulmen, *Politischer Mehrwert*, 453–54.

34. Carl Schmitt, *The Concept of the Political*, 53. The problem is that of coordinating unity and plurality, a classic problem in the history of thought. Carl Schmitt, *La Unidad del Mundo*, transl. A. Truyol y Serra (Madrid: Ateneo, 1951), 15: "There are diverse aspects to the problem of unity. Even the number one is a problem for mathematics, and unity is a theological, philosophical, moral and political problem of immense proportions. So too, in consequence, are duality and plurality." Pasquale Pasquino compared Schmitt to Thomas Aquinas on this point. See Pasquale Pasquino, "Bemerkungen zum 'Kriterium des Politischen' bei Carl Schmitt," *Der Staat* 25 (1986), 397.

35. Carl Schmitt, *The Concept of the Political*, 57: "Should that interest group also want to become cultural, ideological, or otherwise more ambitious, and yet remain strictly nonpolitical, then it would be a neutral consumer or producer co-operative moving between the poles of ethics and economics. It would know neither state nor kingdom nor empire, neither protection nor obedience, and would altogether lose its political character."

36. Schmitt, *La Unidad del Mundo*, 16–17: "Not every well-functioning, centralized organization is the ideal of human order. It must not be forgotten that the ideal unity also applies for the kingdom of the Good Shepherd, but not for every human organization. Abstract unity, as

such, can lead to a surplus of good or of evil. Even Satan's kingdom is a unity, and Christ himself, speaking of the devil and of Beelzebub, took evil's unity for granted."

37. Carl Schmitt, *The Concept of the Political*, 57.

38. Schmitt, *La Unidad del Mundo*, 32.

39. Schmitt, *La Unidad del Mundo*, 21: "If unity in itself is a good thing, then duality in itself is evil and dangerous. 'Binarius numerus infamis,' says St. Thomas Aquinas. The duality of the modern world (1952) is effectively evil and dangerous. This tension is unbearable to all, as an unsustainable state of transition. The unbearable dualistic tension urges a decision."

40. Schmitt, *La Unidad del Mundo*, 24: "The odd numbers (three, five, etc.) are preferable over even numbers because they make balancing easier. It is quite possible that the current duality of the world is closer to a plurality than to a definitive unity and that the forecasts of 'one world' are too hasty."

41. Schmitt, *Constitutional Theory*, 381: "This international legal community is not a contract, nor is it based on a contract. It is also not an alliance and still less a federation. It does not have a constitution in the distinctive sense. It is, instead, the reflex of the politically plural universe, which expresses itself in individual, generally recognized rules and considerations. In other words, it is a pluralistic universe understood as a multitude of political unities that exist alongside one another."

42. Carl Schmitt, "Die Raumrevolution: Durch den totalen Krieg zu einem totalen Frieden," *Das Reich* 19 (1940), 29 Sept., 1940: "The only value of the Versailles experiment is that of negative knowledge: there is no peace in Europe without a European spatial order. There can only be peace in the spatial dimensions and economic structure of the large area that corresponds to this time."

43. Carl Schmitt, "Die Raumrevolution": "In reality, large space can only be an area of freedom for the people and broad autonomy and decentralization. Only then is there peace."

44. Carl Schmitt, *Völkerrechtliche Großraumordnung mit Interventionsverbot für raumfremde Mächte: Ein Beitrag zum Reichsbegriff im Völkerrecht* (Berlin/Wien/Leipzig: Deutscher Rechtsverlag, 1941), 36–37: "Only until large spaces of international law are recognized, prohibiting the intervention of foreign powers and the sun sets on the idea of an empire, can a bounded coexistence be thought of in a distributed land, and the principle of nonintervention can develop its ordering effect on a new international law." Also in Carl Schmitt, "Raum und Großraum im Völkerrecht," *Zeitschrift für Völkerrecht* 24 (1941), 145–79, in note 204 he added: "While 'space' retains its general, neutral, physical-mathematical meaning, for us 'large space' is a current, particular, historical-political concept. The source and origin of the term 'large space' rests, not at the state level, but at the technical, industrial, economic and organizational levels."

45. Schmitt, *Völkerrechtliche Großraumordnung*, 47: "Today, we think in terms of 'global' and large spaces."

46. Schmitt, *Völkerrechtliche Großraumordnung*, 47.

47. Schmitt, *Völkerrechtliche Großraumordnung*, 5: "Above the abstract and general concept of State and its territorial representations, I think it is necessary to present the following ideas to the science of international law: the specific concept of large space and, ordered towards this, the concept of a principle of large space in international law." Günter Maschke, keeping in mind Schmitt's practical supposed intentions, more than the text, stated that the central idea in Schmitt is, however, Germany's hegemonic power. *Aussprache* in Jean L. Feuerbach, "La theorie du 'Großraum' chez Carl Schmitt," in *Complexio Oppositorum: Über Carl Schmitt*, ed. H. Quaritsch (Berlin: Duncker & Humblot, 1988), 421. Also in Günter Maschke, *Der Tod des Carl Schmitt* (Wien: Karolinger Verlag, 1987), 30. Volker Neumann also defends this thesis in his book, *Der Staat im Bürgerkrieg: Kontinuität und Wendung des Staatsbegriffs in der politischen Theorie Carl Schmitt* (Frankfurt/New York: Campus Verlag, 1980), 421.

48. Thus he indicated, for example, how it does not allow for some types of relationships that, nevertheless, enrich international law: "The possibility of real borders (not just inter-State) 'divided-zones' or 'divided-borders' is shut off from territorial thought linked to the State." Schmitt, *Völkerrechtliche Großraumordnung*, 40. And also: "The State cannot go beyond the alternative between inter-State and intra-State relations. This rests on the decisionist structure

of the concept of State, which leads all specific questions of order regarding international law to a hopeless impasse." Schmitt, *Völkerrechtliche Großraumordnung*, 63. Also see Schmitt, "Raum und Großraum im Völkerrecht," 152. Schmitt described the specific issues that the concept of State in its evolution as political unity has created for Legal Science in Carl Schmitt, "The Plight of European Jurisprudence," transl. G. L. Ulmen, *Telos* 83 (1990), 35–70.

49. Schmitt, *Völkerrechtliche Großraumordnung*, 53. Schmitt, "Raum und Großraum im Völkerrecht," 153. He also referred to this in the article, Carl Schmitt, "Staat als ein konkreter, an eine geschichtliche Epoche gebundener Begriff," in *Verfassungsrechtliche Aufsätze*, ed. C. Schmitt (Berlin: Duncker & Humblot, (1958), 375–86.

50. Schmitt, *Völkerrechtliche Großraumordnung*, 41.

51. Schmitt, *Völkerrechtliche Großraumordnung*, 32: "Individualist liberalism and supra-national universalism are two polar-opposites of the same worldview."

52. Schmitt, "Raum und Großraum im Völkerrecht," 178: "The political antithesis of 'large space' is not 'small space.' That has long been outdated. The real opposite is universal govern-ment and its organizational aspirations."

53. Carl Schmitt, "Großraum gegen Universalismus: Der völkerrechtliche Kampf um die Monroedoktrin," in *Positionen und Begriffe im Kampf mit Weimar-Genf-Versailles, 1923–1939*, ed. C. Schmitt (Hamburg: Hanseatische Verlagsanstalt, 1940), 296: "The univer-salists were fanatics because they could not free themselves from the liberal democratic ideolo-gy of Western powers." Also Schmitt, "Raum und Großraum im Völkerrecht," 162–63: "An international law that surpasses State sovereignty, and with it, a legitimacy and guarantee of the 'status quo,' is derived from the market's power. It is not particularly European, as the French 'status quo,' but rather is universal." A sharp critique of Schmitt's international thought from the point of view of this ideological position that Schmitt's criticizes is William Hooker, *Carl Schmitt's International Thought: Order and Orientation* (Cambridge: Cambridge University Press, 2009). He tries to demonstrate that Schmitt's positions and concepts in this area repre-sent a failure.

54. Schmitt, *Völkerrechtliche Großraumordnung*, 66.

55. Feuerbach, "La théorie du Grossraum chez Carl Schmitt," 401–18.

56. On this point, Schmitt clearly indicated that: "The ideal of a global unity in which the world functions perfectly reflects the current technical-industrial way of thinking. We must not confuse this technical ideal with that of Christianity." Schmitt, *La Unidad del Mundo*, 17.

57. Comparing the State and the Church, Schmitt, in one of his earlier writings, stated: "The Church aspires to catholicism, with respect to the State; canon law theorists unanimously highlight that the State as such does not exist in any place, that there are only particular States that are the product of history." Carl Schmitt, *Der Wert des Staates und die Bedeutung des Einzelnen* (Tübingen: J. C. B. Mohr/Paul Siebeck, 1914), 44.

58. Carl Schmitt, "The Visibility of the Church: A Scholastic Consideration," in *Roman Catholicism and Political Form*, transl. G. L. Ulmen (Westport, CT: Greenwood Press, 1996), 51.

59. On this point, Schmitt put his theory of "Großraum" up against theories of dominating space in international law, which, despite taking space into account, are not concrete. Schmitt, "Raum und Großraum im Völkerrecht," 149. Schmitt, *Völkerrechtliche Großraumordnung*, 62: "The understanding of space as a two-dimensional surface, profound and superficial, corre-sponds to calling legal science a 'theory of space' even today. This equates the concepts of country, land, territory and region, without distinction, as State-sanctioned spaces in the sense that any of the cases can be considered empty space limited by borders. This conception transforms what is, for concrete order thinking, the home and farm into a cadastral area, turning natural regions into jurisdictions or districts, demarcations, spheres of competency or however they are now referred to."

60. Schmitt, *Völkerrechtliche Großraumordnung*, 7: "For our concept of large space, empty mathematically neutral space is surpassed, and in its place, a dynamic and qualitative magni-tude emerges." Also see Schmitt, *Völkerrechtliche Großraumordnung*, 61.

61. Schmitt, *Völkerrechtliche Großraumordnung*, 13 and 20.

62. Schmitt, *Völkerrechtliche Großraumordnung*, 20. Schmitt's notes on the United States of America, taken at a conference in Madrid in 1943, provide much insight on this point. RW 265-K8. Mat. 5.

63. Schmitt, *Völkerrechtliche Großraumordnung*, 22 and 30. Also, Schmitt, "Großraum gegen Universalismus," 297.

64. Schmitt, *Völkerrechtliche Großraumordnung*, 66. As an example that this concept—and, in general, all of the concepts that Schmitt brings to light—is not exhausted by its reference to a specific situation or a legitimization of current politics, is how a concept, born from historical reflection becomes independent, becomes a discursive category that conceptualizes any sociopolitical reality. For a National Socialist interpretation of Schmitt's theory of *Großraum* see Mathias Schmitz, *Die Freund-Feind-Theorie Carl Schmitts: Entwurf und Entfaltung* (Köln, Opladen: Westadt Verlag, 1965), 199–214.

65. Schmitt, *Völkerrechtliche Großraumordnung*, 5–7 and 20.

66. For the history of this concept, see: Schmitt, "Raum und Großraum im Völkerrecht," 146–47. In these pages, he cited Friederich Naumann—and one of his writings *Mitteleuropa* (1915)—as inspiration for this concept, though he did not actually use it in his work.

67. Schmitt, *Völkerrechtliche Großraumordnung*, 6.

68. Schmitt, *Völkerrechtliche Großraumordnung*, 7 and 65. Schmitt specifically referenced Viktor von Weizsäcker, *Der Gestaltkreis: Theorie der Einheit von Wahrnehmen und Bewegen* (Leipzig: G. Thieme, 1947). The term *Leistungsprinzip* appears in many places. One can establish links between this concept and Friedrich Ratzel's *Lebensraum*, who, as mentioned earlier, influenced Schmitt. Friedrich Ratzel, *Erdenmacht und Völkerschicksal* (Stuttgart, Alfred Kroner, 1940), 25. Although he does not mention this explicitly, he does quote Ratzel in Schmitt, *Völkerrechtliche Großraumordnung*, 67. However, Schmitt does not integrate this term in his own theory in its usual way. He always utilizes other terms, *Großraum*, *Leistungsraum*, which cannot be exchanged for *Lebensraum*. In Carl Schmitt, "Gespräch über den neuen Raum," in *Estudios de Derecho Internacional en homenaje a Barcia Trelles*, ed. C. de Miguel (Zaragoza: Universidad de Santiago de Compostela, Zaragoza, 1958), 264, he uses the term *Lebensraum* in an ironic manner. He even frees himself from the objection that this term typically sustains. He also uses it in short articles that serve as explanations of National Socialist legislation, for example in Carl Schmitt, "Die Nationalsozialistische Gesetzgebung und der Vorbehalt des 'ordre public' im Internationalen Privatrecht," *Zeitschrift der Akademie für deutsches Recht* 35 no. 4 (1936), 207. Thus, he refers to *Lebensordnung* as: "Ehe, Familie und Haus," meaning, marriage, family, and home; or, on the same page, as "Ehe, Familie, Eigen und Erbe," meaning, marriage, family, property, and legacy. What is common to all of these terms, and what interests us, is the idea of designating a particular space, that is to say, a qualified space. However, within the concept of *Lebensraum* there are connotations that do not appear in the description of the terms Schmitt used. It implies a Darwinian theory of struggle for life, which is essential in fighting for space and not just for biological organisms but also for State entities. Herder introduced the concept of *Lebensraum* to the field of politics—*Ideen zur Philosophie der Geschichte der Menschheit*—and it is closely related to the romantic and historicist concepts of the State within organicist thought. However, Schmitt is more of an institutionalist thinker than an organicist. Moreover, Schmitt displayed his differences with respect to the concept of *Lebensraum* characteristic of the National Socialist discussion. This is what appears in Carl Schmitt's responses to interrogations in Nuremberg on April 18, 1947. *Nachlaß* RW 265. K 61. Mt. 15. Also RW 265. K. 344. Mt. 9. The following is quoted from a fragment of a response to the question, *Wie weit haben Sie die theoretische Untermauerung der hitlerischen Großraumpolitik gefördert?* "I began with the concept of large spaces and negated the biological point of view and its arguments. Similarly, I avoided speaking of race, because that problematic word was totally reserved for Hitler. . . . The awareness of the question relative to the concept of space has, for me, been a criterion for the scientific orientation of the problem of large spaces." The following studies are also interesting: Joseph W. Bendersky, *Carl Schmitt: Theorist for the Reich* (Princeton, NJ: Princeton University Press, 1983) and "Carl Schmitt at Nürenberg," *Telos* 77 (1987), 91–129. In the former, the author made the following analysis: "Schmitt did not provide the theoretical foundations for Nazi foreign policy. Hitler had formulated his ideas long before a jurist he did not know had even thought about *Raumthe-*

orie, and Schmitt's concept soon met with sharp criticism from National Socialist theorists. The source of Hitler's expansionary policies was the racial doctrine of 'Lebensraum.' This concept, already inherent in *Mein Kampf*, had received further explication from racial theorists like Alfred Rosenberg and was reinforced by the writings of the nazified geopolitical school of Haushofer. At the heart of these theories were the biological concept of race and the goal of establishing a racial empire in Europe. Although Schmitt mentioned national groups, his concept has nothing to do with either biological racism or with 'Lebensraum.' He had essentially disregarded, let alone challenged, the 'Lebensraum' doctrine. He had advisedly stayed away from Nazi theories since his rebuke in 1936." Bendersky, *Carl Schmitt: Theorist for the Reich*, 259. This is similarly explained by Günter Maschke, *Zum Leviathan vom Carl Schmitt*, in his introduction to Carl Schmitt, *Der Leviathan in der Staatslehre des Thomas Hobbes* (Köln: Hohenheim, 1982), 206–7. However, Bernd Rüthers interpreted this as a quintessential National Socialist concept in his study *Carl Schmitt im Dritten Reich: Wissenschaft als Zeitgeist-Verstärkung?* (München: Beck, 1990), 83–92. However, as already commented, in my view, Schmitt is more institutionalist than organicist and the concept of *Lebensraum* utilized by National Socialism is more encapsulated within the organicist tradition.

69. Schmitt, *Völkerrechtliche Großraumordnung*, 61. Also Schmitt, "Raum und Großraum im Völkerrecht," 148–49.

70. Schmitt, *Völkerrechtliche Großraumordnung*, 64–65.

71. Schmitt, *Völkerrechtliche Großraumordnung*, 61.

72. Schmitt, *Völkerrechtliche Großraumordnung*, 36: "The concept of large spaces pertains to that of empire."

73. Schmitt, *Völkerrechtliche Großraumordnung*, 36.

74. Schmitt, *Völkerrechtliche Großraumordnung*, 45 and 53. Also " Schmitt, "Raum und Großraum im Völkerrecht," 177.

75. Schmitt, *Völkerrechtliche Großraumordnung*, 37. Also Schmitt, "Raum und Großraum im Völkerrecht," 178: "Large space remains an area of freedom and autonomy for its people. Only because of this is it superior to the forms of universalist government, and only by it is there peace."

76. Schmitt, *Völkerrechtliche Großraumordnung*, 48–49. Also Schmitt, "Raum und Großraum im Völkerrecht," 177.

77. Schmitt, *Völkerrechtliche Großraumordnung*, 67.

78. This was published in 1962 in the *Revista de Estudios Políticos*, no. 122. Only much later, in a 1990 German version, in a translation by Günter Maschke in *Schmittiana II*.

79. "Cambio de estructura en el Derecho Internacional," *Revista de Estudios Políticos*, June 1943, annex.

80. Carl Schmitt, "The New Nomos of the Earth," in Carl Schmitt, *The Nomos of the Earth in the International Law of the Jus Publicum Europaeum* (New York: Telos Press, 2003), 353. To Schmitt, this division appeared superficial in that both terms are relative to the position from which the description is made. Schmitt, "The New Nomos of the Earth," in *The Nomos of the Earth*, 353. Schmitt prefers this example to that of the contrast between land and sea.

81. Schmitt, *La Unidad del Mundo*, 20–22. Also Schmitt, "The New Nomos of the Earth," in *The Nomos of the Earth*, 354–55.

82. Schmitt, "The New Nomos of the Earth," in *The Nomos of the Earth*, 355: "The third possibility also is based in the concept of a balance, but not one sustained and controlled by a hegemonic combination of sea and air power. A combination of several independent Grossräume or blocs could constitute a balance, and thereby could precipitate a new order of the earth." On this point, we must remember what amity lines are: "These lines limit, in the case of the sixteenth century, a belligerent space for vicious power struggles, so that injuries to the law and the damages committed in said space, delineated by the line, are not cause for war between European colonial powers; their actions can disturb neither pacts nor peace." Carl Schmitt, *Völkerrechtliche Großraumordnung*, 57.

83. Carl Schmitt, "El Orden del Mundo después de la Segunda Guerra Mundial," *Revista de Estudios Políticos* 122 (1962), 19–38.

84. Carl Schmitt, "El Orden del Mundo después de la Segunda Guerra Mundial," 21.

85. Carl Schmitt, "El Orden del Mundo después de la Segunda Guerra Mundial," 23.

86. "Übernahme der industriellen Produktionsmitteln." Carl Schmitt, *Land und Meer* (Köln: Hohenheim, 1981), 71, in a note to the text. Schmitt described the new *nomos* of the earth in "El Orden del Mundo después de la Segunda Guerra Mundial," 33, as follows: "At the beginning of my lecture, I used the word *nomos* as the characteristic designation for the division and concrete distribution of the earth. If you ask me now, in this sense of the term *nomos*, what is the *nomos* of the earth today, I can clearly respond: it is the division of the earth in developed or underdeveloped industrial regions, along with the immediate question of who can give aid to whom in their development and who accepts this aid from whom in their development. This distribution is, today, the true constitution of the earth."

87. Carl Schmitt, "The Legal World Revolution," transl. G. L. Ulmen, *Telos* 72 (1987), 73–89, 79.

88. This trend comes to be the demise of the State, according to Ulmen, *Politischer Mehrwert*, 302.

89. Schmitt, "The Legal World Revolution," 79.

90. Schmitt, "The Legal World Revolution," 80.

91. Thus, Schmitt expressed his thoughts specifically referencing the moment after World War II in which there were two main world powers: "The political bottleneck that progress confronts within such Grossräume is overcome in the same way as in a federal State or confederation of States." Schmitt, "The Legal World Revolution," 80.

92. Schmitt, *La Unidad del Mundo*, 17–19. In the same way, in Schmitt, *Völkerrechtliche Großraumordnung*, 328, he affirmed: "The question is determined by the specific economic and industrial structure."

93. Schmitt, "El Orden del Mundo después de la Segunda Guerra Mundial," 34.

94. Schmitt, "El Orden del Mundo después de la Segunda Guerra Mundial," 35. In this way, Schmitt emphasized the responsibility of political power. Thus, in his "Theory of the Partisan: Intermediate Commentary on the Concept of the Political," transl. G. K. Ulmen, *Telos* 127 (2004), 68: "In today's clash between East and West, especially the gigantic race for the incommensurably great new spaces, it is above all a question of political power over our planet, no matter how small it may appear. Only he who dominates an earth that has become so tiny will be able to appropriate and to use the new spaces." Hence Quaritsch, *Positionen und Begriffe Carl Schmitt*, 114: "Hope: that was the first and last proposal of Carl Schmitt."

95. Quaritsch, *Positionen und Begriffe Carl Schmitts*, 36–58.

96. Schmitt, "Staat als ein konkreter, an eine geschichtliche Epoche gebundener Begriff," 385: "In the complicated system of organized interests, each group finds its lobby and lobbyists. The real question is: in which corner of this complex maze can one find a shelter for objective reason. Whoever understands that question will not be too quick to participate in the liquidation of the remains of the inherited State. It is also necessary to reflect on the fact that today the supporter of totalitarianism is not the State, but a party."

97. From concrete order thinking, the form of political unity, the State, appears as an institution and, while it exists, it is the institution par excellence. See Schmitt, "Raum und Großraum im Völkerrecht," 176.

98. Ellen Kennedy, "Politischer Expressionismus: Die kulturkritischen und metaphysischen Ursprünge des Begriffs des Politischen von Carl Schmitt," *Complexio Oppositorum: Über Carl Schmitt*, ed. H. Quaritsch (Berlin: Duncker & Humblot, 1988), 248: "The rise and fall of States as the organizing concept and the reality of European politics is the driving force in Schmitt's work." Ernst-Wolfgang Böckenförde also expresses the same opinion in "Der Begriff des Politischen als Schlüssel zum Staatsrechtlichen Werk Carl Schmitts," in *Complexio Oppositorum: Über Carl Schmitt*, ed. H. Quaritsch (Berlin: Duncker & Humblot, 1988), 293.

99. Carl Schmitt, *Ex Captivitate Salus: Experiencias de los años 1945–1947*, transl. A. Schmitt (Santiago de Compostela: Porto y Cia., 1960), 67ff.

100. Schmitt, *Ex Captivitate Salus*, 24. Schmitt describes the State of the twentieth century, in *La defensa de la Constitución*, 99: "The State transforms into 'self-organization of the society.' The usual distinction between State and society, government and nation, disappears, as has been indicated, from the moment in which all of the concepts and institutions (law, budget, administrative autonomy) that have been constructed on said premise, begin to bring new problems to light. But at the same time, a vast and more profound transformation is

happening. The organization of society into State: the State and society should be fundamentally identical; thus, all social and economic problems become political problems and no distinction between specific political-State and apolitical-social zones can be made. The society turned State, becomes an economic State, a cultural State, a State with foresight, a benefactor State, a philanthropic State; the State which results from society's self-organization cannot really separate itself from society, and it encompasses all things social, that is to say, all that is related to human nature." Also see Carl Schmitt, "Weiterentwicklung des totalen Staats in Deutschland," in *Verfassungsrechtliche Aufsätze* (Berlin: Duncker & Humblot, 1958), 361. Schmitt distinguishes between two types of total State. The one that we have just described is total in the quantitative sense. Everything becomes the State. There is another type of total State, which is a State in the qualitative sense, meaning that which has very intense, total means of exercising power. See Schmitt, "Weiterentwicklung des totalen Staats in Deutschland," 361.

101. Schmitt, "Staat als ein konkreter, an eine geschichtliche Epoche gebundener Begriff," 384: "That question constituted the main difference of opinion between Johannes Popitz and me for years. Even his last scientific-theoretical work, a 35-page typewritten manuscript, references a dispute with my thesis on the epochal dependence of the concept of State. Popitz states that the concept of State should be referred to as a concept with universal validity." This idea already appears in *Der Begriff des Politischen*, 1927, as we have seen, and it will be a constant in his later writings, *Völkerrechtliche Großraumordnung*, 1940, "Der Staat als ein konkreter, an eine geschichtliche Epoche gebundener Begriff," 1941, "Raum und Großraum in Völkerrecht, 1941, Ex Captivitate Salus," 1945, "El Orden del Mundo después de la Segunda Guerra Mundial," 1962, "Die legale Revolution," 1978.

102. Schmitt, "Staat als ein konkreter, an eine geschichtliche Epoche gebundener Begriff," 380. In Schmitt, *Völkerrechtliche Großraumordnung*, 59, he expresses this thought with even more clarity: "Die eigentliche Modernität jenes Zeitalters (16. Jh.) liegt nämlich darin, daß die raumrevolutionäre Veränderung des mittelalterlichen Weltbildes wie sie im 16. Jh. eingetreten und im 17. Jh. wissenschaftlich vollendet ist, uns eine Vergleichungsmöglichkeit bietet, um die heutige Veränderung des Raumbildes und der Raumvorstellungen besser und tiefer zu erfassen."

103. Schmitt, *The Leviathan in the State Theory of Thomas Hobbes*, 47: "A state is not a state unless it can put an end to that kind [state of nature] of a war." Also see, Schmitt, *The Nomos of the Earth*, 110–11; Schmitt, "Staat als ein konkreter, an eine geschichtliche Epoche gebundener Begriff," 376; *Carl Schmitt, Glossarium: Aufzeichnungen der Jahre 1947–1951* (Berlin: Duncker & Humblot, 1991), 19: "The State is essentially the result of religious civil wars and overcoming them brings about the neutralization and secularization of denominations, in other words, doing away with theology."

104. Carl Schmitt, "Reich-Staat-Bund," in *Positionen und Begriffe im Kampf mit Weimar-Genf-Versailles, 1923–1939*, ed. C. Schmitt (Hamburg: Hanseatische Verlagsanstalt, 1940), 191: "The concept of State destroyed the old empire." Also Schmitt, "Staat als ein konkreter, an eine geschichtliche Epoche gebundener Begriff," 375–76.

105. Schmitt, "Staat als ein konkreter, an eine geschichtliche Epoche gebundener Begriff," 380. Schmitt, *The Leviathan in the State Theory of Thomas Hobbes*, 71–72: "For Hobbes it was relevant for the state to overcome the anarchy of the feudal estate's and the church's rights of resistance as well as the incessant outbreak of civil war arising from those struggles by confronting medieval pluralism, that is, power claimed by the churches and other 'indirect' authorities, with the rational unity of an unequivocal, effective authority that can assure protection and a calculable, functioning legal system. To such rational state power belongs the assumption of total political responsibility regarding danger and, in this sense responsibility for protecting the subjects of the state." Also Schmitt, "Der Staat als ein konkreter, an eine geschichtliche Epoche gebundener Begriff," 377–78.

106. As an example of a non-State mode of thought, he used Santi Romano, who goes beyond the State mode of forming concepts. See Carl Schmitt, "Führung und Hegemonie," *Schmollers Jahrbuch für Gesetzgebung, Verwaltung und Volkswirtschaft im Deutschen Reich* 63 (1946), 517. He also expressed this idea in *Der Begriff des Politischen: Text von 1932 mit einem Vorwort und drei Corollarien* (Berlin: Duncker & Humblot, 1979), 10, Vorwort.

107. Schmitt, "Der Staat als ein konkreter, an eine geschichtliche Epoche gebundener Begriff," 376: "The emergence of the concept of State as a normal concept for the form of a political organization of all peoples and times will soon reach its end, along with the period of statehood. However, it is still present today and, hence, from the beginning, there has been no question regarding the historical-concrete and specific character of the concept of State as a representation of the political order linked to European history from the sixteenth to the twentieth centuries."

108. Schmitt, *The Concept of the Political*, 20: "In one way or another 'political' is generally juxtaposed to 'state' or at least is brought into relation with it. The state thus appears as something political, the political as something pertaining to the state—obviously an unsatisfactory circle."

109. There are many criticisms in this regard. To name a few: Christian Meier, "Zu Carl Schmitts Begriffsbildung. Das Politische und der Nomos," in *Complexio Oppositorum: Über Carl Schmitt*, ed. H. Quaritsch (Berlin: Duncker & Humblot, 1988), 539. Heinz Laufer, "Homo homini homo: Das anthropologisches Glaubensbekenntnis eines Doktrinärs," *Politische Ordnung und menschliche Existenz: Festgabe für Erich Voegelin zum 60. Geburtstag*, ed. A. Dempf, H. Arendt, und J. Engel-Hansi (München: C. H. Beck, 1962), 320–42. Böckenförde, "Der Schlüssel zum staatsrechtlichen Werk Carl Schmitts," 293. Rüdiger Kramme, *Helmuth Plessner und Carl Schmitt: Eine historische Fallstudie zum Verhältnis von Anthropologie und Politik in der deutschen Philosophie der zwanziger Jahre* (Berlin: Duncker & Humblot, 1989), 195. The thesis that Adam attempts to prove is featured in, *Rekonstruktion des Politischen* and follows along the same vein.

110. Schmitt, *Constitutional Theory*, 169. He makes it clear that although in *Constitutional Theory* he speaks of the bourgeois *Rechtsstaat*, that affirmation can be applied to any form of political unity, whatever it may be. On the other hand, there is an implicit claim that any State action—of the form of political unity—is political. This claim also appears in Schmitt, *Constitutional Theory*, 178: "For nothing that affects the State can be nonpolitical." With this statement, Schmitt situates himself on a formal, rather than material, level. Because of their object, State decisions are specified as economic, juridical, and so on. However, because of their intentions, they are always political.

111. Carl Schmitt, "Das Problem der innerpolitischen Neutralität des Staates," in *Verfassungsrechtliche Aufsätze*, ed. C. Schmitt (Berlin: Duncker & Humblot, 1958), 57.

112. Schmitt spoke clearest on the State in the following quotes: Schmitt, *The Concept of the Political*, 19: "In its literal sense and in its historical appearance the state is a specific entity of a people." Also Schmitt, *Constitutional Theory*, 239. Schmitt aptly relates the concepts of form, unity, and being. All unity is form and vice-versa, but additionally, all being has form. Thus, every political form is a unity and being. There must always be a relationship between these elements. With regard to this quote, it must be noted that by considering the people as the subject of State determination, he finds himself within a system of modern constitutionalism. Schmitt, *Constitutional Theory*, 100–101. Schmitt, "Der Staat als ein konkreter, an eine geschichtliche Epoche gebundener Begriff," 379. Schmitt, *The Nomos of the Earth*, 140–210.

113. Carl Schmitt, "Die vollendete Reformation: Bemerkungen und Hinweise zu neuen Leviathan Interpretationen," *Der Staat* 4 (1965), 61: "(The most important question with regard to Hobbes is) his place in the so-called process of secularization, progressive de-Christianization and de-divinization of public life." Ulmen provided interesting insight in Gary L. Ulmen, "Politische Theologie und politische Ökonomie," in *Complexio Oppositorum: Über Carl Schmitt*, ed. H. Quaritsch (Berlin: Duncker & Humblot, 1988), 343: "According to Schmitt, Hobbes found a conceptual and political systematic alternative to the decision-making monopoly of the Catholic Church, and thus ended the Reformation. More precisely: Hobbes was able to recognize that any dispute between the spiritual-ecclesiastical and worldly-political in the present is always a political struggle which radicalizes until posing the question of self-affirmation."

114. Schmitt, *The Leviathan in the State Theory of Thomas Hobbes*, 37: "The decisive step occurred when the state was conceived as a product of human calculation. Everything else—for example, the development from the clock mechanism to the steam engine, to the electric motor, to technical or biological processes—are the results of the evolution of technology and scientif-

ic thinking and do not require any new metaphysical resolution." Schmitt viewed the history of State Mechanicalism in the Cartesian conception of the body as a machine. A model of "total State." Carl Schmitt, "Der Staat als Mechanismus bei Hobbes und Descartes," *Archiv für Rechts- und Sozialphilosophie* 30, no. 4 (1937), 622–32. On occasion, he rescued Hobbes's thought from falling into Mechanicalism. See Schmitt, "Die vollendete Reformation," 64.

115. Schmitt, *The Leviathan in the State Theory of Thomas Hobbes*, 50: "In view of such technically complete armatures, the question of right and wrong breaks down. . . . Considering the leviathan as a great command mechanism of just or unjust states would ultimately be the same as 'discriminating' between just and unjust machines."

116. Schmitt, *The Leviathan in the State Theory of Thomas Hobbes*, 56: "on the basis of universal freedom of thought—*quia cogitatio omnis libera est*—he leaves to the individual's private reason whether to believe or not to believe and to preserve his own *judicium* in his heart, *intra pectus suum*. But as soon as it comes to public confession of faith, private judgment ceases and the sovereign decides about the true and the false." Schmitt's theory is developed by Reinhart Koselleck, *Critique and Crisis: Enlightenment and the Pathogenesis of Modern Society* (Cambridge, MA: MIT Press, 1988) by means of a conversation with Schmitt.

117. Schmitt, *Constitutional Theory*, 198: "Religion as the highest and the absolute thing becomes the affair of the individual. Everything else, every type of social formation, church as well as State, becomes something relative, and it can derive its value only as a means of assistance of every absolute value, which is alone definitive."

118. Schmitt, *The Leviathan in the State Theory of Thomas Hobbes*, 61.

119. Schmitt, *The Leviathan in the State Theory of Thomas Hobbes*, 61: "But when public power wants to be only public, when state and confession drive inner believe into the private domain, then the soul of a people betakes itself on the 'secret road' that leads inward. Then grows the counterforce of silence and stillness. At precisely the moment when the distinction between inner and outer is recognized, the superiority of the inner over the outer and thereby that of the private over the public is resolved."

120. Schmitt, "Führung und Hegemonie," 7. On this point, Peterson makes a direct criticism of Schmitt, which is of interest because it clearly includes Schmitt in the process of secularization. Thus, he stated in a letter on July 13, 1938: "[T]he controversy regarding 'indirect potestas' can only be understood when one has given up being a Christian and converted to paganism." Quoted in Barbara Nichtweiß, *Erik Peterson: Neue Sicht auf Leben und Werk* (Freiburg: Herder, 1992), 735.

121. Schmitt, "Coloquio sobre el poder y el acceso al poderoso," 11: "The process of forming the anteroom of which we speak develops through infinitesimal and minimal principles at every step, in the big and small, everywhere where men exercise power over other men. To the same extent that an area of power is brought together, an anteroom for this power is also immediately organized. Each increase of direct power thickens and strains the atmosphere of indirect influences."

122. This criticism is tied to the historical circumstances of the decadence of the Weimar Constitution. Carl Schmitt, "Der bürgerliche Rechtsstaat," *Abendland* 3 (1928), 201–3.

123. One must keep in mind, however, that although *Rechtsstaat* tries to hide this, this type of State is based on, and bases all of its Law, on one decision: "a decision in the sense of bourgeois freedom: personal freedom, private property, contractual liberty, and freedom of commerce and profession. The State appears as the strictly regulated servant of society. It is subordinated to a closed system of legal norms, or it is simply identified with this system of norms, so that it is nothing but norm or procedure. Despite its legal and norm-bounded character, the Rechtsstaat in fact always remains a *State*, so it still contains another distinctly *political* component besides the Rechtsstaat one." Schmitt, *Constitutional Theory*, 169.

124. Schmitt, "Der bürgerliche Rechtsstaat," 201: "With that, individual freedom is unlimited in principle, while the State and its powers are limited. It is the individual that grants power to the State."

125. Schmitt, *Constitutional Theory*, 181. Carl Schmitt, *The Crisis of Parliamentary Democracy*, transl. E. Kennedy (Cambridge, MA: MIT Press, 2000), 42.

126. Schmitt, *Constitutional Theory*, 187: "A logically consistent and complete Rechtsstaat aspires to suppress the political concept of law, in order to set a 'sovereignty of the law' in the

place of a concrete existing sovereignty. In other words, it aspires, in fact, to not answer the question of sovereignty and to leave open the question of which political will makes the appropriate norm into a positively valid command."

127. Schmitt, *Constitutional Theory*, 170.

128. Schmitt, "Der bürgerliche Rechtsstaat," 201: "This principle liberal defense runs throughout the entire organization of the State." At this point it is necessary to consider the question of whether or not one can continue referring to the *bourgeois Rechtsstaat* as a Modern State. Or if, actually, the State has taken a step toward its own dissolution such that the beginnings of its formation as a State can no longer be recognized. The latter corresponds to Schmitt's interpretation.

129. Schmitt, "Der bürgerliche Rechtsstaat," 201.

130. With respect to this point Schmitt, "Der bürgerliche Rechtsstaat," 201: "The bourgeois *Rechtsstaat* is a 'status mixtus' which consciously balances conflicting principles, not in the interest of political unity, but of individual liberty."

131. Schmitt marked a critical dimension of this description with sarcastic expressions. Thus he stated, in Schmitt, *Constitutional Theory*, 173: "The concept of the bourgeois Rechtsstaat receives a more precise sense if one is not just content with the general principles of bourgeois freedom and the protection of justice in general but, instead, sets up certain *organizational criteria* and elevates them to being the defining feature of the true Rechtsstaat."

132. Schmitt, *Constitutional Theory*, 174.

133. The ideal, for the bourgeois *Rechtsstaat*, is the general judicial configuration of the entire life of the State. But this idea is problematic. See Schmitt, *Constitutional Theory*, 176.

134. Schmitt, "Der bürgerliche Rechtsstaat," 201: "The two principles of the bourgeois *Rechtsstaat*, individual liberty and separation of powers, are apolitical. They do not pertain to a form of the State, but rather to organizational methods from within the State."

135. Schmitt, *Constitutional Theory*, 235, quoting Mazzini.

136. F. Tönnies enters the discussion with Schmitt on this point in Ferdinand Tönnies, "Demokratie und Parlamentarismus," *Schmollers Jahrbuch* 51 (1927), 1–44.

137. Schmitt, *Constitutional Theory*, 255–67.

138. Schmitt, *The Crisis of Parliamentary Democracy*, 9: "Every actual democracy rests on the principle that not only are equals equal but unequals will not be treated equally. Democracy requires, therefore, first homogeneity and second—if the need arises—elimination or eradication of heterogeneity."

139. Schmitt, *Constitutional Theory*, 248: "The danger of a radical implementation of the principle of identity lies in the fact that the essential presupposition, substantial similarity of the people, is misperceived. There is not really the maximum degree of identity. Certainly however, the minimum degree of government is present. The consequence is that a people regress from the condition of political existence into one that is subpolitical, thereby leading a merely cultural, economic, or vegetative form of existence and serving a foreign, politically active people."

140. Schmitt, *The Crisis of Parliamentary Democracy*, 26–27. Also Carl Schmitt, "Der Begriff der modernen Demokratie in seinem Verhältnis zum Staatsbegriff," *Archiv für Sozialwissenschaft und Sozialpolitik* 51, no. 3 (1924), 822.

141. Schmitt, *The Crisis of Parliamentary Democracy*, 13. Also Schmitt, *Constitutional Theory*, 257.

142. Schmitt, *Constitutional Theory*, 258.

143. Schmitt, *Constitutional Theory*, 266: "It is clear that all democratic thinking centers on ideas of immanence. Every departure from immanence would deny this identity. Every type of transcendence that is introduced into a people's political life leads to qualitative distinctions of high and low, above or below, chosen etc." Democracy is a "Weltanschauung": "And, if democracy really has nothing to do with a conception of the world, then it cannot achieve the 'perfect truth' of the State's personality, nor can it be more than a form of state among many in the context of political and constitutional techniques. Schmitt, "Der Begriff der modernen Demokratie in seinem Verhältnis zum Staatsbegriff," 823.

144. Schmitt, "Volksentscheid und Volksbegehren: Ein Beitrag zur Auslegung der Weimarer Verfassung und zur Lehre von der unmittelbaren Demokratie," in *Beiträge zum ausländischen*

öffentlichen Recht und Völkerrecht 2 (Berlin: W. de Gruyter & Company, 1927), 49: "A people remain in political and social reality to the extent that they exist as a people politically. Despite any decrease in competency, they always remain essentially a magnitude superior to individual determinations. In this sense, a quantitative minority can appear as a people and dominate public opinion when it has a genuine political will compared to a disinterested majority with no political will."

145. Schmitt, *The Crisis of Parliamentary Democracy*, 28.

146. Schmitt, *Constitutional Theory*, 271. There is a noticeable difference between Schmitt and Tönnies on this point. The latter defines democracy with the characteristic by which Schmitt claimed it invalid. See Tönnies, *Demokratie und Parlamentarismus*, 13.

147. Schmitt, "Der bürgerliche Rechtsstaat," 201–2.

148. Schmitt, "Der bürgerliche Rechtsstaat," 202: "Democracy today is a democracy without *demos*, without a people. The democratic principle requires that that a people responsibly decide and govern. However, the methods by which the present democracy seeks to establish a sovereignty for the people are not democratic, but rather liberal."

149. Schmitt, *The Crisis of Parliamentary Democracy*, 3: "It counts for a great deal that even today it functions better than other untried methods, and that a minimum of order that is today actually at hand would be endangered by frivolous experiments. Every reasonable person would concede such arguments. But they do not carry weight in an argument about principles. Certainly no one would be so undemanding that he regarded an intellectual foundation or a moral truth as proven by the question, What else?"

150. Schmitt, *Constitutional Theory*, 334.

151. Schmitt, *Constitutional Theory*, 329.

152. In *VII Deutschen Soziologentag*, in the discussion on "Presse und öffentliche Meinung," Schmitt was questioned on the concept of opinion. Schmitt responded: "It is my opinion that the specific word against 'opinio'—not contrary—, was anciently dogma or belief, but now after two centuries of bourgeois liberalism, it is action," in *Verhandlungen des Siebenten deutschen Soziologentages vom 28. Sept. bis 1. Okt.1930. Schriften der Deutschen Gesellschaft für Soziologie* (Tübingen: J C B Mohr, 1931), 56–59. Also see: Pasquino, "Bemerkungen zum 'Kriterium des Politischen' bei Carl Schmitt," 395.

153. Schmitt, *The Crisis of Parliamentary Democracy*, 11.

154. Schmitt, *La defensa de la Constitución*, 109: "[D]emocracy is destroyed when the axiom to which the defeated minority submits in advance of the outcome of an election (and does not seek to impose its own will) is invalidated. Therein, the minority recognizes the will of the majority as its own. Now, if in making these defeats impossible, the representation of minorities is organized by the system of proportional representation, it is important to be consistent, allowing for numerous parties, even the smallest, to be taken into consideration."

155. Schmitt, *La defensa de la Constitución*, 111.

156. Schmitt, *La defensa de la Constitución*, 112.

157. Carl Schmitt, "Reichs und Verwaltungsreform," *Deutsche Juristen Zeitung* 36, no. 1 (1931), 6, note 3: "A pluralistic, polycratic and federal construct, all at the same time—what a wretched empire!" Also Carl Schmitt, *Staatsgefüge und Zusammenbruch des zweiten Reiches. Der Sieg des Bürgers über den Soldaten* (Hamburg: Hanseatische Verlagsanstalt, 1934), 45–46. In Bentin's opinion, it is likely he took the term polycracy from Johannes Popitz. See: Lutz-Arwin Bentin, *Johannes Popitz und Carl Schmitt. Zur wirtschaftlichen Theorie des totalen Staates in Deutschland* (München: Beck, 1972), 91. For a criticism of pluralism, see: Thor von Waldstein, *Die Pluralismuskritik in der Staatslehre von Carl Schmitt* (Bochum: Bochum University Press, 1989), 52. There is a "democratic" critique of pluralism that, in some ways, is not far from Schmitt's thought. See Adam, *Rekonstruktion des Politischen: Die Krise der Staatlichkeit. 1912–1933*, 53.

7. PRECEDENTS OF THE POLITICAL THEOLOGY

1. Ernst Topitsch, "Kosmos und Herrschaft: Ursprünge der politischen Theologie," *Wort und Wahrheit: Monatsschrift für Religion und Kultur* 19 (1955), 19–30. Also, Hans Maier, "Politische Theologie? Einwände eines Laien," *Stimmen der Zeit* 183 (1969), 73–91.

2. Maier, "Politische Theologie? Einwände eines Laien," 76.

3. Saint Augustine, *City of God*, VI, 5. Álvaro d'Ors points out that this expression, as part of Sacred Science, first appeared in Panaetius of Rhodes. Indeed, in the *Placita Philosophorum* of Pseudo-Plutarch, Plutarch himself distinguishes the religion's preceptors: the philosophers, the poets and the legislatives. See Álvaro d'Ors, "Teología Política, una revisión del problema," *Revista de Estudios Políticos* 205 (1976), 41–79.

4. Maier, "Politische Theologie? Einwände eines Laien," 76.

5. Eusebius of Cesarea, *Life of Constantine* (New York: Oxford University Press, 1999).

6. Erik Peterson, "Monotheism as a Political Problem" (1935) in: *Theological Tractates*, Erik Peterson (Stanford, CA: Stanford University Press, 2011), 68–106.

7. Peterson tries to show the illicit way that political theology was practiced in ancient and medieval times, and concludes that the possibility of orthodox Christian Political Theologies should be liquidated. A discussion of Schmitt's *Political Theology* from 1922 was implicit in this short treatise.

8. Augustine, *City of God*, XIX, 17.

9. For an example of this, see the book of Martin Aurell, *Des chrétiens contre les croisades: XIIe et XIIIe siècle* (Paris: Fayard, 2013).

10. Takashi Shogimen, *Ockham and Political Discourse in the Late Middle Ages* (Cambridge: Cambridge University Press, 2007), 159ff.

11. Francis Oakley, "The Absolute and Ordained Power of God and King in the Sixteenth and Seventeenth Centuries: Philosophy, Science, Politics, and Law," *Journal of the History of Ideas* 59, no. 4 (1998): 669–90.

12. "Quae divina sunt imperiatoriae potestati non esse subiecta." San Ambrosio, *Patrologia Latina* 16, 1039 a.

13. Looking at these examples is difficult to support Victoria Kahn's thesis on the early modern period as a total break from the older form of political theology that entailed the theological legitimization of the State. Even if the contemporary revision of this epoch aims to view things otherwise, following the texts it is difficult to avoid this fact. See Victoria Kahn, *The Future of Illusion: Political Theology and Early Modern Texts* (Chicago: University of Chicago Press, 2014).

14. Carl Schmitt, *Political Theology: Four Chapters on the Concept of Sovereignty*, transl. G. Schwab (Chicago: University of Chicago Press, 2005). Although he did not invent this "name": Spinoza had already used it as an adjective in his *Theological-Political Treatise*. In any case, we find this expression in other minor treatises of that period, for example in Simon van Heenvliedt's Theologico-Politica Dissertatio (Utrecht: Jacob Watermam, 1662).

15. In this regard, see Michele Nicoletti, *Trascendenza e Potere: La teologia politica di Carl Schmitt* (Brescia: Morcelliana, 1990), 17–39, in the first part of "Un ponte sopra l'abisso: Le radici della Teologia Politica." Also Matthias Kaufmann, *Recht ohne Regel? Die philosophischen Prinzipien in Carl Schmitt Staatsund Rechtslehre* (Freiburg: Alber, 1988), 28; Álvaro d'Ors, "Teología Política, una revisión del problema," 41, 63.

16. In Ernst-Wolfgang Böckenförde's opinion, political theology is not an independent science, but rather, as Carl Schmitt understood it, is found within the framework of juridical research; it could be considered as an instance of political theory. He says as much in Ernst-Wolfgang Böckenförde, "Politische Theorie und Politische Theologie," *Revue européenne des sciences sociales* 19, nos. 54–55 (1981), 236.

17. Hans Barion, "Weltgeschichtliche Machtform? Eine Studie zur Politischen Theologie des II. Vatikanischen Konzils," in *Epirrosis: Festschrift für Carl Schmitt zum 65. Geburtstag* (Düsseldorf, 1953), II, 13–59.

18. José María Beneyto, *Politische Theologie als Politische Theorie: Eine Untersuchung zur Rechts und Staatstheorie Carl Schmitts und ihrer Wirkungsgeschichte in Spanien* (Berlin: Duncker & Humblot, 1983).

19. In our day, this is the case of John Milbank, "The Program of Radical Orthodoxy," in *Radical Orthodoxy? A Catholic Inquiry*, ed. L. P. Hemming (Aldershot, UK: Ashgate, 2000); William T. Cavanaugh, *Theopolitical Imagination: Discovering the Liturgy as a Political Act in an Age of Global Consumerism* (London: T & T Clark, 2002); Slavoj Žižek, Eric L. Santner and Kenneth Reinhardt, *The Neighbor: Three Inquiries in Political Theology* (Chicago: University of Chicago Press, 2005); Giorgio Agamben, *The Kingdom and the Glory: For a Theological Genealogy of Economy and Government* (Stanford, CA: Stanford University Press, 2011); Paul W. Kahn, *Political Theology. Four New Chapters on the Concept of Sovereignty* (New York: Columbia University Press, 2011); Michael Foucault, *Du gouvernement des vivants: Cours au Collège de France 1979–1980* (Paris: Gallimard/Seuil, 2012).

20. Carl Schmitt, *La Unidad del Mundo*, transl. A. Truyol y Serra (Madrid: Ateneo, 1951), 37.

21. "A historical truth is true only once." Carl Schmitt, "Gespräch über den neuen Raum," in *Estudios de Derecho Internacional en homenaje a Barcia Trelles*, ed. C. de Miguel (Zaragoza: Universidad de Santiago de Compostela, Zaragoza, 1958), 275, 280. This same statement appears many times throughout Schmitt's work. For example, in a letter from June 15, 1961, cited in Armin Mohler, "Carl Schmitt und die 'konservative Revolution,'" in *Complexio Oppositorum: Über Carl Schmitt*, ed. H. Quaritsch (Berlin: Duncker & Humblot, 1988), 145, as well as in Carl Schmitt, "Der Aufbruch ins Weltall: Ein Gespräch zu dritt über die Bedeutung des Gegensatzes von Land und Meer," *Christ und Welt* 8, no. 25 (June 23, 1955), 10. And in Carl Schmitt, "The Plight of European Jurisprudence," transl. G. L. Ulmen, *Telos* 83 (1990), 59, the same idea appears: "A historical truth is true only once. The concept of the historical is itself subject to transformations and reinterpretations; its realizations in various areas of intellectual life take many different forms."

22. Referring to Ferker, the founder of *Tagebüche*, he noted, "He has found, and this is essential, a contemporary form of religiosity within the reason of an exclusive positivism and within a faith without objective content." Carl Schmitt, "Die Buribunken," *Summa: Eine Vierteljahresschrift* 4 (1918), 98.

23. As proof of this thesis, Schmitt refers to the work of Reinhart Koselleck, *Critique and Crisis: Enlightenment and the Pathogenesis of Modern Society* (Cambridge, MA: MIT Press, 1988). See Carl Schmitt "Besprechung der Bücher von Max Weber: 'Gesammelte Politische Schriften' und von R. Koselleck: 'Kritik und Krise—ein Beitrag zur Pathogenese der bürgeliche Welt,'" in *Das Historisch-Politische Buch* 7, no. 2 (1959), 53, and 7, no. 10 (1959), 301–2.

24. Carl Schmitt, "Die geschichtliche Struktur des heutigen Weltgegensatzes von Ost und West," in Armin Mohler ed., *Freundschaftliche Begegnungen: Festschrift für Ernst Jünger zum 60. Geburtstag* (Frankfurt, Vittorio Klostermann, 1955), 151.

25. A. Mohler, "Carl Schmitt und die konservative Revolution," 144–45.

26. Each of his books is the fruit of this conception. They each represent a response to a concrete situation and some of them were even developed through dialogue with friends. Thus, for example, according to what Josef Pieper told me (in a September 1992 conversation in Münster), Schmitt explained what would later become his book *Land and Sea* in one or two hours. Indeed, Pieper was present at the telling. *Ex Captivitate Salus* was conceived as a series of letters personally addressed to the reader. The majority of his books are responses to the then contemporary political situation.

27. For thinking this opposition between philosophy of history and theology of history see Karl Löwith, *Meaning in History: The Theological Implications of the Philosophy of History* (Chicago: Chicago University Press, 1949). In his study of Schmitt's thought, Armin Adam notes how he manifests the road to secularization in the philosophy of history, in which the philosophy of history really comes to substitute eschatology, becoming theology itself. *Armin Adam, Rekonstruktion des Politischen: Carl Schmitt und die Krise der Staatlichkeit, 1912–1933* (Weiheim: V. C. H. Acta Humaniora, 1992), 38. The road toward secularization advances from the eschatological, going on to the theology of history to end in the Enlighten-

ment's creation, the philosophy of history. This is the same thesis that Löwith exposes in the cited book. He notes this in "Drei Stufen Historischer Sinngebung," *Universitas* 5, no. 8 (1950), 928. In this sense, it can be said that Carl Schmitt abandoned the "horizon of modernity," given that he reflected on history as theology of history.

28. Schmitt, *La Unidad del Mundo*, 32; and Carl Schmitt, "Tres posibilidades de una visión cristiana de la historia," *Arbor* 62 (1951), 237.

29. Schmitt, *La Unidad del Mundo*, 36: "That concrete irruption of the eternal in time; the framework of the divine in humanity is what made the singularity of the historical possible, as well as our idea of history."

30. Schmitt, "Drei Stufen historischer Sinngebung," 930.

31. Schmitt, *La Unidad del Mundo*, 36: "History is not a course of natural-scientific, biological rules and norms or of any other kind. Its essential and specific content is found in events that happen only once without repetition. Here, experiments or functionalisms are not valid, nor unreal conditional prayers that entertain combinations of what would have happened if this or that fact would not have happened. . . . Historic events happen only once and their uniqueness is destroyed by the philosophy of the history of rationalism."

32. Schmitt, *La Unidad del Mundo*, 36: "The singularity of human actions is only intelligible as it relates to the infinite singularity of the central events in Christian history."

33. Schmitt, "Tres posibilidades de una visión cristiana de la historia," 241.

34. "Christianity turned, in the proper sense, human being on his head. . . . [I]t simply directed man's view from the objectivity of the past to the future found beyond this world." Schmitt, "Die Buribunken," 104.

35. Carl Schmitt, *Glossarium: Aufzeichnungen der Jahre 1947–1951* (Berlin: Duncker & Humblot, 1991), 45: "For God, any future is something that has already been and what concerns us at present is like the light of a distant star which, despite its perceived light, has long been extinguished; it is like a light that keeps beaming."

36. Schmitt, "Tres posibilidades de una visión cristiana de la historia," 241.

37. Schmitt, "Tres posibilidades de una visión cristiana de la historia," 239.

38. Schmitt, "Tres posibilidades de una visión cristiana de la historia," 238. The German version of this book, Schmitt, "Drei Stufen historischer Sinngebung," 928, points to the idea that it is a commentary on Löwith's work. The two versions are not identical so I have used both.

39. Carl Schmitt, "A Pan-European Interpretation of Donoso Cortés," transl. M. Grzeskowiak, *Telos* 125 (2002), 107. Also Schmitt, *La Unidad del Mundo*, 34. In addition, Schmitt, "Drei Stufen historischer Sinngebung," 929. See Alexander Demandt, "Staatsform und Feindbild bei Carl Schmitt," *Der Staat* 27 (1988), 25. Also Schmitt, "Tres posibilidades de una visión cristiana de la historia," 238–39: "Despite all the Hegelian-Marxist-Stalinist dialectic of history, we effectively have no other means of historical self-understanding."

40. Schmitt, *La Unidad del Mundo*, 35.

41. *Katechon* is a central concept in Carl Schmitt's thought. It was also important in Augustine's *City of God*, XX, 19. Cited in multiple places, it is easy to detect the meaning that Schmitt intended for it. Thus, it appears in: *Land and Sea*, transl. S. Draghici (Washington, DC: Plutarch Press, 1997), 8, referring to the Byzantine Empire, which prevented the Arabs from conquering Italy, making the extermination of ancient and Christian culture impossible; Schmitt, *Land and Sea*, 43, referring to Rudolph II, the German king, who, rather than being an active hero, simply delayed and contained the Thirty Years War; Carl Schmitt, *Ex Captivitate Salus: Experiencias de los años 1945–1947*, transl. A. Schmitt (Santiago de Compostela: Porto y Cia., 1960), 35, 36, in discussing the religious idea contained in European action. Also Schmitt, *La Unidad del Mundo*, 34, 35 and Carl Schmitt, *Political Theology II: The Myth of the Closure of Any Political Theology*, transl. M. Hoelzl and G. Ward (New York: Polity Press, 2014), 92, in discussing the Christian Empire; in addition Schmitt, "Drei Stufen historischer Sinngebung," 929, or in the Spanish translation, "Tres posibilidades de una visión cristiana de la historia," 239. The idea of the Antichrist implicitly appears in this historical category. When the idea of *Katechon* faded out, the Antichrist appeared in the form of secularization, identified with secularism or secular humanism: this idea appeared in *Carl Schmitt, Theodor Däublers "Nordlicht": Drei Studien über die Elemente, den Geist und die Aktualität des Werkes*

(München: Georg Müller, 1916), 65 for the first time. It appears many times in Schmitt, *Glossarium*, 12, 30, and 63. One of the most well-known quotes is the following, which is noted here for the interest that it garners in trying to understand Schmitt's political universe: "On the *Katechon*: It is the only way for me to understand history as Christian and encounter its full meaning. . . . I would like to hear from you: who today is the *Katechon*? It cannot be considered Churchill or John Foster Dulles. . . . Its place has never been empty, otherwise we would not be here anymore," Schmitt, *Glossarium*, 63. Among those who have occupied the place of the *Katechon*, Schmitt elsewhere cited Hegel and Savigny and he explained why in the following line: "These two are genuine Katechon halters (*Aufhalter*) in the true sense of the word, both were halters who freely or even without free collaboration accelerated the function-alization without loopholes." Carl Schmitt, *Die Lage der europäischen Rechtswissenschaft*, in *Verfassungsrechtliche Aufsätze*, ed. C. Schmitt (Berlin: Duncker & Humblot, 1958), 429. There is no English translation of this note. A long reference to *Katechon* also appears where he summarized almost everything said on the matter in Carl Schmitt, "Beschleuniger wider Wil-len, oder: Problematik der westlichen Hemisphäre," *Das Reich* 19, no. 4 (1942). On the idea of *Katechon* in Carl Schmitt, Álvaro d'Ors, *De la guerra y de la paz* (Madrid: Rialp, 1954), 188–90 and 203. Also Hermann Schmidt, "Der Nomosbegriff bei Carl Schmitt," *Der Staat* 2 (1963), 98; Von Meden, *Ausprache zur*, Günter Maschke"Die Zweideutigkeit der Entschei-dung: Thomas Hobbes und Juan Donoso Cortés im Werk Carl Schmitts," in *Complexio Oppo-sitorum: Über Carl Schmitt*, ed. H. Quaritsch (Berlin: Duncker & Humblot, 1988), 227: "Clear-ly, for Carl Schmitt, *Katechon* is a key concept as far as I can see in this diary. Donoso Cortés had already outlined this concept in his discourse on dictatorship that Schmitt so admired."

42. Schmitt, "Drei Stufen historischer Sinngebung," 929.

43. Schmitt argues with historical examples: "The medieval kingdom of German lords his-torically understands itself as *Katechon*. Even Luther understood this, thus Calvin took a decisive turn by making the *Katechon* no longer the Empire, but the preaching of the word of God." Schmitt, "Drei Stufen historischer Sinngebung," 929–30.

44. d'Ors, *De la Guerra y de la Paz*, 189.

45. Schmitt, *Land and Sea*, 45.

46. This is what is present when Schmitt argues that any political decision is ultimately resolved in the decision for good or evil in the sense that it represents an approach taken (or not) to the coming of the Antichrist, the end times. Carl Schmitt, "Coloquio sobre el poder y el acceso al poderoso," *Revista de Estudios Políticos* 52, no. 78 (1954), 14.

47. d'Ors, *De la Guerra y de la Paz*, 195–99.

48. Schmitt, *Glossarium*, 63.

49. On this point, editions of *Der Begriff des Politischen* vary. In the 1933 edition, 45, Schmitt claimed, "It could be explained (the relationship between political theory and theologi-cal dogmas) because they are both essentially measured by an ontological-existential way of thinking; and also because of their common methodological presuppositions." In the 1932 edition, which he re-edited, Carl Schmitt, *The Concept of the Political*, transl. G. Schwab (Chicago: Chicago University Press, 2007), 64, he claimed: "The connection of political theo-ries with theological dogmas of sin which appear prominently in Bossuet, Maistre, Bonald, Donoso Cortés, and Friedrich Julius Stahl, among others, is explained by the relationship of these necessary presuppositions." See also Heinrich Meier in *Carl Schmitt und Leo Strauss und der Begriff des Politischen: Zu einem Dialog unter Abwesenden*, 64.

50. Schmitt, *Political Theology*, 36.

51. Schmitt, *Political Theology II*, 39–40.

52. Schmitt, *Political Theology*, 43.

53. Schmitt, *Political Theology II*, 83–84.

54. Schmitt, *Political Theology II*, 43–44.

55. Schmitt, *Political Theology II*, 85–86

56. Saint Augustine, *City of God*, XIX, 17.

57. Schmitt, *Political Theology II*, 97.

58. Schmitt, *Political Theology II*, 114.

59. Schmitt, *Political Theology II*, 115.

60. Schmitt, *Political Theology II*, 86: "The entire Christian eon is not a long march but a single long waiting, a long interim between two simultaneities, between the appearance of the Lord in the time of the Roman Caesar Augustus and the Lord's return at the end of time. Within this long interim, there emerge continually numerous new worldly interims, larger or smaller, which are literally between times. For even highly disputed dogmatic questions concerning orthodoxy often remain in doubt for generations."

61. *Der Begriff des Politischen: Text von 1932 mit einem Vorwort und drei Corollarien* (Berlin: Duncker & Humblot, 1979), 15, Vorwort. This Foreword has not been included in the English translation. Also Carl Schmitt, "Die vollendete Reformation: Bemerkungen und Hinweise zu neuen Leviathan Interpretationen, " *Der Staat* 4 (1965), 55: "Hood demonstrates that Hobbes was not anticlerical. It must also be stated that his famous mandate to silence theologians, during the time of the religious civil war, did not come from Hobbes, but from Albericus Gentilis." Also Carl Schmitt, *Ex Captivitate Salus*, 74: "Thus, the *jus publicum europaeum* was born from the religious civil wars of the sixteenth and seventeenth centuries. In the beginning there was a slogan pronounced against theologians, a call to silence, which a founder of modern international law directed towards theologians: *Silete theologi, in munere alieno*! Such was the cry of Albericus Gentilis regarding the controversy of just war. Even today, I can hear him shout." Also see *The Nomos of the Earth in the International Law of the Jus Publicum Europaeum* (New York: Telos Press, 2003), 158–59.

62. Schmitt, "The Plight of European Jurisprudence," 35–70. This study stems from a conference that took place in the following cities: Bucharest (1943), Budapest (1943), Madrid (1944), Barcelona (1944), Coimbra (1944), and Leipzig (1944).

63. Schmitt, "The Plight of European Jurisprudence," 44.

64. Schmitt, "The Plight of European Jurisprudence," 66.

65. Schmitt, *Ex Captivitate Salus*, 76.

66. Schmitt, *Political Theology II*, 115. Consistent with this approach, Helmut Willke describes the process of secularization, *Ironie des Staates: Grundlinien einer Staatstheorie polyzentrischer Gesellschaft* (Frankfurt: Suhrkamp, 1992), 25–26.

67. Schmitt, *Ex Captivitate Salus*, 79.

68. Carl Schmitt, "Die Rechtswissenschaft als letztes Asyl des Rechtsbewußtseins," *Universitas* 5, no. 5 (1950), 523.

69. Carl Schmitt, "The Legal World Revolution," transl. G. L. Ulmen, *Telos* 72 (1987), 73–89, 74.

70. Carl Schmitt, *Die Tyrannei der Werte* (Hamburg: Lutherisches Verlagshaus, 1979),19. And in Schmitt, *Ex Captivitate Salus*, 74–75: "The jurists leaving the Church was no secession to a sacred mountain, rather the reverse: an exodus from a sacred mountain to the realm of the profane. Upon leaving, the jurists took with them, openly or secretly, some sacred things. The State was adorned with things of mock ecclesiastical origin. The power of temporal princes was carried out with attributes and arguments of a spiritual origin."

71. Schmitt, *Die Tyrannei der Werte*, 21: "Values and a theory of values cannot establish legitimacy; they can only evaluate."

72. In the footnotes of Schmitt, *Political Theology II*, 142–43 (footnote 6, chapter 1 in the translation), Schmitt explains the temporal, thematic and systematic relationship that *Politische Theologie* (1922) has with *Politische Romantik* (1919), *Die Diktatur von den Anfängen des modernen Souveranitätsbegriffes bis zum proletarischen Klassenkampf* (1921) and the two final chapters of *Über die geistesgeschichtliche Lage des heutigen Parlamentarismus* (1923). All of these works are closely related to the concept of sovereignty. For more on this subject see d'Ors, "Teología Política: Una revisión del problema."

73. Schmitt, *Glossarium*, 80: "I will keep from speaking to theologians because I know the deplorable and poor luck of the great Donoso Cortés. It involves a total presence, hidden by history's veil."

74. Schmitt, *Glossarium*, 71: "May I speak of Catholic issues as a layman, not as a theologian? In order to be instructed, just as Donoso Cortés? 'Ubi nihil vales, ibi nihil velis.' Me, as a jurist, that is to say, a first-rate de-theologized scientist? Poor Donoso."

75. Schmitt, *Political Theology II*, 109.

76. Alfred Schindler und Frithard Scholz, "Die Theologie Carl Schmitts," in *Der Fürst dieser Welt*, ed. Jacob Taubes (München/Paderborn: Finck/Schöningh, 1983), 162.

77. Schmitt, *Political Theology*, 5.

78. Schmitt, "Die vollendete Reformation. Bemerkungen und Hinweise zu neuen Leviathan Interpretationen," 64–65.

79. Carl Schmitt, "Coloquio sobre el poder y el acceso al poderoso," 7: "Power is its own autonomous magnitude, even against the consensus it has created, and now I would like to show that it is also against its own power. Power is an objective magnitude with its own laws, in contrast to the human individual who, at a precise moment, can have power in his hands."

80. He says the same thing about Hobbes in Carl Schmitt, *The Leviathan in the State Theory of Thomas Hobbes: Meaning and Failure of a Political Symbol*, transl. by G. Schwab and E. Hilfstein (Westport, CT: Greenwood Press, 1996), 32–33. For Hobbes, God is above all power. In Schmitt, there is a common theme of a juridical-theological reflection on God that is in no way religious. Gary L. Ulmen also recognizes this distiction in " "Politische Theologie und politische Ökonomie," in *Complexio Oppositorum: Über Carl Schmitt*, ed. H. Quaritsch (Berlin: Duncker & Humblot, 1988), 362.

81. Carl Schmitt, "Coloquio sobre el poder y el acceso al poderoso," 14: "God is the highest power and the highest being. All power is from Him and is and remains in his essence, divine and good. If the devil had power, this power, in this way, it would be divine and good. Only the will of the devil is evil. However, even despite this evil, demonic will, power in itself remains divine and good."

82. Schmitt, "Die vollendete Reformation," 56 and 68; Schmitt, *Der Begriff des Politischen*, 122, Hinweise. Although in Schmitt, "Coloquio sobre el poder y el acceso al poderoso," 9 he recognizes that it is impossible for whoever holds power to totally free himself from indirect powers. When speaking to indicate the indirect power of the Church, he is attacking clericalism, in other words, an indirect power that tries to make itself immediately effective, as if it were direct without participating in its assumed responsibility.

83. Nicoletti, *Trascendenza e potere: La Teologia politica di Carl Schmitt*, 55.

84. Schmitt, *Ex Captivitate Salus*, 68–69: "Two names from the era of religious civil wars (Bodin and Hobbes) have become, for me, names of people, alive and present, names of brothers, to which I am related, regardless of the century. The invisible hand that guides us towards books, for the past thirty years, has taken me time and again to these books, and time and again has made me open the books in a significant place, even when I had not moved from the library. At the moment, I have nothing more than my memory. But both thoughts and formulations are as familiar as a brother's way of speaking and thinking. They have encouraged my thought and kept it awake when the positivism of my generation oppressed me and a blind cry of safety sought to paralyze me." Also see: Helmut Rumpf, *Carl Schmitt und Thomas Hobbes, Ideelle Beziehungen und aktuelle Bedeutung mit einer Abhandlung über die Frühschriften Carl Schmitts* (Berlin: Duncker & Humblot, Berlin, 1972).

85. Schmitt, "Die vollendete Reformation," 51.

86. Schmitt, "Die vollendete Reformation," 53: "Der Leviathan ist doch seit Jahrtausenden eines der stärksten Bilder der politischen Theologie und der theologischen Politik."

87. Schmitt, "Die vollendete Reformation," 53.

88. Schmitt, "Die vollendete Reformation," 52. Also see Jacob Taubes, " Statt einer Einleitung: Leviathan als sterblicher Gott: Zur Aktualität von Thomas Hobbes," in *Der Fürst dieser Welt. Carl Schmitt und die Folgen*, ed. J. Taubes (München/Paderborn: Finck/Schöningh, 1983), II, 9–15.

89. Schmitt, "Die vollendete Reformation," 56–64.

90. Schmitt, *Der Begriff des Politischen*, 122–23, Hinweise. This also appears in Schmitt, "Die vollendete Reformation," 63.

91. Schmitt, "Die vollendete Reformation," 61: "The epochal significance of Thomas Hobbes consists in that he conceptually recognized the purely political significance of the claim to spiritual decision."

92. Schmitt, "Die vollendete Reformation," 64: "He has realized that any struggle between the spiritual-ecclesial and the earthly-political becomes a political struggle at any moment." On this point, Schmitt's interpretation of Hobbes must be taken into account. It is clear that Hobbes

takes a decisive step toward secularization. He carries out (*vollendet*) the reform. However, his intention was not to secularize, but to reestablish order. Reality "called" for secularization if it wanted to return to peace. Thus Schmitt claims, "Die vollendete Reformation," 64: "[A] political struggle remains formal until the question of political assertiveness arises, such that the sharp differences between the spiritual, earthly and combination of the two ('res mixtae') have been decided, that is to say, until it responds to the formal question of: 'Who decides?'"

93. Carl Schmitt, "On the Counterrevolutionary Philosophy of the State," in *Political Theology: Four Chapters on the Concept of Sovereignty*, transl. G. Schwab (Chicago: University of Chicago Press, 2005), 53. Also Schmitt, "On the Counterrevolutionary Philosophy of the State," 55: "Such moral disjunctions represent contrasts between good and evil, God and the devil; between them an either/or exists in the sense of a life-and-death struggle that does not recognize a synthesis and a 'higher third.'" Also Schmitt, "On the Counterrevolutionary Philosophy of the State," 55: "[A]s far as the most essential issues are concerned, making a decision is more important than how a decision is made."

94. Schmitt, "On the Counterrevolutionary Philosophy of the State," 55.

95. Juan Donoso, "Ensayo sobre el catolicismo, el liberalismo y el socialismo," in *Obras Completas*, ed. J. Juretschke (Madrid: BAC, 1946), II, 504.

8. POLITICAL THEOLOGY

1. Carl Schmitt, "The Visibility of the Church: A Scholastic Consideration," in *Roman Catholicism and Political Form*, transl. G. L. Ulmen (Westport, CT: Greenwood Press, 1996), 51: "What rightly can be considered and perceived as human personality exists only in the realm of mediation between God and the mundane world. A man totally dedicated to God is as little an individual as one totally immersed in the mundane world. Individuality coexists only in that God keeps the person in the world. The person is unique in the world and thus also in the community. His relation ad *se ipsum* is not possible without a relation *ad alterum*. To be in the world means to be with others. From a spiritual standpoint, all visibility is construed in terms of a constitution of community."

2. Carl Schmitt, *Political Theology II: The Myth of the Closure of Any Political Theology*, transl. M. Hoelzl and G. Ward (New York: Polity Press, 2014), 109: "This is exactly what is at stake in my Political Theology. The scientific conceptual structure of both of these faculties [theology and jurisprudence] has systematically produced areas in which concepts can be transposed, among which harmonious exchanges are permitted and meaningful."

3. Schmitt, *Political Theology II*, 66: "Political theology is indeed a polymorphous phenomenon, and, moreover, there are two different sides to it, a theological and a political one. Each is directed to its specific concepts. This is already given in the *compositum* of the phrase. There are many political theologies because there are, on the other hand, many different religions, and, on the other, many different kinds and methods of doing politics. In such a twofold and bipolar field, a serious discussion is only possible when the arguments, questions and answers are precisely defined."

4. Schmitt, *Political Theology II*, 109. See Hans Maier's comment, "Politische Theologie? Einwände eines Laien," *Stimmen der Zeit* 183 (1969), 74. Also, Hugo Ball, "Carl Schmitts Politische Theologie," *Hochland* 21 (1924), 282, claims that ultimately political theology means that the question regarding the facts and the structure of the juridical and political system is ultimately always a conscious or unconscious theological issue.

5. On this point, there are scholars who label Schmitt as dogmatic, in the sense that he makes a statement that, like the reference to structural parallelism, is neither necessary nor verifiable. For example, José María Beneyto, *Politische Theologie als Politische Theorie: Eine Untersuchung zur Rechts und Staatstheorie Carl Schmitts und ihrer Wirkungsgeschichte in Spanien* (Berlin: Duncker & Humblot, 1983), 76. Others, for example, qualify this assertion as unquestionable or absolutely certain. Thus, Hans Barion, "Weltgeschichtliche Machtform? Eine Studie zur Politischen Theologie des II: Vatikanischen Konzils," in *Epirrosis: Festschrift für Carl Schmitt zum 65. Geburtstag* (Düsseldorf, 1953), II, 17. Also Mathias Kaufmann, *Recht*

ohne Regel? Die philosophischen Prinzipien in Carl Schmitt Staatsund Rechtslehre (Freiburg: Alber, 1988), 28. Also on this matter, see Ernst-Wolfgang Böckenförde, "Die Entstehung des Staates als Vorgang der Säkularisation," *Säkularisation und Utopie: Ernst Forsthoff zum 65. Geburtstag* (Stuttgart/Berlin/Köln/Mainz: Kohlhammer, 1967), 75–94.

6. Carl Schmitt, *Political Theology: Four Chapters on the Concept of Sovereignty*, transl. G. Schwab (Chicago: University of Chicago Press, 2005), 37.

7. Especially in *Der Wert des Staates und die Bedeutung des Einzelnen* (1914), *Politische Romantik* (1919), *Die Diktatur* (1921). Schmitt, *Political Theology*, 37–38.

8. The concept of secularization appears in Schmitt from his early works. See Michele Nicoletti, "Die Ursprünge von Carl Schmitts 'Politischer Theologie,'" *Complexio Oppositorum: Über Carl Schmitt*, ed. H. Quaritsch (Berlin: Duncker & Humblot, 1988), 109–28, and "Alle radici della teologia politica di Car Schmitt: Gli scritti jovanili (1910–1917)," *Annali dell'Instituto storico italo-germanico in Trento* (Bologna: Società editrice il Mulino, 1984), 256–316. Following Nicoletti, this concept undergoes a fundamental change from his first works to the last, in which it acquires its final meaning. The first time the concept of secularization appears is in *Der Wert des Staates und die Bedeutung des Einzelnen* (Tübingen: J. C. B. Mohr/Paul Siebeck, 1914), 81. The second time is in *Theodor Däublers "Nordlicht": Drei Studien über die Elemente, den Geist und die Aktualität des Werkes* (München: Georg Müller, 1916) where, in the opinion of Nicoletti, it acquires the meaning of: "a polarity, a parallel between historical and ontological dimensions." Nicoletti, "Die Ursprünge von Carl Schmitt 'Politische Theologie," 120. The concept openly appears outlined in "Die Zeitalter der Neutralisierungen und Entpolitisierungen," the conference published for the first time in *Europäische Revue*, 1929 and after was included in *Der Begriff des Politischen*. In these writings secularization appears as a reality that is historical-objective, not subjective. Nicoletti, "Die Ursprünge von Carl Schmitt 'Politischer Theologie,'" 12.

9. Thus Helmuth Quaritsch points out in "Carl Schmitt: Una introduzione," *Behemoth* 8 nos. 1–2 (1993), 28: "[I]n spiritual struggle, the possession of a concept is as important as the conquest of a fortress in war."

10. Carl Schmitt, "The Age of Neutralizations and Depoliticizations," in Carl Schmitt, *The Concept of the Political*, transl. G. Schwab (Chicago: Chicago University Press, 2007), 81.

11. Schmitt, "The Age of Neutralizations and Depoliticizations," 85.

12. Carl Schmitt, *Political Romanticism*, transl. Guy Oakes (Cambridge, MA: MIT Press, 1986), 99.

13. Schmitt, *Political Theology II*, 124.

14. Schmitt, "The Age of Neutralizations and Depoliticizations," 91.

15. Schmitt, "The Age of Neutralizations and Depoliticizations," 95.

16. Schmitt, *Political Theology II*, 128–30.

17. Schmitt, *Political Theology II*, 54.

18. Schmitt refers to this main thesis at many points. Thus, for example, among many others, Schmitt, *Political Theology II*, 42, 66, 109 and 148. Gary L. Ulmen, in *Politischer Mehrwert: Eine Studie über Max Weber und Carl Schmitt* (Weinheim: V C H, Acta Humaniora, 1991), 254–55: "Schmitt's political theory can be understood in a political theology sense, but placing both at the same level means falsely taking his method of analysis for what he is trying to prove with said method."

19. Hans Blumenberg, *Die Legitimität der Neuzeit* (Frankfurt: Suhrkamp Verlag, 1966). Jean-Claude Monod, *La querelle de la sécularisation: Théologie politique et philosophies de l'histoire de Hegel à Blumenberg* (Paris: Vrin, 2002) is particularly interesting to follow the discussion between Carl Schmitt and Hans Blumenberg on the topic of secularization.

20. Three of Schmitt's books—contemporary to *Political Theology*—show different analogies between the two realms and in some cases in both directions. In *Political Romanticism* (1919), 82–99, we find an analogy between the occasionalist God of Malebranche's metaphysics transferred to the romantic spirit and politics. In *Dictatorship: From the Origin of the Modern Concept of Sovereignty to Proletarian Class Struggle* (1921) (Cambridge: Polity, 2014), 34–79 we find the transposition of the papal *plenitudo potestatis* to the practice of royal commissars. In *Roman Catholicism and Political Form* (1923) he even evokes analogies between the two realms in the opposite direction. Carl Schmitt, *Roman Catholicism and Political*

Form, transl. G. L. Ulmen (Westport, CT: Greenwood Press, 1996), 18: "Church is the consummate agency of the juridical spirit of the true heir of Roman jurisprudence"; and Schmitt, *Roman Catholicism*, 19: "The Catholic Church is the sole surviving contemporary example of the medieval capacity to create representative figures."

21. In Graham Hammill, "Blumenberg and Schmitt on the Rhetoric of Political Theology," in *Political Theology and Early Modernity*, ed. Graham Hammill and Julia R. Lupton (Chicago: University of Chicago Press, 2012), 84–101, Graham Hammill points out the significance of Blumenberg's article "An Anthropological Approach to the Contemporary Situation of Rhetoric" in *After Philosophy: End or Transformation?*, ed. K. Baynes, J. Bohman, and T. McCarthy (Cambridge, MA: MIT Press, 1987), 454, from 1971 for a new and precise criticism of Schmitt. In this article, Blumenberg conceives rhetoric as a metaphorical practice: "a mode of understanding circumstances, events and problems by means of other circumstances, events and problems that seem to resemble them." What are described here are the Schmittian theopolitical analogies. Implicitly, he is admitting that Schmitt's political theology is pure rhetoric.

22. Blumenberg, *Die Legitimität*, 19: "Der Aufweis der Verwandlung, Umbildung, Verformung, Überführung in neue Funktionen einer identifizierbaren, im Prozess sich durchhaltenden Substanz."

23. As is the case of Ernst H. Kantorowicz, *The King's Two Bodies: A Study in Medieval Political Theology* (Princeton, NJ: Princeton University Press, 1997).

24. Blumenberg, *Die Legitimität*, 73: "Säkularisierung ist eine theologische bedingte Unrechtskategorie."

25. In his correspondence with Hans Blumenberg, Carl Schmitt advocates for continuity against discontinuity, since only continuity allows the juridic experience and juridic conceptualization. Alexander Schmitz and Martin Lepper, eds., *Hans Blumenberg, Carl Schmitt: Briefwechsel* (Frankfurt: Suhrkamp, 2007), 125: Letter of November 27, 1974.

26. This is the thesis that Victoria Kahn tries also to show, appealing to literature and art as a force for secular liberal culture in Early Modernity. Victoria Kahn, *The Future of Illusion: Political Theology and Early Modern Texts* (Chicago: University of Chicago Press, 2014).

27. See Paul W. Kahn, *Political Theology: Four New Chapters on the Concept of Sovereignty* (New York: Columbia University Press, 2011), 108.

28. Schmitt, *Political Theology*, 45.

29. Schmitt, *Political Theology*, 37–52

30. Schmitt, *Political Theology*, 47–52.

31. Schmitt, *Political Theology*, 38–42.

32. This also appears in: Jacob Taubes, "Statt einer Einleitung: Leviathan als sterblicher Gott. Zur Aktualität von Thomas Hobbes," in *Der Fürst dieser Welt: Carl Schmitt und die Folgen*, ed. J. Taubes (München/Paderborn: Finck/Schöningh, 1983), II, 9–15; Ball, "Carl Schmitts Politische Theologie"; Johann B. Metz, "Politische Theologie in der Diskussion," *Stimmen der Zeit* 184 (1969), 289–308; Alfred Schindler and Frithard Scholz, "Zum Ursprung politische Theologie. Einführende Bemerkungen," in *Der Fürst dieser Welt: Carl Schmitt und die Folgen*, ed. J. Taubes (München/Paderborn: Finck/Schöningh, 1983), 153–73; Wolfgang Hübener, "Carl Schmitt und Hans Blumenberg oder über Kette und Schuß in der historischen Textur der Moderne," in *Der Fürst dieser Welt: Carl Schmitt und die Folgen*, ed. J. Taubes (München/Paderborn: Finck/Schöningh, 1983), 57–76; Peter Koslowski, "Politischer Monotheismus oder Trinitätslehre? Zu Möglichkeit und Unmöglichkeit einer christlichen Politischen Theologie," *Der Fürst dieser Welt: Carl Schmitt und die Folgen*, ed. J. Taubes (München/Paderborn: Finck/Schöningh, 1983), 26–44; Maier, "Politische Theologie? Einwände eines Laien"; Hans Hirt, "Monotheismus als politisches Problem?," *Hochland* 35 (1937–1938) 319–24; Richard Faber, "'Nemo contra deus nisi deus ipse' Gegen Hans Blumenberg politische Polytheologie," in *Der Prometeus Komplex: Zur Kritik der Politologie Eric Voegelin und Hans Blumenberg*, ed. Richard Faber (Würzburg, Königshausen+Neumann, 1984), 75–87; Ernst Topitsch, "Kosmos und Herrschaft: Ursprünge der politischen Theologie," *Wort und Wahrheit: Monatsschrift für Religion und Kultur* 19 (1955), 19–30; d'Ors, "Teología política: Una revisión del problema"; Beneyto, *Politische Theologie als Politische Theorie*.

33. Erik Peterson refers to this meaning of political theology in "Kaiser Augustus im Urteil des antiken Christentums: Ein Beitrag zur Geschichte der politischen Theologie," in *Der Fürst*

dieser Welt: Carl Schmitt und die Folgen, ed. J. Taubes (München/Paderborn: Finck/ Schöningh, 1983), 175–80. Also Hirt, "Monotheismus als politisches Problem?," 323–24.

34. For example, Álvaro d'Ors, "Teología Política: Una revisión del problema," *Revista de Estudios Políticos* 205 (1976), 69, seems to indicate that this is one of the possible interpretations of Schmitt's text. Also Beneyto, *Politische Theologie als Politische Theorie*, 133–64. This is understood in another part of the same work: "Thus, religion is at the service of politics, political theology opens itself to theological politics." Beneyto, *Politische Theologie als Politische Theorie*, 81.

35. Koslowski, "Politischer Monotheismus oder Trinitätslehre?," 32.

36. Koslowski, "Politischer Monotheismus oder Trinitätslehre?," 32.

37. Ernst-Wolfgang Böckenförde, "Politische Theorie und Politische Theologie," *Revue européenne des sciences sociales* 19, no. 54–55 (1981), 237.

38. Koslowski, "Politischer Monotheismus oder Trinitätslehre?," 32.

39. Koslowski, "Politischer Monotheismus oder Trinitätslehre?," 33.

40. Böckenförde, "Politische Theorie und Politische Theologie," 238.

41. Böckenförde, "Politische Theorie und Politische Theologie," 236–37.

42. Koslowski, "Politischer Monotheismus oder Trinitätslehre?," 32.

43. Koslowski, "Politischer Monotheismus oder Trinitätslehre?," 34

44. Koslowski, "Politischer Monotheismus oder Trinitätslehre?," 34

45. Koslowski, "Politischer Monotheismus oder Trinitätslehre?," 35

46. Schmitt, *Political Theology II*, 109.

47. Koslowski, "Politischer Monotheismus oder Trinitätslehre?," 34.

48. Koslowski, "Politischer Monotheismus oder Trinitätslehre?," 32.

49. Koslowski, "Politischer Monotheismus oder Trinitätslehre?," 34.

50. Koslowski, "Politischer Monotheismus oder Trinitätslehre?," 35.

51. And referring to the *The Visibility of the Church*, he noted the following: "In my essay I do not talk about an affinity between the church and certain forms of political unity (monarchy or democracy). The essay defends the unique political form of the Roman church as the historical and visible representation of Christ." Schmitt, *Political Theology II*, 142. Summing up all of these statements together, it does not seem possible to speak of a secularization of eschatology in Schmitt.

52. Erik Peterson, "Monotheism as a Political Problem," in *Theological Tractates* (Stanford, CA: Stanford University Press, 2011), 68–106. Peterson based this book on two previously published articles: Erik Peterson, "Göttliche Monarchie," in Erik Peterson, *Theologische Quartalschrift* (1931), 537–64; and "Kaiser Augustus im Urteil des antiken Christemtums: Ein Beitrag zur Geschichte der politischen Theologie," *Hochland* (1932), 289–99. Newly published in Jacob Taubes, *Der Fürst dieser Welt* (München: Fink/Schöningh, 1983), 174–80.

53. Peterson, "Monotheism," 104.

54. Peterson, "Kaiser Augustus," 174. My translation.

55. Barbara Nichtweiss, *Erik Peterson: Neue Sicht auf Leben und Werk* (Freiburg, Herder, 1992), 724–36.

56. Nichtweiss, *Erik Peterson*, 736.

57. Montserrat Herrero, ed., *Carl Schmitt und Álvaro d'Ors Briefwechsel* (Berlin: Duncker & Humblot, 2004), 277. Letter without date, probably written between June and July 1976: "Mein lieber Freund Don Álvaro: nur einige Zeilen, um Ihnen zu danken für den meisterhaften Artikel über die politische Theologie. Ich verstehe Ihre Verbitterung angesichts der Oberflächlichkeit und allgemeinen Ignoranz, die Diskussion des Problems der 'politischen Theologie' beherrscht. Peterson ist ein skandalöser Fall; sein Buch von 1935 ist der Widerruf seines Vortrags von 1925; es ist eine Rückkehr zum Protestantismus in seinen pietistischen Ursprüngen und zum Bultmannianismus; es ist die Friedenserklärung mit Karl Barth und dem 'religiösen Sozialismus.' Das gesamte Problem Petersons entwickelt sich unter dem Zeichen des 'Skandals' Kierkegaard. Die Freude über die Rückkehr des verlorenen Sohnes (1930) war unmäßig; es gibt hier eine schockierende Parallele zum Fall Max Scheler. Der Minderwertigkeitskomplex der deutschen Katholiken war immens; es ist eine Tommissensche Verwechslung, von einem 'renouveau catholique' nach 1918 zu sprechen; es war das genaue Gegenteil. Der französische 'renouveau catholique' ist eine Antwort auf die *Séparation* und den

französischen kämpferischen Laizismus; das Aufkommen des Katholizismus von Weimar (1919) war im Gegensatz dazu eine Anerkennung der Römischen Kirche als verfassungsrechtliche Körperschaft! Und die *katholische* Partei, das 'Zentrum' war eine homogen *katholische* Partei und nicht wie die Christliche Demokratie, 'Parität.' 'Parität" ist die alte deutsche Tradition nach 1648 bis heute! Verzeihen Sie meine Eiferung, lieber Don Álvaro. Ihre Publikation ist auf jeden Fall ein gutes Werk."

58. Schmitt, *Political Theology II*, 122.

59. Eusebius of Cesarea, *Life of Constantine* (Oxford: Oxford University Press, 1999).

60. See Herrero, *Carl Schmitt und Álvaro d'Ors*, 45–54: d'Ors's letter from April 1, 1973: "Ich hatte seit einiger Zeit die Absicht, wiederum das Problem der politischen Theologie zu untersuchen, indem ich natürlich von Ihren alten und neueren Schriften ausgehen wollte, aber auch von anderen Darstellungen derselben Idee; zum Beispiel, Kantorowicz, *The King's Two Bodies*, dessen Untertitel gerade auf die mittelalterliche Politische Theologie anspielt. Ihr Buch hat als neuer Impuls gewirkt, mehr über dieses Thema zu lesen und zu schreiben." Herrero, *Carl Schmitt und Álvaro d'Ors*, 263.

61. Álvaro d'Ors, "Teología política: Una revisión del problema," in *Sistema de las ciencias IV*, (Pamplona: Servicio de Publicaciones de la Universidad de Navarra, 1977), 99.

62. d'Ors, "Teología política, una revisión del problema," *Revista de Estudios Políticos* 205 (1976), 96.

63. Schmitt, *Political Theology II*, 122–25.

64. Henri de Lubac, *Corpus Mysticum: The Eucharist and the Church in the Middle Ages* (Notre Dame, IN: University of Notre Dame Press, 2006). He was also friends with Peterson. Nichtweiss, *Erik Peterson*, 873.

65. William T. Cavanaugh, *Theopolitical Imagination: Discovering the Liturgy as a Political Act in an Age of Global Consumerism* (London: T & T Clark, 2002).

66. As Heinrich Meier supposes: Heinrich Meier, *Die Lehre Carl Schmitts: Vier Kapitel zur Unterscheidung Politischer Theologie und Politischer Philosophie* (Stuttgart, Weimar: J. B. Metzler Verlag, 1994).

67. Peterson, *Kaiser Augustus*, 174.

68. This critique is found in Schmitt, *Political Theology II*, chapter 3, 103–15. In reference to this criticism, see the work of Nichtweiss, *Erik Peterson*, and Nicoletti, "Alle radici della 'teologia politica' di Carl Schmitt: Gli scritti jovanili (1910–1917)." Also see Koslowski, "Politischer Monotheismus oder Trinitätslehre?" 27. Also Hirt, "Monotheismus als politisches Problem?" 323–24, criticizes Peterson very differently from the way Schmitt does. He does not attempt to recover his position, as in Schmitt's case, but to invalidate it with previous arguments from the Council of Nicaea. One of the reasons he uses to argue in his critique is that it cannot be said that there was a time in the history of Christianity in which monotheism did not imply a belief in the Trinity. The doctrine of the Trinity belongs to the ancient faith of the Church and, read strictly, cannot be made to defend a concept of God that might make sense for a ruler.

69. Schmitt, *Political Theology II*, 148.

70. Nichtweiss, *Erik Peterson*, 810, claims that Peterson's primary intention was to liberate Christian doctrine from the prevailing *Reichstheologie* and only indirectly to criticize Schmitt, who was not part of that movement. See also A. Dempf, "Erik Petersons Rolle in der Geisteswissenschaft," *Neues Hochland* 54 (1961–1962), 24–31. Quoted in Michael J. Hollerich, "Introduction" to Erik Peterson, *Theological Tractates* (Stanford, CA: Stanford University Press, 2011), xi–xxxi, xxv: "Arianism was a cipher for the political theology of Christians who had been bewitched by Hitler and his regime in its early days." Dempf thought that Peterson's war against Arianism was, in his final days, a war against Hitler's regime. In the end, Peterson's booklet was also, in Schmitt's opinion, a theo-political attempt to distance himself from Hitler's regime in 1935 under the mark of a "pure" theology. It is not easy to free oneself from the political consequences of every act, even in the case of theology, as Peterson's example shows. Schmitt, *Political Theology II*, 38: "This was seen then as contemporary criticism and protest; as a well-disguised and intelligently masked allusion to the cult of the Führer, the one-party system and totalitarianism. The book's motto contributed to that; it was a sentence by St. Augustine—'Pride too as has certain desire for unity and omnipotence, but in the realm of

temporal things, where all things are transient like a shadow—who warns against the false striving for unity which originates in the worldly lust for power." This sentence shows the extent to which Schmitt considered the motto of Peterson's work in the right sense and not in the sense in which Geréby, following Jacob Taubes, considered it. A rare hypothesis, impossible to prove, floats about that it was a message to his friend Schmitt to avoid the Nazi temptation. György Geréby, "Carl Schmitt and Erik Peterson on the Problem of Political Theology: A Footnote to Kantorowicz," in Azid Al-Azmeh and János M. Bak, *Monotheistic Kingship: The Medieval Variants* (Budapest: Central European University Press, 2005), 49. Geréby and Taubes were supposing that Schmitt used political theology to support Nazism in the same way that Peterson neglects political theology to avoid a relationship with it, but that was not Schmitt's idea in 1922. Moreover, Nichtweiss asserts that, given the fact that many of Peterson's writings are inspired by Schmitt's ideas, it is impossible that he primarily intend to criticize Schmitt in order to take distance from Nazism. Nichtweiss, *Erik Peterson*, 812.

71. Schmitt, *Political Theology II*, 42: "My own book *Political Theology*, from 1922, was known to Peterson through many conversations. The book does not deal with theological dogma, but with problems in epistemology and in the history of ideas: the structural identity of theological and juridical concepts, modes of argumentation and insights."

72. Michele Nicoletti holds the same opinion in his analysis of the Peterson-Schmitt discussion. M. Nicoletti, "Erik Peterson e Carl Schmitt: Ripensare un dibattito," in *Erik Peterson: La presenza teologica di un outsider*, ed. Giancarlo Caronello (Roma: Libreria Editrice Vaticana, 2012), 534.

73. Schmitt, *Political Theology II*, 38, 98–103. Peterson's views on this matter can be seen in G. Caronello's book, quoted above, as well as in Nichtweiss's book also quoted above; Roger Mielke, *Eschatologische Öffentlichkeit: Öffentlichkeit der Kirche und Politissche Theologie im Werk von Erik Peterson* (Göttingen: Vandenhoeck & Ruprecht, 2012). As Mielke asserts, Peterson confronted political totalitarianism with an apocalyptical concept and image of the church as an independent public sphere, which is mainly disseminated through worship.

74. Nichtweiss, *Erik Peterson*, 785. The theological situation of the Triniatrian dogma was, in the words of Hirt, as follows: "In particular, the decision of the Council of Nicaea, at the time of the Arian controversy, prohibited the future use of the dogma of the Trinity, which defines the essence of God, for the legitimacy of the Roman state, especially to justify Caesar's government. In short, it prohibited the use of faith and specifically the theory of the Trinity to justify a political purpose." Hirt, "Monotheismus als politisches Problem?," 310.

75. Schindler and Scholz, "Zum Ursprung politische Theologie: Einführende Bemerkungen," 154–56.

76. This is an error he thought he saw repeated at the beginning of the Nazi era in Germany. As mentioned in previous pages, Peterson's work, in Nichtweiss's opinion, was a position against the realization of such in the National Socialist German Reich. In July 1933, a "Sondertagung des katholischen Akademikerverbandes" was held in Maria Laach with the theme "Das nationale Problem des Katholizismus," which Schmitt attended. Peterson struggled against this movement. Nichtweiss, *Erik Peterson*, 811.

77. Schmitt, *Political Theology II*, 122–25.

78. Koslowski, "Politischer Monotheismus oder Trinitätslehre?," 35.

79. Gregory of Nazianzus's argument is an attempt to overcome the conceptions of the Trinity that were inherited from Neoplatonism, and it placed emphasis on unity and hypostasis. Against these emphases, St. Gregory's Trinitarian theory speaks of unity in multiplicity. However, we see that Schmitt forced this thesis because it does not have the markedly dualist character that he attributes to it and that he takes to the extreme relating this formulation with Goethe's aphorism and Lenz's fragment, "Catherine of Siena." Transcribed below is the central part of the exhibition of *Oratio theologica* III, 2 in the Latin version: "At nos unius principatum colimus; unius autem principatum dico, non quem persona una circumscribit (fieri enim potest ut quod unum est, si a seipso dissideat, secumque discordet, multa fiat), sed quem aequalis naturae dignitas constituit, et voluntatis consensio, motusque identitas, atque ad unum, eorum, quae ex ipso sunt, conspiratio (id quod in rebus procreatis fieri nequit), ita ut, etiamsi numero differant, essentia tamen et natura minime distinguantur. Quocirca unitas, principio in binarium mota, in Trinitate constitit," Migne, *Patrologiae Graecae*, 36, 76 A/B.

80. *Oratio theologica* III, 2. Schmitt, *Political Theology II*, 122.

81. Schmitt, *Political Theology II*, 122–23.

82. *El Sofista*, 249–54.

83. Schmitt, *Political Theology II*, 123.

84. Schmitt, *Political Theology II*, 123.

85. Schmitt, *Political Theology II*, 124.

86. In God there is no possibility for this friend-enemy distance. Gregory of Nazianzus's definitive phrase, which Schmitt used to support his political theory of enmity, is written in the conditional: "*(fieri enim potest ut quod unum est, si a se ipso dissideat, secumque discordet, multa fiat)*." He does not say that this happens in the Trinity, but that the condition of possibility for it to happen exists in the finite world. What is not real in God, however, is real in the reality created with the damage of sin.

87. Schmitt, *Political Theology II*, 124–25.

88. Schmitt, *Political Theology II*, 125

89. Schmitt, *Political Theology II*, 126. This refers to Goethe's text in book 20 of *Dichtung und Wahrheit* (Berlin: Deutsche Buch Gesellschaft, 1967), 665. As in Schmitt, *Political Theology II*, 126, also in Carl Schmitt, "Clausewitz als politischer Denker: Bemerkungen und Hinweise," *Der Staat* 6 (1967), 494, Goethe's quote is attributed to book 4 of *Dichtung und Warheit*, which again shows that Schmitt quoted from memory.

90. Momme Mommsen, "Zur Frage der Herkunft des Spruches 'Nemo contra deum nisi deus ipse,'" *Goethe-Jahrbuch: Vierteljahresschrift der Goethe Gesellschaft* 13 (1951), 97, 98. Also see, Carl Schmitt, "Clausewitz als politischer Denker: Bemerkungen und Hinweise," *Der Staat* 6 (1967), 478–502.

91. Jakob Michael Reinhold Lenz, *Werke und Schriften*, ed. B Titel and H. Haug (Stuttgart: Goverts, 1966), II, 435.

92. Schmitt, *Political Theology II*, 126–27.

93. Faber, "'Nemo contra deus nisi deus ipse': Gegen Hans Blumenberg politische Polytheologie," 76.

94. Hans Blumenberg, *Arbeit am Mythos* (Frankfurt Suhrkamp Verlag, 1979). The fourth part of the book is entitled: *Gegen einen Gott nur ein Gott*, 433–567. The most straightforward reference to Schmitt is on pages 578–604.

95. Faber, "'Nemo contra deus nisi deus ipse': Gegen Hans Blumenberg politische Polytheologie," 79.

96. d'Ors, "Teología Política, una revisión del problema," *Revista de Estudios Políticos* 205 (1976), 69: Carl Schmitt even introduced in the divine Trinity a seed of the political . . . the reduction of essential trinitarianism to a Hegelian dialectic dualism falls under a demonic parody of the Holy Trinity." And Beneyto, *Politische Theologie als Politische Theorie*, 101: "Thus, Carl Schmitt's political theology becomes a 'political Christology:' the structure of the unity-duality of the political modulates intra-Trinitarian 'stasiology,' that is to say, the enmity between God the Father and the Son of God made man."

97. André Doremus, "Théologie, politique et science dans la problématique de la théologie politique," *Cahiers Vilfredo Pareto: Revue européenne des sciences sociales* 16, no. 44 (1978), 58.

98. Schmitt, *Political Theology II*, 33. Schmitt's interpretation of political Christology is puzzling. Thus, different explanations are possible, some of which have already been mentioned. Ulmen expresses this in *Politischer Mehrwert*, 141–42.

99. See Ingeborg Villinger, *Carl Schmitts Kulturkritik der Moderne: Texte, Kommentar und Analyse des "Schattenrisse" des Johannes Negelinus*, (Berlin: Akademie Verlag, 1995), 171-191, in the *Schattenrisse* commentary on Wilhelm Oswald.

100. Schmitt, *Political Theology II*, 75.

101. Schmitt, *Political Theology II*, 123: "Even the sheer listing of numerous examples of such opposition provides a rich resource for the observation of political and politico-theological phenomena. At the heart of the doctrine of Trinity we encounter a genuine politico-theological *stasiology*. Thus the problem of enmity and of the enemy cannot be ignored."

102. Schmitt, *Political Theology II*, 128–29.

103. Schmitt, *Political Theology II*, 130.

104. Schmitt, *Ex Captivitate Salus*, 54.

105. Schmitt, *Ex Captivitate Salus*, 48.

106. Schmitt, *Roman Catholicism and Political Form*.

107. Schmitt, "The Visibility of the Church," 57: "The unity of God assumes the form of a legal succession in the historicity of a mediation through mortal man, because only in this way could it be made visible in time. One God. One Church."

108. Ernst H. Kantorowicz, *The King's Two Bodies: A Study in Medieval Political Theology*.

Bibliography

WORKS BY CARL SCHMITT

1907

"Berlin 1907." *Schmittiana I: Eclectica* 17, nos. 71–72 (1988), 14–20.

1910

Über Schuld und Schuldarten: Eine terminologische Untersuchung. Breslau: Schletter'sche
Buchhandlung, 1910.

1912

"Don Quijote und das Publikum." *Die Rheinlande* 22 (1912), 348–50.
"Der Wahnmonolog und eine Philosophie des Als-ob." *Bayreuther Blätte*, Juniheft (1912),
239–41.
Gesetz und Urteil: Eine Untersuchung zum Problem der Rechtspraxis. Berlin: Otto Liebman,
1912.
"Der Spiegel." *Die Rheinlande* 22 (1912), 61–62.

1913

"Schopenhauers Rechtsphilosophie außerhalb seines philosophischen Systems." *Monatsschrift
für Kriminalpsychologie und Strafrechtsreform* 10, no. 1 (1913), 27–31.
"Juristische Fiktionen." *Deutsche Juristen Zeitung* 18, no. 12 (1913), 804–6.
*"Schatterisse." Carl Schmitts Kulturkritik der Moderne: Texte, Kommentar und Analyse des
"Schattenrisse" des Johannes Negelinus*, ed. Ingeborg Villinger. Berlin: Akademie Verlag,
1995.

1914

Der Wert des Staates und die Bedeutung des Einzelnen. Tübingen: J. C. B. Mohr/Paul Siebeck,
1914.

1916

Theodor Däublers "Nordlicht": Drei Studien über die Elemente, den Geist und die Aktualität des Werkes. München: Georg Müller, 1916.

1917

"Recht und Macht." *Summa: Eine Vierteljahresschrift* 1 (1917), 37–52.
"Die Sichtbarkeit der Kirche: Eine scholastische Erwägung." *Summa: Eine Vierteljahresschrift* 2 (1917), 71–80. ["The Visibility of the Church: A Scholastic Consideration." In *Roman Catholicism and Political Form*, transl. G. L. Ulmen (pp. 45–61). Westport, CT: Greenwood Press, 1996.]

1918

"Die Buribunken." *Summa: Eine Vierteljahresschrift* 4 (1918), 89–106.

1919

Politische Romantik. München/Leipzig: Duncker & Humblot,1919. [*Political Romanticism*, transl. Guy Oakes. Cambridge, MA: MIT Press, 1986.]

1921

"Politische Theorie und Romantik." *Historische Zeitschrift* 123 (1921), 377–97.
Die Diktatur: Von den Anfängen des modernen Souveränitätsgedankens bis zum proletarischen Klassenkampf. München/Leipzig: Duncker & Humblot, 1921. [*Dictatorship: From the Origin of the Modern Concept of Sovereignty to Proletarian Class Struggle*, transl. M. Hoelzl and G. Ward. Cambridge: Polity, 2014.]

1922

Politische Theologie: Vier Kapitel zur Lehre von der Souveränität. Berlin, München/Leipzig: Duncker & Humblot, 1922. [*Political Theology: Four Chapters on the Concept of Sovereignty*, transl. G. Schwab. Chicago: University of Chicago Press, 2005.]
"Die Staatsphilosophie der Gegenrevolution." *Archiv für Rechts und Wirtschaftsphilosophie* 16 (1922) 121–31. ["On the Counterrevolutionary Philosophy of the State." In *Political Theology: Four Chapters on the Concept of Sovereignty*, transl. G. Schwab (pp. 53–67). Chicago: University of Chicago Press, 2005.]

1923

Die geistesgeschichtliche Lage des heutigen Parlamentarismus. München/Leipzig: Duncker & Humblot, 1923. [*The Crisis of Parliamentary Democracy*, transl. E. Kennedy. Cambridge, MA: MIT Press, 2000.]
Römischer Katholizismus und politische Form. Hellerau: Jakob Hegner, 1923. [*Roman Catholicism and Political Form*, transl. G. L. Ulmen. Westport, CT: Greenwood Press, 1996.]

1924

"Der Begriff der modernen Demokratie in seinem Verhältnis zum Staatsbegriff." *Archiv für Sozialwissenschaft und Sozialpolitik* 51, no. 3 (1924), 817–23.

"Romantik." *Hochland* 22, no. 2 (1924), 157–71.

1925

"Der Status quo und der Friede." *Hochland* 23, no. 1 (1925), 1–9.
"Besprechung des 'Essai sur l'emploi du sentiment religieux comme base d'autorité politique' von Marie-Anne Cochet. *Deutsche Literaturzeitung* 47 (1925), 2308–10.
"Illyrien: Notizen von einer dalmatinischen Reise." *Hochland* 23, no. 3 (1925), 293–98.
"Die Kernfrage des Völkerbundes." *Schmollers Jahrbuch für Gesetzgebung, Verwaltung und Volkswirtschaft im Deutschen Reiche* 48, no. 4 (1925), 1–26.

1926

"Der Gegensatz von Parlamentarismus und moderner Massendemokratie." *Hochland* 23 (1926), 257–70.
"Zu Friedrich Meineckes 'Idee der Staatsräson,'" *Archiv für Sozialwissenschaft und Sozialpolitik* 56, no. 1 (1926), 226–34.

1927

"Der Begriff des Politischen." *Archiv für Sozialwissenschaft und Sozialpolitik* 58, no. 1 (1927), 1–33.
"Donoso Cortés in Berlin." *Wiederbegegnung von Kirche und Kultur in Deutschland: Eine Gabe für Karl Muth*. München: Kösel und Pustet, 1927, 338–73. [Carl Schmitt, "Donoso Cortés in Berlin." transl. M. Grzeskowiak, *Telos* 125 (2002), 87–99.]
"Volksentscheid und Volksbegehren: Ein Beitrag zur Auslegung der Weimarer Verfassung und zur Lehre von der unmittelbaren Demokratie." *Beiträge zum ausländischen öffentlichen Recht und Völkerrecht* 2. Berlin: W. de Gruyter & Company, 1927.

1928

Verfassungslehre. München/Leipzig: Duncker & Humblot, 1928. [*Constitutional Theory*, transl. J. Seitzer. Durham, NC: Duke University Press, 2007.]
"Der Völkerbund und Europa." *Hochland* 25 (1928), 345–54.
"Der bürgerliche Rechtsstaat." *Abendland* 3 (1928), 201–3.

1929

"Der unbekannte Donoso Cortés." *Hochland* 27, no. 12 (1929), 491–96. [Carl Schmitt, "The Unknown Donoso Cortés." transl. M. Grzeskowiak, *Telos* 125 (2002), 80–86.]
"Die europäische Kultur im Zwischenstadium der Neutralisierung." *Europäische Revue* 5, no. 8 (1929), 517–30. ["The Age of Neutralizations and Depoliticizations." In Schmitt, *The Concept of the Political*, transl. G. Schwab (pp. 81–96). Chicago: University of Chicago Press, 2007.]

1930

Der Völkerbund und das politische Problem der Friedenssicherung. Leipzig: Teubner, 1930.
"Staatsethik und pluralistischer Staat." *Kantstudien* 35, no. 1 (1930), 28–42.
Hugo Preuss: Sein Staatsbegriff und seine Stellung in der deutschen Staatslehre. Tübingen: J. C. B. Mohr, 1930.
"Das Problem der innerpolitischen Neutralität des Staates." *Mitteilungen der Industrie- und Handelskammer zu Berlin* 28, no. 9 (1930), 471–77.

1931

Der Hüter der Verfassung. Tübingen: Mohr/Siebeck, 1931. [*La defensa de la Constitución.* Barcelona: Labor, 1931.]
"Die Wendung zum totalen Staat." *Europäische Revue* 7, no. 4, 241–50.
"Presse und öffentliche Meinung: Diskussionsbeitrag auf dem deutschen Soziologentag in Berlin." *Schriften der deutschen Gesellschaft für Soziologie* 7 (1931), 56–59.
"Reichs und Verwaltungsreform." *Deutsche Juristen Zeitung* 36, no. 1 (1931), 5–11.
"Freiheitsrechte und institutionelle Garantien der Reichsverfassung." *Rechtswissenschaftliche Beiträge zum 25 jährigen Bestehen der Handels Hochschule Berlin.* Berlin: Verlag von Reimar Hobbing, 1931.

1932

Legalität und Legitimität. München/Leipzig: Duncker & Humblot, 1932. [*Legality and Legitimacy,* transl. J. Seitzer. Durham, NC: Duke University Press, 2004.]
Der Begriff des Politischen. München/Leipzig: Duncker & Humblot, 1932. [*The Concept of the Political,* transl. G. Schwab. Chicago: University of Chicago Press, 2007.]
"Gesunde Wirtschaft im starken Staat." *Mitteilungen des Vereins zur Wahrung der gemeinsamen wirtschaftlichen Interessen in Rheinland und Westfalen* 1, no. 21 (1932), 13–32.

1933

Der Begriff des Politischen. Hamburg: Hanseatische Verlagsanstalt, 1933.
Staat, Bewegung, Volk: Die Dreigliederung der politischen Einheit. Hamburg: Hanseatische Verlagsanstalt, 1933. ["State, Movement, People: The Triadic Structure of Political Unity." In *State, Movement, People: The Triadic Structure of Political Unity,* transl. S. Draghici (pp. 3–54). Washington, DC: Plutarch Press, 2001.]
Carl Schmitt, "Reich-Staat-Bund." In *Positionen und Begriffe im Kampf mit Weimar-Genf-Versailles, 1923–1939,* ed. C. Schmitt (pp. 190–98). Hamburg: Hanseatische Verlagsanstalt, 1940.
"Völkerrechtliche Formen des modernen Imperialismus." *Königsberger Auslandsstudien* 8 (1933), 117–42. ["Forms of Modern Imperialism in International Law," transl. by M. Hannah. In *Spatiality, Sovereignty and Carl Schmitt: Geographies of the Nomos,* ed. S. Legg (pp. 29–45). Abingdon, UK: Routledge, 2011.]
"Machtpositionen des modernen Staates." *Deutsches Volkstum* 15, no. 2 (1933), 225–30.
"Frieden oder Pazifismus?" *Münchener Neueste Nachrichten* 86, no. 308 (November 11, 1933).
"Weiterentwicklung des totalen Staats in Deutschland." In *Verfassungsrechtliche Aufsätze.* Berlin: Duncker & Humblot, 1958, 359–71.

1934

Über die drei Arten des rechtswissenschaftlichen Denkens. Hamburg: Hanseatische Verlagsanstalt, 1934. [*On the Three Types of Juristic Thought,* trans. J. W. Bendersky. Westport, CT: Praeger Publishers, 2004.]
Staatsgefüge und Zusammenbruch des zweiten Reiches: Der Sieg des Bürgers über den Soldaten. Hamburg: Hanseatische Verlagsanstalt, 1934.
"Nationalsozialistisches Rechtsdenken." *Deutsches Recht* 4, no. 10 (1934), 225–29.
"Der Führer schützt das Recht: Zur Reichstagsrede Adolf Hitlers vom 13. Juli. 1934." *Deutsche Juristen Zeitung* 39, no. 15 (1934), 945–50.

1936

I caratteri essenziali dello stato nazionalsozialista. Panorama: Circolo Juridico di Milano, 1936.

"Die deutsche Rechtswissenschaft im Kampf gegen den jüdischen Geist." *Deutsche Juristen Zeitung* 41, no. 20 (1936), 1193–99.

"Die geschichtliche Lage der deutschen Rechtswissenschaft." *Deutsche Juristen Zeitung* 41, no. 1 (1936), 15–21.

"Die Nationalsozialistische Gesetzgebung und der Vorbehalt des 'ordre public' im Internationalen Privatrecht." *Zeitschrift der Akademie für deutsches Recht* 35, no. 4 (1936), 204–11.

1937

"Der Staat als Mechanismus bei Hobbes und Descartes." *Archiv für Rechts- und Sozialphilosophie* 30, no. 4 (1937), 622–32.

"Totaler Feind, totaler Krieg, totaler Staat." *Völkerbund und Völkerrecht* 4 (1937), 139–45.

"Der Begriff der Piraterie." *Völkerbund und Völkerrecht* 4 (1937), 351–54.

1938

Die Wendung zum diskriminierenden Kriegsbegriff. München/Leipzig: Duncker & Humblot, 1938.

Der Leviathan in der Staatslehre des Thomas Hobbes: Sinn und Fehlschlag eines politischen Symbols. Hamburg: Hanseatische Verlaganstalt, 1938. [*The Leviathan in the State Theory of Thomas Hobbes: Meaning and Failure of a Political Symbol*, transl. G. Schwab and E. Hilfstein. Westport, CT: Greenwood Press, 1996.]

1939

Völkerrechtliche Großraumordnung mit Interventionsverbot für raumfremde Mächte: Ein Beitrag zum Reichsbegriff im Völkerrecht. Berlin/Wien/Leipzig: Deutscher Rechtsverlag, 1939. [I have quoted by Berlin/Wien/Leipzig: Deutscher Rechtsverlag, 1941.]

"Großraum gegen Universalismus: Der völkerrechtliche Kampf um die Monroedoktrin." *Zeitschrift der Akademie für Deutsches Recht* 6, no. 7 (1939), 333–37. ["Grossraum versus Universalism: The International Legal Struggle over the Monroe Doctrine." transl. M. Hannah, in *Spatiality, Sovereignty and Carl Schmitt: Geographies of the Nomos*, ed. S. Legg. Abingdon, UK: Routledge, 2011.]

"Inter Pacem et bellum nihil medium." *Zeitschrift der Akademie für deutsches Recht* 6, no.18 (1939), 593–95.

"Der Reichsbegriff im Völkerrecht." *Deutsches Recht* 9, no. 11 (1939), 341–44. (Included in *Völkerrechtliche Großraumordnung.*)

"Neutralität und Neutralisierungen." *Deutsche Rechtswissenschaft, Vierteljahresschrift der Akademie für Deutsches Recht* 4, no. 2 (1939), 97–118.

1940

Positionen und Begriffe im Kampf mit Weimar-Genf-Versailles 1923–1939. Hamburg: Hanseatische Verlagsanstalt, 1940.

"Die Raumrevolution: Durch den totalen Krieg zu einem totalen Frieden." *Das Reich* 19 (September 29, 1940).

"Reich und Raum: Elemente eines neuen Völkerrechts." *Zeitschrift der Akademie für deutsches Recht* 7, no. 3 (1940), 201–3. (Included in *Völkerrechtliche Großraumordnung.*)

"Der neue Raumbegriff." *Raumforschung und Raumordnung* 11–12 (1940), 440–42 (Included in *Völkerrechtliche Großraumordnung.*)

1941

"Raum und Großraum im Völkerrecht." *Zeitschrift für Völkerrecht* 24 (1941), 145–79.
"Staatliche Souveranität und freies Meer: Über den Gegensatz von Land und See im Völkerrecht der Neuzeit." *Das Reich und Europa.* Leipzig Koehler & Amelang, 1941, 91–117. [First part corresponding with *Staat als ein konkreter, an eine geschichtliche Epoche gebundener Begriff.* In *Verfassungsrechtliche Aufsätze*, ed. C. Schmitt (pp. 375–86). Berlin: Duncker & Humblot, 1958.]
"Das Meer gegen das Land." *Das Reich*, March 10, 1941.

1942

Land und Meer: Eine weltgeschichtliche Betrachtung. Leipzig: Reclam, 1942. [*Land and Sea*, transl. S. Draghici. Washington, DC: Plutarch Press, 1997.] [I have also quoted the Günter Maschke edition, *Land und Meer*, Köln: Hohenheim, 1981, because of their *Nachbemerkung* and some interesting notes.]
"Beschleuniger wider Willen oder: Die Problematik der westlichen Hemisphäre." *Das Reich*, April 19, 1942.

1943

Cambio de estructura en el derecho internacional. Madrid: Instituto de Estudios Políticos, 1943.

1946

"Führung und Hegemonie." *Schmollers Jahrbuch für Gesetzgebung, Verwaltung und Volkswirtschaft im Deutschen Reich* 63 (1946), 513–20.

1949

"Maritime Weltpolitik: Besprechung eines Buches von Egmon Zechlin." *Christ und Welt* 2 (1949).
"Donoso Cortés in gesamteuropäischer Interpretation." *Die neue Ordnung* 3, no. 1 (1949), 1–15. [Carl Schmitt, "A Pan-European Interpretation of Donoso Cortes." transl. M. Grzeskowiak, *Telos* 125 (2002), 100–15.]

1950

Die Lage der europäischen Rechtswissenschaft. Tübingen: Internationaler Universitätsverlag, 1950. ["The Plight of European Jurisprudence," transl. G. L. Ulmen, *Telos* 83 (1990), 35–70.]
Ex Captivitate Salus: Erfahrungen der Zeit 1945–1947. Köln: Greven Verlag, 1950. [*Ex Captivitate Salus: Experiencias de los años 1945–1947*, transl. A. Schmitt. Santiago de Compostela: Porto y Cia., 1960.]
Donoso Cortés in gesamteuropäischer Interpretation: Vier Aufsätze. Köln: Greven Verlag, 1950.
Der Nomos der Erde im Völkerrecht des Jus Publicum Europaeum. Köln: Greven Verlag, 1950. [*The Nomos of the Earth in the International Law of the Jus Publicum Europaeum.* New York: Telos Press, 2003.]
"Existentielle Geschichtsschreibung: Alexis de Tocqueville." *Universitas* 5, no. 10 (1950), 1175–78.

"Die Rechtswissenschaft als letztes Asyl des Rechtsbewußtseins." *Universitas* 5, no. 5 (1950), 523–28.

"Das Problem der Legalität." *Die neue Ordnung* 4, no. 3 (1950), 270–75. ["The Question of Legality." In *State, Movement, People*, transl. S. Draghici (pp. 55–81). Washington, DC: Plutarch Press, 2001.]

"Drei Stufen Historischer Sinngebung." *Universitas* 5, no. 8 (1950), 927–31.

1951

La Unidad del Mundo, transl. A. Truyol y Serra. Madrid: Ateneo, 1951. [It was first published in Spanish, one year later in German, "Die Einheit der Welt." *Merkur*, 6 (1952), 1–11.

"Tres posibilidades de una visión cristiana de la historia." *Arbor* 62 (1951), 237–41. (Not identical with "Drei Stufen Historischer Sinngebung.")

"Justissima tellus: Das Recht als Einheit von Ordnung und Ortung." *Universitas* 6, no. 3 (195), 283–355.

"Recht und Raum." In *Tymbos für Wilhelm Ahlmann: Ein Gedenkbuch herausgegeben von seinen Freunden*. Berlin: Walter de Gryter & Co., 1951, 241–51.

"Raum und Rom: Zur Phonetik des Wortes Raum." *Universitas* 6, no. 9 (1951), 963–67.

"Dreihundert Jahre Leviathan." *Die Tat*, April 5, 1951. Also in *Universitas* 7, no. 2 (1952), 179–81.

1953

"Nehmen, Teilen, Weiden: Ein Versuch, die Grundfragen jeder Sozial- und Wirtschaftsordnung vom 'nomos' her richtig zu stellen." *Gemeinschaft und Politik: Zeitschrift für soziale und politische Gestaltung* 1, no. 3 (1953), 18–27. Also in *Rechtsstaatlichkeit und Sozialstaatlichkeit* 118. Darmstadt: Wissenschaftliche Buchgesellschaft, 1968, 489–504. ["Appropriation, Distribution, Production." In Carl Schmitt, *The Nomos of the Earth in the International Law of the Jus Publicum Europaeum*, transl. and annot. G. L. Ulmen. New York: Telos Press Publishing, 2003.]

1954

Gespräch über die Macht und den Zugang zum Machthaber, Günther Neske, Pfullingen, Württemberg, 1954. ["Coloquio sobre el poder y el acceso al poderoso." *Revista de Estudios Políticos* 52, no. 78 (1954), 3–20.]

"Besprechungen der Bücher von Ernst Sauer: 'Souveränität und Solidarität' und von Rudolf Bindschedler: 'Rechtsfragen der europäischen Einigung.'" *Das Historisch-Politische Buch* 2, no. 7 (1954), 217–18.

1955

"Der neue Nomos der Erde." *Lebendiges Wissen*, Neue Folge 2 (1955), 281–88. Also in *Gemeinschaft und Politik: Zeitschrift für soziale und politische Gestaltung* 3, no. 1 (1955), 7–10. ["The New Nomos of the Earth." In *The Nomos of the Earth in the International Law of the Jus Publicum Europaeum*, transl. G. L. Ulmen. New York: Telos Press Publishing, 2006.]

"Besprechungen der Bücher von Herbert von Borch: 'Obrigkeit und Widerstand: Zur politischen Soziologie des Beamtentums,' von F. J. P. Veale: 'Der Barbarei entgegen' und von Georg Schwarzenberger: 'Machtpolitik.'" *Das Historisch-Politische Buch* 3 (1955), 72; 200–201; 259.

"Die geschichtliche Struktur des heutigen Weltgegensatzes von Ost und West." In *Freundschaftliche Begegnungen: Festschrift für Ernst Jünger zum 60. Geburtstag*, ed. Armin Mohler (pp. 135–67). Frankfurt, Vittorio Klostermann, 1955.

"Der Aufbruch ins Weltall: Ein Gespräch zu dritt über die Bedeutung des Gegensatzes von Land und Meer." *Christ und Welt* 8, no. 25 (June 23, 1955).

1956

Hamlet oder Hekuba: Der Einbruch der Zeit in dem Spiel. Düsseldorf, Köln: Eugen Diederichs, 1956.
"Besprechungen der Bücher von Karl Griewank: 'Der neuzeitliche Revolutionsbegriff,' von Max Weber: 'Wirtschaft und Gesellschaft' und 'Staatssoziologie.'" *Das Historisch-Politische Buch* 4, no. 4 (1956), 110; 7 (1956), 195–96; 5 (1956), 70–71.
"Antwort auf eine Umfrage 'Bücher von Morgen.'" *Christ und Welt* 9, no. 49 (December 6, 1956).

1957

"Die andere Hegel-Linie: Hans Freyer zum 70. Geburstag." *Christ und Welt* 10, no. 30 (1957), 30.

1958

Verfassungsrechtliche Aufsätze aus den Jahren 1924–1954: Materialen zu einer Verfassungslehre. Berlin: Duncker & Humblot, 1958.
"Besprechung des Buches von Johannes Winckelmann: 'Gesellschaft und Staat in der verstehenden Soziologie Max Webers.'" *Das Historisch-Politische Buch* 6, no. 4 (1958), 102.
"Gespräch über den neuen Raum." In *Estudios de Derecho Internacional en homenaje a Barcia Trelles*, ed. C. de Miguel (pp. 263–82). Zaragoza: Universidad de Santiago de Compostela, Zaragoza, 1958.

1959

"Nomos-Nahme-Name." In *Der beständige Aufbruch: Festschrift für Erich Pryzwara*, ed. S. Behn (pp. 92–105). Nürenberg: Verlag Glock & Lütz, 1959. ["Nomos-Nahme-Name." In *The Nomos of the Earth in the International Law of the Jus Publicum Europaeum.* New York: Telos Press, 2003.]
"Besprechung der Bücher von Max Weber: 'Gesammelte Politische Schriften,' und von R. Koselleck: 'Kritik und Krise—ein Beitrag zur Pathogenese der bürgeliche Welt.'" *Das Historisch-Politische Buch* 7, no. 2 (1959), 53; 10 (1959), 301–2.

1960

"Der Gegensatz von Gemeinschaft und Gesellschaft als Beispiel einer Zweigliedrigen Unterscheidung: Betrachtungen zum Schicksal solcher Antithesen." *Estudios Jurídico Sociales* (I, pp. 165–76). Zaragoza: Universidad de Santiago de Compostela, 1960.
"Besprechung des Buches von W. J. Mommsen: 'Max Weber und die deutsche Politik, 1890–1920.'" *Das Historisch-Politische Buch* 8, no. 6 (1960), 180–81.

1962

"El Orden del Mundo después de la Segunda Guerra Mundial." *Revista de Estudios Políticos* 122 (1962), 19–38.

1963

Theorie des Partisanen: Zwischen Bemerkung zum Begriff des Politischen. Berlin: Duncker & Humblot, 1963. ["Theory of the Partisan: Intermediate Commentary on the Concept of the Political," transl. G. L. Ulmen, *Telos* 127 (2004), 11–78.]

1964

"Besprechung des Buches von F. C. Hood: 'The Divine Politics of Thomas Hobbes. An Interpretation of Leviathan.'" *Das Politisch-Historische Buch* 12, no. 7 (1964), 202.

1965

"Die vollendete Reformation: Bemerkungen und Hinweise zu neuen Leviathan Interpretationen." *Der Staat* 4 (1965), 51–69.
"Besprechung des Buches von P. C. Mayer-Tasch: 'T. Hobbes und das Widerstandsrecht.'" *Das Historisch-Politische Buch* 13, no. 7 (1965), 202.

1967

"Clausewitz als politischer Denker: Bemerkungen und Hinweise." *Der Staat* 6 (1967), 478–502.
"Die Tyrannei der Werte." In *Säkularisation und Utopie: Festschrift für Ernst Forsthoff.* Stuttgart: W. Kohlhammer Verlag, 1967. [Re-edited *Die Tyrannei der Werte.* Hamburg: Lutherisches Verlagshaus, 1979.]

1970

Politische Theologie II: Legende von der Erledigung jeder Politischen Theologie. Berlin: Duncker & Humblot, 1970. [*Political Theology II: The Myth of the Closure of Any Political Theology*, transl. M. Hoelzl and G. Ward. New York: Polity Press, 2014.]
"TV-Demokratie-Die Agressivität des Fortschritts." *Deutsches Allgemeines Sonntagsblatt* 23, no. 26 (1970).

1978

"Die legale Weltrevolution: Politischer Mehrwert als Prämie auf juristische Legalität und Superlegalität." *Der Staat* 17 (1978), 321–340. ["The Legal World Revolution," transl. G. L. Ulmen, *Telos* 72 (1987), 73–89.]

1991

Glossarium: Aufzeichnungen der Jahre 1947–1951, ed. E. F. von Medem. Berlin: Duncker & Humblot, 1991.

OTHER WORKS

Agamben, Giorgio. *The Kingdom and the Glory: For a Theological Genealogy of Economy and Government.* Meridian: Crossing Aesthetics, 2011.
Altmann, Rüdiger. "Der Feind und der Friede." *Merkur: Deutsche Zeitschrift für europäisches Denken* 22, no. 9 (1968), 777–85.

Armin, Adam. *Rekonstruktion des Politischen: Carl Schmitt und die Krise der Staatlichkeit, 1912–1933.* Weinheim: V. C. H. Acta Humaniora, 1992.

Aurell, Martin. *Des chrétiens contre les croisades: XIIe et XIIIe siècle.* Paris: Fayard, 2013.

Bachofen, Johann J. *Mutterrecht.* Dortmund: Karl Schwalvenberg Verlag, 1947.

Ball, Hugo. "Carl Schmitts Politische Theologie." *Hochland* 21 (1924), 261–86.

Barion, Hans. "Kirche oder Partei? Römischer Katholizismus und politische Form." *Der Staat* 4 (1965), 131–76.

———. "Weltgeschichtliche Machtform? Eine Studie zur Politischen Theologie des II. Vatikanischen Konzils." In *Epirrosis: Festschrift für Carl Schmitt zum 65. Geburtstag* (II, pp. 13–59). Düsseldorf, 1953.

Becker, Helmuth. *Die Parlamentarismuskritik bei Carl Schmitt und Jürgen Habermas.* Berlin: Duncker & Humblot, 1994.

Bendersky, Joseph W. *Carl Schmitt: Theorist for the Reich.* Princeton, NJ: Princeton University Press, 1983.

———. "Carl Schmitt at Nürenberg." *Telos* 77 (1987), 91–129.

Beneyto, José M. *Politische Theologie als Politische Theorie: Eine Untersuchung zur Rechts und Staatstheorie Carl Schmitts und ihrer Wirkungsgeschichte in Spanien.* Berlin: Duncker & Humblot, 1983.

Benoist, Alain. *Carl Schmitt: Bibliographie Seiner Schriften und Korrespondenzen.* Berlin: Akademie Verlag, 2003.

Bentin, Lutz-Arwin. *Johannes Popitz und Carl Schmitt: Zur wirtschaftlichen Theorie des totalen Staates in Deutschland.* München: Beck, 1972.

Bielefeld, Heiner. *Kampf und Entscheidung: Politischer Existenzialismus bei Carl Schmitt, Helmuth Plessner und Karl Jaspers.* Würzburg: Königshausen & Neumann, 1994.

Blumenberg, Hans. *Die Legitimität der Neuzeit.* Frankfurt: Suhrkamp Verlag, 1966.

———. *Arbeit am Mythos.* Frankfurt Suhrkamp Verlag, 1979.

———. "An Anthropological Approach to the Contemporary Situation of Rhetoric." In *After Philosophy: End of Transformation*, ed. K. Baynes, J. Bohman, and T. McCarthy. Cambridge, MA: MIT Press, 1987.

Böckenförde, Ernst-Wolfgang. "Politische Theorie und Politische Theologie." *Revue européenne des sciences sociales* 19, nos. 54–55 (1981), 233–45.

———. "Konkretes Ordnungsdenken." *Historisches Wörterbuch der Philosophie*, ed. J. Ritter and K. Gründer (VI, pp. 1312–15). Basel: Schwabe Verlag, 1984.

———. "Politisches Mandat der Kirche?" *Stimmen der Zeit* 184 (1969), 361–73.

———. "Die Entstehung des Staates als Vorgang der Säkularisation." *Säkularisation und Utopie: Ernst Forsthoff zum 65. Geburtstag* (pp. 75–94). Stuttgart/Berlin/Köln/Mainz: Kohlhammer, 1967.

———. "Der Begriff des Politischen als Schlüssel zum Staatsrechtlichen Werk Carl Schmitts." In *Complexio Oppositorum: Über Carl Schmitt*, ed. H. Quaritsch (pp. 283–300). Berlin: Duncker & Humblot, 1988.

Bonald, Louis-Gabriel-Ambroise. *Oeuvres complètes de Bonald*, ed. l'abbé Migne (3 vols). Paris: Migné, 1859.

Brunner, Otto. *Land und Herrschaft: Grundfragen der territorialen Verfassungsgeschichte im Mittelalter.* Brünn/München/Wien: Rudolf M. Rother Verlag, 1943.

Cavanaugh, William T. *Theopolitical Imagination: Discovering the Liturgy as a Political Act in an Age of Global Consumerism.* London: T & T Clark, 2002.

Cristi, Renato. *Le libéralisme conservateur: Trois essais sur Schmitt, Hayek et Hegel*, transl. N. Burge. Paris: Ed. Kimé, 1993.

Croce, Mariano, and Salvatore, Andrea. *The Legal Theory of Carl Schmitt.* Abingdon, UK: Routledge, 2013.

Cumin, David. *Carl Schmitt: Biographie politique et intellectuelle.* Paris: Cerf, 2005.

Demandt, Alexander. "Staatsform und Feindbild bei Carl Schmitt." *Der Staat* 27 (1988), 23–32.

Donoso Cortés, Juan. *Obras Completas*, ed. J. Juretschke. Madrid: BAC, 1946.

Doremus, André. "Théologie, politique et science dans la problématique de la théologie poli-tique." *Cahiers Vilfredo Pareto. Revue européenne des sciences sociales* 16, no. 44 (1978), 54–65.

Estévez, José A. *La crisis del Estado de derecho liberal: Schmitt en Weimar*. Barcelona: Ariel, 1989.

Faber, Richard. "'Nemo contra deus nisi deus ipse' Gegen Hans Blumenberg politische Poly-theologie." In *Der Prometeus Komplex: Zur Kritik der Politologie Eric Voegelin und Hans Blumenberg*, ed. Richard Faber (pp. 75–87). Würzburg: Königshausen+Neumann, 1984.

Feuerbach, Jean L. "La theorie du 'Großraum' chez Carl Schmitt." In *Complexio Oppositorum: Über Carl Schmitt*, ed. H. Quaritsch (pp. 401–18). Berlin: Duncker & Humblot, 1988.

Fijalkowski, Jürgen. *Die Wendung zum Führerstaat: Ideologische Komponenten in der politis-chen Philosophie Carl Schmitts*. Köln/Opladen: Westdeutscher Verlag, 1958.

Flickinger, Hans G. *Die Autonomie des Politischen: Carl Schmitt Kampf um einem beschädigten Begriff*. Weinheim: Akademie Verlag, 1990.

Foucault, Michael. *Du gouvernement des vivants: Cours au Collège de France 1979–1980*. Paris: Gallimard/Seuil, 2012.

Freund, Julien. *L'essence du politique*. Paris: Sirey, 1965.

Galli, Carlo. *Genealogia della politica: Carl Schmitt e la crisi del pensiero político moderno*. Bologna: Il Mulino, 1996.

Geréby, György. "Carl Schmitt and Erik Peterson on the Problem of Political Theology: A Footnote to Kantorowicz." In *Monotheistic Kingship: The Medieval Variants*, ed. Azid Al-Azmeh and János M. Bak (pp. 31–61). Budapest, Central European University Press, 2005.

Gerhardt, Volker. "Politisches Handeln: Über einen Zugang zum Begriff der Politik." In *Der Begriff der Politik: Bedingungen und Gründe politischen Handelns*, ed. Volker Gerhardt (pp. 291–309). Stuttgart: J. B. Metzlersche Verlagsbuchhandlung, 1990.

Goethe, Johann W. *Dichtung und Wahrheit*. Berlin: Deutsche Buch Gesellschaft, 1967.

———. *Paralipomena zu den Annalen,* Jubiläums-Ausgabe *Sämtliche Werke*, ed. E. von der Hellen. Stuttgart: J. G. Cotta, 1902–1907.

Gottfried, Paul. *Carl Schmitt*. London: The Claridge Press, 1990.

Gottmann, Jean. *La politique des etats et leur geographie*. Paris: Librairie Armand Colin, 1952.

Habermas, Jürgen. "Die Schrecken der Autonomie: Zu zwei frühen Publikationen des deuts-chen Staatsrechtslehrers Carl Schmitt." *Babylon: Beiträge zur jüdischen Gegenwart* 1 (1986), 108–17.

Hammill, Graham, and Julia R. Lupton. *Political Theology and Early Modernity*. Chicago: University of Chicago Press, 2012.

Hefele, Hermann. "Zum Problem einer Politik aus dem katholischen Glauben." *Abendland* 2, no. 4 (1927), 195–97.

———. "Zum Problem des Politischen." *Abendland* 3, no. 7 (1928), 203–5.

Hepp, Robert. "Der harmlose Clausewitz." *Zeitschrift für Politik* 25, no. 3 (1978), 303–18; and no. 4, 390–429.

Herrero, Montserrat, ed. *Carl Schmitt und Álvaro d'Ors Briefwechsel*. Berlin: Duncker & Humblot, 2004.

———. "Posiciones ante el derecho de Carl Schmitt." In Carl Schmitt, *Posiciones ante el derecho*, ed. and transl. M. Herrero. Madrid: Tecnos, 2012.

Heydte, Friedrich A. von der. "Heil aus der Gefangeschaft? Carl Schmitt und die Lage der europäischen Rechtswissenschaft." *Hochland* 43 (1951), 288–94.

Hirt, Hans. "Monotheismus als politisches Problem?" *Hochland* 35 (1937–1938), 319–24.

Hofmann, Hasso. *Legitimität gegen Legalität: Der Weg der politischen Philosophie Carl Schmitts*. Neuwied/Berlin: Luchterland, 1964.

Holczhauser, Vilmos. *Konsens und Konflikt: Die Begriffe des Politischen bei Carl Schmitt*. Berlin: Duncker & Humblot, 1990.

Hooker, William. *Carl Schmitt's International Thought: Order and Orientation*. Cambridge: Cambridge University Press, 2009.

Hübener, Wolfgang. "Carl Schmitt und Hans Blumenberg oder über Kette und Schuß in der historischen Textur der Moderne." In *Der Fürst dieser Welt: Carl Schmitt und die Folgen*, ed. J. Taubes. München/Paderborn: Finck/Schöningh, 1983, 57–76.

Hüsmert, Ernst. "Die letzten Jahre von Carl Schmitt." *Schmittiana I: Eclectica* 17, nos. 71–72 (1988), 40–45.

Jünger, Ernst. *Radiaciones. Diarios de la Segunda Guerra Mundial.* Barcelona: Tusquets, 1992.

———. *El Trabajador. Dominio y figura.* Barcelona: Tusquets, 1990.

———. *Ernst Jünger-Carl Schmitt. Briefwechsel.* Stuttgart: Klett-Cotta Verlag, 1999.

Kahn, Victoria. *The Future of Illusion: Political Theology and Early Modern Texts.* Chicago: University of Chicago Press, 2014.

Kahn, Paul W. *Political Theology: Four New Chapters on the Concept of Sovereignty.* New York: Columbia University Press, 2011.

Kantorowicz, Ernst H. *The King's Two Bodies: A Study in Medieval Political Theology.* Princeton, NJ: Princeton University Press, 1997.

Kaiser, Joseph H. "Die Dialektik der Repräsentation." In *Festschrift für Carl Schmitt zum 70. Geburtstag,* ed. H. Barion, E. Forsthoff, and W. Weber (pp. 71–80). Berlin: Duncker & Humblot, 1959.

———. "Konkretes Ordnungsdenken." In *Complexio Oppositorum: Über Carl Schmitt,* ed. H. Quaritsch (pp. 318–31). Berlin: Duncker & Humblot, 1988.

Kaufmann, Matthias. *Recht ohne Regel? Die philosophischen Prinzipien in Carl Schmitt Staats- und Rechtslehre.* Freiburg: Alber, 1988.

Kempner, Robert M. W. *Ankläger einer Epoche: Lebenserinnerungen.* Frankfurt a. M. Ullstein, 1983.

Kennedy, Ellen. "Carl Schmitt und die 'Frankfurter Schule': Deutsche Liberalismuskritik im 20. Jahrhundert." *Geschichte und Gesellschaft* 12 (1986), 380–419.

———. "Politischer Expressionismus: Die kulturkritischen und metaphysischen Ursprünge des Begriffs des Politischen von Carl Schmitt." In *Complexio Oppositorum: Über Carl Schmitt,* ed. H. Quaritsch (pp. 233–51). Berlin: Duncker & Humblot, 1988.

Kervégan, Jean-François. *Hegel, Carl Schmitt: Le politique entre spéculation et positivité.* Paris: PUF, 1992.

Kierkegaard, Søren. *La répétition: Oeuvres complètes V.* Paris: Éditions de l'Orante, 1972.

Kodalle, Klaus M. *Politische als Macht und Mythos: Carl Schmitts Politische Theologie.* Stuttgart: Kohlhammer, 1973.

Koenen, Andreas. *Der Fall Carl Schmitt: Sein Aufstieg zum "Kronjuristen des dritten Reiches."* Darmstadt: Wissenschaftliche Buchgesellschaft, 1995.

Koselleck, Reinhart, Otto Brunner, and Werner Conze. *Geschichtliche Grundbegriffe: Historisches Lexikon zur politisch-sozialen Sprache in Deutschland.* Stuttgart: Klett-Cotta, 1990.

Koselleck, Reinhart. *Critique and Crisis: Enlightenment and the Pathogenesis of Modern Society.* Cambridge, MA: MIT Press, 1988.

———. *Futures Past.* New York: Columbia University Press, 2004.

Koslowski, Peter. "Politischer Monotheismus oder Trinitätslehre? Zu Möglichkeit und Unmöglichkeit einer christlichen Politischen Theologie." *Der Fürst dieser Welt: Carl Schmitt und die Folgen,* ed. J. Taubes (pp. 26–44). München/Paderborn: Finck/Schöningh, 1983.

Kramme, Rüdiger. *Helmuth Plessner und Carl Schmitt: Eine historische Fallstudie zum Verhältnis von Anthropologie und Politik in der deutschen Philosophie der zwanziger Jahre.* Berlin: Duncker & Humblot, 1989.

Krauss, Günther. "Erinnerungen an Carl Schmitt." *Criticón* 1, no. 95 (1986), 127–30; 2, no. 96 (1986), 180–86.

Krockow, Christian Graf von. *Die Entscheidung: Eine Untersuchung über Ernst Jünger, Carl Schmitt und Martin Heidegger.* Frankfurt: Campus Verlag, 1990.

Kuhn, Helmut. "Besprechung des Buches Carl Schmitt-Der Begriff des Politischen." *Kantsstudien* 38 (1933), 191–93.

Laak, Dirk van. *Gespräche in der Sicherheit des Schweigens: Carl Schmitt in der politischen Geistesgeschichte der frühen Bundesrepublik.* Berlin: Akademie Verlag, 1993.

———. *Der Nachlaß Carl Schmitts: Verzeichnis des Bestandes im Nordrhein-Westfälischen Hauptstaatsarchiv.* Siegburg: Republica, 1993.

Laufer, Heinz. "Homo homini homo: Das anthropologisches Glaubensbekenntnis eines Doktrinärs." *Politische Ordnung und menschliche Existenz: Festgabe für Erich Voegelin zum 60. Geburtstag*, ed. A. Dempf, H. Arendt, and J. Engel-Hansi (pp. 320–42). München: C. H. Beck, 1962.

———. *Das Kriterium des politischen Handelns: Versuch einer Analyse und konstruktiven Kritik der Freund-Feind-Unterscheidung auf der Grundlage der Aristotelischen Theorie der Politik.* Frankfurt: Johann Bernecker, 1962.

Legg, Stephen, ed. *Spatiality, Sovereignty and Carl Schmitt: Geographies of the Nomos.* Abingdon, UK: Routledge, 2011.

Lenz, Jakob Michael Reinhold. *Werke und Schriften*, ed. B. Titel and H. Haug. Stuttgart: Goverts, 1966.

Löwith, Karl. "Politischer Dezisionismus." In Karl Löwith, *Der Mensch inmitten der Geschichte: Philosophische Bilanz des 20. Jahrhunderts* (pp. 19–48). Stuttgart: J. B. Metzler Verlag, 1990.

———. "Der okkassionelle Dezisionismus von Carl Schmitt." In, Karl Löwith, *Sämtliche Schriften* (VIII, pp. 32–71). Stuttgart: J. B. Metzlersche Verlagsbuchhandlung, 1984.

———. *Meaning in History: The Theological Implications of the Philosophy of History.* Chicago: University of Chicago Press, 1949.

McCormick, John P. *Carl Schmitt's Critique of Liberalism: Against Politics as Technology.* Cambridge: Cambridge University Press, 1997.

Maier, Hans. "Politische Theologie? Einwände eines Laien." *Stimmen der Zeit* 183 (1969), 73–91.

Marquard, Odo. "Grenzbegriff." In *Historisches Wörterbuch der Philosophie*, ed. J. Ritter and K. Gründer (I, p. 871). Basel: Schwabe, 1971–2007.

Maschke, Günter. "Drei Motive im Anti-Liberalismus Carl Schmitts." In *Carl Schmitt und die Liberalismuskritik*, ed. K. Hanser and H. Lietzmann (pp 55–79). Opladen: Springer, 1988.

———. "Die Zweideutigkeit der Entscheidung: Thomas Hobbes und Juan Donoso Cortés im Werk Carl Schmitts." *Complexio Oppositorum: Über Carl Schmitt*, ed. H. Quaritsch (pp. 192–221). Berlin: Duncker & Humblot, 1988.

———. *Der Tod des Carl Schmitt.* Wien: Karolinger Verlag, 1987.

———. *Staat, Großraum, Nomos: Arbeiten von Carl Schmitt aus den Jahren 1917–1970.* Berlin: Duncker & Humblot, 1995.

———. "Zum Leviathan vom Carl Schmitt." Introduction to Carl Schmitt, *Der Leviathan in der Staatslehre des Thomas Hobbes* (pp. 206–7). Köln: Hohenheim, 1982.

Mehring, Reinhard. *Pathetisches Denken: Carl Schmitts Denkweg am Leitfaden Hegels: Katholische Grundstellung und antimarxistische Hegelstrategie.* Berlin: Duncker & Humblot, 1989.

———. *Carl Schmitt zum Einfuhrung.* Hamburg: Iunius Verlag, 1992.

———. *Carl Schmitt: Aufstieg und Fall.* München: Verlag C. H. Beck, 2009. Translated as *Carl Schmitt: A Biography.* Cambridge: Polity Press, 2014.

Meier, Christian. "Zu Carl Schmitts Begriffsbildung: Das Politische und der Nomos." In *Complexio Oppositorum: Über Carl Schmitt*, ed. H. Quaritsch (pp. 537–56). Berlin: Duncker & Humblot, 1988.

Meier, Heinrich. *Carl Schmitt, Leo Strauss und "Der Begriff des Politischen": Zu einem Dialog unter Abwesenden.* Stuttgart: Metzler Verlag, 1991.

———. *Die Lehre Carl Schmitts: Vier Kapitel zur Unterscheidung Politischer Theologie und Politischer Philosophie.* Stuttgart: J. B. Metzler Verlag, 1994. Translated as *The Lesson of Carl Schmitt: Four Chapters on the Distinction between Political Theology and Political Philosophy*, expanded edition. Chicago: Chicago University Press, 2011.

Metz, Johann B. "Politische Theologie in der Diskussion." *Stimmen der Zeit* 184 (1969), 289–308.

Mohler, Armin. "Rechts-Schmittisten, Links-Schmittisten und 'Establishment'-Schmittisten." *Criticon* 98 (1986), 265–67.

———. "Carl Schmitt und die 'konservative Revolution.'" In *Complexio Oppositorum: Über Carl Schmitt*, ed. H. Quaritsch (pp. 129–51). Berlin: Duncker & Humblot, 1988.

Monod, Jean-Claude. *La querelle de la sécularisation: Théologie politique et philosophies de l'histoire de Hegel à Blumenberg*. Paris: Vrin, 2002.

Migne, *Patrologiae Grecae*, Tomus 36.

Milbank, John. "The Program of Radical Orthodoxy." In *Radical Orthodoxy? A Catholic Inquiry*, ed. Lawrence P. Hemming. Aldershot, UK: Ashgate, 2000.

Mommsen, Momme. "Zur Frage der Herkunft des Spruches 'Nemo contra deum nisi deus ipse.'" *Goethe-Jahrbuch: Vierteljahresschrift der Goethe Gesellschaft* 13 (1951), 86–104.

Neumann, Volker. *Der Staat im Bürgerkrieg: Kontinuität und Wendung des Staatsbegriffs in der politischen Theorie Carl Schmitt*. Frankfurt: Campus Verlag, 1980.

Nichtweiss, Barbara. *Erik Peterson: Neue Sicht auf Leben und Werk*. Freiburg: Herder, 1992.

Nicoletti, Michele. "Die Ursprünge von Carl Schmitts 'Politischer Theologie.'" In *Complexio Oppositorum: Über Carl Schmitt*, ed. H. Quaritsch (pp. 109–28). Berlin: Duncker & Humblot, 1988.

———. *Trascendenza e Potere: La teologia politica di Carl Schmitt*. Brescia: Morcelliana, 1990.

———. "Alle radici della 'teologia politica' di Car Schmitt: Gli scritti jovanili 1910–1917." In *Annali dell'Instituto storico italo-germanico in Trento* (pp. 256–316). Bologna: Società editrice il Mulino, 1984.

———. "Erik Peterson e Carl Schmitt: Ripensare un dibattito." In *Erik Peterson: La presenza teologica di un outsider*, ed. G. Caronello (pp. 517–38). Roma: Libreria Editrice Vaticana, 2012.

Noack, Paul. *Carl Schmitt: Eine Biographie*. Berlin: Propyläen Verlag, 1993.

Oakley, Francis. "The Absolute and Ordained Power of God and King in the Sixteenth and Seventeenth Centuries: Philosophy, Science, Politics, and Law." *Journal of the History of Ideas* 59, no. 4 (1998), 669–90.

Ors, Álvaro d'. *De la guerra y de la paz*. Madrid: Rialp, 1954.

———. "Teología Política: Una revisión del problema." *Revista de Estudios Políticos* 205 (1976), 41–79.

———. *Una introducción al estudio del derecho*. Madrid: Rialp, 1963.

———. *Escritos varios sobre el derecho en crisis*. Roma: Consejo Superior de Investigaciones Científicas, 1973.

———. "El 'Glossarium' de Carl Schmitt." In *Estudios sobre Carl Schmitt*, ed. D. Negro Pavón (pp. 17–48). Madrid: Fundación Cánovas del Castillo, 1995.

———. *Ensayos de teoría política*. Pamplona: Eunsa, 1979.

———. "La función de la propiedad en el ordenamiento civil." In *Historia del Derecho Privado: Trabajos en Homenaje a Ferrán Valls i Taberner* (pp. 2841–65). Barcelona: PPU, 1989.

Ors, Eugenio d', *Nuevo Glosario II*. Madrid: Aguilar, 1947.

Pasquino, Paquale. "Bemerkungen zum 'Kriterium des Politischen' bei Carl Schmitt." *Der Staat* 25 (1986), 385–98.

———. "Die Lehre vom 'pouvoir constituant' bei Emmanuel Sieyès und Carl Schmitt: Ein Beitrag zur Untersuchung der Grundlagen der modernen Demokratietheorie." In *Complexio Oppositorum: Über Carl Schmitt*, ed. H. Quaritsch (pp. 371–85). Berlin: Duncker & Humblot, 1988.

Pattloch, Peter P. *Recht als Einheit von Ordnung und Ortung: Ein Beitrag zum Rechtsbegriff in Carl Schmitts "Nomos der Erde."* Aschaffenburg: Pattloch Verlag, 1961.

Peterson, Erik. "Kaiser Augustus im Urteil des antiken Christentums: Ein Beitrag zur Geschichte der politischen Theologie." In *Der Fürst dieser Welt: Carl Schmitt und die Folgen*, ed. J. Taubes (pp. 175–80). München/Paderborn: Finck/Schöningh, 1983.

———. "Monotheism as a Political Problem." In *Theological Tractates*. Stanford, CA: Stanford University Press, 2011, 68–106.

Pieper, Josef. "Notizen." *Hochland* 46 (1954), 342–45.

———. *Noch wußte es niemand: Autobiographische Aufzeichnungen 1904–1945*. München: Kösel Verlag, 1976.

Plessner, Helmuth. *Die Stufen des Organischen und der Mensch: Einleitung in die philosophische Anthropologie*. Berlin: de Gruyter, 1975.

————. *Macht und Menschlicher Natur*. Berlin: Ernst von Hippel, 1931.

Portinaro, Pier Paolo. *La crisi dello jus publicum europaeum: Sagio su Carl Schmitt*. Milano: Ed. di Communità, 1982.

Przywara, Erich. *Humanitas: Der Mensch gestern und morgen*. Nürnberg: Glock und Lutz, 1952.

————. *Mensch*. Nürnberg: Glock und Lutz, 1958.

Quaritsch, Helmut. *"Positionen und Begriffe" Carl Schmitts*. Berlin: Duncker & Humblot, 1989.

————. *Antworten in Nürnberg*. Berlin: Duncker & Humblot, 2000.

Ratzel, Friedrich. *Erdenmacht und Völkerschicksal*. Stuttgart: Alfred Kroner, 1940.

Rumpf, Helmut. *Carl Schmitt und Thomas Hobbes: Ideelle Beziehungen und aktuelle Bedeutung mit einer Abhandlung über die Frühschriften Carl Schmitts*. Berlin: Duncker & Humblot, 1972.

Rüthers, Bernd. *Carl Schmitt im Dritten Reich: Wissenschaft als Zeitgeist-Verstärkung?* München: Beck, 1990.

Savigny, Friedrich C. von. *Grundgedanken der Historischen Rechtsschule*. Frankfurt: Vittorio Klostermann, 1965.

Schelsky, Helmut. "Der Begriff des Politischen und die politische Erfahrung der Gegenwart." *Der Staat* 22 (1983), 321–45.

Scheuerman, William E. *Carl Schmitt: The End of Law*. Lanham, MD: Rowman & Littlefield, 1999.

Schindler, Alfred, and Frithard Scholz. "Zum Ursprung politische Theologie: Einführende Bemerkungen." In *Der Fürst dieser Welt: Carl Schmitt und die Folgen*, ed. J. Taubes (pp. 153–73). München/Paderborn: Finck/Schöningh, 1983.

Schmidt, Hermann. "Der Nomosbegriff bei Carl Schmitt." *Der Staat* 2 (1963), 81–108.

Schmidt, Heinz W. "Vom Geistesgrund und der Feindschaft im Begriff des Politischen bei Carl Schmitt." In *Epirrosis: Festschrift für Carl Schmitt zum 65. Geburtstag* (II, pp. 651–64). Düsseldorf, 1953.

Schmitz, Mathias. *Die Freund-Feind-Theorie Carl Schmitts: Entwurf und Entfaltung*. Köln, Opladen: Westadt Verlag, 1965.

Schmitz, Alexander, and Martin Lepper, eds. *Hans Blumenberg, Carl Schmitt: Briefwechsel*. Frankfurt: Suhrkamp, 2007.

Schneider, Peter. *Ausnahmezustand und Norm: Eine Studie zur Rechtslehre von Carl Schmitt*. Stuttgart: Deutsche Verlagsanstalt, 1957.

Shogimen, Takashi. *Ockham and Political Discourse in the Late Middle Ages*. Cambridge: Cambridge University Press, 2007.

Schwab, Georg. "Enemy oder Foe: Der Konflikt der modernen Politik." In *Epirrosis: Festschrift für Carl Schmitt zum 65. Geburtstag* (II, pp. 665-82). Düsseldorf, 1953.

————. *The Challenge of Exception: An Introduction to the Political Ideas of Carl Schmitt between 1921 and 1936*. Berlin: Duncker & Humblot, 1970.

Sternberger, Dolf. *Drei Wurzeln der Politik*. Frankfurt am Mainz: Suhrkamp, 1995.

————. *Schriften IV: Staatsfreundschaft*. Frankfurt am Mainz: Insel Verlag, 1980.

Strauss, Leo. "Anmerkungen zu Carl Schmitt 'Der Begriff des Politischen.'" In *Carl Schmitt, Leo Strauss und "Der Begriff des Politischen": Zu einem Dialog unter Abwesenden*, ed. H. Meier (pp. 97–26). Stuttgart: Metzler Verlag, 1991.

Taubes, Jacob. "Statt einer Einleitung: Leviathan als sterblicher Gott. Zur Aktualität von Thomas Hobbes." In *Der Fürst dieser Welt: Carl Schmitt und die Folgen*, ed. J. Taubes (II, pp. 9–15). München/Paderborn: Finck/Schöningh, 1983.

Tierno, Enrique. *Cabos sueltos*. Barcelona: Bruguera, 1982.

————. *Escritos 1950–1960*. Madrid: Tecnos, 1971.

Tommissen, Piet. "Contributions de Carl Schmitt à la polémologie." *Cahiers Vilfredo Pareto: Revue européenne des sciences sociales* 16, no. 44 (1978), 141–70.

————. "Über Carl Schmitts 'Theorie des Partisanen." In *Epirrosis: Festschrift für Carl Schmitt zum 65. Geburtstag* (II, pp. 709–25). Düsseldorf, 1953.

Tönnies, Ferdinand. "Demokratie und Parlamentarismus." *Schmollers Jahrbuch* 51 (1927), 1–44.

Topitsch, Ernst, "Kosmos und Herrschaft: Ursprünge der politischen Theologie." *Wort und Wahrheit: Monatsschrift für Religion u nd Kultur* 19 (1955), 19–30.

Ulmen, Gary L. *Politischer Mehrwert: Eine Studie über Max Weber und Carl Schmitt.* Weinheim: V C H, Acta Humaniora, 1991.

———. "Politische Theologie und politische Ökonomie." In *Complexio Oppositorum: Über CarlSchmitt,* ed. H. Quaritsch (pp. 341–69). Berlin: Duncker & Humblot, 1988.

———. *Verhandlungen des Siebenten deutschen Soziologentages vom 28. Sept. bis 1. Okt. 1930: Schriften der Deutschen Gesellschaft für Soziologie* (pp. 56–59). Tübingen: J C B Mohr, 1931.

Vattimo, Gianni. "Invento la politica di amico-nemico." *La Stampa,* April 17, 1987.

Villinger, Ingeborg. *Verortung des Politischen: Carl Schmitt in Plettenberg.* Hagen: v. d. Linnepe, 1990.

———. *Carl Schmitts Kulturkritik der Moderne: Texte, Kommentar und Analyse des "Schattenrisse" des Johannes Negelinus.* Berlin: Akademie Verlag, 1995.

Voegelin, Eric, *The New Science of Politics.* Chicago: University of Chicago Press, 1987.

Vollrath, Ernst. *Grundlegung einer philosophischen Theorie des Politischen.* Würzburg: Königshausen & Neumann, 1987.

Waldstein, Thor von. *Die Pluralismuskritik in der Staatslehre von Carl Schmitt.* Bochum: Bochum University Press, 1989.

Weber, Samuel. "Taking Exception to Decision: Walter Benjamin and Carl Schmitt." *Diacritics* 22, nos. 3–4 (1992), 5–18.

Weiss, Konrad. *Der christliche Epimetheus.* München: Edwig Runge, 1933.

Weizsäcker, Viktor von. *Der Gestaltkreis: Theorie der Einheit von Wahrnehmen und Bewegen.* Leipzig: G. Thieme, 1947.

Willke, Helmut. *Ironie des Staates: Grundlinien einer Staatstheorie polyzentrischer Gesellschaft.* Frankfurt: Suhrkamp, 1992.

Wenzel, Uwe-Justus. "Die Dissoziation und ihr Grund." In *Die Autonomie des Politischen: Carl Schmitt Kampf um einem beschädigten Begriff* (pp. 13–36). Weinheim: Akademie Verlag.

Žižek, Slavoj, Eric L. Santner, and Kenneth Reinhardt. *The Neighbor: Three Inquiries in Political Theology.* Chicago: University of Chicago Press, 2005.

Index

acclamation, 86–88, 211n74, 213n95–214n106
Adam, Armin, 206n124, 207n147, 209n29, 209n39, 210n51, 210n52, 210n56, 211n68, 213n97, 213n98, 214n107, 222n65, 222n70, 222n73, 230n30, 237n109, 240n157, 242n27
Adams, Paul, 18
Agamben, Giorgio, 242n19
Albertus Magnus, 145
Altmann, Rüdiger, 228n146
Ambrosius, Aurelius, 241n12
amity line, 42, 115, 194n130, 225n100, 226n131, 234n82
Andric, Ivo, 17
Anschütz, Gerhard, 15, 215n123
Augustine of Hippo, 113, 143–144, 146, 150, 151, 168, 169, 171, 175, 199n24, 241n3, 241n8, 243n41, 244n56, 251n70
Aurell, Martin, 241n9

Bachofen, Johann, 21, 185n8, 186n19
Ball, Hugo, 2, 11, 247n4, 249n32
Balthasar, Hans Urs von, 187n36
Barion, Hans, 15, 18, 210n59, 210n60, 241n17, 247n5
Becker, Werner, 2
Bendersky, Joseph W., 1, 12, 184n15, 233n68, 234n69
Beneyto, José M., 219n30, 242n18, 247n5, 249n32, 250n34, 253n96

Benjamin, Walter, 12, 13, 184n16, 217n12
Benoist, Alain de, 1
Bentin, Lutz-Arwin, 199n21, 205n104, 240n157
Blumenberg, Hans, 2, 162–163, 168, 169, 172, 173, 184n14, 248n19, 249n21, 249n22, 249n24, 249n32, 253n93, 253n94, 253n95
Bodin, Jean, 5, 65, 66, 98, 113, 114, 120, 153, 175, 246n84
Bonald, Louis Gabriel Ambroise de, 35, 74, 155, 208n1–208n5, 244n49
Bossuet, Jacques-Bénigne, 244n49
Brunner, Otto, 197n5, 223n83
Bynkershoek, Cornelius van, 114

Caamaño, José, 18
Cabral de Moncada, Luis, 2
Caronello, Giancarlo, 252n72, 252n73
Cavanaugh, William T., 242n19, 251n65
charisma, 87, 214n100
church, 8, 10, 12, 14, 26, 41, 43, 62, 76, 81, 83, 126, 144–146, 151, 154, 155, 156, 165, 168, 169, 170, 171, 174, 175–176, 208n8, 210n41, 213n97, 223n78, 232n57, 232n58, 236n105, 237n113, 238n117, 245n70, 246n82, 247n1, 249n21, 250n51, 251n63, 251n68, 252n73, 254n107
Cicero, Marcus Tullius, 28, 89, 116, 188n48, 214n110, 214n112

271

About the Author

Montserrat Herrero is Associate Professor of Political Philosophy at the University of Navarra (Spain) and Principal Investigator of the Religion and Civil Society project at University of Navarra's Institute for Culture and Society. She is author of *La política revoluciona via de John Locke* (at press); *Ficciones políticas: El eco de Thomas Hobbes en el ocaso de la modernidad* (2012); and *El nomos y lo político: La filosofía política de Carl Schmitt* (2007); and editor of *Carl Schmitt und Álvaro d'Ors Briefwechsel* (2004). She has also translated several of Schmitt's books into Spanish, collected as *Carl Schmitt: Posiciones ante el derecho, Estudio preliminar, traducción y notas de Gesetz und Urteil, Über die drei Arten des rechtswissenschaftlichen Denkens, Freiheitsrechte und institutionelle Garantien der Reichsverfassung* (2012).